STUDIES IN

AFRICAN AMERICAN HISTORY AND CULTURE

edited by

GRAHAM RUSSELL HODGES
COLGATE UNIVERSITY

A GARLAND SERIES

Lawrence William Towner, photo courtesy of Rachel Towner Raffles

A GOOD MASTER WELL SERVED

MASTERS AND SERVANTS IN COLONIAL MASSACHUSETTS, 1620–1750

LAWRENCE WILLIAM TOWNER

GARLAND PUBLISHING, INC.
A MEMBER OF THE TAYLOR & FRANCIS GROUP
NEW YORK & LONDON / 1998

Library of Congress Cataloging-in-Publication Data

Towner, Lawrence W. (Lawrence William), 1921–1992.
A good master well served : masters and servants in colonial
Massachusetts, 1620–1750 / Lawrence William Towner.
        p.   cm. — (Studies in African American history and
culture)
    Includes bibliographical references and index.
    ISBN 0-8153-2787-0 (alk. paper)
    1. Indentured servants—Massachusetts—History. 2. Master
and servant—Massachusetts—History. 3. Massachusetts—
History—Colonial period, ca. 1600–1775. 4. Afro-Americans—
Massachusetts—History—17th century. 5. Afro-Americans—
Massachusetts—History—18th century. I. Title. II. Series.
    HD4875.U5T69 1997 ₁₉₉ꙮ
    306.3'63'0974709032—dc21   96-54889

Printed on acid-free, 250-year-life paper
Manufactured in the United States of America

Contents

Dissertations and Gatekeepers
Why It Took Forty-Five Years for a Ph.D. Thesis to be Published

"A Good Master Well Served: A Social History of Servitude in Massachusetts 1620-1750" was received with unusual enthusiasm by knowledgeable scholars who read the dissertation soon after it was completed in 1954. Clifford Shipton, Director of the American Antiquarian Society, told Towner "I have never seen a better doctoral dissertation." Early readers were all struck by the same quality. "I think your research has been exhaustive," wrote Edmund Morgan, "that you have made extensive use of the most valuable collection of sources now available—the court records. . .The work as it stands is a thoroughly documented study of servitude in Massachusetts. . ." When Oscar Handlin read the thesis in 1960 he wrote, "I can't think of any significant body of sources you have missed, nor do I think there are significant factual gaps."[1]

More than three decades later, Marcus Rediker, reading the same manuscript for a university press considering publication, had a similar reaction. "To put the matter bluntly, this is one of the most thoroughly researched dissertations one is likely to find in any field. . . Towner's painstaking work in the newspapers and court records of Massachusetts is especially impressive, and his corroborative use of official ministerial and other documents rounds out his story in impressive ways. . . The sheer recovery of such massive amount of material about servants—notoriously difficult objects of research—would itself be a major accomplishment." More than that, the thesis was "the work of a serious professional in full control of his materials." Rediker was struck, after more than thirty years, by "the remarkable ways" the study "has stood the test of time. It reads less like a work of the 1950s than something much more recent. Part of this of course, is owing to the author's prescient decision to do a 'social history' long before social history had made its explosive appearance within the discipline."[2]

Why, then, did Bill Towner—as Lawrence William Towner (1921-1992) was known to everyone—never publish his dissertation as a book? Why, especially in light of the fact that it won him the kind of recognition that brought him very rapidly to positions at the peak of the historical profession? In 1955, the year the thesis was accepted at Northwestern University, Towner, an instructor, then an assistant professor at M.I.T.(1950-55) who had not published as much as an article, was appointed Associate Editor (later Editor) of the William *and Mary Quarterly,* (1955-1962), the leading journal in the fast emerging field of early American history, and Associate Professor at the College of William and Mary. After six years in Williamsburg, replacing Douglass Adair, a brilliant editor who had left the journal somewhat in disarray, he put it on the road to being one of the best edited historical journals in the country.[3] He spent the summer of 1960 on a grant and the academic year 1961-62 on a fellowship in Cambridge offered by Oscar Handlin at the Center for the Study of the History of Liberty in America to revise the dissertation. Then in the Spring of 1962 he was appointed director of the Newberry Library, a post he held until his retirement in 1986.[4]

It would be easy to say he was swallowed up by the extraordinary professional demands of the positions he held, not once, but twice in his career, and let it go at that. At Williamsburg, besides editing the *Quarterly* (with minimum editorial assistance), he taught two courses, created and directed a new graduate program, and occasionally served as acting Director of the Institute of Early American History (founded in 1943). At the Newberry he turned an ailing independent research library of uncertain future into one of the great humanities research centers of the country, building its rare book collections, creating four research centers, making the library a pace setter for American libraries in one field after another, and testifying in Washington as a spokesman for the humanities in public life. Bill and Rachel Towner had a family of four children in Williamsburg and Rachel arrived at the Newberry in the Fall of 1962 pregnant with twin boys. Family always loomed large in their lives even in an elegant Newberry town house in which the Towners entertained endless rounds of potential donors, trustees, and visiting scholars.[5]

A job may be engulfing but decisions about scholarship, while personal, complex and multi-layered, inevitably are taken in a context of the expectations of the profession and the academic and political climate. At a time when the historical profession is sponsoring conferences on "The Specialized Scholarly Monograph in Crisis," when recent Ph.D.s are under unprecedented pressures to publish, the subject of why one scholar did not publish his dissertation thirty and forty years ago may be of larger interest (although a young Ph. D. today might well ask, if she could have as successful and as creative a career as Bill Towner, why stop to publish a thesis?) It is, I suppose, a cautionary tale, for young scholars as well as for gatekeepers of the profession, or enablers as they think of themselves: thesis directors, book and journal editors, peer reviewers, givers of grants and fellowships, and advice-givers of all sorts.

Bill Towner and I were friends from our graduate student days at Northwestern in the late '40s, pen pals through the pains of thesis writing and job hunting in the '50s and we renewed our friendship after 1964 when I moved to Illinois. We had not played much of a role in each other's dissertations when we were writing and revising them. So, in the 1970s when my own research interests in artisans coincided with his and I read his thesis for the first time, I was bowled over by this buried trove of treasures and the surefootedness of his command of an extraordinary body of sources. I was never disappointed whether I looked at it for apprenticeship to understand George Robert Twelves Hewes, a Boston shoemaker in the Revolution, or the recreation of servants to understand Boston's apprentice holiday Pope's Day, the American Guy Fawkes Day.[6] I reflected on the question over the years and especially after his retirement in 1986. I was happy then to recommend the manuscript to Rutgers University Press which sent him a contract to publish it after receiving Rediker's report. I posed the question in conversations with Bill when I wrote the introduction to a volume of his essays on history, libraries and the humanities whose publication he agreed to shortly before his death. To answer the question I have since gone over his personal correspondence in the Newberry Archives—correspondence with his sponsor Ray Allen Billington, with Handlin and other academics, with his friends, with me—and his correspondence with parents and with editors at the *William and Mary Quarterly* who edited his first articles, and I was not prepared for what I found.

Bill Towner was a graduate student at Northwestern from 1947 to 1949, who researched and wrote his thesis from 1950 through 1954, and worked on revising it in 1960-62. The context of the decade and a half after World War II in which Bill began his career eludes today's young historians: of a suddenly booming historical profession in which a handful of elite university departments (and their graduates) set the standards for the profession; of the rapid emergence of early American history as a major field of inquiry with its own journal, and since 1943 its own research center in which a few major figures also called the tunes; of the pouring of intellectual energies into a rejection of the long regnant, Progressive paradigm of American history identified with Charles Beard, Frederick Jackson Turner, and Vernon Louis Parrington—all taking place in an academic climate increasingly fouled by the impact of the Manichean struggles of the Cold War on American intellectual life.[7]

Bill Towner was a midwesterner born in St Paul, Minnesota, the son of Cornelia and Earl Towner, an accountant with Bell Telephone. He got a B.A. from Cornell College in Iowa (1942). He was a tenth generation Towner in America, descended from seventeenth century settlers in Connecticut, a lineage he rarely revealed. He became an historian in the last glow of Progressive history fed by liberal political upsurges of the post-war years, both little appreciated. He had been politicized by his experiences in the war, a time when FDR spoke of the four freedoms and Henry Wallace of the "age of the common man." He returned from serving as a pilot in the China-Burma-India theater with an abiding contempt for Chiang Kai-shek and an anger at America's unrelenting support for corrupt regimes without support from their own people. George McGovern, our fellow teaching assistant who had served as a bomber pilot in the European theater, expressed his commitment to social justice as a Methodist minister until he found a more congenial outlet in history and then politics. As a left-wing New Yorker at Columbia for my Masters in 1946-47, I was attracted to Northwestern, by, among other things, a letter a majority of the history faculty sent to Henry Wallace urging him to run as a third party candidate in 1948. I was also appalled one day at the newspaper kiosk at the Columbia subway station when out of the corner of my eye I caught my M.A. director staring at me to see what paper I would buy. At Northwestern, Bill liked to recall, he and I turned out leaflets on a messy mimeograph machine against the Mundt-Nixon bill, a harbinger of the witchhunt.[8]

Ray Allen Billington, our mentor, a historian of the frontier, was a sophisticated follower of Turner who gave talks about the indispensable role of third parties in American history and at the American Historical Association lambasted Samuel Flagg Bemis, a patriotic diplomatic historian, for defending the rising political hysteria as "cool-headed alarm."[9] We showed our progressivism by our choice of dissertation topics: McGovern on the struggles of Colorado miners with John D. Rockefeller, Martin Ridge (later editor of the *Journal of American History*) on Ignatius Donnelly, the Populist leader, I on the artisans and yeomen who were the grass roots of the Jeffersonian Democratic Republican party in New York. Bill chose the servants of Massachusetts, a term he used to embrace apprentices, white indentured servants, and slaves, all notoriously unstudied even by the progressives and rarely linked.

Billington was not interested in building a "school" of interpretation, but like his Harvard mentor, Arthur Schlesinger Sr., the pioneer of social history, encouraged students to pursue their own interests and interpretations. He subjected us to a grueling initiation in a hands-on year-long seminar but after that he was primarily a source of inspiration, endless encouragement and a link to the "old boy" network that dominated hiring (at a time when there was no such thing as a published A.H.A. job listing). At the time Northwestern had no specialist in colonial history, as Bill explained to Douglass Adair, seeking "outside help and guidance" in choosing a thesis topic. The result was once in the field doing research he was "somewhat at sea," as were most of us.[10] He had the good fortune to win over Clifford "Ted" Shipton who became a second mentor. Director of the American Antiquarian Society's massive project that put 50,000 titles of early American imprints on microcard, Shipton was beyond compare in his mastery of New England sources. He thought Bill's thesis "a necessity" and "was willing to give me all the time I need to bring it to completion." Shipton could not have been more different from Billington. His multi-volume biographies of the graduates of Harvard College breathed empathy for colonial elites and Tories. As Bill told the story:

He listened to my problems with patience and kindliness and then made a suggestion: "Read all eight volumes of the *Records and Files of the Quarterly Courts of Essex county, Massachusetts*. Report back in a *week* with the questions your reading raised."

That was the beginning. Two years later, having in the meanwhile been sent to every county court house in the state, having been forced through every issue of every newspaper and hundreds of sermons, but still baffled by one aspect of my research problem, I turned to him for additional sources. "You have reached the place in your work where you have got to stop research," Ted wrote on November 19, 1952. 'The problem now is to make it available. The secret of accomplishing anything in the historical field is *controlled superficiality and sloppiness*."[11]

Bill's thesis was anything but superficial or sloppy. He had no models—which is often an advantage. There was no study of servants in a given locale, embracing all strata of servants and certainly none that linked white and black servants. Richard B. Morris's recent *Government and Labor in Early America* (1946) was a monumental work, based on ten years exploring 20,000 court cases from Maine to Florida. But three-fifths of the book was devoted to free labor with chapters on wage regulation, concerted action by artisans, and maritime labor relations. In the section on bound labor Morris focused on the sources of servants and their legal status, framing the entire study in the context of mercantilism. Abbot Emerson Smith's work was devoted to the English trade in indentured servants and the transportation of convict labor, almost all of whom went to the middle and southern colonies.[12]

Towner's research and the organization of his materials were informed by a kind of open-minded progressivism. He was interested in presenting the experiences of ordinary people, not in an institutional history of servitude. He organized his data functionally as it seemed to grow out of the lives of servants. First, there was the inevitable context under the gawky chapter heading, "Factors Influencing Conditions of Labor and Other Institutions of Servitude," which broke with the Progressive tradition by playing on the persistence of the English heritage, rejecting the allegedly liberalizing influence of the frontier (to

Billington's delight) while emphasizing the shaping role of Puritan ideals (*pace* Perry Miller, Samuel Eliot Morison and Edmund Morgan). His analytical categories, however, were unexpected: there was a "servant elite" of apprenticed and indentured servants (both with terms fixed by contract) and the "servant lower classes" made up of poor boys and girls put out to servitude by Overseers of the Poor, debtors, war prisoners, criminals, Indians and Negroes, the latter slaves for life but "servants" in the euphemism of the day. They had to be looked at both separately and for their commonalities. Then, taking the entire period from 1620 to 1750, the thesis blossomed with the whole array of these servants at work and at leisure. Two final chapters were devoted to servant protest, the first to legal action in the courts, verbal abuse, and crimes against masters, the second to the servant runaways. The dissertation shot beyond Progressive history in its attentiveness to blacks as well as whites, women as well as men, and in its insights into a panoply of individual resistance to "the master class," the sort of day-to-day resistance and cultural formation scholars of slavery in the South would not develop until the 1970s.

The level of documentation in the thesis was unusual. Towner visited every lower court in Massachusetts, examined some 1,400 court cases, and recovered some 7,000 servants; he had read every issue of every Massachusetts newspaper to 1750, every sermon, tract and broadside that impinged on his subject. Weighing his evidence judicially, measuring numbers carefully without falling into a trap of only analyzing what could be quantified, he offered generalizations that conveyed a command of subject and context. He then subordinated his proof, piling up example after example in dense footnotes and in thirteen appendices.[13]

What happened to doctoral dissertations in the 1950s? The prevailing professional wisdom was that they were invariably too long, cumbersome, and overburdened with documentation; they all could be boiled down and the reader referred to the original for documentation. Moreover, there was no thesis that could not profit from revision; with some distance the author would see his subject in greater perspective. A book was what counted for advancement, articles were O.K. but only as a spin-off or leftover from the thesis. These certainly were the assumptions Billington conveyed.

Bill was buoyed by the reaction to his thesis of Shipton and Edmund Morgan, then at Brown University on his way to Yale, and already a leading figure in the study of Puritan society. Morgan thought it could be "of considerable use to scholars" as it was but urged a revision in which Towner "kept the servants before the reader as human beings," advising him to "reduce the number of examples and present the ones you retain in much more detail," a demanding but very doable proposal which recognized the spirit of the enterprise. Bill appreciated Morgan's advice but he faced "the necessity of 'getting something out'" and hoped to get it published "more or less as it stands." If he could not get a publisher, "I think I'll have to tear the entire thing down and approach it substantially as you suggest."[14]

With uncommon self-confidence, Bill submitted his unrevised manuscript to two publishers: Houghton Mifflin, which as a trade publisher, rejected it, and Harvard University Press which dallied. The press director apologized, "the trouble is we have had a great deal of difficulty in obtaining the services of scholarly readers competent in your field." The thesis was so original, that, in effect, it was in a non-existent field. Two readers eventually responded with customary Ivy League diffidence: one thought Towner overdid servant protest, should come down past the Revolution and deal with the ex-servant while the other thought while the monograph " certainly fills a gap. . . it would be rather a pity for the Harvard Press to publish the book until it had been ripened a bit." It was a blow and Bill, assuming he would have to expand the coverage, had already drafted a proposal to the Social Science Research Council to do a study of labor in Massachusetts that would go up to 1800, and include free as well as unfree workers, a daunting task.[15]

He was saved by the offer of the double job as editor of the *Quarterly* and teacher at William and Mary. Bill put off a decision on revision. After five years at Williamsburg, Bill lamented he had "not had time to lay a hand" on the thesis.[16] But the 1950s, we can now see, was not a time when there was any clamor, professional or popular, for a young historian to put his hand to scholarship in this field. Colonial labor history was an oxymoron. Labor history in the first two hundred years of American history was simply not a field—neither to colonialists nor to labor historians who defined their field as dealing with unions and strikes of industrial workers. Richard B. Morris's massive work, as Graham Hodges has noted, "languished as a 'neglected classic'." Carl Bridenbaugh's little book on craftsmen made more of a splash in the museum world than among academics.[17] Black history was not in the mainstream and when scholars at last opened a debate about slavery, they focused on the ante-bellum era, 1830-1860, or the early sources of racism. Intellectual history was "in" as were biographies and definitive editions of the papers of the founding fathers—Jefferson, Adams, Washington, Franklin and Hamilton. In the 1950s the Institute of Early American History sponsored conferences at Williamsburg on the "needs and opportunities for specialized study" in the fields of early American science, education, and American Indian and white relations and later in the arts and technology, the latter two the closest it would get to artisans and laborers.[18]

Jesse Lemisch's experience writing a dissertation at Yale, 1958-1962, on the politics of merchant seamen in the Revolutionary era suggests something of the reigning scholarly values of the fifties and early sixties "before the sixties became 'The Sixties'," as he puts it. "There are no sources," his advisor, Edmund Morgan told him at first. "Later," Lemisch writes, "Morgan good-naturedly liked to tell the story on himself: 'That is the last time I'll ever say that to a graduate student'." The thesis, completed in 1962, and now reprinted in this same series by Garland Publishing, dealt with the seamen in only one city, New York, and in the preface Lemisch felt he had to apologize that it was "frankly fragmentary," acknowledging that the "the study will have greater depth when approached on the continental scale," a grandiose idea. He did in fact go on to highly successful articles embracing Jack Tar in the streets of other cities, Jack Tar in British prisons, and then embarked on the life history of one Jack Tar in the post-war era. Somehow, when it came to the study of class, class formation and class conflict, it was not enough for a young historian to offer a case study of his subject in one place and for one time period, as it was for more conventional subjects.[19]

At the time historians of early America were more interested in taking down the Progressive paradigm. The year Bill's thesis was accepted, 1955, was the year Louis Hartz's book announced that America was "born free" and Robert Brown's book declared that colonial Massachusetts was an equalitarian "middle class" society and a political democracy. In the late fifties Charles Beard was demonized and "class" was suspect as a category of analysis. "My University of Chicago colleague Daniel Boorstin," Lemisch recalls, "enjoyed what he called my 'sea stories' but could not abide my introduction of the notion of class." Richard Morris's 70-page chapter, "Concerted Action among Workers" (still without peer), was out of sync in the Age of Eisenhower. What John Higham called "the cult of consensus" was depositing a layer of ice freezing out history that challenged the mood of celebrating the "American Century." Lemisch's striking demonstration of the possibilities of "history from the bottom up" did not appear until 1968 and the landmark "new" social histories of small New England communities not until 1970. The new history did not gain momentum until the upheavals of the late 1960s.[20]

Colonial Williamsburg Inc., moreover, was hardly a hospitable climate for the study of servitude. The restoration presented a colonial town in which black waiters served tourists at replicas of colonial taverns, but in which interpreters scarcely mentioned slaves—who had comprised half the population of the town—and white craft apprentices wore cute colonial garb.[21] It was literally decades before the interpretive program applied Thad Tate's monograph on the Negro in colonial Williamsburg written as a member of the research staff. Contemporary Williamsburg was no more congenial. If in *Brown vs. the Board of Education* (1954) the Supreme Court had made desegregation the law of the land, Williamsburg held on to its old ways. Bill was founder and co-chair of an interracial study group which he later called "my most treasured experience." So far, he wrote, "no crosses have been burned in my yard."[22]

In 1959 as Bill confronted the prospect of revision, he called it "the goddamn thesis;" by early 1960 he "had about decided to settle for a quick rewrite without substantial alterations." Shipton, in fact, had "offered to publish the thing as is in the A.A.S. Proceedings and then bring it out as a separate [book]," a remarkable offer in light of its size and dense documentation. "But I am not content with it as it is," Bill wrote. He changed his mind with the prospect of a summer grant from Oscar Handlin, Director of the Center for the Study of the History of Liberty at Harvard.[23]

Oscar Handlin (1915–) had a formidable reputation. At Harvard since 1939, he was already "the leading authority on immigration," the author of a pathbreaking monograph on the Irish in Boston and of a work of synthesis on the assimilation of immigrants which won the Pulitzer Prize in 1951.[24] He was the chief editor of the canonical *Harvard Guide to American History* . And in a pathbreaking monograph on the role of the Massachusetts government in the economy and in interpretive articles on the origins of slavery and Confederation politics, he had established his authority in early American history.[25] He was nothing if not a synthesizer and was unmistakably cool to the Progressive paradigm. A regular contributor to *Commentary*, among other magazines, he was, an admiring biographer writes, "fervently anti-communist" and later in the 1960s found student radicals and "New Left historians especially distasteful." In Handlin's graduate seminars the mood was one of "laissez faire," as Richard Bushman, one of his many productive, independent-minded students wrote; there was "no sense of forbidden or preferred paths." But as Director of the Center for the Study of the History of Liberty in America (1958-67), he and his wife, Mary, had laid out an agenda for historical research in a prospectus published as *The Dimensions of Liberty*. Handlin valorized the achievement of liberty in three spheres: free government, social mobility and voluntary associations. The Center proposed "to commission a large number of autonomous monographs" to test some nine "propositions or hypotheses," for example, "the social structure of the United States encouraged social mobility." Fellowships would also be awarded to historians whose scholarship might contribute to the new synthesis.[26]

Handlin took Bill's dissertation seriously. It was "a promising manuscript" which "could be made into a valuable book." There was no need for further research and he did not have to extend the time-frame; "the job before you is one of interpretation and presentation." Bill had asked for support for a summer. Handlin wrote he "would like to persuade you," to commit yourself to finishing the job even if it should take longer than the summer." The study "ought to be set within the context of the dominant social assumptions of Massachusetts," but more important it had to grapple with the "meaningful changes in the status of servitude" and "relate the changes in the conditions of servitude to the developing changes in ideas about society, about freedom, and status." If Bill agreed, Handlin wrote, "I would like you to undertake to stick to the job until it was finished. If you do, I will go through the whole manuscript once more editing it carefully and making specific suggestions. . . ." [27]

Bill was persuaded all too quickly. It was a time when there were almost no other fellowships to revise dissertations and when a manuscript with a nod from Handlin would be published by Harvard University Press. "I am willing to commit myself to extensive revision and rewriting of my manuscript," Bill replied, not realizing what he was letting himself in for. He would try to make "the relationship of the institution to the society of which it was a part," which he granted was "only barely implicit" in his dissertation, explicit and central.[28] He wrote to Billington with enthusiasm; he was turning down Shipton's offer to publish the thesis as is. The fellowship "may break the log jam in my own thinking about my abilities as a writer," a confession of insecurity that will come as a surprise to the countless historians to whom Bill had played midwife as a superb editor, and to all who knew him in his later articles and essays as a stylist of clarity, grace, and wit.[29]

Once Bill agreed, Handlin assumed the role of editor for which he was justly renowned. He responded with a seven-page letter with general suggestions for "extensive revision" followed by a four-page supplement with specific suggestions and from then on Bill would try to come to grips with Handlin's critique. To cope with what he identified as "the central flaw" in the dissertation, Handlin proposed that Towner "recast" his material in a chronological framework, the first period from 1620 to 1680, the second from 1680 to 1750, breaking at a point where it seemed to him major societal changes were reshaping the institution. He outlined ten chapters in which a "reorganization" of Towner's seven chapters could be constructed. The proposal would have resulted in such new chapters as "Signs of Strain in the System" and "Efforts to Maintain the Traditional Conceptions of Servitude."[30] The consequence would no doubt have been a far more analytical monograph focusing on the institution of servitude in the context of a changing society, but it would have been at the expense of a rich compelling portrait of colonial life in which servant agency and resistance were central. Thus where Towner ended with two chapters on protest, Handlin wanted this distributed through the manuscript and subsumed at the end within a final chapter on "conditions of servitude." In his discussion of protest, Handlin warned "you ought to take care of one of the points made by one of the readers [for Harvard Press] namely that although some [servants] could protest in the forms you indicate, the preponderant number accepted their conditions and acquiesced in them."[31]

Not surprisingly, Bill had a difficult time accommodating his data to what he told Handlin were his "penetrating suggestions." "My 'writing' is going very slowly," he told his friend, Bill Abbot, near the end of his summer's grant. "Six years away from the material has been too long, and while I could have edited the ms. in its original form in relatively short order, I am finding that recasting it is quite a job. I have worked out a tentative outline (Oscar's didn't quite work)." When he reported to Handlin on his progress late in the Fall of 1960, he was contrite. "You undoubtedly knew that I would flounder for a time with your outline, my manuscript, scissors, stapler and blue pencil. I did so flounder." After drafting three unsuccessful versions of one chapter, he wrote, "I scrapped my thesis and the chapters I'd written and returned to your outline with my *notes*." But after arranging his notes chronologically, he found that 1660 rather then 1680 made a better cutting point. He then revised Handlin's outline. Bill asked Handlin for a fellowship to spend the 1961-62 academic year at the Center and Handlin granted it.[32]

The year in Cambridge was exhilarating but restructuring the manuscript and writing his first article came hard. He spent a good part of the fall working on a paper for the A.H.A. convention which became the article, "A Fondness for Freedom," for the *Quarterly*. Reviewers of a draft were laudatory; Shipton said it was "excellent, as you would expect," and Handlin who had "discussed it with him in the process of its composition" thought it was "a first rate piece of work." He hoped the *Quarterly* would publish it quickly so as not to compete with Towner's book which Handlin expected would be "out a year from now." But Bill was nervous about his first article—"I do not feel proud of it at all," he wrote of a draft—and was making substantive revisions even in the galley proofs. "If I had published a lot," he apologized to the Associate Editor, "maybe I would not be so fearful of every word but since this may be the only publication for a long time, I'd like to feel really good about it." His comment was prescient. [33].

Handlin's pressure was not enough. Past the half-way point in his fellowship, in February, 1962, Bill told his father he was only "half way into the book," still structuring seven chapters which took him up to 1720. "But that is only the first draft," and the first chapter "had to be expanded," the third "rewritten completely" and the sixth was "only fragmentary." Meanwhile, he had taken on a paper on Boston's poor apprentices, an essay with a table of 1,000 indentures, some 90 pages in all, which he was writing, then proofreading for publication by the Colonial Society of Massachusetts through the Spring. In mid-April he reported to his dad "time is running out on me and I feel a little panicked." Then in May—as Newberry made him a finalist for its directorship, "the cliff hanging weeks" began. After he landed the job in June, he returned to work feverishly on the manuscript. "I have one more chapter to go," he wrote late in July "and am taking one over to Handlin today." When he arrived at the Newberry his mood was so upbeat he could boast to a reporter of the achievements of his productive year: "the entire first draft of a book," four articles, two book reviews and he was father of twins.[34]

But the manuscript was just that, a "first draft," and when he began his pressure-cooker job at the Newberry, in the time he set aside for scholarship it was easier to respond to a request for an article for the twentieth anniversary issue of the *Quarterly* than to work on the large, recalcitrant manuscript. In August, 1963, when he dispatched "The Sewall-Saffin Dialogue about Slavery" he told his father "Sent off a copy to Oscar Handlin at Harvard and he likes it too (it's a chapter in a book I am doing for him)."[35] But the book never came off and hung very heavily on his shoulders for years. Bill had no trouble revising articles for sympathetic editors at the *Quarterly* who tried to help him say what he wanted to say; he could stick to a scholarly article for more than a decade, as he did with "Last Wills and True Confessions," prepared for a festschrift to Shipton; it was difficult completing a book for an intimidating editor not on his wavelength.

At about the same time Bill was in Cambridge, I avoided what could have been a similar experience with Handlin with my own scholarship, in an episode which throws some light on Handlin as well as on alternative standards in publishing at the time. My dissertation on the Democratic Republicans of New York, completed in 1958, was ridiculously long, 970 pages, and got only as far as 1797. Billington advised me to take the story up to 1801, the end of the Federalist era, as I originally intended, and then condense the entire manuscript to a 400-

page book. I was dubious and in 1960 was blessed by a godfather in Julian Boyd, editor of *The Jefferson Papers,* who read it and wrote me a nine-page letter expressing his enthusiasm for the texture of early American politics a close study of a single state could reveal. The materials "should not be compressed" much more than I had already done, Boyd insisted, for two reasons. "Since you have explored New York politics at the grass-roots level and have engaged in an extensive probing of economic and social factors, the materials you present are necessary to sustain your interpretations." Moreover, one of the "significant findings" was "the clear distinction in value as between the different kinds of evidence to be employed in feeling out what Jefferson used to call 'the tone of my constituents'." He hoped that I would "vigorously resist" the demands of a publisher to cut it. Billington acquiesced. The letter was an open sesame to publication by the Institute.[36]

While revising, I applied for support from Handlin for a sequel volume, "The New York Jeffersonians: The Testing, 1797-1801" whose ten chapters I outlined. At an interview in New York City in June, 1962, Handlin held out the prospect of a fellowship if I added to the Democratic Republicans of New York, the Democratic Republicans of Pennsylvania and the Democratic Republicans of New Jersey. I reported this with some astonishment to Billington: "he said he 'could get more mileage for his money' out of [such a] project, i.e., he could answer more questions which he is interested in." I held back. There was no offer. The interview in the Mayflower Donut Shop in Manhattan stuck with me because the proposal amazed me: a book to fit another scholar's agenda which showed no appreciation for the kind of book I wanted to write (which in the end I did not write anyway). The Institute brought out the New York study in 1967, a book of 636 pages, and another scholar's book on the New Jersey Jeffersonians. [37]

For Bill, if the fellowships of 1960 and 1961-62 did not lead to the completion of a manuscript, they bore rich fruit in the articles which point to the direction a revision would have taken. His article on servant protest, developing the themes of chapters six and seven of the thesis, has become a classic. In one masterful chart (modestly placed in a footnote), he laid out "Servant Protest by Type of Protest, 1629-1750" covering three types of protest (legal, unruly, runaways) for five groups of servants in four time periods. Where Handlin had decided that protest was atypical, Towner argued convincingly that Cotton Mather's characterization of Negro slaves "as having a 'Fondness for Freedom' applied to all ranks of servitude." He also showed the way in which "the misbehavior of servants" shaped the institution, "making the system of servitude unattractive. . .to masters" and paving the way for a body of anti-slavery opinion.[38] The articles that followed took up Handlin's challenge to contextualize his data but did so in his own way. He dealt with the first Massachusetts debate over slavery,[39] Boston's poor children put to servitude 1734-1805 by the Overseers of the Poor,[40] and the changing patterns of servant behavior and the attitudes to them revealed by the confessions of criminals in execution sermons and broadsides.[41] Towner's sympathies were never far below the surface. Halfway through "A Fondness for Freedom" the reader senses the author has boldly inverted the values of Puritan society by defining as protest "acts which today are described as delinquency or criminality." Acts of aggression against individuals were "protests against society and its proscriptions." E.P Thompson would have been enthusiastic even if Oscar Handlin might have demurred.

In the late 1960s Towner was enthusiastic about the "new" social history. Indeed, he invited Kenneth Lockridge, pathbreaker of New England community studies, to the Newberry to think through what became in 1974 the Center for Family and Community History whose institutes trained a new generation in the mysteries of quantitative, social science history. But by the late '70s as the fund-raising pressures of his job mounted and he suffered bouts of serious illness, Bill shelved the book. He joked that with his reputation "he could not afford to publish," a quip that masked some pain. At what point he abandoned the project, I am not sure. In the early '80s when he and Rachel moved from their empty-nest Newberry town-house into a small Newberry apartment he destroyed his dissertation notes and, I believe, his partially revised manuscript, which is nowhere to be found. "It was the only way I could put it all behind me," he said to me.

As I think about the four research centers Bill established at the Newberry—for the study of the history of cartography, Indian history, family and community history and the Renaissance—none has a research agenda, save perhaps for making full use of the Newberry's rich resources in these fields. In the decade I served as co-chair of the committee on fellowships, someone might have asked of a proposal, "can that be done at the Newberry?" but I can't imagine a fellow later sending a completed chapter to the director of a center which had to meet his or her approval.

Bill entered retirement in 1986 already engrossed in a new research project: a study of Samuel Willard's *A Compleat Body of Divinity. . .* (Boston, 1726), the book Perry Miller regarded as the *summa* of seventeenth century Puritan thought. Bill proposed a study of the 450 subscribers, a massive social history of readership. "I do not know where the study will lead me," he wrote—but he was excited once again to be on the cutting edge of scholarship in a field that was opening up, the history of the book.[42]

There is an unhappy coda to the saga of the dissertation. In retirement Bill had an offer in 1989 to publish his original thesis from Rutgers University Press which was also interested in publishing Lemisch's 1962 thesis on seamen in a series, "Class and Culture." But the enthusiasm of the series editors and a young house editor in recovering gems of an earlier era, the glowing encomium from Rediker, who had won recognition as a young practitioner of the new labor history, and my support were not enough to overcome his ambivalence about his original work.

The offer was to publish the dissertation with an introduction of from 25 to 50 manuscript pages dealing with the scholarship of the last thirty years in the field—a daunting task. Bill was excited by Rediker's praise. "Your review," he wrote, "has made my day. Day hell, it made my season if not indeed my year. I thank you. I feel like a retired fire horse who has heard the old fire bell in the night." But he had "lingering doubts." "Can I really let it go without revision?. . .Will it ruin my reputation?" He took steps to go ahead, receiving warm approval from Richard Leopold who had served on his dissertation committee. He gathered up the required three copies of the manuscript, looked into illustrations and pondered the suggestions by the Rutgers house editor to edit his 1950's language to meet current sensibilities about race and gender, marking the references page by page. But he was sick. He suffered from the increasing burdens of emphysema which, he wrote the Rutgers editor, "has eaten deeply into my energy, my courage and my will." He was irritated by her well-meaning editorial suggestions. "I have thought about and rejected the idea of editing the text," he wrote her, "to change Negroes to Blacks (or for that matter to African Americans and Indians to Native Americans, a misnomer). I may edit out a few wenches however, unless they are quotes." The editor, he groused to me, also did not get the irony intended by using Cotton Mather's injunction as the title, "A Good Master Well Served."[43]

But 1989 was a bad year. He spent three weeks in the hospital with a bacterial pneumonia during which there was a scare of death. Then after the building in which they lived was sold, he and Rachel moved again. In February, 1990, he decided not to return the contract. He gave the series editor his reasons. Apologizing for his delay, he explained the year 1989 had been a "total loss" and he was "largely incapacitated." But even if he were healthy, "I probably would not proceed with" the project, giving the reasons "I could not do the book you wanted." He thanked the house editor for "providing me with the exciting prospect of seeing the dissertation in print." In a hand-written letter to me he let his hair down: "the thematic guts have been revealed" in articles, he had made "subtle refinements" in "A Fondness for Freedom" which he "believed the whole dissertation deserves but can never get." Revisions were necessary and they required time and "in the time I have left I want to do other things *and* to do the book right would take *too much.*" He thanked me—"I love you for pushing me on it." As we talked about the issue of revision later when I was doing his biography for the introduction to his collected essays, he was rueful: "Oscar wanted me to organize the dissertation chronologically and it would not work." His experience with Handlin had made him lose confidence in his original vision of the subject. "I could not do the book you wanted," he told the Rutgers series editor. He could have said the same thing to Handlin. In retrospect, he was not blessed by gatekeepers who wanted him to do the book they wanted.[44]

The same thing almost happened with a collection of his essays on history, libraries and the humanities which a committee of associates and friends at the Newberry meeting in the early '90s had great pleasure in selecting for publication as a gift to Bill. Bill gave a skeptical blessing to the project, approved the selections, talked to me for hours so that I got my introduction and head notes right and summoned up his strength to go over my text with undiminished editorial acumen. Then he withdrew his approval for publication, thanking the committee. This time, however, Rachel Towner prevailed and he reinstated his blessing; in his last days he joked with me about a "sexy" dust jacket for the book. The University of Chicago Press published the volume posthumously to warmly appreciative reviews by librarians and historians.[45]

A Good Master Well Served will now find its audience, thanks to the good judgment of Graham Hodges, as editor for Garland Publishing. It is "a terrible, terrible shame," Rediker wrote, "that the ms. has gone so long unpublished."[46] Nothing quite like it has ever appeared. Surveying the state of colonial labor history in 1984, Richard Dunn pointed out that "before World War II, colonial historians took little interest in the topic." Immediately after the war Richard B. Morris and Abbot Emerson Smith "opened the subject to fruitful inquiry." But "in the thirty-five years since World War II much more excellent work has been done, particularly on colonial slave labor not dealt with by Morris or Smith. Yet in some respects the history of American colonial labor is almost untouched."[47] And in an encyclopedic survey of American economic history in 1985, John McCusker and Russell Menard could say "the literature on the legal aspects of servitude is fairly complete but we know much less about the actual functioning of master-slave relationships. . . Apprenticeship in the colonies, the practice of binding out children to learn trades or to work as live in servants in farm households needs to be studied. Our impression is that it was primarily an urban institution, although variations on apprenticeship were developed to care for orphans in the countryside, but we know too little to be certain. We would like to know how common it was and could benefit from better information about its institutional arrangements and functions."[48]

Towner's dissertation speaks to all of these issues and to still others in social history. It should please those many readers who like reading doctoral dissertations for the fullness of documentation that alone conveys a rich texture of experience and who would like to share a masterful historian's joy in the recovery of a lost history.

Newberry Library
November, 1997
Alfred F. Young

NOTES

1. Lawrence W Towner [hereafter LWT] to Ray Billington, Mar. 5, 1960 [re Shipton]; Shipton to LWT, Aug. 24, 1953; Edmund Morgan to LWT, Jan. 25, 1955; Oscar Handlin to LWT, Feb. 29, 1960, Newberry Library Archives, Lawrence W. Towner Papers, hereafter cited as Newberry Archives. The letters cited from Towner's papers are either in Personal Correspondence where they are arranged in folders by name of the correspondent or are in Box 6 of Towner's post-retirement papers.

2. Marcus Rediker, "Reader's Report on Lawrence W. Towner's A Good Master Well Served..." n.d. [1988], Newberry Archives, folder, Rutgers University Press.

3. Conversation with Thad Tate, former Director of the Institute of Early American History, Oct. 2, 1997; Keith B. Berwick, "A Peculiar Monument: The Third Series of the *William and Mary Quarterly,* " William and Mary Quarterly, ser. 3, vol.2l (1964), 8-l0. The [London] *Times Literary Supplement,* Feb.1, 1963, spoke of Towner as "a young mid-westerner" who had "has been editing [the Quarterly] with distinction."

4. Alfred F. Young, "Introduction: Bill Towner, " in Robert W. Karrow, Jr and Alfred F. Young, eds., *Past Imperfect: Essays on History, Libraries and the Humanities* (Chicago: University of Chicago Press, 1993), xv-xxxviii.

5. Towner, "A History of the Newberry Library, " in *Humanities Mirror: Reading at the Newberry, 1887-1987*, comp. and ed., Rolf Achilles, (Chicago, Newberry Library, 1987), 17-26.

6. Alfred F. Young, "George Robert Twelves Hewes (1742-1840):A Boston Shoemaker and the Memory of the American Revolution, " *William and Mary Quarterly* 3rd. ser., XXXVIII (1981), 561-623. I have also found his thesis a rich source for a biography in progress of Deborah Sampson Gannett, a Massachusetts servant who served in the Continental army.

7. For the growth of the profession, John Higham, *History: The Development of Historical Studies in the United States* (Englewood Cliffs, N.J., Prentice Hall, 1965; for the politics of history, Peter Novick, *That Noble Dream: The "Objectivity Question" and the American Historical Profession* (Cambridge: Cambridge University Press, 1988) and Jesse Lemisch, *On Active Service in War and Peace: Politics and Ideology in the American Historical Profession* (Toronto, New Hogtown Press, 1975).

8. James W. Towner, comp, *Extracts from A Genealogy of the Towner Family* (n.d. 1948, n.p.); Alfred F. Young, "An Outsider and the Progress of a Career in History, " *William and Mary Quarterly.* 3rd ser., 52 (1995), 499-512;

Robert Sam Anson, *McGovern: A Biography* (New York, Holt, Rinehart and Winston, 1972), chs. 1-4, captures a little bit of this spirit.

9. Towner, "Ray Allen Billington, " in Towner, *Past Imperfect,* , 217-223, originally in *Westerner's Brand Book* (Chicago Coral) 20: no. 4 (June 1963.

10. LWT to Douglass Adair, Aug. 9, 1949, Newberry Archives.

11. Towner, "Clifford Kenyon Shipton, " in Towner, *Past Imperfect*, 224-228, original in *Proceedings* (American Antiquarian Society) 84, pt. 1 (1974), 24-29. LWT to Billington, Mar. 9, 1950; LWT to Shipton, Mar. 28, 1950, Shipton to LWT, Nov. 11, 1952, Aug. 24, 1953. Newberry Archives.

12. Richard B. Morris, *Government and Labor in Early America* (New York: Columbia University Press, 1946). For Towner's use of Morris, see LWT to Alfred Young, Aug. 26, 1950, Newberry Archives. I was surprised when I read Bill's copy of Morris that he had not marked it up; Abbot Emerson Smith, *Colonists in Bondage: White Servitude and Convict Labor in America, 1607-1776* (Chapel Hill: University of North Carolina Press for the Institute of Early American History, 1947). Marcus Jernegan, *Laboring and Dependent Classes in Colonial America, 1607-1783* (1931) was a collection of essays in which only the essays on the education of poor children and poor relief were relevant.

13. The thirteen appendices are available in the microfilm edition of "A Good Master Well Served, " (Ann Arbor: University Microfilms, 1955). They are A. Apprentice Contracts [listing terms of servitude]; B. Contract Servants [listing terms]; C Free Whites-Servitude for Crime; D. White Servants-Time added for Crime Except Running Away; E. Indians Made Servants for Crime and Debt; F. Indian Servants Having Time Added for Crime; G. Runaways Brought to Court; H. A Sampling of Cases Where Masters Owned More Than One Servant; I. Covenant Servants; J. Relative Frequency of Appearance [of servants] in Records [7066 Servants] A Bar Graph. K. Servants Having Illegitimate Children; L. Negro Children Offered as Gifts in Boston Newspapers; M. Skilled Negroes [arranged by trade]

14. Morgan to LWT, Jan. 25, 1955, LWT to Morgan, Jan. 31, 1954 [misdated, 1955?], LWT to Morgan May 31, 1955. Brown was considering Towner for a job. Morgan supported him for the Institute job, Morgan to LWT, Feb. 4, 1955. Newberry Archives.

15. Craig Wylie to LWT, June 3, 1954; Thomas J. Wilson [Harvard Press] to LWT, Mar. 28, 1955. Two unsigned readers reports, forwarded sometime after May 5, 1955; LWT to Howard Bartlett, Jan. 6, 1955. Newberry Archives.

16. LWT to Oscar Handlin, Dec. 14, 1959, Newberry Archives.

17. Carl Bridenbaugh, *The Colonial Craftsman* (Chicago: University of Chicago Press, 1950); for Morris's delayed influence, see Graham Hodges, "In Retrospect: Richard B. Morris and *Government and Labor in Early America* (1946), " *Reviews in American History* 25 (1997), 360-38 and Morris, "Preface" to *Government and Labor* (Boston, Northeastern University Press, 1981 edn.), vii-xii; Christopher Tomlins, "Why Wait for Industrialism? Work, Legal Culture and the Example of Early America: An Historiographical Argument, " *Labor History* (forthcoming) analyzes Morris's work and the failure of historians of labor to cope with pre-industrial labor history. I am indebted to Tomlins for sharing this ms. with me.

18. The Institute published: Whitfield J. Bell, Jr. *Early American Science: Needs and Opportunities for Study* (Williamsburg, 1955); William N. Fenton, *American Indian and White Relations to 1830* (Williamsburg, 1957); Bernard Bailyn, *Education in the Forming of American Society* (Williamsburg, 1960).

19. Jesse Lemisch, "Author's Postscript" to "Jack Tar in the Streets: Merchant Seamen in the Politics of Revolutionary America" in Michael McGiffert, ed., *In Search of Early America: The William and Mary Quarterly, 1943-1993* (Williamsburg, 1993), 136-37. The original article was published in the *Quarterly* 3d. ser., XXV (July, 1968), 371-407; "Listening to the 'Inarticulate': William Widger's Dream and the Loyalties of American Revolutionary Seamen in British Prisons, " *Journal of Social History,* III (Fall, 1969), 1-29; "The American Revolution and the American Dream: A Short Life of Andrew Sherburne, a Pensioner of the Navy of the Revolution," (Unpublished Ms.); for an autobiographical account, Lemisch, "Looking for Jack Tar in the Scholarly Darkness" (Paper, Jack Tar in History Conference, Halifax, Nova Scotia, 1990).

20. Alfred F. Young, "American Historians Confront the Transforming Hand of Revolution," in Ronald Hoffman and Peter Albert, eds. *The Transforming Hand of Revolution: Reconsidering the American Revolution as a Social Movement* (Charlottesville: University of Virginia Press, 1996), 422-438, on "The New Left" historians, 438-447 on "The New Social History."

21. Mike Wallace, *Mickey Mouse History and other Essays on American Memory* (Philadelphia: Temple University Press, 1996), 3-32; Richard Handler and Eric Gable, *The New History in an Old Museum: Creating the Past at Colonial Williamsburg* (Durham: Duke University Press, 1997).

22. Thad Tate, *The Negro in Eighteenth-Century Williamsburg (Williamsburg:* (Williamsburg: Colonial Williamsburgh, dist., University Press of Virginia, 1965); LWT to Billington, Mar. 5, 1960, Newberry Archives; LWT

to his father and mother [Earl and Cornelia Towner], July 7, 1963, in possession of Rachel Towner.

23. LWT to Billington, Mar. 5, 1960, Newberry Archives. It is not clear when Shipton made the offer or when Bill turned it down.

24. Quotation from Higham, *History*, 225; Handlin, *Boston's Immigrants: A Study in Acculturation* (Cambridge: Harvard University Press, 1941); Handlin, *The Uprooted: The Epic Story of the Great Migrations that Made the American People* (Boston: Little Brown, 1951).

25. Oscar and Mary Flug Handlin, *Commonwealth. A Study of the Role of Government in the American Economy: Massachusetts, 1774-1861* (Cambridge, Harvard University Press, 1947); Oscar and Mary Flug Handlin, "Origins of the Southern Labor System, " *William and Mary Quarterly* 3d ser. VII (1950); LWT to Billington, Feb. 25., 1951, Newberry Archives. 26. Andrew Shankman, "Oscar Handlin, " in Clyde Wilson, ed., *Twentieth Century American Historians* (Detroit, 1983), 191-97, quotation at 196; Maldwyn Jones, "Oscar Handlin" in Marcus Cunlife and Robin Winks, ed., (New York: Harper and Row, 1969), 270-72, is critical of Handlin's "present-mindedness;" Richard Bushman, "Introduction" to Bushman, et al, eds., *Uprooted Americans: Essays in Honor of Oscar Handlin* (Boston: Little Brown, 1979), ix-xvi; Oscar and Mary Flug Handlin, *The Dimensions of Liberty* (Cambridge, Harvard University Press, 1961), 5-8.

27. Handlin to LWT, Feb. 29, 1960, Newberry Archives.

28. LWT to Handlin, Mar. 8, 1960, Newberry Archives.

29. LWT to Billington, Mar. 5, 1960, Newberry Archives.

30. Handlin to LWT, May 25, 1960, Newberry Archives. Handlin reported on Towner's monograph as "part of our investigations of the political and institutional elements in the development of American liberty." See Center for the Study of the History of Liberty in America, "Report for the Year 1960-61" (Cambridge, 1961, 4pp.).

31. Handlin to LWT, May 27, 1960, Newberry Archives.

32. LWT to William Abbot, Aug. 11, 1960, LWT to Handlin, Nov. 28, 1960, Handlin to LWT May 17, 1961 [granting a fellowship for 1961-62], Newberry Archives.

33. Shipton to Jack P. Greene [visiting editor] Nov. 30, 1961, Handlin to Greene, Dec. 11, 1960, LWT to Greene, Nov. 19, 1961, LWT to Greene, Dec. 14, 1961, LWT to Elizabeth Suttell, Feb. l0, 1962. Correspondence file for "A Fondness for Freedom," *William and Mary Quarterly* Archives, kindly provided by Philip Morgan and Patricia Higgs.

34. His progress can be traced in the letters of LWT to his father and mother, Feb. 12, Mar. 9, Mar. 23, May 25, July 19, July 22, 1962, correspondence in possession Rachel Towner. Conversations Rachel Towner with Alfred Young, October and November, 1992. Dale Vincent, "Newberry's New Librarian..." *Chicago Sun Times*, Sept. 17, 1962.

35. LWT to his father, Aug. 19, 1963, correspondence in possession of Rachel Towner. See also the correspondence file for "Sewall Saffin Dialogue, " *William and Mary Quarterly* Archives. Conversation Alfred Young with William Abbot, Nov., 1997.

36. Julian Boyd to Alfred Young, Jan. 19, 1960; Billington to Young, Jan. 31, 1960, in the author's possession.

37. Young to Billington, June 12, 1962, reporting the interview; correspondence of Handlin and Young, Dec. 22, 1961- Dec. 14, 1962 in the author's possession. Young, *The Democratic Republicans of New York: The Origins, 1763-1797* (Chapel Hill: University of North Carolina Press for the Institute of Early American History, 1967); Carl Prince, *New Jersey's Jeffersonian Republicans: The Genesis of an Early Party Machine, 1789-1817* (Chapel Hill, 1967).

38. Towner, "'A Fondness for Freedom': Servant Protest in Puritan Society, " *William and Mary Quarterly,* 3d. ser., 19 (1962), 201-19, reprinted in Towner, *Past Imperfect*, 3-21.

39. Towner, "The Sewall-Saffin Dialogue on Slavery," *William and Mary Quarterly,* 3d. ser., 21 (1964), 40-52, reprinted in Towner, *Past Imperfect,* 22-35.

40. Towner, "The Indentures of Boston's Poor Apprentices, 1734-1805, " *Colonial Society of Massachusetts, Publications*, 43 (1966), 417-33, reprinted in Towner, *Past Imperfect,* 36-55.

41. Towner, "True Confessions and Dying Warnings in New England, " in *Sibley's Heir: A Volume in Memory of Clifford Kenyon Shipton*, Publications of the Colonial Society of Massachusetts, vol. 59, *Collections,* (Andover: Colonial Society of Massachusetts, 1982), 523-39. The article, originally written in 1963, was revised in 1969, submitted in 1975 and proof read in 1981. See "True Confessions" folder, Newberry Archives.

42. LWT, "Research Project Description," Third Draft, Jan. 14, 1987 and the correspondence to historical societies in a folder "Willard Project." "The History of the Book" has since become a major project at the American Antiquarian Society.

43. Milton Cantor [series editor with Bruce Laurie] to LWT, Feb. 24, 1988, LWT to Cantor, Mar. 7, Nov. 13, 1988, Marcus Rediker "Reader's Report, " n.d. but Dec. 4, 1988; Cantor to LWT, Dec. 27, 1988, Richard Leopold to LWT, Jan. 27, 1989; Marlie Wasserman [Rutgers Press editor] to LWT, Jan. 28, Mar. 10, 1989; LWT to Rediker, Feb. 13, 1989, Rediker to LWT, Mar. 3, 1989. Two pages of page references on yellow foolscap have Towner's notes. All Newberry Archives, "Rutgers" folder.

44. LWT to Milton Cantor, Feb. 28, 1990; LWT to Marlie Wasserman, Feb. 28, 1990; Cantor to LWT, Mar. 10, 1990; LWT to Alfred Young, Jan. l0, 1990; Newberry Archives. Conversations of Rachel Towner with Alfred Young, Oct., 1997.

45. LWT to Richard Brown, Charles Cullen, Robert W. Karrow, Kenneth Nebenzahl, Paul Saenger and Alfred Young, Sept. 3,1990. Newberry Archives.

46. Rediker, "Reader's Report;" for use of Towner's scholarship, see Rediker, "Good Hands, Stout Heart and Fast Feet: The History and Culture of Working People in Early America," in Geoff Ely and William Hunt, eds., *Reviving the English Revolution: Reflections and Elaborations on the Work of Christopher Hill* (London, Verso Press, 1988), 221-49.

47. Richard Dunn, "Servants and Slaves: The Recruitment and Employment of Labor," in Jack P. Greene and J.R. Pole, eds., *Colonial British America: Essays in the New History of the Early Modern Era* (Baltimore: Johns Hopkins University Press, 1984), 157-58.

48. John J. McCusker and Russell R. Menard, *The Economy of British America, 1607-1789* (Chapel Hill: University of North Carolina Press for the Institute of Early American History, 1985), 243-44.

Abbreviations

A.H.R.	*The American Historical Review*
C.S.M. *Pubs.*	*Publications* of the Colonial Society of Massachusetts
E.I. *Colls.*	*Collections* of the Essex Institute
Jour. Pol. Econ.	*The Journal of Political Economy*
M.H.S. *Colls.*	*Collections* of the Massachusetts Historical Society
M.H.S. *Proc.*	*Proceedings* of the Massachusetts Historical Society
N.E.Q.	*The New England Quarterly*
Sessions	General Sessions of the Peace

Psal. LI. 14. *Deliver me from Blood-Guiltiness, O God, thou God of my Salvation: and my Tongue shall sing aloud of thy Righteousness.* Isa. I. 18. *Come now and let us Reason together, saith the Lord: though your sins be as scarlet, they shall be as white as snow: though they be red like crimson, they shall be as wool.*

The last SPEECH and dying ADVICE of
poor Julian,

Who was Executed the 22d of *March*, 1733. for the Murder of Mr. *John Rogers* of *Pembroke.* Written with his own Hand, and delivered to the Publisher the Day before his Execution.

FRom my Childhood to Twenty Years of Age, I liv'd in a Family where I was learnt to Read and say my Catechism, and had a great deal of Pains taken with me.—— And in my younger Years I was under some Convictions and Awakenings, and concern'd about the Condition of my Soul ;—— and I had many Warnings in the Providence of God to turn from my Sins—— But I have (and I desire to lament it) abused God's Patience and Goodness to me, and apostatised from God and good Beginnings, and now I have forsaken God, he has forsaken me, and I acknowledge he has been just in leaving me, so that I have gone from bad to worse, till for my Sins I am now to die.

Whereas I have been charged with and tried for burning my Master's Barn, I now declare as a dying Man that I did not do it, nor was I any way privy to it.

I acknowledge I deserve to die, and would confess especially my Drunkenness and Sabbath-breaking, which have led me to this great Sin for which I now die.

I desire therefore that all, and especially Servants, would take Warning by me ; I am a dying Man, just going to leave this World, and the Thoughts of it terrify me, knowing how unfit I am to appear before my Judge.

O beware of sinning as I have done—— Beware of Drunkenness, of Sabbath-breaking, and of running away from your Masters, and don't put away the Thoughts of Death and of Judgment : I once put these Things far away, but now they are near, and I am going to appear before my great and terrible Judge, which surprizeth me beyond what I am able to express.

If you have been instructed and catechized from your Childhood, and joined your selves to Assemblies in which the Lord Jesus Christ is most purely worshipped, then let me warn and charge you to beware of casting off the Things that are good, lest God leave you to your selves, and you go on in Sin till you come to the greatest Wickedness.

O take Warning by me all of you, I intreat you—— See and fear and do no more so wickedly as I have done.

O let me once more intreat you all, especially Servants, to beware of the Sin of Drunkenness, and be obedient to your Masters ; don't run away from them, nor get Drunk, for if you do it will bring you to Ruine as it has done me.

I call to you now as one come from the Dead, to turn from your evil Ways while you have Time, and not put off your Repentance to another Day, lest you then call and God will not answer you.

My Master often told me that my Sins would bring me to this, but I little thought that it would be so.

I return my hearty Thanks to the Rev. Ministers who have taken Pains to assist me in preparing for my latter End. And as I desire to be forgiven, so I forgive all Mankind.

These Things I declare freely and voluntarily, and desire Mr. *Fleet* to Print the same for the Benefit of the Living : And I do hereby utterly disown and disclaim all other Speeches, Papers or Declarations that may be printed in my Name, as Witness my Hand this 21st. of *March*, 1733.

Julian.

Witness

Zach. Trescott.

Printed and Sold by T. Fleet, at the Heart and Crown in Cornhill, Boston.

A Good Master Well Served

An Exhortation to young and old to be cautious of small Crimes, left they become habitual, and lead them before they are aware into thofe of the moft heinous Nature. Occafioned by the unhappy Cafe of *Levi Ames*, Executed on *Bofton*-Neck, *October* 21ft, 1773, for the Crime of Burglary.

I.

BEWARE young People, look at me,
 Before it be too late,
And fee Sin's End is Mifery :
 Oh ! fhun poor *Ames's* Fate.

II.

I warn you all (beware betimes)
 With my now dying Breath,
To fhun Theft, Burglaries, heinous Crimes ;
 They bring untimely Death.

III.

Shun vain and idle Company ;
 They'll lead you foon aftray ;
From ill-fam'd Houfes ever flee,
 And keep yourfelves away.

IV.

With honeft Labor earn your Bread,
 While in your youthful Prime ;
Nor come you near the Harlot's Bed,
 Nor idly wafte your Time.

V.

Nor meddle with another's Wealth,
 In a defrauding Way :
A Curfe is with what's got by ftealth,
 Which makes your Life a Prey.

VI.

Shun Things that feem but little Sins,
 For they lead on to great ;
From Sporting many Times begins
 Ill Blood, and poifonous Hate.

VII.

The Sabbath-Day do not prophane,
 By wickednefs and Plays ;
By needlefs Walking Streets or Lanes
 Upon fuch Holy days.

VIII.

To you that have the care of Youth,
 Parents and Mafters too,
Teach them betimes to know the Truth,
 And Righteoufnefs to do.

IX.

The dreadful Deed for which I die,
 Arofe from fmall Beginning ;
My Idlenefs brought poverty,
 And fo I took to Stealing.

X.

Thus I went on in finning faft,
 And tho' I'm young 'tis true,
I'm old in Sin, but catcht at laft,
 And here receive my due.

XI.

Alas for my unhappy Fall,
 The Rigs that I have run !
Juftice aloud for vengeance calls,
 Hang him for what he's done.

XII.

O may it have fome good Effect,
 And warn each wicked one,
That they God's righteous Laws refpect,
 And Sinful Courfes Shun.

An Exhortation to young and old
by courtesy of the Historical Society of Pennsylvania

1. Factors Influencing Conditions of Labor and the Institution of Servitude

The servant class which emerged in the present area of Massachusetts before 1750 included whites, Indians and Negroes. The social structure within the servant class ran from the highly mobile "voluntary" apprentices at the top to an ethnically determined caste of red and black servants and slaves at the bottom. Between the extremes, one grouping shaded off almost imperceptibly into the next: so that, in a social scale each varied little from its nearest neighbors. All servants had one thing in common: each was bound to serve a master in his lawful commands regardless of the servant's own particular desires or inclinations, for the sanctions of custom, religion, and the law held him subservient to his master's wishes.

Being servants, at the beck and call of a kindly, stern, or tyrannical master, their lives tended to be very much alike, regardless of the status they held within their class. For example, the apprentice frequently did menial tasks for his master unconnected with his training in a craft, while the Negro or Indian slave not infrequently became a skilled artisan. Moreover, the servants not only spent their working hours under supervision, but were responsible to their masters for their actions at all times. They ate, slept, played, and worshipped under their masters' roof, or at least under their masters' jurisdiction. Hence, distinctions within the class were blurred even though in the end an apprentice or other white servant became a free man, while the Negro and his offspring remained in bondage.

There were five major factors which influenced the conditions of labor in the period prior to 1750, and which shaped the institution of servitude as it emerged in Massachusetts: an economic need for labor, the land system, custom, a desire to maintain a homogeneous population, and religion. These forces may be isolated for the purpose of analysis, but they were essentially interrelated, and they varied in their degree of influence as the colonial scene changed.

3

Of the above factors, the economic need for labor was of signal importance. The passage from the Old World to the New was accompanied by a profound change in the relationship of man to land: the New World was a vast area of unexploited land—raw, rich, almost unpopulated land. This was the great economic fact of colonial America.[1] Without an ever increasing labor force to apply to that land, the returns would be limited to what a man alone could do; and generations would pass without perceptibly raising the standard of living, or indeed without equaling that which the immigrants had been accustomed to in the home country. A man's hands, and his children's hands, could not do the work alone, and yet there was no reliable labor pool from which he could draw the help he needed. Land was cheap, opportunity was great, and men were few. The corollary to the great expanse of undeveloped land was a chronic labor shortage throughout the seventeenth and eighteenth centuries.

This chronic labor shortage can be demonstrated in several ways. First, there were laws designed, in part at least, to assure the would-be employer that those laborers on the scene would be available and at a "reasonable" wage. It was recognized that a free man would take up land for himself at the first opportunity, and not a little seventeenth-century legislation was designed to keep the landless laborer landless. Furthermore, even if the free man were prohibited from taking up land when and where he chose, thus keeping him available in a labor pool, if he were left uncontrolled, he would demand wages in excess of what seemed reasonable to the transplanted Englishman from the relatively crowded motherland. Seventeenth-century laws and institutions attempted to limit these demands with specific wage scales, suits at law, and other social pressures.[2]

Secondly, the existence of a labor shortage is demonstrated by the complaints of those who lived in the period. There is the almost apocryphal story by John Winthrop where a servant offered to hire his master so the latter could earn back the wages in cattle that his servant proposed to charge him. In the same chronicle, Winthrop relates that a servant, having completed his term of service, charged such extortionate prices that he would not work "but for ready money." Soon having saved twenty-five pounds, he retired to England. When his savings were squandered, the former servant returned once more to this Eldorado, where gold could not be picked up off the streets, but where it could be earned by the sweat of one's brow much more quickly than in England.[3]

Other evidence of a shortage of labor is abundant. Seventeenth-century correspondence is filled with requests for servants.[4] And in the eighteenth century, newspaper help-wanted notices indicate a persistent demand, Just as other advertisements show the existence of a brisk market by their offerings of blacks, whites and reds for sale.[5] The shortage of workers was such that the children of the poor were sought avidly, and by the 1740s specially printed blanks were made not only for the recording of their contracts but for *requests* made to the overseers as well.[6]

The shortage of labor was not only general in terms of a demand for muscle-power, but particular, in that skilled workers were needed. Artisans, such as shipwrights, were occasionally excused from military duty so that they might carry on in their occupations.[7] Plymouth Colony at one time even forbade the employment of skilled labor by foreigners and strangers until the wants of the colony had been supplied.[8] Town and colony governments offered inducements in the form of houses, land, and monopoly, to millers, blacksmiths and others.[9] Servants, of whatever type were permitted over all opposition to practice skilled trades.[10] Apprentices were not infrequently enticed to leave their masters,[11] and unless servants were securely bound, masters might find the pressures of the community forcing them to relinquish their hold upon their laboring men.[12] Newspaper advertisements asked for skilled servants of all types, farmers, blocksmiths, boys to keep accounts;[13] and men scoured the countryside looking for able mechanics and tradesmen. "I haue at last met with a miller," wrote Wait Winthrop from Boston, "which I hope will proue [*sic*] extraordinary for that and anything else about the house . . .;"

> he must be treated not as an ordinary servant, [he went on to say] but as one that deserues well, which, if I mistake not, he will do, if you be not rash and angry on every little occation, but overlook little mistakes, if any.[14]

This dearth of workingmen gave considerable advantage in bargaining power to the unbound American worker. As the economy became more free, that is as the society moved away from restrictive medieval and mercantilist price-wage legislation, the would-be employer was forced to offer higher wages, better working conditions, or better apprenticeship terms. He could not expect domestic labor to bind itself out save under exceptional circumstances once a free market existed. If he wanted cheap labor, unquestionably under his control, he was forced to turn more and more to other races, or foreign whites, or social deviants from his own community who lost their bargaining power as a consequence of their deviations. The term "servant" could be applied to fewer native workers as the decades passed on: the term "laborer" took its place.[15]

This shortage of skilled and unskilled labor—labor needed for such simple tasks as cutting wood on up the scale to the more complex crafts—accounts to a very great extent for the existence of a bound labor system in the Massachusetts area. It accounts for the early importation of Negroes, for the use of Indian war captives as slaves, and for the trading of captive Indians for the more tractable blacks. It accounts too, for the growth of a trade in servants, sporadic and unorganized in the seventeenth century, more systematic and commercial in the eighteenth century.

The same shortage of labor, combined with the economic necessity of avoiding high institutional costs for prisons and poor houses, accounts for the practice of binding out domestic criminals, debtors, poor children, and other persons considered social liabilities. In this way, criminals and debtors reimbursed society and the individuals whom they had wronged, while poor children and others were transformed from social liabilities to social assets as they worked, learned trades, or at least did not appear as burdens on the tax rolls.[16]

The second major factor influencing the conditions of labor and the institution of servitude was the land system adopted in the early history of the Massachusetts and Plymouth colonies—a system kept more or less intact throughout the period of this study. Simply stated, this system provided that the land should be settled by communities, not individuals, and that the dwelling units should be gathered into a town while the farm lands were scattered about the periphery of the settled area. This mode of settlement was admirably suited to the climate and terrain in which the New Englanders lived, and it conformed to the needs of protection against the Indians, on the one hand, and the protection of the essentially community-minded culture and religion on the other.[17]

The land system affected the institution of servitude in three ways. In the first place, most farms were too small and infertile for the employment of large numbers of workers in the production of a staple crop.[18] As a consequence, there was a tendency for servants to work with their masters in groups of two or three at the most—more of a family-farm and family-relationship than obtained in the large plantation with many servants or slaves. In turn, of course, this limited the demand for labor as compared with the South. Secondly, the land system, in its emphasis on community rather than individual settlement, limited the use of free land as a reward for the importer of servants or as an inducement for prospective servants. Originally the practice of the Pilgrims and Puritans had been similar to that of other local governments along the seacoast. A man paying his own passage, or that of others, was allowed a certain acreage, or head right, to be disposed of as he chose.[19] Early in the 1630's, however, both Plymouth and Massachusetts curtailed this policy.

Plymouth was the first to modify its head right system. It began by segregating its grants to ex-servants at Scituate or some other place "where it may be usefull" to the colony.[20] In 1636, the Pilgrims reduced the acreage provided by the government for discharged servants to five acres, granted only if the person was found "fit" to occupy it.[21] On the same day Governor and Council gathered into their own hands the right to approve or disapprove all who wanted to be housekeepers or build cottages.[22] Shortly thereafter, prospective masters were warned that if they covenanted with servants to give them land at the end of service, it would be at their own expense. The colony was to be free of any such agreements.[23]

Massachusetts showed even less liberality with regard to land grants for service than Plymouth. The Bay colony never made statutory provision for ex-servants to have land except indirectly, when it ruled in 1634 that no one was to have land allotted in any plantation unless he proved faithful to his master during his time of service.[24] Later, in 1636, the General Court added a penalty for turning a man loose or giving him a lot until his time was served out as covenanted.[25]

Both colonies, then, failed to recognize the need for laborers (who might be induced to migrate under the promise of free land at the end of service) as paramount to the religious and social structure of the communities they were creating. It is indeed significant that after 1640, only two cases of servants having land promised to them by indenture could be found in Plymouth or Massachusetts.[26]

In this failure to use free land as a magnet to attract servants, the colonists refused to recognize fully the need for labor. On the other hand, they could not ignore the labor shortage. Once the servant in the colony had been freed, the land policy tended to push him into a general labor force by making it more difficult for him to set up on his own. The land system, then, had its compensations. A crisis in Massachusetts politics in 1634 illustrates this relationship between land grants and labor. The proposed members of the land committee, it appeared, were lowerclass voters. John Winthrop and John Cotton convinced them that such business should be left to their betters. The leaders feared that if the "inferiour sort" were given too large allotments of land, workers might be encouraged to neglect their trades, thus increasing the labor shortage.[27]

The land system, then, influenced the institution of servitude in several ways. It tended to keep the numbers small in any one household, and at the same time, it kept the numbers imported down to a minimum when it failed to provide land bounties or "head-rights" for importers. Finally, the land system tended to keep those laborers already in the colonies from getting land, thus maintaining them in a labor pool.

The third major factor influencing the conditions of labor and the institution of servitude was custom: the institutions which the colonizers carried in their minds, and indeed on their ships, as they came to American shores. For centuries, Englishmen had been accustomed to at least one form of unfree labor, apprenticeship. And even though the system of apprenticeship was beginning to be subject to various pressures in old England, Parliament in the sixteenth century had strengthened it by general legislation nationwide in scope making the courts of law responsible for its enforcement. It was ideally suited to the new world in the absence of other forms of manual training; and with modifications made necessary by other forces—primarily the demand for labor—it was established.[28]

Parliamentary legislation, in the Poor Act of 1601, moreover, strengthened the bound labor system by establishing a lesser breed of apprentice, one bound by order of the justice of the peace for service terminating at twenty-one and twenty-four years for girls and boys respectively. This procedure, designed as a poor-relief measure, was admirably suited to colonial needs both for its legal purpose and as a means of supplying cheap labor. With modifications, poor apprenticeship was adopted by the Puritan and Pilgrim colonists and retained in the provincial period.[29]

Apprenticeship, however, was not the only form of bound labor in old England. The long hire, ranging from seasonal and yearly hirings to long-term arrangements of many years, was frequently resorted to. In fact, under the terms of the famous Elizabethan Statute of Artificers, yearly hirings were required in many trades, while otherwise unemployed individuals without social or economic standing were forced to serve by the year in husbandry. The long hire came to America, too.[30] Thus custom played its part.

The fourth factor influencing the conditions of labor and the institution of servitude was the very real desire to maintain a homogeneous population. While the demand for labor, any sort of labor, was great, Pilgrims, Puritans, and their descendants did not live by bread alone. Indeed, the economic man was hedged about by all sorts of scruples, which led him to enter an injunction against the indiscriminate importation of any beast of burden able to walk on two legs and use its hands. From the days of Bradford and Winthrop, who protested strongly against the admission of undesirables to their heavenly cities, certain types of immigration, certain sources of labor, were restricted in their use.

Bradford, with the servant population in mind, complained against the invasion of Plymouth by "wicked persons and profane people . . . ," while Winthrop wrote disparagingly of some who had crossed the ocean as servants and "never had any show of religion in them. . . . "[31] The eighteenth century saw no decrease in the desire to maintain high standards among imported servants even though the religious scruples of Bradford or Winthrop no longer dominated society. Thus James Franklin's newspaper complained in 1725:

> the Masters of Vessels going to Ireland &c. knowing the great Want of Servants here, pick up all the Vagabonds they can find to make up a cargo, Fellows and Wenches brought up to no other Employments than the *picking* St. Patricks *Vermin, and driving them out of their strong Holds* . . . they serve us for no other Purposes than to plague their Masters and Mistresses and debauch their Children. This gives us an ill Opinion of Foreigners, especially those coming from *Ireland,* when the truth of it is, the best of them stay at home for want of Encouragement to go abroad, and generally the very *Scum* of the Nation, both Freemen and Servants, visit the Plantations.

Signed "Homespun Jack," this article went on to suggest the encouragement of the better sort of artificers and farmers by lending them money, without interest, to help them cross the ocean.[32]

This desire to maintain a homogeneous population may be seen writ large in the expulsion of deviants such as Roger Williams, Anne Hutchinson, and the Quakers, who violated religious orthodoxy. Even in the eighteenth century, the Scotch-Irish, with their presbyterian church polity, found themselves less than cordially welcomed by the orthodox ministry and their followers.[33] However, other factors played a more important part in the discrimination against deviates of the servant and laboring class.

First among the non-religious discriminations was the refusal of the New Englanders to allow the sweepings of English prisons to be sold on their shores. No shortage of labor was acute enough to compensate them for the danger of having their communities overrun by such malefactors. As a consequence, many a shipmaster was forced to post a bond that he would take his criminal cargo elsewhere when he sought haven in a Massachusetts port. It is apparent that few English criminals entered the labor market.[34]

A second discrimination motivated by the desire to maintain homogeneity was based on racial considerations. The demand for labor was not strong enough either to silence the criticism of the importation of Negroes, or to eliminate the importation fee, despite the Crown's positive instructions to the contrary.[35] Indeed, racial prejudice was a prime factor in the anti-slavery sentiment expressed in the early eighteenth century. This sentiment, in turn, led to the establishment of a bounty to be paid to importers of white servants, and eventually to the founding of a society designed to encourage the importation of servants of the white race instead of Negroes.[36]

Religion, the fifth major factor shaping conditions of labor, influenced the institution in three interconnected ways. It provided a justification for the existence of higher and lower orders in society, and more specifically, justification for servitude itself. Second, it emphasized the family nature of the institution, thus requiring the legal and moral extension of the family to include servants working for a master. Third, religion imposed certain moral restrictions and definitions upon both parties to the relationship restraining the rapacity of the master in exploiting the servant, and restraining the servant from making excessive demands upon the master. In short, religion provided a pattern of rights and obligations within the master-servant relationship for their mutual guidance.

Religious justification for the existence of higher and lower orders in society occupied the attention of John Winthrop aboard the *Arbella* in 1630. He proposed, in his "Modell of Christian Charity," that "God Almithie in his most holy and wise providence hath soe disposed of the Condicion of mankinde, as in all times some must be rich some poore, some highe and eminent in power and dignities; others meane and in subjeccion."[37]

Much later, Samuel Willard, pastor of Boston's South Church and vice president of Harvard, examined this condition of subjection, particularly that between master and servant. While he found it incompatible with man's existence before the fall from grace, it came, he thought, as a fruit of that fall: the curse which attended man's disgrace made servitude unavoidable and necessary.[38]

Biblical justification was to be found for the existence of order and subjection in this world. The Fifth Commandment, "Honor thy father and thy mother," showed the New Englanders that God had ordained orders in society, some high and some low. "And tho all Orders which Men may ordain, are not approved by God; yet that there should be Orders is His revealed Will and Pleasure: Rom. 13.1. *The Powers that be are ordained of God.*"[39] In fact, the status of servitude was ordained by Christ.[40]

Having justified the existence of servitude, what was the nature of the institution? For this too, religion had an answer: it was a family institution. This fact is clearly demonstrated in the extensive works on master-servant relationships written in Massachusetts around the end of the seventeenth century.[41] Samuel Willard described the de facto situation as one which is "OEconomical" in nature. Since this was true, both the right of ruling and the duty of serving was limited to that which was proper to a family.[42] Cotton Mather, too, recognized this essentially domestic nature of society and saw three kinds of relations within it: *conjugal,* or that between man and wife; *parental,* or that between parent and child; and *herile,* or that between master and servant.[43]

The colonial governments enforced the beliefs of religious leaders that young men and women, along with older people of little property and casual morality, should live under the direction of a father or master, who would instruct them in the proper religious beliefs and fend off the dangers of loose living and idleness by supervising their every behavior.[44] This attitude justified their reaching beyond the poor in worldly goods to include the poor in spirit among the sources of bound labor. But more than the extension of servitude to larger groups, this concept of domestic government, as applied to the servant class, provided a rationalization of the institution by bringing it within the realm of natural relations between superior and inferior as established by God, and within the basic unit of society, the family.

As an institution, not only founded on the religious principle of orders in society, but included within the divinely established family, servitude became in itself a divine institution. As such, the totality of master-servant relations was subject to God's will and supported by his awesome might.

Samuel Willard explored this relationship at length, and in a well-documented sermon laid forth the proper behavior of both parties. He reduced the necessary rules to the "Law of Nature on the Moral Law," wherein it was shown to be "very lawful" for some to attain the position of masters and some that of servants. Like all other activities of man, servitude was capable of being improved to God's glory. In fact, the glorification of God through the perfecting of master-servant relationships was the Lord's command.[45]

In order to accomplish this improvement of the institution of servitude, masters had duties to perform which were equally obligatory in God's eyes as the duties of the servant. The obligation of demonstrating Christian love to those under one's authority was primary: even the "poorest Slave hath a right to it. . . . "

> The meanest Servant is in some respect as good as his Master, altho' Providentially made far Inferiour to him. They had both one Father; are made of the same Metal, and cast in the same Mold of Humanity. . . .[46]

In short, both have immortal souls, and it must be remembered that the difference in condition between them is only temporary with regard to the endless limit of eternity.[47]

This love of one's subordinates, made necessary by the fathership of God and the brotherhood of man, was to manifest itself in the command over one's servants and the care one was to take for them. The command or dominance one had was limited and did not extend to the "Arbitrary Power" of life and death, a function reserved to the Civil Government.[48] Moreover, one should not ask his servant to perform sordid, sinful, or illegal things, for surely the master would be sinning through his servant.[49] Christian command was further to manifest itself in the forbearance from "*scurrilous & undue threatnings*" and a prudent and humane exercise of the privilege and duty of correction.[50] Finally, when servants appeared to fall into error, they were to have full liberty "to plead their Innocency," and were not to be forbidden to speak in order to justify their actions.[51]

Care, the second manifestation of the master's love for his servant, was important too. One should be particularly concerned with servants' souls, for they were as precious to Christ as any others. With the authority of a head of a family, the master would have to answer for the souls under his roof. He must, therefore, provide instruction as well as time for reading the Word and for "secret" religious "performances."[52] Care for the bodies must also be just and equal. Recognizing that there was little danger of the servant's material wants being over-supplied, emphasis was placed where possible evil might lie. All servants were to have good and wholesome food, adequate apparel, and suitable nursing in time of sickness.[53] All these were obligations upon the master for the improvement of servitude to God's glory.

"THERE *is a Reciprocal Duty of Servants towards their Master*": Willard warned,

> And it is to be paid to them . . . because they are their Masters, let them be otherwise what they will; and they are to adore the Providence of God, in disposing them to a better or worse Condition in this regard; and if they suffer hard things in

it, to consider, that Servitude it self was bro't in by Sin, and is a part of that Death which Good as well as Bad must undergo in this World; hence that, 1 Pet.2,18. *Servants, be Subject to your masters with all fear, not only to the good and gentle but also to the froward.*[54]

Included in the obligation thus imposed upon servants by man's sinful nature was the necessity of showing reverential fear to the master, a cheerful obedience to all lawful commands, "DILIGENCE *and Faithfulness in discharging of the Service that is incumbent on them,*" and "PATIENCE & *Submission.*"[55]

Patience and submission were extremely important in improving the institution, particularly in a society were servants were not famous for their recognition of established authority. Injury was to be brought to the magistrate for redress: it was not for the inferior to seek to settle his own claims by raising his hand against his superior.

And if he have no door open to obtain regular Succour from Men, he ought with Patience to commit it to God, who hath said, that He is the Avenger of all such.[56]

It was Cotton Mather in *A Good Master Well-Served . . .* , who worked out in greatest detail the divinely imposed duties of servants to masters. His writing was bent to the task of convincing the subordinate that in serving man he was serving God. "Whatsoever *Service* you do for your *Masters* (or *Mistresses*)," he wrote, "do it as a Service unto the Lord Jesus Christ."[57] And remember, that when you break the commands of him, who is set over you in this life, you break the commands of God.[58] "Yield," therefore, "unto your *Masters* . . . that Reverence, which is due from a *Servant* unto a Master." Because it is God's will that you are in this lower order, "don't think much of that *Inferiority,* which is to be confess'd by you, as long as you are *Servants.*" After all, he that is "in the Lord" and yet a servant is the "Lord's free-man."[59]

Having established the necessity of subordination, Mather drew up a list of do's and don'ts for Christian servants. The first necessity was reform, for they had ordinarily been so truculent that the term servant had almost become synonymous with knave or villain.[60] They were admonished, therefore, to beware of sullenness, sauciness and impudence, which were "most abominable." Running away, of course, was disgraceful, and lying, laziness, thievishness, drunkenness, wantonness, betraying maaster's secrets, impairing his estate, and carrying tales concerning the master's household or personal affairs were dangerous. And, Mather added, for their own sakes and their masters, avoid evil company.[61]

Positive exhortations to be good were not lacking either. Diligence in a servant was to be much admired; in fact, one was to seek to be universally serviceable. Faithfulness and a reverent attitude toward one's master was also greatly to be desired. Complete subordination to the will of the master, in other words, was the practical end sought in the inferior side of the reciprocal relationship,[62] although the divine end was not forgotten.

Samuel Willard summed up the central purpose, as he saw it, of the improvements required in the institution by religion.

> LET all such as stand in this Relation; *Take heed to themselves, that they do serve God thus in it, as they hone to give up their Account with Joy another Day.* Let *Masters* consider, They have a Master in Heaven, who will reckon with them e're long; and if they have abused their Power, or neglected their Duty, it will be ill for them. And let *Servants* remember; That whatsoever Entertainment their Service finds from their Earthly Masters, God will accept and crown their Faithfulness in it; and if they have served Christ, and done it as to him, great will be their Reward in Heaven: And how hard soever it may at present seem unto them, yet when Christ shall say, Well done good and faithful *Servant,* it will never Repent them.[63]

Religion, then, provided a justification for orders within society, reenforced the family nature of servitude, and set up a pattern of behavior for all Christian masters and servants to obey. It undoubtedly was a potent force in ameliorating the conditions of service whether for slave or servant, and it provided an ideal by means of which both master and servant could measure their own and each other's behavior.

The five factors influencing the conditions of labor and servitude—an economic need for labor, the land system, customary institutions, a desire for homogeneity, and religion—were operative throughout the entire period with varying intensity. They were, of course, interactive in shaping the institution of servitude, and they sometimes cooperated and sometimes worked at cross purposes. The economic need for labor, for example, influenced the institution positively in that it made necessary the development of indentured servitude and other forms of master-servant relationships based on imported labor. On the other hand, the desire for a homogeneous population, as well as the peculiar land system of the New England colonies, lessened the effectiveness of the economic demand by restricting, but not prohibiting, the importation of alien peoples, and by limiting the inducements which could be offered to voluntary immigrants. Practices and institutions to which the colonists had been accustomed in the Old World served as patterns for different phases of servitude, but the scarcity of labor required innovations which at best were but casually reminiscent of the English labor pattern. Religion too played its part. It provided a justification for the subservience implicit in the institution, on the one hand, but it emphasized on the other, that the relationship was religious and moral as well as economic. In addition, religious attitudes reenforced the essentially domestic nature of New England servitude by bringing master-servant behavior within the realm of the divinely ordained and divinely regulated family. Servitude, in the present area of Massachusetts before 1750, was a complex phenomenon and a product of complex forces.

NOTES

1. This relationship was modified in New England by two basic factors: the Indians who hemmed in the whites until the end of the seventeenth century (along with the French in the eighteenth), and the socio-religious complex which to a great extent dictated community rather than individual settlement, thus restraining individuals from taking up land in the interior. However, even along the sea coast and the Connecticut River in the first period, and between the two areas as well as beyond the Connecticut in the second, much labor was needed. For example, see Samuel Davis, "Notes on Plymouth, Massachusetts," in Massachusetts Historical Society, *Collections* (Boston, 1815–), Second Series, III, 162–163.

2. For restrictions on taking up land see below, page 10. For wages and labor shortage see E.A.J. Johnson, *American Economic Thought in the Seventeenth Century* (London, 1932), 128, 205, 206–207, and "Some Evidence of Mercantilism in the Massachusetts-Bay," *New England Quarterly,* I (Sept., 1927), 371–395.

3. James Kendall Hosmer, ed., *Winthrop's Journal "History of New England" 1630–1649* in the *Original Narratives of Early American History Series,* James Franklin Jameson, ed. (Nev, York, 1908), II, 228 (1645); 97 (1643). Hereafter cited as *Winthrop's Journal.* The particular cause at this time was war in England which "kept servants from coming to us. . . . " *Ibid.,* II, 228.

4. For examples, see M.H.S. *Winthrop Papers 1498–* (Boston 1929–), III, 247 (1636), 268–269 (1636); IV, 6–7 (1637/8), 64, 65–66 (1638); V, 5–8 (1644/5); M.H.S., 5 *Colls.,* I, 200–201 (1633).

5. The proportion of help-wanted notices is roughly 15% before 1740, 85% from 1740–1750. Some 126 persons and seven groups of undetermined size were advertised for in the newspapers between 1720/1 and 1750. The earliest example occurred in the *Boston Gazette* for Dec. 26, 1720–Jan. 2, 1720/1. Hereafter cited as *Gazette.* For others before 1740 see *ibid.,* July 28–Aug. 4, 1735, Sept. 19–26, 1737; Apr. 24–May 1, 1738 (repeated); Sept. 11–18, 1738; *Boston Evening-Post,* July 11, 1737; Feb. 6, 1738; July 10, 1738; Dec. 3, 1739 (hereafter cited as *Evening-Post*); *Boston News-Letter,* Sept. 21, 1738 (hereafter cited as *News-Letter*); *The New-England Courant,* Nov. 12–19, 1722; Sept. 23–30, 1723 (hereafter cited as *Courant*). For those appearing between the years 1740–1750 inclusive, see the files of the *New England Weekly Journal* (hereafter cited as *N.E. Journal*), *Evening-Post, News-Letter, Gazette,* and *The Boston Weekly Post-Boy* (hereafter cited as Post-Boy). For groups advertised for, see: *Post-Boy,* Jan. 29, 1739; *News-Letter,* Feb. 13, 1746; June 4, 1747; *Evening-Post,* Mar. 23, 1741; June 21,1742 (repeated); June 2, 1746 (repeated); Jan. 26, 1747 (repeated), Besides being repeated in several issues of one paper, some were advertised in more than one. See, for examples: *Post-Boy,* Jan. 26, 1747 and *Evening-Post,* Jan. 26, 1747 (repeated); *Gazette,* Feb. 13, 1750 and *News-Letter,* Mar. 1, 1750; *Post-Boy,* May 4, 1741 *Gazette,* May 4–11, 1741, *News-Letter,* Apr. 16–24, 1741, and the *N.E. Journal,* May 5, 1741. For servants offered for sale, see all newspapers, *passim.*
6. MSS. and printed forms, "Boston Indentures, 1734–1805," I (1734–1751), 182 ff, and II, 105 ff. Hereafter cited as MSS. Boston Indentures.
7. Nathaniel B. Shurtleff, ed., *Records of the Governor and Company of Massachusetts Bay in New England* (Boston, 1853–1854), I, 258 (1639). Hereafter cited as *Mass. Recs.*
8. William Brigham, ed., *The Compact with the Charter and Laws of the Colony of New Plymouth* . . . (Boston, 1836), 28 (1626). Hereafter cited as Brigham, *Laws.*
9. Victor S. Clark, *History of Manufactures in the United States* (New York, 1929), I, chapter III, *passim.* See especially 39–41, 47–53. William B. Weeden *Economic and Social History of New England 1620–1789* (New York, 1890), I, 80–81.
10. See chapter V, below.
11. Richard B. Morris, *Government and Labor in Early America* (New York, 1946), 414–419.
12. See, for example, *Courant,* Nov. 23–30, 1724; George F. Dow, ed., *Records and Files of the Quarterly Courts of Essex County Massachusetts 1636–1683* (Salem, 1911–1921), VI, 151 (1669). Hereafter cited as *Essex County Court.*
13. See chapter V, below.

14. Wait Winthrop to John Winthrop (his son), Boston, Oct. 11, 1714. M.H.S., 6 *Colls.*, V, 301–302. In 1748, a pamphleteer could still write that many more laborers were needed to achieve prosperity in the province. Mylo Freeman (pseud.), *A Word in Season To all True Lovers Of Their Liberty and their Country, Both of which are NOW in the Utmost Danger of Being Forever Lost* (Boston, 1748), 11.

15. See chapter II, below.

16. Moreover, the shortage of labor accounts in part for the fact that throughout the entire period, freemen were impressed briefly for particular projects. In the seventeenth century, they built forts and embattlements, developed roads, and performed other socially useful tasks. For examples see: Nathaniel B. Shurtleff, ed., *Records of the Colony of New Plymouth In New England* (Boston, 1855–1857), I, 6 (1632/3). Hereafter cited as *Plym. Recs.* See also; *Mass. Recs.*, III, 102–103 (1646); Morris, *Government and Labor . . .*, 7–10, 303; Clark, *Manufactures . . .*, I, 33–34. In the eighteenth century, similar levies were made upon free Negroes in larger communities as they were called out to clean "houses of easement," dig drainage ditches, and in general, to do the dirty work no one else wanted to do. This service was in lieu of military training, from which the blacks were excluded. Lorenzo Johnston Greene, *The Negro in Colonial New England 1620–1776* (New York, 1942), 303–304. See also: Record Commissioners of the town of Boston, *Reports* (Boston, 1881–1909), XIII, 8, 41–43, 59–60, 82–83, 105–109, 145; XV, 132–136, 251; XVII, 29, 68 (hereafter cited as *Boston Records*); Boston Public Welfare Department, MSS file 1720 (Sept. 3, 1720).

17. For a brief summary of the land system, see Ray Allen Billington, *Westward Expansion A History of the American Frontier* (New York, 1949), 68 ff. For a more detailed examination see Roy Hidemichi Akagi, *The Town Proprietors of the New England Colonies. A Study of Their Development, Organization, Activities, and Controversies, 1620–1770* (Philadelphia, 1924).

18. For exceptions, particularly in size of grants, see Billington, *Westward Expansion . . .*, 68. For larger farms being worked see chapter V, below.

19. *Mass Recs.*, I, 43 (1629). An early example was Thomas Beard, shoemaker, who paid his own way to the Bay. The instructions from the company were to the effect that he was to be given fifty acres, but he and others like him (as well as those getting land as servants) were to be liable to some service certain days of the year if they were not adventurers in the common stock. *Ibid.*, 405 (1629). For head rights and general land policy, for servants in other colonies see Abbott Emerson Smith, *Colonists in Bondage: White Servitude and Convict Labor in America 1607–1776* (Chapel Hill, 1947), 15–16, 376 (n,26), 238–241, 296–297, 300–301.

20. *Plym. Recs.*, I, 23 (1633/4). Ex-servants were evidently not considered good neighbors by the Pilgrims. Duxbury residents, for example, petitioned in 1638 that no land be granted in that place without the approval of three leading citizens. The reason given was that the church there was very weak and could not expect help from the many ex-servants already there. *Ibid.*, 184. Apparently this attitude was widespread, for the General Court forced the towns to provide land for those servants who had it coming to them in the towns where they lived, or were settled as inhabitants, unless there were no lands available. *Ibid.*, II, 69 (1643/4).
21. *Ibid.*, I, 44 (1636).
22. *Ibid.*
23. David S. Pulsifer, ed., *Records of the Colony of New Plymouth, Laws 1623–1682* (Boston, 1861), 18 (1636). Hereafter cited as Pulsifer, *Laws*. Plymouth continued to honor the claims of "old servants" and "ancient freemen" throughout the seventeenth century. See: *Plym. Recs.*, III, 216 (1661); IV, 18 (1662 twenty-seven individuals), 128 (1666); V, 125–126 (1673); VI, 18 (1679, two cases) . Not many cases from the earlier period are extant. For examples, see *ibid.*, I, 15–16 (1633, twenty-five acres unmanured land by indenture), 30 (1634, two servants discharge masters of all covenants except land), 43 (1636, ex-servant sells land due by indenture for six bushels of corn), 43 (1636, sells land due for service for fifty shillings), 102 (1638, granted twenty-five acres due for service), 69 (1643/4, the same).
24. *Mass. Recs.*, I, 127.
25. *Ibid.*, 186. Few grants to ex-servants could be found. Undoubtedly many acquired land, but few for service. For examples see: *Boston Records,* IV, 7 (1634, three acres); *Mass. Recs.*, I, 255 (1638/9, a lot). For others, see appendices in Towner, "A Good Master Well Served . . . " (Ph.D. diss., Northwestern University, 1954).
26. *Essex Institute Historical Collections* (Salem, 1859–), LVIII, 264 (1730). Hereafter cited as E.I. *Colls.* This is an indenture of Elizabeth McMeans and her son, William, to John Mitchell for four years after arrival at Salem, and to age twenty-one, respectively. Mitchell was to pay passage, and keep. As freedom dues they were to receive land, corn and clothes according to the "custom of the country." If Mitchell stuck to the letter of his bargain, they received no land, for the custom was clearly opposed to it. For the other case see Pulsifer, *Records of the Colony of New Plymouth in New England, Printed by order Or the Legislature of the Commonwealth of Massachusetts. Deeds* (Boston, 1861), 216 (1651). Hereafter cited as Pulsifer, *Deeds.*
27. *Winthrop's Journal,* I, 143–144. Cotton argued successfully that the Lord's order among the Israelites was to have all such business committed to the elders, and that the residents of Boston should do the same. A new election was held.

28. See 5 Eliz., c. 4 (1562/3); Paul H. Douglas, *American Apprenticeship and Industrial Education,* in *Columbia University Studies,* XCV, ii (New York, 1921), chapter I. For Massachusetts apprenticeship see below, chapter II.
29. See: 43 Eliz., c. 2 (1601); and chapter III, below.
30. For examples of the long hire in a family which later came to America, see: *Winthrop Papers,* I, 24, William Bettes covenanted in 1604 to serve for lls. per year and his clothing; in the next few years, two girls came to serve by the year at 33s.4d., a boy at lls. per year, and a men at L4 per year. In 1604, John Prior agreed to serve for four years in return for meat, drink, clothes, and 20s. at the end of his time.
31. *Bradford's History "of Plimoth Plantation"* (Boston, 1900),476 (1642). Hereafter cited as *Bradford's History. Winthrop's Journal,* II, 307–308 (1646). Winthrop warned against indiscriminate immigration in 1630, in a letter to his son saying, "people must come well provided, and not too many at once. Pease may come if he will, and such others as you shall think fitt, but not manye, and let those be good, *and but fewe servante and those vsefull ones." Winthrop Papers,* II, 305–307. Italics mine.
32. *Courant,* Jan. 4–11, 1725. More effective than such complaints was the intolerable burden Irish immigrants placed upon the poor rates. Possible laborers, they were prohibited from landing without the captain's bond that none would become public charges. Thus did the rate-payer override the user of manpower. For bonds, see: MSS. Suffolk County, Records of the Court of General Sessions of the Peace, II, 170–171 (1717), 30 cases, II, 210– 218 (1718), five cases. Hereafter cited as MSS. Suffolk Sessions. See also *Boston Records,* XV, 3, 7, 10, 11, 54, 79, 81, 148, 314 (1736–1742), and C.K Shipton, "Immigration to New England, 1680–1740." *Journal of Political Economy,* XLIV (Apr., 1936), 234–239. For a study, which emphasizes the shift from religious and social exclusiveness to economic causation in immigration restriction see: Emberson E. Proper, *Colonial Immigration Laws,* in *Columbia University Studies,* XIII, ii (New York, 1900), 727–217.
33. For the Scotch-Irish see Charles Knowles Bolton, *Scotch-Irish Pioneers In Ulster and America* (Boston,1910),136 ff., 180 ff., and Henry Jones Ford, *The Scotch-Irish in America* (Princeton, 1915), 192 ff.
34. James D. Butler, "British Convicts Shipped to American Colonies", in *The American Historical Review,* II (Oct. 1896), 12–33. For bonds required, see *Boston Records,* XV, 206, 212–213 (1739), and 261, 266–267 (1740). Smith says few were wanted in America. See his *Colonists in Bondage . . . ,* 103–104, Morris, *Government and Labor. . . . ,* 326, agrees that New England received few convicts. However, the *Evening-Post* carried a story on May 24, 1736

concerning a vagabond from Virginia. "It is thought," the paper said., "he is a *Convict,* and not the only one of that tribe among us."

35. For criticism of importation, see below, chanter VII. The Crown's instructions were printed in the *News-Letter,* June 1–8, 1732. Massachusetts had an importation fee from 1705–1750. See *Acts and Resolves, Public and Private of the Province of the Massachusetts Bay* . . . (Boston, 1869–1922), I, 578–579; II, 517–518, 981. Hereafter cited as *Acts and Resolves.* But see Greene, *The Negro in Colonial New England* . . . , 50–52. It should be noted that there is little evidence for the deliberate breeding of slaves. See below, chapter VI.

36. For the definite connection between the impost on Negroes and the bounty on whites, see: M.H.S. *Journals of the House of Representatives of Massachusetts* (Boston 1919–), II, 25 (1718); VIII, 322 (1728). Hereafter cited as *House Journals.* A society for the encouragement of immigration of Protestant Foreigners was formed in 1750. See *Post-Boy,* July 9, 1750 and Oct. 1, 1750. For the whole movement in the 1740's and 1750's see Erna Risch "Joseph Crellius, Immigrant Broker," *N.E.Q., XII* (June, 1939), 241–267.

37. John Winthrop, "A Modell of Christian Charity," in Perry Miller and Thomas H. Johnson, eds., *The Puritans* (New York, 1938), 195.

38. Samuel Willard, *A Compleat Body of Divinity* . . . (Boston, 1726), 613 (second pagination).

39. *Ibid.,* 598 (second pagination). Willard develops the idea in this sermon that the duties of the several orders thus ordained were originally written in men's hearts, but the apostasy has blurred them so that those in superior position sometimes seek boundless power, and conversely, those in inferior positions refuse to bear any yoke or obey any commands. Benjamin Wadsworth reminded his listeners, or readers, that "*the Christian Religion does not dissolve or destroy, those various Relations or Capacities which are common among men.*" *The Well-Ordered Family* . . . (Boston, 1712J, 3.

40. Cotton Mather, *A Family Well-Ordered* . . . (Boston, 1699), 67.

41. Samuel Willard, *A Compleat Body of Divinity* . . . sermons CLXXIX, and CLXXXVIII. Cotton Mather, *A Good Master Well-Served* . . . (Boston, 1696), *A Family Well-Ordered* . . . and *The Servant of Abraham: With Motives for the Instruction of Servants* (Boston, 1716). Benjamin Wadsworth, *The Well-Ordered Family* . . . .

42. Willard, *A Compleat Body of Divinity* . . . , 613 (second pagination).

43. C. Mather, *A Good Master Well-Served* . . . , 46; and *A Family Well-Ordered* . . . , 66.

44. Edmund S. Morgan, *The Puritan Family, Essays on Religion and Domestic Relations in Seventeenth-Century New England* (Boston, 1944), particularly chapter V.

45. Willard, *A Compleat Body of Divinity* ..., 614 (second pagination), cites 1 Corinthians, 7, 20–22.
46. Willard, *loc. cit.*
47. *Ibid.,* 615 (second pagination). Wadsworth, although he recognized freedom was more to be desired than servitude, stated that there was no difference between the two statuses with regard to their spiritual priviliges and duties. *The Well-Ordered Family* ..., 2.
48. Willard, *loc. cit.* C. Mather, *A Good Master Well-Served* ..., 15–16.
49. Willard, *loc. cit.* C. Mather, *A Good Master Wel-Served* ..., 10.
50. Willard, *loc. cit.* He wrote: "Utmost Severity is not to be used, when more gentle Treatment is as probable to attain the end. ... And we are not to make *Asses* of our Servants, whilst they may be treated as *Men.*" See also: C. Mather, *A Good Master Well-Served* ..., 16; Wadsworth, *The Well-Ordered Family* ..., 105–106, 107. "If he's so foolhardy, high and stout as not to be mended by words; then correction should be us'd for his reformation." But, qualified Wadsworth, this correction should not be administered in a rage or a passion, nor unless positive of the fault.
51. Willard, *loc. cit.* In chapter VII, below, It is shown that there was little need to fear that servants would fail to speak out in their own behalf.
52. Willard, *A Compleat Body of Divinity* ..., 615–616 (second pagination). C. Mather, *A Good Master Well-Served* ..., 16–18. Mather considered these duties to include teaching, catechising, requiring of them to please God, and praying for them. Wadsworth, who urged religion also, saw a very practical result to be obtained. A truly converted servant, he thought, would not run away, and would be more profitable. *The Well-Ordered Family* ..., 105–106, 109–111.
53. Willard. *A Compleat Body of Divinity* ..., 616 (second pagination). Wadsworth went further than Willard by including under care of the body, proper time for eating, sleeping, spiritual refreshment, *and* "on proper occasions some short space for relaxation and diversion. ... " Moreover, he damned the failure to provide adequate care as an "unmerciful, wicked and abominable thing." *The Well-Ordered Family* ..., 104. See also, C. Mather, *A Good Master Well-Served* ..., 13–15.
54. Willard, *loc. cit.*
55. *Ibid.* He wrote, "no lawful Command, tho' possibly in it self ingrateful, should be refused by them, nor disputed against by them, nor done with a murmuring and discontented mind."
56. *Ibid.,* 617 (second pagination).
57. C. Mather, *A Good Master Well-Served* ..., 33.
58. *Ibid.,* 39.
59. *Ibid.,* 35.

60. *Ibid.*
61. *Ibid.,* 15–16, 23, 31, 37, 38, 42, 44, 49.
62. *Ibid.,* 45, 42, 37, 38. "*Servants,* your *Tongues,* your *Hands* your *Feet,* are your *Masters,* and they should move according to the Will of your *Masters.*"
63. Willard, *A Compleat Body of Divinity . . . ,* 617 (second pagination).

2. The Servant Elite: Apprentices and Indentured Servants

There were two categories of voluntary servants in the servant class in Massachusetts prior to 1750: apprentices and indentured servants. Apprenticeship was essentially an educational institution in which a master imparted his skill or knowledge to a trainee in exchange for labor. Indentured servitude was essentially an economic institution in which a master provided certain economic goods—transportation, food, clothing, housing, and some end-payment—in exchange for labor. Although ideally distinct from each other, in practice they over-lapped because of certain characteristics which they had in common. Both types of servitude were voluntary, and in both, the particular conditions of service were determined in part by the bargaining of two parties, the master and the servant. In both, the terms of service were recorded in an indenture or contract, and in each case, the servant lived with his master as a part of his master's household and was responsible to him for his every action twenty-four hours a day, seven days a week. Yet they were distinct, and of the two, apprenticeship was ordinarily superior in terms of rewards offered, and in terms of social respectability.

When Josiah Franklin, tallow chandler in early eighteenth-century Boston, placed his son, Benjamin, as an apprentice, he illustrated many characteristics of apprenticeship as it existed in Massachusetts. In the first place he demonstrated the almost universal acceptance of this means of acquiring a skill. Benjamin was the tenth son to be put out as an apprentice in Josiah's immediate family. Second, this was clearly an alternative to going on to higher formal education, for Josiah had intended his son as a tithe to the church, but he found the college education too costly for his means. Third, he illustrated the variety of crafts available to the prospective apprentice in the larger community, if not in the small town. Of the ten sons, nine were apprenticed to different trades, and Benjamin himself was taken to many different tradesmen to view their work and to judge which would be most pleasing to his tastes. Fourth, he showed the partly voluntary, partly involuntary nature of the system. Benjamin's expressed wish was to go to sea, but this was forbidden. In that sense, the choice was voluntary only on the part of the father. On the other hand, the boy was not forced to choose any one particular trade, and in that sense his choice was his own. Fifth, Benjamin's being placed on trial with a cutler, his uncle, illustrated the apparently common practice of an adjustment period prior to the signing of a contract during which the prospective servant lived with and served his prospective master, but during which either could withdraw if conditions were not satisfactory. Finally, Benjamin's experience indicated the role that bargaining power played in determining the particular conditions of servitude. Benjamin's uncle demanded a fee for taking the youth as an apprentice. This Josiah was unwilling to pay, and the negotiations were broken off. Instead of being apprenticed to his uncle, the youth was then indentured to James, his brother, who agreed to pay journeyman's wages the last year of the nine-year apprenticeship.[1]

Probably most children during the colonial period were raised to be farmers or farmers' wives, receiving their basic instruction in the home,[2] but for any who aspired to a position in society outside of farming, some formal training was necessary, Those who were to become ministers, of course, went to college, as did most who became teachers;[3] but others, like Benjamin Franklin, served an apprenticeship to a master, who acted *in loco parentis* for a specified number of years, giving training, keep, and some form of end-payment in exchange for service.

This system of education was as old as recorded history.[4] When the first immigrants came to New England in the seventeenth century, English apprenticeship had passed through the stages of guild and town regulation and had become the subject of Parliamentary legislation.[5] English law required a minimum number of years (seven) and a minimum age at which one could attain freedom (twenty-four). Moreover, it required the enrollment of contracts or indentures before the local courts, and established a proportion to be observed between journeymen and apprentices so as to limit the latter and encourage the employment of the former.[6]

The settlers at New Plymouth, Salem, and Boston, however, conceived the institution as dependent not upon law, but upon custom and the bargain agreed to between contracting parties, for only the most general legislation, applicable to all temporary servants, and some legislation applicable to perpetual servants, was enacted in the first generation or more. The variously called Statute of Apprentices or

Statute of Artificers of England was neither enforced in America, nor re-enacted there.

Plymouth, it is true, did require the enrollment of contracts for servants on her record books in 1638, and the Puritans in Massachusetts Bay asked that servants be taught to read the capital laws and learn the catechism.[7] Further they advised that servants having served faithfully seven years should not be sent away empty handed,[8] while they prohibited selling a servant his time before the contracted period was up.[9] But otherwise, neither colony regulated the relationship between apprentice and master by law.

The reasons for the failure to define the apprenticeship system in the specific terms of the Statute of Artificers in New England are conjectural. England's law was designed, in the first place, to bolster a system of production and a pattern of relationships no longer compatible with the facts of economic growth. That is, the government sought to maintain medieval restrictions on a growing capitalistic economy, and thereby protect the trades from overcrowding by limiting apprenticeship, and to provide work for journeymen.[10] New England, however, had comparatively little artisan production on the one hand, and no labor surplus on the other. Her economy required freedom, not restriction, labor exploitation, not labor protection. While she introduced some medieval-type legislation, she did not return to the Middle Ages.

Secondly, the Puritan colonies relied consciously or unconsciously upon custom to guide them in establishing institutions. Customary patterns of behavior undoubtedly had the force of law. Finally, where custom failed them, they relied upon the *Bible*. The three thousand miles of ocean between the old and the new allowed for innovation which new circumstances required, or for the demise of old laws incompatible with new situations. For example, prior to the parliamentary legislation of 1562, the guilds or towns had performed the function of regulation in old England, but neither was particularly effective in Massachusetts. The shoemakers and fanners of Boston, and the coopers of Boston and Charlestown formed short-lived guilds before 1650, but guild organization was the exception not the rule.[11] The coopers were able to get Boston to pass an ordinance requiring local enrollment of indentures, and prohibiting practice of the trade without seven years' apprenticeship. Enforced upon occasion by the town government, this ordinance resulted in at least two persons being required to give up cooperage, but the enrollment of indentures was haphazard and incomplete.[12] A later attempt on the part of ship carpenters in 1675 to deter a non-apprenticed worker, by carrying him through town on a pole, met with five shillings damage plus fees of court assessed to each participant.[13] Most significant of all, the provincial General Court was silent on the question of regulating ordinary apprenticeship, although those bound out at the instance of the overseers of the poor or selectmen were protected by general laws.[14]

Apprenticeship, then, was a system of training for which the individual paid with his labor and perhaps a fee. Omitting from consideration variant types loosely styled apprentices—poor children bound out by the authorities[15] and an occasional servant so designated in order to indicate his servile status[16]—a general pattern does emerge, one shaped by custom but considerably modified by the individual parties concerned.

A parent with more sons than he could profitably employ, or whose son preferred a different trade or means of livelihood, would inquire concerning the opportunities in the area sometime after the boy's twelfth to fourteenth year. Having located a receptive master, the son might very well be placed with him on trial, during which time both the boy and the master could get out of the arrangement. He might or might not stay at home during this trial period, but he would be under the master's supervision during the day at least.[17]

If all parties, the father, the master, and possibly the boy, were satisfied, the next step would be to draw up a written agreement which would specify the mutual obligations each was to assume.

Variously styled as contracts, covenants, but most frequently as indentures, the form was well known, and by the late seventeenth century at least, widely used. It was to be found, for example, in the *Boston Almanac for 1692* and in an eighteenth-century secretary's guide. Printed indentures were generally available in the eighteenth century.[18] Frequently notary publics or even school teachers wrote up the contract for the parties involved.[19]

A typical indenture in form and terminology, if not in exact terms, was that between William Pearce and John Cromwell.

> [This] indenture wit[nesseth that] Wm. Pearce son of Richard Pearce-late dec. of his free voluntary will & with consent & aprobation of Elizabeth his mother, hath put himself apprentice to John Cromwell of Salem in ye county of Essex, Slathener, the science or trade of a slathener which he now useth, to be taught & with him after the manner of an apprentice to dwell & serve from the 25th day of December last past, unto the full end & term of eight years from thence next following & fully to be compleat & ended, by all which

terme of eight yeares the sd apprentice, the sd John Cromwell
& Hannah his wife, well & truly shall serve, theire secreats
shall keepe close, theire commandments lawful, & honest
every where he shall gladly doe, hurt to his said master or Mrs.
he shall not doe nor suffer to be don, but shall lett if he may
or immediately admonish his sd Master or Mrs thereoftaverns
he shall not frequent, from the service of his Master &
Mistress day or night, he shall not absent or prolong himselfe,
but in all things aa a good & faithfull apprentice, shall beare
& behave himself toward his sd. Master & Mrs & all his
duering the terme aforesd: Ye said John Cromwell to his sd
apprentice- the science or art of a slatherner which he now
useth shall teach & informe or cause to be taught & informed
the best waye that he may or cann: & alsoe shall teach his
apprentice or cause him to be taught to read & wright:
apparell, meate-drink-washing & lodging & all other
necessaryes meete & convenient for an apprentice, as well in
sickness as in health- for & duering ye time aforesd. & at the
end thereof to dismiss his sd. apprentice, with doble apperall
throughout, both linen & woolen, one sute for Lord's dayes,
& one sute for working days. In witness whereof the p[ar]ties
to these indentures have sett to theire hands seales
interchangeably each to the other this 19th day of February in
ye year of our Lord God one thousand six hundred seventy six
1676. . . . [20]

There were certain general conditions. The boy lived with his
master, who provided him with all the necessaries of life—food,
clothing, washing, and lodging. In addition, the master obliged himself
to teach the apprentice his art or "mystery," so that when the boy was
freed, he would be able to employ the necessary skills of the trade to
earn his living. In exchange, the boy promised to serve the master for a
set number of years, and to obey him in all his lawful commands.
There were certain things he promised not to do: he would not contract
matrimony, or commit fornication,[21] he would not destroy his master's
property, nor divulge his secrets; he would not absent himself without
leave, nor haunt taverns and ale-houses. Secondly there were some very
specific terms. The apprentice was to serve a particular number of years
from a given date; the master was to teach him a specific trade.

Accepting the above as the norm, we have an institution
determined primarily by custom, and incidentally, quite in accordance
with English statutory law. But it was in the variations from the norm,

extremely numerous, that the true characteristics emerge: that is to say, an agreement between two independent parties.

Take the number of years of service. The norm, or that number which the largest group of known apprentices contracted for, was seven. Yet, there were twice as many who varied from it, with more serving less than seven years, than those serving more.[22] For example, Mathew Legroe, slain in the Indian Wars of the late seventeenth century, had been bound as an apprentice to learn a trade in 1675, for two years and six months.[23] At the other end, there was one Charles Attwood whose father bound him for thirteen years so that he could not only learn to dress leather and make gloves, but also to read, write, and cast accounts well enough to keep a merchant's books.[24] As a rare exception there was Richard Handy of Plymouth County, who agreed to serve a master until he felt that he had fully attained the skill of a cooper. Richard, not the master, was to decide when that time had arrived; yet in other respects he was to behave as an apprentice.[25] Even more illustrative of this bargaining, however, is the case of John Sampson, aspirant to the shipwright's craft. He had a choice between a shipwright wllling to take him for a minimum of five years' service, and a local housewright who would train him in his trade in return for three years' servitude. Sampson chose the longer period with the shipwright.[26]

Another element of the contract which varied from case to case was the payment of a fee to the master for accepting the apprentice in the first place. This practice, common enough in England, particularly in the more exclusive trades, was not unknown in America, although the recorded instances are few.[27] Mention has already been made of the elder Franklin's unwillingness to pay a fee to the cutler with whom Benjamin was placed on trial. The fact that the demand came from a relative of Franklin's would indicate that the practice was not unknown, but it should be kept in mind that the man was a recent immigrant from England.[28] Other cases show a variety in fees expected, from the delivery of a whole crop of Indian corn, beans and pumpkins (including half the work of harvesting)[29] to cash fees ranging upward from sixty pounds.

Those highly placed could command even larger sums. Wllliam Stoddard, an eighteenth-century Boston merchant, asked one hundred pounds and a bond of five hundred pounds for the apprentice's fidelity.[30] Similarly, another merchant, named Joshua Winslow, wrote to Richard Wilson in 1740:

> When Cap Cary went hence, he mentioned to me the taking
> your Son Apprentice for 7 years & I accordingly gave him

Incouregement I would do it on Condition I might have 150£
Sterling with him, which I had with my last & which the
Boarding & taking Care of a Lad for that Time is fully worth
however on Receipt of your Letter I told Capt Steel I would
take him & leave it with you to make such further allowance
as you thought reasonable, he is now with me & bound for
Seven Years from the 1st May I shall do my utmost to
Instruct him & hope he will do well; he is somewhat thick of
Hearing w[hi]ch i8 a great disadvantage.[31]

A third mayor area of variation existed in the degree of formal
"book learning" the individual apprentice was to get. Much has been
written about the Puritan contribution to organized education, and there
exists no need to reproduce it here.[32] It is enough to admit that schools
were ordinarily available, and that all children were to be able "perfectly
to read the English tongue, and [to have] knowledge of the Capital
laws . . . "[33] Many masters contracted to see that their apprentices
learned reading, writing, and in some cases arithmetic. For example,
Andrew Stewman became the servant of a sailmaker in Salem in
1739/40. His master, beyond teaching him his trade, covenanted to
teach Andrew to read, write, and "Cypher to the rule of Three if he be
capable to learn."[34] That this was not the usual provision, even in the
eighteenth century, is suggested by the petition of Francis Worden
about his apprentice in 1727. It was his view that training in a trade,
providing clothes, and teaching to read, write and cypher was "more
than is Comonly practiced to be put in Indentures. . . . "[35] Some even
obliged themselves to keep their charges in school, or to allow
schooling at the parent's expense to be taken from the time which
ordinarily would be the master's.[36]

Yet a fourth area of variation arose over the payment of freedom
dues, or end-payment. It has already been pointed out that land was
rarely given to servants of any kind as part of their contract, although
some apprentices were among the exceptions.[37] Even so, they were not
turned away empty handed. The most common freedom dues were
clothing—two suits, one for the Lord's day and one for working days.[38]
That this was an important consideration may be seen in the specific
listing made in one agreement in 1687. The apprentice was to have
"double clothes throughout as: Jackets, coats, Waistcoates, Briches,
Drawers, trousers, Shirts, neck-clothes, Hatts, stockings shoes, gloves,
Hankerchiefs . . . "[39] Many other variations occurred. Some of them
were: money, produce of some kind, books, instruments, guns, and one
suit instead of two.[40]

Miscellaneous differences cannot be overlooked, either, for they illustrate even better the impact of individuals on custom. Some of them are: a provision for non-transfer of the servant without his assent, a limitation to a particular geographical area, the providing of part of the servant's keep by the parents, the prohibition or limitation of employment in menial work or work unconnected with the trade, provision for an alternate trade, the inclusion of an agreement for a period of service as a workman at the end of the apprenticeship, and finally, even a specification that a child could visit his parents on Sundays.[41]

An examination of particular agreements, as opposed to the above general variations, is equally instructive as to the individual nature of these contracts. Some were quite complex: in 1639, Dearmont Mathews signed an agreement with a master whereby he would work for six years at an annual wage of four pounds and one pig. At the end of his time he was to receive a piece of land, three suits and six shirts. His son, Tegg, was part of the agreement, for he was apprenticed to the same master for ten years. During that time Tegg was to have two years of schooling but the remaining eight were to be spent with the father.[42] Another case the same year involved one John Bourne who agreed to serve a master for six years if the master would undertake to teach him, at his coming to New England, the trade of a shipwright. If not, he would serve only four years.[43] Finally, at the end of the century, Joseph Barber became an apprentice to Joseph Markes until the age of twenty-one. The usual provisions were included in the indenture, and the boy was to be taught the trade of a "lining and wooling" weaver. But, the indenture continues, "if the sd. Joseph like not to learn the sd. trade, his sd. master Joseph engage to pay to the sd Joseph Barber Ten pounds in good Silver Money & a good gun at the end of his apprenticeship."[44]

The cases enumerated above indicate that apprenticeship contracts were subject to considerable variation from the generally accepted norm, but they do not tell the entire story. Combined with custom, the contracts set the framework within which the relationship between master and servant would function, but they did not determine the day-to-day pattern of behavior. Here there was room for even further variation, as the two persons involved worked out a way of life together. An irascible master or a truculent apprentice might conceivably make of the situation a living hell. On the other hand, if both individuals were moderate in their demands upon one another, it could prove to be a satisfactory experience for all concerned. It was this possibility of minute variation between the two extremes which impresses one with the immense variety of relationships which must have developed in this intimate association.

While the element of education was the distinguishing factor of apprenticeship, the second category of voluntary servitude was more directly economic in its function. Essentially, it represented an exchange of guaranteed labor for certain economic goods, whether transportation, wages, keep, end-payment, or all four. As a voluntary arrangement defined by a contract, this form of master-servant relationship came to be called indentured servitude.

The institution of indentured servitude arose in response to a particular need: a labor shortage in a community whose source of manpower was three thousand miles away. The problems involved were: to provide sufficient inducement to the worker to come to the New World, to provide him with transportation, and to secure the would-be employer an adequate return on his investment if he paid the transportation. As the system had developed by the early eighteenth century, transportation, keep, and a small end-payment were inducement enough to get many individuals to come, while a promise to work for a certain number of years (recorded in an enforceable contract) was considered sufficient guarantee of an adequate return on the part of the master. In its simplest form then, it was an exchange of transportation costs plus keep for labor.

Unlike apprenticeship, indentured servitude did not have a body of custom and tradition to give it form and content; it was essentially an innovation. However, there were certain practices current in old England which gave the colonists something to build upon. In the first place, apprenticeship training was not completely divorced from the idea of bound labor in exchange for certain economic goods. After all, the apprentice not only earned his education, he also worked to compensate the master for food, clothing, medical care, and housing. Moreover, in the case of apprentices bound out by the overseers of the poor, there is little doubt but that in many instances they were simply bound laborers whose training in a craft was of little significance. Thirdly, both types of apprenticeship had accustomed the colonists to the idea of a labor contract, or indenture. Why not substitute transportation to America for training in a trade? In the fourth place, the English were familiar with the custom of hiring for long periods, enforceable by law, even when the employee was not a youth, but an adult. The idea of the contract, of keep in exchange for service of some duration, combined with the problem of a costly sea voyage to a labor-scarce community, produced a variety of experiments in master-servant relationships resulting ultimately in a satisfactory solution to a serious problem.

There were several experimental solutions to the problem of a labor shortage which may be considered under the general heading of indentured servitude: company servants, servants on share, servants working for absentee masters, redemptioners, and servants drawn voluntarily from the white population in New England.

The first three of these experimental types were tried and discarded during the first decades of settlement in the seventeenth century. The early companies sent contract labor to work full time under the supervision of company members, or sent them on shares, their production to be divided between the company and share holder.[45] Private individuals, moreover, assumed the total risk of dilatory workers, desertion, or death, as they became absentee masters of servants shipped to Massachusetts where they worked without supervision of a master, or under the occasional eye of their master's friends.[46] None of these proved satisfactory. Company servants, as such, ceased to exist after the first few years. Private servants, without supervision of their masters, soon followed suit with only a rare exception in the later seventeenth century.[47] In at least one instance, all three devices proved disastrous, as a large number of company and private servants had to be freed to fend for themselves because of a shortage of provisions and shelter.[48]

The fourth experimental type, which may be considered under indentured servitude, was the redemptioner—the person who sought to sell his service to the highest bidder in the New World in order to reimburse the captain of his vessel for his transportation. Few came in this manner to the area between Massachusetts Bay and Cape Cod, although their numbers were apparently large elsewhere in the colonies.[49] The earliest redemptioner recorded in Massachusetts was in 1640, and curiously enough, it was for passage not to the New World, but from there to London where he had been bequeathed fifty pounds by his grandfather. He agreed to serve for seven years if he did not produce his passage money within six days after arrival.[50] That same year, a man came to Massachusetts on redemption terms and sold his services to John Winthrop, who agreed to pay him wages in addition to his passage. In fact, Winthrop agreed to pay wages equal to that offered by any other employer.[51]

The paucity of records concerning further redemptioners indicates that this type of servant, one who ordinarily had some worldly goods at his disposal, went elsewhere than to the ports ot Salem, Boston, and Plymouth. In fact, it was not until the eighteenth century that a third redemptioner showed up in the records. A woolcomber named Joseph Basker, hearing that there were good opportunities in his trade, ventured to come to New England in 1715. He agreed to pay a shipper five pounds in Bristol or eight pounds in New England for his transportation. Little other evidence on redemptioners could be found through 1750.[52]

More important and more persistent than the four experimental types of indentured servitude discussed above was the fifth: a voluntary servitude drawn from the white population in New England. It is common knowledge that seventeenth-century New England, with its emphasis on religion and its close cultural ties with its mercantilist motherland, sought to regulate its economy with regard to the just price, forestalling, regrating, usury, and wages.[53] Closely related to these regulations were laws designed to assure the master of his locally-hired servants, and of course, to assure the servant of employment, keep, and protection from abrupt dismissal in the midwinter's cold. Both Plymouth and Massachusetts imposed upon the servant contract minimum periods of duration (six months in Plymouth, a year in Massachusetts) and at the same time forbade selling a servant his time or dismissing him before his contract was up.[54]

Many New Englanders were willing to engage themselves for time beyond the limits thus imposed. Without capital and without tools, servents young in years and experience no doubt found it comforting to be able to rely upon the wisdom, capital, and patience of a family man who would ward off the evils of hunger, cold, and the Indians, and who would provide care in time of smallpox or other disabling calamity. Mothers with too many daughters to stir the soup, fathers with too many sons to work the house plot and ten acres, were glad to exchange the services of their children for a "cow calf and one half its increase," to say nothing of getting rid of the immediate responsibility of their children's supervision. Young men and women with little capital could get wages, a promise of a few acres of land (in the early days of settlement) or twelve bushels of Indian corn, two suits, and a musket at the end of their servitude, as well as bits of household or yeomanry education.[55]

Although individuals persisted in binding themselves out as servants to their neighbors throughout the entire period of this study, the numbers were few after the early decades of colonization.[56] Some, of course, were bound out by parent or guardian too, but even so, the numbers of American-born white servants decreased as the opportunities to serve on wages became stronger, and the restrictions of the laws became weaker. In time, those who might have served thus became the free laboring class, aa is testified to by the increasing reference to free laborers in the later decades of settlement.[57] In order to secure voluntarily bound, white, non-apprenticed labor, the would-be employer had to turn to the old world.

The ultimate solution to the problem of acquiring bound white servants, then, was not company servants, servants on shares, servants of absentee masters, or redemptioners, nor was it to be found in a reliance upon the local population. Instead, the answer was to be the transportation of men, women, and children for personal use or for sale from across the Atlantic.

Initially, the transportation itself was not a commercial venture, but rather an obstacle for the individual employer to overcome in the most convenient way he could manage. In other words, the typical seventeenth-century manner of acquiring servants from abroad rested upon the individual initiative of particular persons meeting a particular need for labor. Servants emigrated with their master, came on specific order to them in New England, or were brought over with a master who had visited the home country. In fact, most indentured white servants in the seventeenth century were brought across the ocean in these individualistic ways.

The *Mayflower* and the *Arbella* each had its own component of young people coming as part of the family of some colonist. Thus the record of the *Mayflower's* passengers includes "Mr. Edward Winslow Elizabeth his wife, & 2 men servants, cared Georg Sowle, and Elias Story . . . ," or "Mr. William Mullines, and his wife; and 2 children Joseph, & Priscila; and a servant Robart Carter."[58] The *Arbella* was not without servants either, as John Winthrop's references to them testify.[59] Engaged in England before leaving, these servants probably did not have more than oral agreements to serve for a certain length of time, and they probably relied upon the morality of the masters and of the community into which they migrated for protection against excessive exploitation, just as the master relied upon the community ties to keep his servants true to him.

On a similarly individual basis, many servants were sent over by friends or business acquaintances of individuals in the New World on request from prospective masters. In 1633, for example, Thomas Gostlin wrote to John Winthrop, Jr., stating that he was sending two servant girls (one for the elder Winthrop), but that he could not find a husband—man or a carpenter as requested.[60] A few years later, Sebastian Paulin was brought over by his uncle under an agreement to become a servant to Robert Keayne for ten years,[61] and, in 1639, one William Leeke agreed to be a "conductor" for the transportation of Edward Jones, prospective servant of Anthony Stanton of Boston.[62]

Still others were picked up by their masters-to-be during a return trip to the old country. The younger Winthrop, after searching New England for iron, made a trip back to old England to hire servants to work it.[63] An intimate glimpse of this particular way of getting servants is afforded in a letter concerning John Coggswell of Ipswich written to the father of a prospective servant in 1653:

> GodmanP[o]well your son it seemes being willing to goe into new England hath spoken with my Kinsman mr John coggswell of Ipswich in new england now with me about his goeing thither as a servant to him for Six yeares my couzzen being to pay for the pasage to giue him meat, drinke, & cloths in a fitting way & ten pounds in money after the expiration of his 6 yeares: & I will Ingage to you for my kinsman well vsinge of your son and that he shall not sell him to any man Else: Because I am unknown to you you may enquire of mr Randall who I am & he will sertifie you soe I rest . . . [64]

Almost a century later, individuals and families were still coming to Massachusetts with their servants. In May of 1716, for example, the ship *Boston Merchants,* docked in Boston with a doctor and his servants, a ropemaker with eight servants, a carpenter with seven; and a few days later, the ship, *Allen,* from London disembarked among others, a merchant with his three men, and two gentlemen with their servants.[65]

Although the employer most frequently solved his need for imported indentured servants in this individualistic way in the seventeenth century, a commercial system of transporting servants gradually grew up in which the voyage to the New World was not an obstacle but the means whereby the entrepreneur could realize a profit from the sale of labor transported at the entrepreneur's expense. In other words, individuals came to realize that there was money to be made in the shipping of servants to the colonies.

Bradford, reflecting in 1642 on the quality of immigrants who had come in the first two decades of settlement, recognized that "men, finding so many godly disposed persons willing to come into these parts, some begane to make a trade of it . . . " and then, unfortunately, he thought, filled up what empty space they had with any persons for whom they could receive passage.[66] At any rate, by 1638, such persons as Mr. Whittingham, who brought Richard Coy and several other servants to New England, did begin to make a trade of it. In a suit for freedom, one of Whittingham's transported servants claimed that ten years was too long to serve in exchange for the service rendered in transportation. The court's reply tells us much about the system already established. The servants had first come from Boston in Lincolnshire to London.

> There Mr. Whittingham kept them upon his own charges from May 1st till June 24th, so that his bringing up to London and charges of his staying there could not be less than 40s., his passage to New England, 51i., making 71i., besides other charges in provisions in addition to what they allowed ordinarily to passengers, all of which could be no less than 81i. This 81i. disbursed in England according to merchant's account, the adventure of his person considered, could not be here worth less than 151i. or 161i., and 161i., for a boy of thirteen years of age to be laid out here for ten year's service cannot any way seem injurious to the servant or of much advantage to the master.[67]

Slowly the practice of purveying servants grew during the seventeenth century, varying, of course, with the economic situation in England and the colonies, and with the political situation at home.[68] In 1653, for example, Mr. James Garret, master of the ship, *Trades Increase* of Charlestown, brought to Massachusetts several persons whom he put out as servants for terms of as much as nine years.[69] Early in the following decade, Boston's mint master and leading goldsmith, John Hull, on business in England, made an investment in servants. "Several children," he recorded in his diary, "I brought over, and all in good health, and so disposed of them, and providentially missed the having of one Sam Gaylor, who was after placed with Master Clark, and fell overboard, and was lost by the way."[70] And in 1676, an enterprising individual, George Cheever, went to the Island of Jersey and brought back to Massachusetts several boys and girls for sale.[71]

By the turn of the century, the system of purveying voluntary labor to America was well organized. While relatively few ships came to New England, as compared with the middle and southern colonies, they came none-the-less with group consignments to the ports of the Province of Massachusetts Bay. This practice, for example, made it possible for Josiah Cotton, son of the better known John, to add to his small income as a teacher in Marblehead by writing indentures for Jersey boys and girls brought to that port in the year 1700.[72] The purveyors of servants, be-sides being ship masters and residents of old England, were men like Boston's merchant, William Little, who sometime in the early eighteenth century chartered half a sloop, picked up Connecticut staves and exchanged them in Ireland for twenty indentured servants.[73]

After the first decade of the eighteenth century, the increased wholesale shipment of servants from abroad may be traced in the newspaper advertisements. Some forty large shipments were advertised between 1716 and 1750.[74] In 1716, for example, *The Boston News-Letter* advertised several persons to be disposed of by a ship captain, including an "Anchor and Ship Smith, House Carpenters, Ship joyners, and carver, Cooper, Shoemakers, Pattoun maker, Naylors, Locksmiths, Currier, Taylor, Book Printer, Silver and Gold Lace weavers, Button Maker, Earthenware pottery Maker, House-keepers, washer women & Cooks."[75] In 1721 *The Boston Gazette* carried a notice of the arrival of the brigantine, *Anne & Rebecca,* Thomas Handrey, commander. Aboard await-ing sale "for at least four year's time" were "Sundry men & women servants that have had the small pox."[76] Near the end of the same decade, *The Boston Gazette* advertised:

> Plads from Glasgow.
> Plads of sundry Sorts both fine & ordinary, Choice Linens of several Sorts, Bed Tickins, Handkerchiefs, & Muslins, with some Young Men & Womens Time of Service, to be Sold at Mr. George Bethune's Warehouse in Merchants Row. Boston.[77]

And ten years later, in 1739, the *John and Mary* disembarked "Several Men and Women Servants, Indented for Four Years . . . ," whose time was to be sold very "Reasonably by *Harris* and *Shower* at their Warehouse on the Town-Dock for ready Money or on Bond."[78]

In the seventeenth century, most of these imported servants came from England, although an occasional individual turned up from Ireland,[79] the Isle of Jersey,[80] Scotland,[81] and the Continent.[82] After the turn of the century, however, England took second place to Northern Ireland, with Scotland running third.[83] At least two good shipments came from the continent, one in 1729 and the other in 1731. The Isle of Jersey continued to be represented, while Wales and Newfoundland contributed a few.[84]

While the experimentation with variant forms of indentured servitude, and the emergence of commercially supplied imported labor indicate some of the characteristics of the conditions of service under which a servant worked, the picture is not complete without a discussion of the concrete terms of the labor contract. These terms were of extreme importance to the prospective immigrant, for he was not anxious to come to America without some foreknowledge of what his life would be like under an unknown master. Thus, John Winthrop, jr., hoping to get some "boyes and young maids of good towardness" to milk the cows, wash the dishes, and polish the boots of himself and friends, learned in 1633 that the youth of England were cautious about coming to the New World except on favorable terms. "I pray you therfore Good Sir," said his correspondent:

> write over . . . that there may be good Satisfaction in these following particulare, and I shal not be wanting in endeavours for your best furtherance. Vizt. What shal be the most of their employment there, whether dayrie, washing, etc. and what should be the Wages, and for how many yeers tyed, whether apparel found, who should provide for theire shipping over, their iourney thither, their diet while they stay for the wind or ships setting forth, and provision in the ship besides ship diet, (for tis said that must be, or it wil go very ill with them.)[85]

Each servant, then, sought the best terms he could get before leaving hearth and home, even if home were a gutter in London's slums. Each prospective master sought the best terms he could get too, for after all, the servant might die halfway through the period of indenture, or worse yet, halfway across the ocean.

In the process of bargaining, as it developed over the years, a pattern of rights and obligations on the part of each party to the labor contract emerged which may be considered as the norm, or the customary terms of the relationship. These terms, as in apprenticeship, were frequently recorded in a contract or indenture—hence the term "indentured servant." The following, in its terms and language, is typical.

> This Indenture made ye Seventh day of February in ye Year of our Lord God One thousand Seven hundred & sventeen Between Ebenezer Kingsby of ye one Party and William Gibb of ye other Party Wittneseth That the sd Ebenezer Kingsby doth hereby Covenant Promise and Grant to and with the sd William Gibb his Exec.s adms. & assigns from ye Day of ye Date hereof untill the first and Next arrivall at Boston In New England & after for & During ye Term of four Years to Serve in Such Service and Imployment as ye sd. William Gibb or his assignes Shall there Employ him according to the Custom of the Country In ye. Like Kind In Consideration whereof ye sd William Gibb do hereby Covenant & Grant to and with the said Ebenezer Kingsby to pay for his Passage and to find &

allow Meat Drink apparell & Lodging with other Necessarys during ye Sd Term and at the End of ye sd Term to pay unto him ye usuall allowance according to ye Custom of ye Country in ye Like Kind In Witness where of ye Partys above menconed to these Indentures have interchangeably Set their hands & Seals ye Day & Year above written.[86]

Thus the servant got his transportation to America, including his keep aboard ship, and probably his keep while awaiting shipment. Secondly, he was to be fed, clothed, housed, and given other necessaries, such as laundry, and care in sickness. Thirdly, he was to receive at the end of his service an unspecified payment, which would be determined by the common practice in the place of his servitude. That was all. The common practice of freedom dues in Massachusetts and Plymouth was two suits of clothes, one for dress and one for work. In exchange, the servant was to serve a stated number of years, in this case four from the date of arrival in Boston. The average was between three to five years. He was to serve in whatever legitimate capacity his master thought fit to employ him, whether menial or skilled, in city or country, on land or at sea. Finally, as the notation of the colonial notary on the above indenture indicates, he was more likely to serve his master's assignes, than his master himself. Most servants were transferable; indeed, most were transferred at least once, while many had three masters or more.[87] This was indentured servitude.

As in apprenticeship, however, the conditions of service of any individual servant were likely to vary considerably from the norm. Take the length of time, for example. A majority of those indigenous laborers who bound themselves as servants did so for less then three years, some only for months. On the other hand, many youths served longer terms than the norm, some as high as eight or nine, and one even for twelve.[88]

Most of these term variations occurred in the seventeenth century when the "long hire" was being enforced, and when the institution was strongly influenced by the minimum age requirements for freedom in the Statute of Apprentices. Thus, the case of the twelve-year term, was a servant who agreed in 1634 to serve until the age of twenty-three.[89] Another, brought to Massachusetts in 1643 without indentures, served more then ten years for his transportation fee of five pounds and sought only to be released from servitude when he was "well over 21 . . ."[90] But even in the eighteenth century years in excess of five were served by imported servants.[91]

A second variation in the conditions of service concerned a servant's transferability. While most servants could be transferred with as much ease as a slave, and could be bequeathed to a new owmer by the old master's will, some were able to get restrictions placed in their indentures prohibiting their transfer without their consent, or assuring their release at the death of their master.[92] Thus, the indenture of John Pitts prevented his mistress from completing his sale to one Benjamin Edwards in Boston in 1711/12,[93] while a seventeenth-century servant was freed from his master's widow shortly after the death of his owner.[94]

The obligations of the master also varied from the norm of transportation, keep, and an end-payment of two suits of clothing. It has already been pointed out in connection with the indigenous laborers that they could command periodic wages in lieu of transportation, and that some of them received land at the end of their terms.[95] However, imported servants, early in the period of settlement, were able to command better terms too. The major leeway in bargaining was in transportation. At first, it appears, transportation was an obligation assumed by the master: he wanted the servant, so he paid the fare. Wages of one kind or another were given, freedom dues were paid (rather larger than those paid later), and in some unusual instances, thc master guaranteed transportation back to England for the servant when his time was up.[96] William Snow, for example, was brought to Plymouth early in 1638. He had agreed to serve for five years in return for which he was to receive his keep and a cow calf, a sow pig, eight bushels of Indian corn, and two suits.[97] Another, Richard Crane, came aa a servant to Massachusetts for three years at more than ten pounds a year. His intention was to return to England at the end of his term.[98]

A contract typical of this class of servant, in which transportation was almost incidental, was signed by a woman for whom passage costs of eight pounds and clothing costs of thirty-five shillings had been paid before she was sent to John Winthrop, jr. by Amos Richardson.

> This Wrighting Wittnesseth that Catharin Leamon Spinster doth binde herselfe a servant in Covenant unto John Winthropp Esqr. with him or his assignes to dwell and abide in all Needfull servis to her best abillitie for the full space of fowre yeares next after these presents, for which servis shee is to haue Forty shillings a yeare wages and meate and drink and Lodging and such like necessaries. . . . [99]

Atypical in its terms, but useful to illustrate the variety which occurred, is the agreement reached in 1636 between two merchants of

Bristol, Abraham Shurt end Giles Elbridge. Shurt agreed to serve Elbridge in New England as a servant (including living with his master and behaving "as a servant ought to") for five years at sixty pounds yearly. He was to receive transportation to and from New England, in addition to meat, drink, lodging, and diet en route.[100] Only as the transportation of servants to New England became regular and commercial in nature did this variation disappear. In other words, wages were no longer paid in addition to transportation: transportation became wages.

Some further variations occurred in the bargains struck between masters and servants. Principally these were in freedom dues, although there were some servants able to secure educational provisions. Freedom dues varied from an ewe goat up to the norm of two suits and beyond to sums as large as ten pounds sterling, and frequently in the seventeenth century included produce or cattle.[101] Only in the early decades, as has been noted above, was land given, although one woman and her son, indenting themselves in 1730 for four years and until the age of twenty-one, respectively, were to get land according to the "custom of the country." Since the "custom of the country" was not to give land, they must have been disappointed at the end of their terms.[102]

What emerged, then, in late seventeenth-century colonial Massachusetts and Plymouth, and in the Province of Massachusetts Bay thereafter, was what is commonly known as an indentured servant. In the early years of settlement, his prototype may have served for transportation, keep, and an end-payment, or for wages in addition. He is easily confused, moreover, with voluntary domestic indenture or "covenant servants,"[103] and he sometimes had to have the words "serve as an apprentice," or "servant or apprentice" in his agreement for lack of a commonly accepted name. By the provincial period, however, he was a "servant by indenture."[104]

Apprenticeship and indentured servitude were the two principal forms of the highest category among bound servents. The former was firmly established among native American children, the latter came to be an institution reserved primarily for imported workers, as Americans became less and less willing to bind themselves to labor service for long periods. To get bound labor without apprenticeship, or excessive wage demands, the prospective employer had to turn elsewhere.

NOTES

1. Henry Steele Commager, ed., *The Autobiography of Benjamin Franklin & Selections from his Writings* (New York, 1944), 12–17.

One of the reasons he did not go to school was the "mean living many so educated were afterwards able to obtain. . . . " *Ibid.,* 12.

2. Farming, as Adam Smith noted, was more worthy of apprenticeship for seven years than many trades less difficult to master. *An Inquiry Into the Nature and Causes of the Wealth of Nations* (New York, 1937), Book I, Chapter Ten, part ii, 126–127. Children were regularly put out to farmers in the area of this study, particularly by the overseers of the poor. See below, chapter III.

3. Some who went to college afterwards served apprenticeship. John Langdon Sibley, *Biographical Sketches of Graduates of Harvard University in Cambridge Massachusetts* (Cambridge, 1837–), VII, 151. Hereafter cited as *Sibley's Harvard Graduates.*

4. Paul H. Douglas, *American Apprenticeship and Industrial Education* in *Columbia University Studies,* XCV, ii (New York, 1921), 12–16.

5. Francis Robert Seybolt, *Apprenticeship & Apprenticeship Education in Colonial New England & New York,* in *Columbia University Teachers College Contributions to Education,* LXXXV (New York 1917), 1–22.

6. Five Eliz c. 4. The effective enforcement of this famous Elizabethan statute, and the poor laws of early seventeenth-century England has been seriously questioned by John U. Nef, *Industry and Government in France and England 1540–1640,* in *Memoirs of the American Philosophical Society Held at Philadelphia For Promoting Useful Knowledge,* XV (Philadelphia, 1940), 25–35, 35–57. However, the disruption of economic revolution had not yet destroyed servitude in England, and it is shown below how the transplanted English sought vigorously and successfully to establish servitude of many shades in Plymouth and Massachusetts.

7. Brigham, *Laws,* 58. Whitmore, *Laws,* 136 (1642). Plymouth required the same by 1671. Brigham, *Laws,* 270.

8. Whitmore, *Laws,* 53 (1641).

9. *Mass. Recs.,* I, 186 (1636). Plymouth's law of 1639 was less rigorous than Massachusetts'. It simply made it more difficult to obtain freedom, but was not a flat prohibition. Brigham, *Laws,* 65.

10. Nef, *Industry and Government . . . , passim.*

11. Morris, *Government and Labor . . . ,* 139–141.

12. *Boston Records* II, 156–157 (law); VII, 21 (1664), 39 (1667/8, enforcement). A greater significance is attached to the law of 1660 by Seybolt, *Apprenticeship, . . .* 24–25. However, indentures appear only infrequently in the printed records, those in manuscript deal primarily with the poor, and apprentices continued to serve less than seven years. The one instance Seybolt cites as evidence actually deals with the poor. *Ibid.,* 24n.

13. Colonial Society of Massachusetts, *Publications* (Boston, 1895–), XXIX–XXX, "Records of the Suffolk County Court," Part II, 602. Hereafter cited as *Suffolk County Court,* I, II. I found no evidence

indicating compliance with the Hat Act of 1732 except its report in the *News-Letter,* Aug. 3–10, 1732.

14. *Acts and Resolves,* I–III, *passim.*
15. See below, chapter III.
16. The term, "apprentice" was frequently used to indicate the relationship of master and servant rather than necessary training provisions. For example, some of the early "apprentices" appear to have been bound servants without compensation except freedom dues or annual wages. See: *Records of the Court of Assistants of the Colony of Massachusetts Bay 1630–1692* (Boston, 1901–1928), II, 17 (1631), 26 (1632). Hereafter cited as *Assistants.* In 1633/4, John Smith, finding himself in "great extremity," bound out as an "apprentice" for ten years. *Plym. Recs.,* I, 23. In 1701, Mary Clifford put herself as an "apprentice or servant" to John and Margaret Pastre for four years. *Boston Records,* X, 51. In 1705/6, John Drisco is listed as an "apprentice or servant." MSS. Suffolk Sessions, I, 121. In 1744, Samuel Stertevant of Plymouth County bound himself as a "servant or apprentice" for eighteen months. Since his master paid seventy pounds for him, he was probably a domestic criminal owing damages and costs and serving it out. MSS. "Edward Winslow Notary Public. Benjamin Drew 1741–1759," 25–26.
17. Franklin, *Autobiography* . . . , 16. MSS. Essex Deeds, VI, 80. MSS. Records of the County of Middlesex, in the Commonwealth of Massachusetts: Transcribed under the Direction of Commissioners of the County of Middlesex, by David Pulsifer, 1851, V, 156. Hereafter cited as MSS. Middlesex County Court. MSS. Suffolk Sessions, III, 314 (1725). Several parents provided in their wills for apprenticeship of their sons after their own deaths. *Essex County Court,* VIII, 2–3 (1680); *Suffolk County Court,* II, 779 (1676/7); *The Probate Records of Essex County Massachusetts* (Salem, 1916–1920), II, 152–153 (1668). Hereafter cited as *Essex Probate.*
18. *Boston Almanac for the Year of Our Lord God 1692* . . . (Boston, 1692), 17–18. Reproduced photographically in M.H.S. "Nichols Reproduction Massachusetts Almanacs," VII. Thomas Hill, *The Young Secretary's Guide: or A Speedy Help to Learning* (seventh edition, Boston, 1730), 100–101. See advertisement for "Blank Bonds, Indentures Ec. to be Sold at the Printing House in Newbury-Street." *Gazette,* Jan. 15–22, 1733.
19. See MSS. Public Notary Books of Stephen Sewall and Mitchell Sewall, and MSS. "Edward Winslow Notary Public. Benjamin Drew 1741–1759," *passim.* For a school teacher writing indentures see *Sibley's Harvard Graduates,* IV, 398–402 (1700).
20. MSS. Essex Deeds, VI, 80.

21. The example given does not mention fornication, but this was a general prohibition. See, for example, *Essex County Court,* IV, 256–257 (1665). ⸺

22. See appendix A in Towner, "A Good Master Well Served . . ." (Ph.D. diss., Northwestern University, 1954).

23. *Essex Probate,* III, 81–82. Note also that the excuse given in Boston for enacting the seven year ordinance was that many youths were serving apprenticeships of only three to four years. *Boston Records,* II, 156–157 (1660).

24. E.I. *Colls.,* XI, 74–80 (1697).

25. *Plym. Recs.,* IV, 194 (1667).

26. Thomas Lechford, "Note Book . . . ," American Antiquarian Society, *Proc.* (Worcester, 1882–), New Series, VII, 303–405 (1641). Hereafter cited as Lechford, *Note-Book.*

27. Morris, *Government and Labor . . . ,* 369–370. In England, Adam Smith noted the common practice of requiring fees for apprenticeship, the occasional maintenance of the apprentice by the parents, and in the case of those unable to pay, the requirement of service beyond the necessary time for learning in exchange for training. *Wealth of Nations . . . ,* Book I, Chapter Ten, Part 1, 102.

28. See above page 24.

29. *Plym. Recs.,* IV, 194 (1667).

30. *Sibley's Harvard Graduates,* IV, 649. Stoddard was willing to settle for sixty pounds if the parents would provide clothes and washing.

31. MSS. Joshua Winslow Copy Book of Letters (1712–1769), 19. Boston, August 26, 1740.

32. However, it should be noted that Seybolt's chapter on education in Plymouth and Massachusetts is somewhat misleading, for he assumes that the legal obligations imposed upon the masters of poor apprentices were equally obligatory on all masters of apprentices. *Apprenticeship . . . ,* 36–51.

33. Whitmore, *Laws,* 16; Brigham, *Laws,* 271 (1671).

34. MSS. Public Notary Books of Stephen Sewall and Mitchell Sewall, II, 56.

35. MSS. Suffolk Sessions, IV, 68–69.

36. See appendix A in Towner, "A Good Master Well Served . . ." (Ph.D. diss., Northwestern University, 1954).

37. See above chapter I. A few, before 1640, and in Plymouth, may have had land, but it is not sure they were apprentices. See appendix A in Towner, "A Good Master Well Served . . ." (Ph.D. diss., Northwestern University, 1954).

38. See appendix A in Towner, "A Good Master Well Served . . ." (Ph.D. diss., Northwestern University, 1954). In 1675 a master was sued for not giving his apprentice two suits and ten pounds at the end

of service "according to the custom of the country. . . ." *Suffolk County Court,* II, 610–611.

39. E.I. *Colls.,* XI, 74–80.
40. See appendix A in Towner, "A Good Master Well Served . . . " (Ph.D. diss., Northwestern University, 1954).
41. *Ibid.* For visiting provisions see Edmund S. Morgan, *The Puritan Family* . . . , 37.
42. Lechford, *Note-Book,* 251–252.
43. *Ibid.,* 203 (1639).
44. MSS. M.H.S. "Miscellaneous Bound Manuscripts," Indenture of Joseph Barber (1694).
45. *Mass. Recs.,* I, appendix, *passim. Winthrop Papers,* III, 201–204 (1635).
46. Sir Mathew Boynton to John Winthrop, jr., 1636, *Winthrop Papers,* III, 247. Boynton was sending two servants, ten sheep, and a ram to Ipswich. He hoped that Winthrop would look after the servants, for though they were honest, they "should haue eyes ouer them espetiallie when they are att soe far a distance from theyr maister. . . ." See also: *Ibid.,* II, 334–335, 337–341 (1630); IV, 249–252 (1640).
47. For the exception see MSS. "Photostatic Copy of Records of County Court, Suffolk 1680–1692," modern penciled pagination followed, II, 245 (1685, two servants). Hereafter cited as MSS. Suffolk County Court.
48. Thomas Hutchinson, *The History of the Colony and Province of Massachusetts Bay,* Lawrence Shaw Mayo, ed. (Cambridge, 1936), I, 19. *Winthrop Papers,* II, 337–341 (1630). Boynton (see note 46 above) apparently found long distance supervision unprofitable, for he discharged his servants in 1637, offering to pay their passage home unless they preferred to use their liberty in Massachusetts, *Ibid.,* 388–389.
49. A.E. Smith, *Colonists in Bondage* . . . , 21–22, 223–225.
50. Lechford, *Note-Book,* 328.
51. *Winthrop Papers,* IV, 322 (1640/41). Winthrop freed the servant after a year, and the man complained that he could have made more in that year than four pounds passage, two pounce tools, plus clothes.
52. Barker claimed he was persuaded to sign a regular indenture as a guarantee of his payment on arrival in America. He was forced to honor the indenture even though he had offered to pay. MSS. Suffolk Sessions, II, 102–103 (1715). For another Bristol redemptioner see MSS. Suffolk Court Files, Vol. 98, folio 131 (1715). John Warren, 31 years old, agreed to serve four years unless he paid his transporter nine pounds within ten days of arrival in New England.
53. E.A.J. Johnson, "Some Evidences . . . ," *passim.*
54. Brigham, *Laws,* 58 (1638); *Mass. Recs.,* I, 88 (1631), 186 (1636).

55. For examples see: (short term), *Plym. Recs.,* I, 8 (1633); II, 6 (1640/1); (long term), *ibid.,* I, 15–16 (1633); Pulsifer, *Deeds,* 32 (1638 servant working for transportation agrees to serve extra year for five pounds). For land, see appendices A and B.

56. Morgan, *The Puritan Family* . . . , 37 (1688, girl for six years); Pulsifer, *Deeds,* 164 (1648, man, five years, for keep and a heifer); MSS. Winthrop Papers, W.19.22 (1650, man, eighteen months for L6:10 and the cure of an arm); Essex County Court, II, 372 (1662, man, term unknown); MSS. "Plymouth Sessions of the Peace," I, 5 (1686, suit against servant for failure to fill his five month's indenture). Hereafter cited as MSS. Plymouth Sessions. Old Colony Historical Society, miscellaneous MSS., "Documents Very Old," I, 25 (1697, boy, three years, one month for keep, a gun, two suits, and one-half interest in a cow); MSS. Public Notary Books of Stephen Sewall and Mitchell Sewall, I, 54 (1705, man, one year in return for keep); MSS. Suffolk Sessions, III, 132–133 (1722 girl to age eighteen); MSS. Suffolk County Court, I, 50 (1680, nine weeks); E.I. *Colls.,* LVI, 289–290 (1717, one summer, apparently for sea service); MSS. "Edward Winslow Notary Public. Benjamin Drew 1741–1759," 25–26 (1744, one year).

57. The late seventeenth century saw many laborers owning property in Suffolk County. See: *Suffolk Deeds* (Boston, 1880–1906), III, V, VIII-XIV, *passim.* In the eighteenth century they became even more numerous. See: MSS. Suffolk Sessions, IV, V, *passim.*; MSS. Middlesex County General Sessions of the Peace, II, III, IV, *passim.* Hereafter cited as MSS. Middlesex Sessions. MSS. Essex County Records of the Court of General Sessions of the Peace, I, n.p. case of John Brown (Dec. 27, 1692), n.p., case of John Bligh, Jan. 23, 1693/4); II, 307, 361–362; IV, 178, 220; V, 682–688; VI, 75. Hereafter cited as MSS. Essex Sessions. MSS. Bristol County General Sessions of the Peace, III, 8, 258–259; IV, 89. Hereafter cited as MSS. Bristol Sessions. MSS. Plymouth Sessions, IV, 7–8, 83–84, 108–109. See also Boston Public Welfare Department, MSS. File 1719 (Sept.-Dec.). There were, of course, servants upon wages who lived in with their masters, though probably not bound. See *News-Letter,* Mar. 7–14, 1734.

58. *Bradford's History,* reproduction of page of MSS. passenger list opposite 531. Fourteen other servants were among the one hundred-odd passengers of the *Mayflower, Ibid.,* 531 ff.

59. *Winthrop's Journal,* I, 25, 30, 38, 42. For other examples see: *Boston Records,* VI, 78 (1633), 82 (ca. 1633); *Winthrop Papers,* III, 201–204 (1635), 251–253 (1636, several); IV, 89 (ca. 1639); *Suffolk County Court,* II, 800–801 (1677); Lechford, *Note-Book,* 378–381 (1640); *Mass. Recs.,* I, 32–33 (1628/9); Cotton Mather, *Magnalia Christi Americana: or, the Ecclesiastical History of New England* . . . (London, 1702), III, 142 (1637).

60. M.H.S., 5 *Colls.*, I, 200–201 (1633).
61. *Winthrop Papers*, III, 352 (1636/7).
62. Lechford, *Note-Book*, 427–428 (1639). See also *Winthrop Papers*, IV, 329–330 (1641); MSS. *Winthrop Papers*, W. 3. 132 (1653).
63. M.H.S., 5 *Colls.*, VIII, 36–37 (1643/4).
64. *Essex County Court*, I, 307–308 (1653); see also VI, 151 (1676)
65. *Boston Records*, XXIX, 233, see also 237–238. E.I. *Colls.*, LVIII, 264 (1730).
66. *Bradford's History*, 476–477.
67. *Essex County Court*, I, 381–382.
68. The classic illustration of this is, of course, *Winthrop's Journal*, II, 31. See also: *Winthrop Papers*, IV, 205–206, 216–217 223–225, and Clifford K. Shipton, "Immigration to New England; 1680–1740," *Jour. Pol. Econ.*, XLIV (Apr., 1936), 225–239, *passim*.
69. *Suffolk Deeds*, IV, 48.
70. "Diaries of John Hull . . . ," American Antiquarian Society, *Archeologia Americana* (Worcester, 1820–), III, 153. Hereafter cited as Hull, *Diary*.
71. E.I. *Colls.*, I, 159–160. For others who brought small numbers of servants not for their own use, but for sale see: Lechford, *Note-Book*, 365–367 (1640); MSS. Suffolk Sessions, II, 90, 91 (1715); MSS. Public Notary Books of Stephen Sewall and Mitchell Sewall, I, 141 (1717/8).
72. *Sibley's Harvard Graduates*, IV, 398–402 (1700).
73. *Ibid.*, V, 528.
74. *News-Letter:* Aug. 19–26, 1717; Sept. 23–30, 1717; Aug. 4–11, 1718; Dec. 15–22, 1716 (two shipments); Aug. 3–10, 1719; Nov. 12–19, 1722; July 17–24, 1729; Sept. 11–18, 1729; Oct. 15–22, 1730; Mar. 26–Apr.2, 1741; Nov. 22, 1750. *Gazette:* May 6–13, 1723; Oct. 21–28, 1728; July 7–14, 1729; Aug. 9–16, 1731; Dec. 27–Jan. 3, 1731/2; May 1–8, 1732; May 14–21, 1733; Sept. 16–23, 1734; June 14–21, 1736; June 20–27, 1737; Aug. 15–22, 1737; July 3–10, 1738; Oct. 30–Nov. 6, 1738; Aug. 24–31, 1741; Nov. 24, 1741; Jan. 11, 1743. *Courant:* Oct. 26–Nov. 2, 1724. *Journal:* Aug. 30, 1737; May 1, 1739; June 23, 1741. *Evening-Post:* May 9, 1743; May 14, 1750. *Post-Boy:* Apr. 28, 1746; Sept. 18, 1749. For another shipload, see *Boston Records*, XV, 316–318 (1741).
75. June 18–25, 1716.
76. Nov. 27–Dec. 4, 1721.
77. Nov. 24–Dec. 1, 1729.
78. *News-Letter*, July 26–Aug. 2, 1739.
79. For examples see: *Essex County Court*, I, 57 (1643); II, 197–198 (1660); VIII, 222–226 (1661); *Mass. Recs.*, III, 294 (1652); *Plym. Recs.*, III, 91 (1655); 220 (1661); MSS. Winthrop Papers, W.3.132 (1653). Some or all of these may have been sent over as prisoners rather than voluntary indenture servants.

80. E.I. *Colls.,* I, 159–160 (1676).
81. For examples see: Samuel Bates, ed., *Records of the Town of Braintree,* 1640–1793 (Randolph, Mass., 1886), 636 (1657). Hereafter cited as *Braintree Records.* See also *Boston Records,* IX, 37 (1652); *Essex County Court,* III, 264–265 (1665); *Assistants,* I, 30 (1674/5); *Suffolk County Court,* II, 847–848 (1677); MSS Middlesex County Court, I, 68 (1654); 84–85 (1655); MSS. Middlesex Court Files, file 16, number 740 (1660/1). These, like the Irish, may very well have been prisoners of war rather then voluntary servants.
82. *Essex County Court,* V, 312 (1674); MSS. Suffolk County Court, I, 228 (1684).
83. The citations for English, Irish, and Scotch servants in the eighteenth century are too numerous to list. However, the statement is based on a search of all Boston newspapers through 1750. See also Clifford K, Shipton, "Immigration to New England, 1680–1740," *Jour. Pol. Econ.,* XLIV (Apr., 1936), 225–239. For sample listings of shipments of Scotch, English, and Irish see: *Gazette,* June 14–21, 1736; *Post-Boy,* Apr. 28, 1746; *News-Letter,* July 26–Aug. 2, 1739.
84. For examples: (The Continent) *Gazette,* July 7–14, 1729; Aug. 9–16, 1731; (Jersey servants) *News-Letter,* Nov. 24–Dec. 1, 1726, and *Gazette,* Jan. 11, 1743; (Welch) *Gazette,* Jan. 2–9, 1738 and *Post-Boy,* Feb. 9, 1741; (Newfoundland) MSS. Suffolk Sessions, II, 90 (1715), and MSS. Public Notary Books of Stephen Sewall and Mitchell Sewall, II, 55–56 (1744).
85. *Winthrop Papers,* III, 126–128.
86. MSS. Public Notary Books of Stephen Sewall and Mitchell Sewall, I, 141. For an almost identical form used in 1682/3 by a New York or New Jersey servant see A.E. Smith, *Colonists in Bondage . . . ,* 18.
87. See appendix B in Towner, "A Good Master Well Served . . . " (Ph.D. diss., Northwestern University, 1954).
88. *Ibid.*
89. *Plym. Recs.,* I, 32 (1634).
90. MSS. Middlesex Court Files, File 6, number 200. Petition of Stephen Mattock.
91. See appendix B in Towner, "A Good Master Well Served . . . " (Ph.D. diss., Northwestern University, 1954).
92. *Ibid.*
93. MSS. Suffolk Sessions, I, 242–243.
94. *Assistants* II, 164. For an eighteenth-century case see MSS. Suffolk Sessions, III, 127–128 (1722).
95. See above, page 33. See also appendix B in Towner, "A Good Master Well Served . . . " (Ph.D. diss., Northwestern University, 1954).

96. See appendix B in Towner, "A Good Master Well Served ... " (Ph.D. diss., Northwestern University, 1954).
97. *Plym. Recs.,* I, 94 (1638).
98. *Winthrop Papers,* IV, 105–106 (1638/9). There was a controversy over whether it was to be for three years or five.
99. *Winthrop Papers,* V, 339 (1649). See also IV, 322 (1640/41).
100. *Boston Records,* XXXVII, 38 (1636). An even more extravagant case was that of Mr. Leader, hired to run the iron works at Saugus. He signed an indenture, as any bound servant did, for seven years. He was to get one hundred pounds per year plus passage for wife, children and three servants. A house was to be built for him, and land was to be available for his horses and cows. Today (and then too, at times) he would be called a factor or agent. Yet he was bound, and he illustrates the flexibility of the institution. *Winthrop Papers,* V, 5–8 (1644/5). His successor, John Gifford bound himself for seven years also, at eighty pounds per year. Typescript, "A Collection of Papers Relating to the Iron Works at Lynn and More Particularly to a Suit Between Mr. John Gifford the Agent For the Undertakers of the Iron Works and The Inhabitants of the Massachusetts Bay Colony Dated 1650 *et. seq.,*" 21. Morgan, *The Puritan Family ... ,* 62, correctly states that the term "Servant" was loosely and widely applied to employees of whatever type. However; the agreement between Shurt and Elbridge shows that some of these highly paid individuals were bound as securely as a poor servant who served for his passage and keep.
101. See appendix B in Towner, "A Good Master Well Served ... " (Ph.D. diss., Northwestern University, 1954).
102. E.I. *Colls.,* LVIII, 264.
103. See appendix I in Towner, "A Good Master Well Served ... " (Ph.D. diss., Northwestern University, 1954).
104. See: *Suffolk Deeds,* IV, 48 (1653); *Plym. Recs.,* I, 23 (1633/4); *Boston Records,* X, 51 (1701); MSS. Suffolk Sessions, I, 12 (1701); Lechford, *Note-book,* 427–428 (1639), *Assistants,* I, 30 (1674/5, two cases). For eighteenth century see appendix B in Towner, "A Good Master Well Served ... " (Ph.D. diss., Northwestern University, 1954).

3. The Poor as a Source of Bound Labor

Somewhat beneath the voluntary apprentice and indentured servant in the social scale of the servant class, yet above the debtor, criminal, and the colored servants, were those children and occasional adults who were forced into servitude by law because they were poor. The "Poor" in Massachusetts and Plymouth colonies, it must be understood, were not exclusively of the pauper class. Instead, the term includes those who simply had insufficient property to ward off charges of idleness, disorderly living, living outside of family organization—in effect, living contrary to the accepted social mores. With some exceptions (particularly in the case of living outside of family government) servitude was reserved only for the children of these social unfortunates. The adults were treated otherwise; nevertheless this class provided a ready reservoir of labor after the early years of settlement, especially in the eighteenth century.

From the first decades in Plymouth snd Massachusetts Bay, the poor presented a problem, at first of minor, then major proportions.[1] Exigencies of a hostile climate, unfriendly Indians, and disease, as well as the vagaries of the economic system worked upon the already significant differences in wealth among the settlers to produce a growing class of indigent or near indigent, who had to rely upon society for support or help.

Private philanthropy at once assumed part of the burden. In the 1630s, one man gave money for wood, another a cow, and a third some heifers.[2] By the 1650s, legacies of ten pounds for a loan fund, fifty pounds for the poor of a particular church, fifty pounds to establish a free school, and even fifty pounds for indigent scholars at Harvard had been left by colonials who knew how badly the money was needed.[3]

The eighteenth century, despite considerable public assumption of responsibility, saw no decline in the necessity of private giving. The morally ubiquitous Cotton Mather was frequently engaged in projects for relieving the impoverished of Boston and neighboring communities.

He gave away food, books, and money to help poor children stay in school; he collected money from others to dispense, and he recorded the activities of persons of like sympathies similarly engaged. His *Diary* for 1713 notes that "The distressed Familles of the Poor to which I dispense, or procure needful Reliefs, are now so many, and of such Daily Occurrence, that it is needless for me here to mention them."[4] By the 1720s, the poor in Boston were so numerous that collections were taken up in such towns as Amesbury, Scituate, Marshfield and Barnstable to provide wood and other necessaries for them.[5]

The ministry not only took note by collecting and distributing goods to the indigent, but also by bringing attention to them in sermons and publications. Cotton Mather urged more concern be taken with the welfare of the inner man than the outer in his *Some Seasonable Advice unto the Poor* published in 1726,[6] while Benjamin Colman, ten years later, preached on the desirability of being generous to those unfortunates of a pious disposition. Reverend Mr. Charles Chauncey, in the same period, took a less charitable position by warning against the creation of a class of the professionally improvident.[7]

Despite Chauncey's grumbles, private gifts continued to be made *The Weekly News-Letter* reported in 1741 that:

> It is humbly propos'd by the Overseers of the POOR, That in Consideration of the distressing Circumstances of the Poor of the Town, occasioned by the Extremity of the present Season, that there be a Collection for their Relief the next Tuesday Evening at the Rev. Dr. Colman's Meeting-House, which they are willing to take the Trouble of distributing to the most suitable Objects in their several Wards.[8]

Later issues show that this was no idle appeal, for from the congregations of fifteen ministers in town, some £1250 was collected.[9] In the same decade, a musical concert was held at Faneuil Hall to raise money for charity.[10]

Private philanthropy was not restricted to the accumulation of stocks to be worked, occasional gifts, and haphazard charity. In Boston at least, charitable societies were formed whose purpose was to provide for the indigent of a particular ethnic group, such as the Scot's Charitable Society organized in Boston in 1657, and the Charitable Irish Society of the eighteenth century, or along strictly religious lines such as the Episcopal Charitable Society organized in 1724.[11]

Despite the vigorous efforts of individuals and voluntary associations, the poor presented problems which required the organized financial and coercive powers of government. At first, the colonial governments assumed the responsibility for administering public care of the poor, and frequently, the financial responsibility as well. By the 1640s, decentralization occurred as the various towns were deemed capable of handling the administrative and financial burdens.[12] Thus, Massachusetts Bay by 1639, and Plymouth, by 1643/44 made statutory what had already been partially implemented according to English custom—local responsibillty for the care of the poor.[13]

This delegation of power to local authorities raised the same problem which plagued English towns: who was a legal inhabitant, and who a mere sojourner for whom the town need not be concerned? Formally, the question was settled in Plymouth in 1642/43, when it established a three-month period during which a destitute, or potentially destitute stranger could be warned from the town without the town's becoming liable for his care.[14] Massachusetts had provided in its original law, that the court, or any two magistrates out of court, could determine the legal settlement of individuals if dispute arose. In 1659 Massachusetts also adopted the three months settlement period.[15]

Despite this formal decision, controversies arose between towns concerning the care of the poor, as John Harmon learned to his sorrow when neither Plymouth nor Taunton wished to support him. In October of 1680, he was ordered to be maintained in Plymouth until the following June. July's court reversed itself and ordered him maintained in Taunton to await the decision of the October session. Then, the court ordered each town to provide one half his care until March. July, 1682, found him wandering from town to town with Dartmouth being charged for his keep until October. A year later the General Court finally decided that he should alternate between Plymouth and Taunton from year to year.[16]

Once accepted as legal inhabitants, the indigent were maintained by the towns, each of which worked out its own methods of care. In some cases, the nearest relative was required to assume total financial responsibility, in others they made the relative personally responsible but paid for the support. Some towns set aside a "poor" stock, which they raised by appropriation or by earmarking certain fines for that purpose. Braintree paid one Timothy Winter for his care of Jacob Pool, in 1686/87, while two years later, Samuel Speere was ordered to build a "house" seven feet by five feet at public expense to "secure his Sister, good-wife Witty being distracted & provide for her. . . ." In Boxford, the selectmen met to "hear of the pooer" and ordered Daniel Black, Jr. to help his father during haying and present the selectmen a bill for it. Boston not only made cash payments to the indigent, but the town provided free medical care by giving doctors who attended them abatements of their taxes. Indeed, Boston had an almshouse as early as 1662, where such poor persons as Mrs. Jane Woodcock, widow, had the liberty of living at the town's pleasure.[17]

During the provincial period, the General Court recognized the continued growth of the poor class by reenacting the settlement laws, increasing the authority of the county courts (even setting up overseers of the poor in the counties), increasing the authority of the overseers of the poor in the town of Boston, passing enabling acts for the creation of workhouses, particularly in Boston, and providing certain funds to be derived from fines for various legal infractions.[18]

That Boston needed special legislation can be seen by reviewing a census taken there in 1742 in the various wards. Out of a population of 16,382 whites and 1,374 Negroes, some 110 persons were being maintained in the almshouse and thirty-six in the workhouse. Of some 1,200 widows 1,000 were considered to be non-rateable or even destitute.[19]

It was from this fairly large and growing body of poor folk, then, that many servants were drawn involuntarily. Both Plymouth and Massachusetts passed legislation early in the 1640s which enabled the towns to place out the children of the poor as "apprentices," with or without their parents' consent.[20]

For example, in Plymouth, one of the many children of Samuel and Elizabeth Edeth was bound out to the age of twenty-one in March of 1646/47. That same year, the town of Rowley put Thomas Abbot, jr., out as an apprentice for seven years, and Salem ordered the son and daughter of Ruben Guppy to be placed as servants until the ages of twenty-one and eighteen, respectively.[21] This practice was continued throughout the seventeenth century with terms of servitude which varied from town to town and servant to servant.[22]

It was during the provincial period that the binding out of pauper children became most significant. The General Court, in November of 1692, re-enacted the law giving the selectmen (or overseers if there were such) the right to dispose of poor children.[23] A decade later, because of a misunderstanding concerning its application, the law was re-enacted and strengthened to include not only the children of those who were receiving alms, but those given abatements in their taxes because of poverty.[24] Subsequently, the act was renewed several times without change until 1741, when the office of county overseer was created to supervise the binding out of poor children living outside of any town jurisdiction.[25]

In Boston by 1691, overseers of the poor were established—men whose function was to keep track of the number of poor in their respective wards, distribute funds for their use, make formal visitations with the selectmen to poll the poor, recommend admittance to the poor house, and supervise that institution as well. Prominent among their functions was the supervision of the putting out of paupers to "apprenticeship."[26] A person wishing for a servant would get his selectmen to certify him to the overseers, as did this resident of Reading in 1742:

> To the Gentlemen the overseers of the pooer in the town of Boston this is tow signefy to you that John Nichols and his wife are parsons of sober Conversations and sutably qulifyed to Bring up a Child agreable to the Gospel in our judments.[27]

If a poor child were available, as in the Nichols' case, the overseers would then bind him out for a period of years determined by the age of the child, girls to age eighteen and boys to twenty-one.[28] By the last years of the 1740s, the Boston overseers had their own indentures printed, so common was the practice. Indeed, in the years 1734–1751, some 247 boys and girls in a ratio of two to one, were disposed of in this manner.[29]

Once they disappear from the town records, it is difficult to separate these poor apprentices from their more fortunate brethren whose parents or guardians took care in choosing a master and trade for them. Their service was certainly more burdensome in point of years, but most apprentices served to age twenty-one, and all children were used for labor on farms or in homes before apprenticeship, poor or not. More than half of the poor apprentices served over nine years, while some served as many as fifteen or sixteen, and others as few as one, three, or four. As many served for twelve years as seven.[30]

As for training provisions, the available indentures show that the children were to be apprentices, that the boys were to be taught reading, writing and arithmetic, the girls reading and writing. While most of the girls were used as household servants, they were sometimes to be taught knitting, sewing, and even spinning (in which case they were to learn arithmetic too). The boys were frequently used as farm labor in such towns as Woburn, Weston, Marlboro, and Braintree, but not a few were put out to such artisans as cordwainers, housewrights, barbers, shipwrights, and cabinet makers.[31] At least one became a successful printer.[32]

End-payments, or freedom dues, varied too. The overwhelming majority were to be provided with the customary two suits of clothing.

A few, however, and for no apparent reason, were to have additional dues of a sum of money. In 1734, for example, an indigent currier's son was bound apprentice to a shoemaker for fifteen years. He was to be taught reading, writing, the trade of shoemaker, and then to be given two suits and thirty pounds in bills of credit.[33] Similarly, in the next few years, three boys were bound out to learn husbandry for sixteen, twenty, and fifteen years each. They were to get, in addition to reading, writing, and arithmetic, freedom dues of two suits, and twenty pounds in bills of credit, seven pounds and ten shillings, and twenty pounds, respectively.[34]

In the seventeenth century, the system seems clearly to have been a convenient way of taking care of the poor, but by the eighteenth century, in Boston at least, it took on the additional function of a labor pool supplying the surrounding towns, and even such "faraway" places as New Hampshire.[35]

The children of paupers or non-rated taxpayers were not the only poor persons put to service in this period. Seventeenth-century Massachusetts and Plymouth colonies, as well as the Province of Massachusetts Bay cast a much wider net.

It is perhaps unfair to these New Englanders to include under the topic of the poor, persons who were ordered into service by the colonial authorities for failure to live under proper family government. There are instances, for example, where persons of some substance lost control of their families by court action, being forced to submit them, and themselves, to another adult's authority,[36] but generally speaking there was a connection between idleness, ill living, and poverty in the Puritan and Pilgrim mind, and this connection found its way into their laws. Clearly, poverty, or even inadequate means left the individual with fewer defenses against the organized community. At any rate, the consciousness of a necessity for family supervision of work, play, religion, and education led the colonists to exercise their authority in placing single persons in family homes, as servants if necessary, and in disrupting improperly regulated families, disposing of their numbers in the same manner.

The family rather than the individual was considered not only the basic unit of the state, but also the fundamental and requisite means of social and religious control.[37] Living outside this unit—not subject to its salutary religious, moral, and economic discipline—was unthinkable in the seventeenth century for adults as well as minors. In the eighteenth century, the same attitude applied to minors only, whether they were capable of self support or not.

Single individuals were, of course, the obvious objects of such solicitude. As possible cancers in the body politic, unrestrained by family responsibilities, likely to be of loose habits, and frequenters of idle gatherings, there was little question but that they needed restraint. From early times, the Puritan authorities were constrained to regulate their behavior, going so far as to place the company servants in artificial families where

> O[u]r earnest desire is, that yow take spetiall care . . . that the cheife in the familie (at least some of them) bee grounded in religion; wherby morning and evening famylie dutyes may bee duely p[er]formed, and a watchfull eye held over all . . . by one or more in each famylie to bee appointed thereto, that soe disorders may bee p[re]vented, and ill weeds nipt before they take too great a head.[38]

These, of course, were already servants, and by nature of servitude, should have lived under authority. Half a decade later, however, in 1636, Massachusetts ordered that each town should dispose into service all single persons within their jurisdiction, and at the same time prohibited the setting of servants free until they had served out the time covenanted.[39]

Plymouth sought the same end, but left the enforcement in the hands of the central governmental authorities rather than transferring it to the towns. In 1633,[40] 1636,[41] and 1640,[42] she enacted legislation designed to assure that all who were permitted to set up by themselves as housekeepers should be reliable God-fearing individuals whose behavior would conform to the accepted pattern.

Economy and humanity undoubtedly were favored, if unconsciously, in the decision to place individuals of improper situation or bearing under the jurisdiction of families rather than institutions. Economy, because institutions were expensive to maintain whereas a servant undoubtedly earned his own keep. Humanity, because institutional life, in those grim days of Bridewells was likely to be more severe, more destructive of the individual psyche than a family hearth no matter how "puritanical."[43]

It was not left to personal inclination, of course, to determine the nature of a truly Christian household. A proper family would have at its head a mature person, well founded in the religious principles of his community, working diligently to improve his estate, God-fearing, respectful of authority, sober, married, and conscious of his obligation to maintain discipline for those under his authority—his children and his servants. Early Massachusetts law required that he take care to see

his children and servants properly taught in the catechism, reading, so
as to be able to read the Bible and the capital laws, and that they be
brought up to some occupation such as husbandry or other trade "if they
will not, or cannot train them up in learning to fitt them for higher
imployments." If the head of the family proved to be neglectful, the
selectmen, after admonition to reform, and finding him still negligent,
could take his children or servants from him, and put them out as
servants, the girls to age eighteen, the boys to twenty-one.[44]

Unwilling to rest with the children and servants, the colonies
determined proper behavior for adults as well. In 1633 and 1639,
Massachusetts and Plymouth prohibited idleness, the latter specifically
referring to the class where they most expected such behavior, the poor.
The grand jurymen were instructed to take a "speciall view and notice of
all manner of persons, married or single . . . that have small meanes
to mayntaine them and are suspected to live idly & loosely. . . . "
No punishment was determined, for the courts were supposed to use
their own discretion.[45]

By the early 1640s, both colonies had decided that few, if any,
individuals could be trusted to live outside of a family, that family
government had to conform to certain standards, and that those families
which did not, could be broken up as far as the children were concerned,
while the adults might expect some punishment for improper behavior.
Servants, moreover, were to be kept in service until their time was up,
and even then, they might not set up for themselves unless approved by
the authorities.

This was no idle legislation. In the late 1630s, Christopher
Osborne and Jeremiah Willis were presented to the Plymouth Court for
"liuing disorderly out of service, contrary to the order of the Court."
Jeremiah, the next month, was given a week's time to find a master.[46]
Shortly after, Anthony Bessie was presented for living alone disorderly
and for taking in a visitor without permission.[47] On the same day,
Joseph Windsor was presented for keeping house alone after six
months' warning to the contrary.[48] Web Adey, presented with others in
1637 for disorderly living, was required to give an account of how he
lived. Apparently his account did not reflect his ordinary behavior, for a
year later he was brought again before the court for living in "idleness
and nastiness" and for working on two Sabbath days. His punishment
was to sit in the stocks during the pleasure of the bench, and to find a
master before the next sitting of the Assistants. His house and garden
were to be rented or sold for the "convenient apparelling" of him during
the service.[49]

The Massachusetts Assistants were equally severe with those who freed servants before their time was up.[50] Several individuals were presented before them for such misbehavior: Captain Stoughton and Rolfe Allen in 1639, John Woodbridge and Christopher Batte in 1640, Thomas Baguley, Abraham Morrell and Samuel Sherman in 1641, and John Beamis in 1643.[51]

Both colonies were willing to separate families too if it was felt that the government of the particular family was insufficient to maintain proper standards. The notorious Billingtons were constantly in legal difficulties in Plymouth. In 1642 and 1643, several children of Francis and Christian were ordered to be put out as servants. Later, one of these children, named Joseph, after attaining freedom, was warned that if he did not improve, the court would find a service for him.[52]

In the Middlesex court, the Charlestown constables were ordered to keep a close watch upon Jonathan Mansfield and his wife for several misdemeanors, and the selectmen were advised to put his children out to service. A year later, the same court approved the selectmen's choosing masters for eight year old John and his twin, Elizabeth, for they found that Jonathan was not capable to raise them "by reason of the misgovernment of himself and wife."[53] A somewhat different case was disposed of there the following year when Samuel Tingsley, Mary Deane, and their five weeks old bastard were to be "disposed of by the Selectmen of Charlestowne, as they shall [think] meet for their abode, labor & maintenance."[54] As a final example in this early period, Salem's Henry Phelps was accused of entertaining Quakers and being intimate with his brother's wife. Which crime was worse, the court did not say, but his son was taken from him and given to his uncle to be placed as apprentice with some religious family.[55]

The determination of the Puritans in Massachusetts Bay to enforce a Christian family pattern upon all who lived under their jurisdiction was considerably strengthened by the attacks made upon the colony under the Restoration. With compromises already forced upon them concerning church membership, the elect moved to nip the rising internal forces of sin, idleness, and profane living, lest God's wrath blast their rule from their hands.

As a first step in this control the General Court declared it was to be understood that included under the definition of idle persons were those "that haue familyes to prouide for, who greatly neglect their callings or mispend what they earne, whereby their familyes are in much want, & are thereby exposed to suffer & to neede releife from others . . . "[56]

Secondly, they warned town officials that failure to enforce the acts of 1636, concerning single persons, and of 1642, regarding the proper education and training of children and servants, would result in the county court's admonishing or fining the selectmen responsible. Further they would place the offending single persons, children, or servants in the house of correction. Accordingly, the constables were served with notices to that effect, deploring the consequences of local neglect and finding that it:

> doth occasion much sinn & prophanes to increase among us, to the dishonnor of God & the ensnaring of many children & servants, by the dissolute liues & practises of such as doe liue from vnder family government, & is a great discouragement to those family governors who conscientiously endeavour to bring vp their youth in all Christian nurture, as the lawes of God & this com[m]onwealth doth require.[57]

The constables were to return a list of those living in this deplorable state of sin to the next session of the county court. Under the threat of penalty, action was achieved. In Middlesex County, for example, the constables in Sudbury, Woburn, Malden, Chelmsford, Lancaster, Reading, Watertown, Groton, Billerica, and Marlborough received printed notices under the above order.[58] The county court received the names of some thirty-odd offenders, three of whom were considered not yet dangerous, but bearing watching.[59] Of those clearly dangerous, some were put under the guidance of masters. Edmund Browne of Sudbury, for example, certified that he had witnessed (as a consequence of the above act) the binding of Joseph Parminter to "bro Emmons."[60] The selectmen of Billerica, on the other hand, found difficulty in disposing of Aaron Jacques according to law and requested the help of the court. He was reported as living from under family government, neglecting his calling, and "much given to idleness: also shifting from house to house; & unfaithful in his covenants & promises with such p[er]sons, with whom he has engaged service."[61] Yet another, Robert Williams, petitioned for clemency maintaining that he had wished to live properly under family control ever since he finished his time with his master, that he had worked for several men since of good repute and at their houses, that he then worked for a man whom he hoped would vouch for his character, " . . . indeed," he wrote, "I am not a sarvent yet [I do] submit myself to family order as a sarvent. . . . "[62]

A decade later Massachusetts further strengthened its enforcement machinery by hinging together all the various determinants of improper family government in its instructions for the newly (1679) created office of tithingman. These officials, to be chosen by selectmen annually from among the "most prudent & discreet inhabitants . . . ," were, among other duties hardly more enjoyable:

> diligently to inspect the manners of all disorderly persons, & whereby [*sic*] more private admonitions they will not be reclaymed, they are . . . to present their names [to the proper authorities] . . . who shall proceed against them as the law directs; as also they are, in like manner, to present the names of all single persons that liue from vnder family government, stubborne and disorderly children & servants, night walkers, typlers, Saboath breakers, by night or by day, & such as absent themselues from the publicke worship of God on the Lords dayes, or whateuer the course or practise of any person or persons whatsoeuer tending to debauchery, irreligion, prophaneness, & atheisme among us, wherein by omission of family gouernement, nurture, & religious dutyes, & instruc[ti]on of children & servants, or idlenes, profligat, vncivill, or rude practises of any sort. . . . [63]

Under the above and earlier legislation, numerous individuals were ordered to service for one abuse or another: Jonathan Birch of Dorchester for living idly unless he provided himself with a master in ten days; Sarah Buckminster, widow, of Boston, for having a child three years after her husbend died; Abigail Roberts of Boston for excessive finery in her clothing and living from under family government; Onesephorous Stanly of Cambridge for abuse to a constable, drunkenness, and "false reports to amuse the people"; William Britt of Boston for idleness; and Wllliam Prouse, for being a vagabond.[64]

Families were even more sorely afflicted than single individuals. Samuel Dunton of Cambridge, for example, had his children taken from him and apprenticed after being convicted of bringing them up in a "rude irreligious, prophane, and barbarous manner. . . ."[65] On the same day in 1674, the Middlesex County Court warned Edmund Parker of Lancaster that he would lose his child if he continued to neglect the worship of God on the Lord's days.[66] A few years later, the Widow Arrington of Cambridge had her children put to service by the selectmen after being convicted of entertaining "Idle and rude persons . . . ," in her house at "unseasonable times."[67]

This practice was sometimes carried out in wholesale lots. A dramatic illustration is to be found in Muddy River (Brookline) where the parents of fourteen girls and boys ranging from age eight to twenty were given thirty days' notice in 1672 to "dispose of their severall children (herein nominated or mentioned) abroad for servants to serve by Indentures for some term of yeares according to their ages and capacities. . . . " Refusal would result in the authorities taking the children and placing them themselves.[68]

A selection from the Hampshire County Court session of March, 1680, perhaps reflects the spirit and tone of these dispositions as well as any:

> Whereas the selectmen of the Town of Northampton made information to this Court relating to the Estate & condition of the family of Robert Lyman, who being in a very Low condition- Accounts of Maintainance & things necessary to supply & bringing up the children- & the Sd. Robert Lyman & his wife appearing in the Co. etc. & showing their earnestnes that their children should not be put out, & this Court finding that what the said Parents Spake to be more out of fond affection & sinful Indulgence then any Reason or Rule, & finding great Reason that care Should be taken upon such accounts Doe therefore order & impower the selectmen of the Town aforesaid, to set out to some convenient Places Three of the said Robt Lymans Children . . . to serve as Apprentices.
> •
> Also Cornelius Merry his children being many & little care about their education, it appearing that their father is a very Vicious, & Rather Learnes them Irreligion rather then any good Literature, & therefore. . . . [the court empowers the selectmen to apprentice two of his children][69]

Finally, the Suffolk Court stepped into the family of Captain James Johnson, accused of disorderly behavior in his family including entertaining persons at unseasonable hours of the night. The Captain was ordered to break up housekeeping and dispose of himself into some "good orderly Family" within the fortnight, or the selectmen of Boston would do it for him.[70]

In the last decades of the seventeenth century, Massachusetts found that non-institutional care of adults was insufficient to meet the problem, and the colonists began to move toward a more formal institutional control. In October, 1682, the General Court, learning of many idle persons in families, and single persons negligent in their callings, as well as some who followed no employment at all, ruled that they were to be set about any employment they were capable of or else to go to the house of correction there to be kept at work.[71]

December of the same year found Boston, where the idle were especially prevalent, voting to set up a work house for families and persons spending their time in idleness and tippling (as well as for the poor).[72] Institutional control in alms house, work house, or house of correction became the dominant pattern in the eighteenth century.

During the provincial period, there was a decided decline in the legal emphasis on family living. It was not until 1703 that a law requiring single persons to reside in a family was enacted, and even then its enforcement was restricted to persons under twenty-one.[73] Adult idleness and dissolute living were still proscribed, of course, but service in a family was no longer the cure: the house of correction, the work house, and supervision at work by selectmen of the town concerned supplanted the earlier discipline.[74] Exceptions to this occurred only when misfits in the social order were sold for charges accumulated in longer stays in detention institutions. Such was the case of Sarah Landers, in 1723, who was sold from the house of correction after being detained there because of being found a "lewd, Idle dissorderly person."[75]

Children were a different matter: for them, service was still the answer. Pauper boys and girls were regularly bound out to service in the eighteenth century,[76] and in 1710 the courts began to move in on the children of the idle, as they had under the period of Puritan control. First, it was made clear that it was not necessary that a person be receiving alms in order to have his dependents taken from him, only that the selectmen or overseers of the poor determine that the parents could not maintain them. This did not apply to rated taxpayers.[77] A decade later, idle disorderly, and vagrant persons having rateable estates, but negligent of themselves or families, could lose their children and have their estates managed for them.[78]

After a strong petition from Boston, a special act was passed in 1735 for her purpose alone. Under its broad provisions, the idle and indigent were to be employed in a work house, and the children of those who were negligent of their care were to be bound out into good families whether the parents were rated to the public taxes or not.[79]

Lest there be any doubt as to the intention of the lawmakers with regard to restoring the control over family behavior, it should be noted that the old educational test was revived. Lower requirements, but a definite age limit put the parent to this social, not economic, test:

Be it further enacted,
That where persons bring up their children in such gross ignorance that they do not know, or are not able to distinguish, the alphabet or twenty-four letters, at the age of

six years, in such case the overseers of the poor are hereby
impowered and directed to put or bind out into good families,
such children, for a decent and Christian education, as when
parents are indigent and rated nothing to the publick
taxes. . . . [80]

How rigorously this was enforced in Boston is unknown, but it
appears significant in light of the fact that the records begun in 1734 of
poor children bound out by the overseers become full only after the act
of 1735 was passed.[81]

Besides the children of the poor, the idle, and the dissolute, a
miscellaneous group of minors found their way into servitude as a
consequence of the acceptance of family government as the norm. Some
of these were defenseless without social protection, such as bastards,
poor orphans, and abandoned children legitimate or otherwise. Others,
orphans with estates, or children without one parent or another, were
not defenseless but were frequently bound out where they might be
raised in a proper family or receive training as apprentices.

A bastard's father, if he could be found, was legally responsible for
the upkeep of the child. He not only had to pay the mother a certain
amount for the lying-in charges, but a specified sum each week or
month for the care of the offspring. Moreover, he was frequently forced
to find sureties for himself to save the town "harmless" of expense
should the child become indigent in the future.[82] At times, a father was
able to persuade the court, after an interval of payments, to permit him
to bind his child out as a servant, thus saving himself any further
obligations. Such was the case with a Mr. Samuel Gookin of
Charlestown in 1678. He petitioned the county court to be relieved
from the care of his bastard son born of one Hannah Steevenson, a
financial responsibility of two shillings per week. The court, finding
the mother unwilling to post a bond to secure Cambridge against any
future charges, ordered the child apprenticed to Michael Fleg of
Watertown until the age of twenty-one. Thereupon Gookin was freed of
his responsibility.[83]

Such disposition by the courts should not be interpreted as a casual
attitude; quite the reverse was the case. In the first place, the courts saw
to it that town taxpayers were protected. In the second place, the mother
was provided for during the child's infancy. Thirdly, the courts made
sure the child was placed with a "substantial" freeholder or citizen. The
case of Samuel Peck's bastard well illustrates this concern. In 1697,
Peck asked that his child be put to service to save himself charges.
Since the mother had no objections, the court approved provided that

the master be prohibited from transferring the child to another without judicial consent. This was not an idle gesture, for the following year the master, one Benjamin Hunt, asked and was refused permission to bind the bastard to a man in Swanzey. Finally, the child was taken from Hunt and bound to one Nathaniel Cooper as an apprentice to be "carefully provided for, well used & instructed in Knowledge & fear of God. . . . "[84]

Poor orphans, without estates to compensate a guardian for maintaining them or to secure a favorable apprenticeship, were ordinarily put out to age eighteen or twenty-one, some to the age of twenty-four, although they were not always secured by a binding contract. Massachusetts law in the seventeenth century required assent of two assistants before absolute binding was permitted unless the orphan were old enough to consent for himself (fourteen), or his parents had signified their intention to bind the child before their demise. In the provincial period they were without that protection, except that they could choose a guardian at the same age.[85] Abandoned children were treated much the same. In 1645, one was bound out to the age of twenty-four unless his father were to return and pay for his keep,[86] another, a century later, was ordered disposed of by the selectmen "to some good family for a small sum . . . or otherwise as they think best."[87]

Children unfortunate enough to lose their fathers, or more rarely, their mothers, were frequently put out to service. Apparently this was done at the discretion of the remaining parent in cases where poverty or other disqualification was not an issue, at the order of authority otherwise. In 1633, for example, Peter Browne died intestate leaving a widow, children of several wives, and an estate of one hundred pounds. One daughter by a former wife was put to John Done for nine years, another to William Gilson for twelve. The widow chose to keep the two children she had had by Browne, and one by her earlier marriage.[88]

Sometimes, the authorities revoked the disposition or refused the wishes of the widow in question. Esther Harrison in 1722 petitioned to the court for release of her children committed to the alms house in Boston by the overseers of the poor. She had a chance to put the boy to a good master, and she needed the girl to look after a still younger child so Esther could work at her trade as a tailor. The overseers objected, and Esther was denied her petition.[89] Another widow with a boy on trial as an apprentice to a tailor, lost her petition against the overseers, who took him and placed him as a poor apprentice to a farmer.[90] In most cases, however, the courts observed the wishes of the parents where they could.[91]

It was from these many varieties of poor folk that considerable bound labor was drawn. Uppermost in the colonial mind was the necessity of having each individual in the community under proper authority and discipline for his own good, as well as the good of society. Paupers had shown that they were incapable of giving their children proper care by the mere fact of their dependence upon charity; those who were less poor revealed a similar deficiency by their inability to pay taxes. Those who failed to give their children education and training, as well as the idle and dissolute, forfeited the right to raise their progeny, because they failed their obligations, if indeed they had not forfeited the right to be considered mature adults. Bastards, orphans, and fatherless children had to be protected, too, and made capable of economic independence. To the Puritan and Pilgrim, guidance in a family under Christian authority was the happiest solution for the unreliable adult and the immature child. It was both natural and economical. To the eighteenth-century provincial mind, institutional care was superior to family living for misbehaving adults, but a home was still best for children. Bound labor, as labor, was essentially a by-product, although in the eighteenth century, an important one.

NOTES

1. There is ample evidence of the existence of a class of poor who lived on or beyond the borderline of pauperism in the early decades of settlement. The elder Winthrop wrote of the poorer sort who stayed in tents during the first winter, and in 1631 Thomas Dudley advised against further poor immigration for "divers years; for we have found by experience that they have hindered, not furthered the work. . . ." *Winthrop Papers,* II, 273 n. This judgment apparently reflected the disposition of the "poore famylyes" for whom stock hed been raised to send them to the Massachusetts Bay. *Ibid.,* II, 207 n. In 1633, despite the earlier experience, John Winthrop wrote to Sir Simonds D'Ewes to tell him thet he could further the work of God by sending over some "poore godly familyes with a yeares provision. . . ." *Ibid.,* III, 139–140. In the same decade the town of Muddy River (Brookline) recognized the existence of the "poorer sort" who had no cattle, while the government of Massachusetts Bay reproved innholders for charging excessive meal prices to the poor, and recognized the responsibility of the public for the maintenance of two poor individuals. *Mass Recs.,* I, 214 (1637); I, 230 (1638); and I, 258 (1639). Plymouth too had its paupers. In the 1640s, the poor without cattle were exempted from sharing the costs of killing wolves, while as early as 1642/43, there was a poor stock in the town of Plymouth. *Records of the Town of Plymouth . . .* (Plymouth, 1889–1903),

hereafter cited as *Plymouth Town Records.* The Weld-Peter Mission to England raised £875 there to send poor children (Irish protestants, and various orphans and bastards from London) to New England. Although the money was enough to send one hundred only twenty were sent in 1643. Others arrived later. C.S.M. *Pubs.,* XXXII, 215.

2. In that order: *Winthrop Papers,* III, 6 (1630/31); Pulsifer, *Deeds,* 32–33 (1638); *Winthrop's Journal,* I, 128 (1634).

3. In that order: Essex Probate, I, 227–228 (1655); *Boston Records,* X, 10–11 (1653); C.S.M. *Pubs.,* XV, 199 (1660). Several private gifts were made in Boston for building an alms house there. *Boston Records,* VII, 7. Eighteenth-century gifts were large too; one amounted to two hundred pounds. *Ibid.,* XII, 217 (1738).

4. Quote from M.H S., 7 *Colls.* VIII, 260. See also *Ibid.,* VII, 529, 580–581; VIII, 45, 150, 179–180, 213–214, 266, 282, 344, 370, 380, 475, 498.

5. *Courant,* Nov. 13–20, 1721, Dec. 25, 1721–Jan. 1, 1722.

6. Cotton Mather, *Some seasonable advice unto the poor; to be annexed unto the kindnesses of God that are dispensed unto them.* (Boston, 1726), p. 1.

7. Benjamin Colman, *The Merchandise of a People Holiness to the Lord . . .* (Boston, 1736), 21–25; *Sibley's Harvard Graduates,* VI, 448.

8. Jan. 29–Feb. 5, 1741.

9. *News-Letter,* Feb. 5–12, 12–19, 1741.

10. *Boston Records,* XVII, 88,

11. Carl Bridenbaugh, *Cities in the Wilderness, The First Century of Urban Life in America, 1625–1742* (New York, 1938), 81–82, 393–394.

12. For example, in 1638, the General Court recorded that "Mary Joanes was consented to bee taken care of by the countrey, & at the countrey's charge." *Mass. Recs.,* I, 230. The following year, the same body recognized its financial responsibility for the care of a Mrs. Jupe, a poor person, "if shee prove sick. . . ." *Ibid.,* I, 258. It should be noted, moreover, that after responsibility was placed upon the towns for the care of their own poor, the colony governments continued to care for those who could not establish claims on a particular town— immigrants, visitors who had no means of support, families of soldiers, poor and sick sailors, etc. Indeed, during the provincial period there was a class of indigent persons designated as "Province Poor," for whom the General Court assumed the burden of care. Frequently such individuals were allowed to live in the Boston Alms House at provincial expense. See: *Boston Records* XV, 21, an account rendered for care of "Province Poor" at the alms house in 1736. See also: *ibid.,* XV, 48 ff. XVII, 23 ff. Occasionally the county courts provided for the poor, as in Suffolk in 1679 and Middlesex in 1672.

See: *Suffolk County Court,* II, 1061–62; MSS. Middlesex County Court, III, 36.

13. Whitmore, *Laws,* 184; Pulsifer, *Laws,* 41.

14. Pulsifer, *Laws,* 40.

15. Whitmore, *Laws,* 184 (1639). *Mass. Recs.,* IV, i, 365. In 1655 the General Court recognized the burden towns were subject to by strangers coming in without the consent of the town authorities. To provide a legal remedy, it enacted that the towns could prohibit the entry of strangers, and that such as were brought in without town consent should not be chargeable to the town, but to the persons responsible for their coming in. *Mass. Recs.,* III, 376–377. Amphia Freedman, probably a Negro, was warned from Charlestown in 1709, Watertown in 1714, and Cambridge in 1715. See MSS. Middlesex Sessions, I, 239, 293, 311. For other warnings out see: MSS. Court Files, Suffolk, Volume 99, p. 60 for twenty-six warnings between 17 Aug., 1714 and 14 June, 1715 in Boston. In Middlesex County, for the year 1743, some forty-one families and forty-one persons were warned. Between 1735 and 1748, approximately 675 warnings are listed. MSS. Middlesex Sessions, III, *passim.*

16. *Plym. Recs.,* VI, 54, 71, 74, 94, 113. For other controversies over settlement see: MSS. Essex Sessions, II, 335 (1717); MSS. Middlesex Sessions, III, 362 (1743), 480–81 (1747); MSS. Suffolk Sessions, V, n.p. (Feb. 6, 1743/4, case of Margaret Philips).

17. In that order: *Braintree Records,* 24, 26; Sidney Perley, ed., *Boxford Town Records 1685–1706* (Salem, 1900), 44 (1688), *Boston Records,* VII, 51 (1669), 64 (1671/2), 76 (1673); Robert W. Kelso, *The History of Public Poor Relief in Massachusetts, 1620–1920* (Boston, 1922), 113–114, Boston Records, VII; 157–158 (1682), 24 (1664/5). Other types of aid were given: *Braintree Records,* 133 (1728, poor man received loan of five pounds); Boston Records, XV, 33 (1737, Boston contributed five pounds for sending poor man back to Jersey); MSS. Middlesex sessions, II, 130 (1727, decision of Chelmsford with regard to Samuel Gould—one room in Mr. Emery's house with fire, three shillings per week paid to creditors, suitable maintenance provided, employed according to his ability to help pay charges, horse provided for riding to meetings); MSS. Essex Sessions, IV, 45 (1720/1, the five sons of a woman ordered to pay six shillings each week for her support).

18. In that order: *Acts and Resolves,* I, 67–68 (1692, the three month period was extended to twelve in 1700/01, *ibid.* 453); II, 1067 (1741); II, 756–757 (1736); I, 380 (1700); II, 756–758 (1736); and I, *passim.* See the sixty three references to forfeitures for the poor, I, 860. Boston did indeed take advantage of the enabling act to set up a workhouse for the poor. For the severe regulation thereof, see: *Boston Records,* XII, 234–240 (1739).

19. M.H.S., 3 *Colls.* I, 152. These widows were not listed, merely, but helped. In 1744, for example, an overseer of the poor distributed £23:11 among fourteen women of his ward. MSS. Boston Public Welfare Dept. Files, file 1744. This leading port town assessed considerable sums for the relief of the poor from the £335:4:3 for poor and "other occasions" of 1689 to the £4000 of 1737. *Boston Records,* VII, 198; XII, 177–178. While Boston undoubtedly had the most poor, other towns were not in the happy state of having none. Plymouth, for example, varied from an appropriation of £5 out of £86:08:00 in 1710 to £60 out of £289 in 1731. *Plymouth Town Records,* II, 38, 275. The town of Billerica, possessed of only fifty families, reported ten poor persons in 1680. MSS. Middlesex Court Files, file 89, no number (Mar. 25, 1680).

20. Plymouth ruled in 1641 that those who had relief from the towns and did not employ their children would have their children put to work or "placed out. . . ." In 1658, those whose parents could not provide "competent and convenient" food and clothes could be put out by two or three townsmen if their parents would not. Pulsifer, *Laws,* 38, 111. Massachusetts was more vague. The introduction to the act discussed training in labor, religion, reading, capital laws, and then stated that those not "able and fitt" to bring up their children and unwilling to put them out, should lose them. *Mass. Recs.,* II, 6–7, 8–9 (1642).

21. In that order: *Plym. Recs.,* II, 112–113; *Essex County Court,* I, 113; E.I. *Colls.,* IX, 151 (fourteen years. An older boy was put out for seven years a year earlier. *Ibid.,* 82–83).

22. For examples of how the terms of service varied see the case of Sarah Durrem, who was to be kept until age eighteen, the town to pay her keepers and give them forty shillings for clothes, *Boston Records,* VII, 135 (1679); child Stock, who was to be kept from the age of twenty weeks to age sixteen or eighteen. Her master was to provide food, clothing, etc , to teach her to read, and to teach her the principles of the Christian religion and housewiferey, For this, the town was to pay thirty pounds. *Ibid.,* IV, 165 (1669/70). In another case, Frances Bacon's child was to be kept until age twenty-one; her master was to be paid ten pounds. *Ibid.,* IV, 212 (1676). Between 1679 and 1682, Boston bound out nine girls for terms ranging from six to fifteen years. Compensation varied from keep and two suits to that plus learning to read, sew, knit and "other housewifery." MSS. "City of Boston . . . Inhabitants-1695 . . . Indentures of Apprentices," numbers 1–4, 8, 10, 13, 16, 17. Two boys were to serve five and eleven years respectively, the first to be educated so as not to lose any education already attained, and the second to learn to read and write. *Ibid.,* 11, 12. Benoni Joanes was put out until age twenty-one, to be taught to read and write, and to get five pounds and two suits of clothes at end of term. MSS. Hampshire County Court, I, 12 (1678). For other poor children bound out see MSS. Middlesex

Court Files, file 45, no number (Apr. 2, 1678, case of the children of Henry and Sarah Stretcher); MSS. Middlesex County Court, III, 218 (1678), 302 (1679); MSS. Hampshire County Court, I, 36 (1680); *Essex County Court,* I, 206 (1650/51); IV, 238–239 (1670); *Assistants,* II, 67 (1637); MSS. Suffolk County Court, II, 202 (1686); *Plymouth Town Records,* I, 12 (two cases, 1642/3); *Essex Probate,* II, 26 (1666).

23. *Acts and Resolves,* I, 67. Males were to be servants until the age of twenty-one, females to eighteen or until married.

24. *Ibid.,* I, 538 (1703).

25. *Ibid.,* I, 654 (1710); II, 73–74 (1717); II, 182 (1720); II, 579 (1731); II, 1053–1054 (1741); II, 1067 (1741).

26. Bridenbaugh, *Cities . . . ,* 234.

27. MSS. Boston Indentures, I, 28. For similar requests see I, 33, 36, 37, 38, 39, 41, 45, 53, 55, *et. seq.* By the 1750s, these assurances were printed and distributed to the selectmen of the various towns from which people applied for servants. *Ibid.,* II, 105 ff.

28. The practice in England was to bind to twenty-one and twenty-four, respectively. See Morris, *Government and Labor . . . ,* 384.

29. MSS. Boston Indentures, I, *passim.* Boston was not the only town in the provincial period to put out poor children. See Perley, *Boxford Town Records . . . ,* 44–45(1693); MSS. Suffolk Sessions, IV, 244–245 (1729, Norton); MSS. "Edward Winslow Notary . . . ," 45 (1744, Plymouth).

30. MSS. Boston Indentures, I, *passim.* One served for twenty years. *Ibid ,* I, 86.

31. *Ibid.*

32. Information received from Dr. Clifford K. Shipton.

33. MSS. Boston Indentures, I, 1 (reverse side).

34. *Ibid.,* I, 1 (1740); 10 (1740); 86 (1745).

35. *Ibid.,* I, 97 (1745).

36. In 1643, William Walcott had his wife, children and estate committed to his father-in-law for disposal. Walcott was to be a servant to the father-in-law. *Essex County Court,* I, 57. Three decades later, Captain James Johnson, complained of for disorderly behavior, including entertaining at unseasonable hours of night, was ordered to break up housekeeping and dispose himself in some "good orderly Family" within a fortnight. Otherwise the Boston Selectmen were to do it for him. *Suffolk County Court,* II, 646–647 (1675).

37. Morgan, *The Puritan Family . . . ,* 78–89. Professor Morgan perhaps puts too much emphasis upon the Puritan nature of this attitude. Puritanism undoubtedly reenforced the emphasis on family living, but it had already long existed in England. The Statute of Artificers, for example, in 1562/3, required family living to age thirty for all single unpropertied persons. 5 Eliz. c. 4. For further examination of family importance see Arthur W. Calhoun, *A Social*

History of the American Family from Colonial Times to the Present (Cleveland, 1917), I, 67–127.

38. *Mass. Recs.,* I, 397 (1629).
39. *Ibid.,* 186. It should be noted that a parenthetical qualification in the law, ("or other wise") probably left room for being forced to live in a family, but not necessarily as a servant. In 1657, Boston, finding much "Inconvenience" because of idleness or sickness of servants released before their time, required those who set them at liberty to secure the town from any charge there arising. *Boston Records, II ,* 141–142.
40. Brigham, *Laws,* 35. This was a prohibition against ex-servants and other single persons setting up for themselves unless they could provide arms and ammunition. Otherwise they were to go back into service.
41. *Ibid.,* 36. Consent of governor and council required before setting up as independent housekeepers In that same year it was enacted that only those servants found "fit to occupy it for themselves" should be allowed land. *Ibid.,* 35.
42. In 1639/40, Plymouth prohibited servants buying out their time and being for themselves unless they had been housekeepers in England or were "meete and fitt to bee so." *Ibid.,* 65.
43. For a graphic description of the seventeenth-century jail in Salem see *Essex County Court,* VIII, 330–338. For an eighteenth-century poor house see *Boston Records,* XII, 232–40.
44. Whitmore, *Laws,* 136 (1642). Plymouth enacted the same law, almost word for word, in 1671. Brigham, *Laws,* 270–271. Children and servants were to show proper respect toward their parents and masters too, or suffer a ten-lash whipping. *Mass. Recs.,* III, 355 (1654). More severe cases were bound out. Ephraim Gale, for example, convicted of "stubborn and wicked actions" towards his parents, was confined to jail until "orderly disposed to service." MSS. Middlesex County Courts, III, 5 (1671).
45. Whitmore, *Laws,* 158; quote from Brigham, *Laws,* 64. Massachusetts allowed magistrates to hear the case, or to transfer it to the county court. Plymouth required determination by the Court of Assistants. An example of the discretion used is the case of Thomas Oddingsal presented for idleness in 1641/42. He was ordered to bring a weekly account of his work to one of the justices. *Essex County Court,* I, 34. On the same day, William Walcott was ordered whipped for a like offense. *Ibid.*
46. *Plym. Recs.,* I, 107 (1638), 109 (1638/9).
47. *Ibid.,* 118 (1638/9).
48. *Ibid.,* But in 1638, "John Tisdall, vpon the good report made of him, & of his good carryage, is allowed to keepe house and plant for himself, p[ro]vided that he so continue his carryage still." *Ibid.,* I, 102.

49. *Ibid.*, 68, 87. He failed to put himself to service, so he was ordered to serve Thomas Prence. His house and lands were sold. *Ibid.*, 91. Adey ended up in prison. *Ibid.*, II, 36 (1641/2). For other cases see *Ibid*, I, 106(1638), 21 (1633/4). The latter case resulted in a man's being put "apprentice" for eight years for having lived an "extravagant" life. He was to receive, at the end of his time, two suits, twelve bushels of corn, and twenty acres of land.

50. It will be remembered that in Massachusetts, the towns were to dispose of those living single. However, the Assistants did, on occasion, bind such persons out. See *Assistants*, II, 67 (1637); 126–127 (1642). Some cases were appealed, as provided by law, to the county courts. See MSS. Middlesex County Court, I, 35 (1653), 180 (1659).

51. *Assistants*, II, 84 and 88, 99, 100, 105, 106, 135–136. But one, dismissed before the law was made, was allowed to have a lot, his service being approved. *Mass. Recs.*, I, 206 (1637).

52. *Plymouth Town Records*, I, 12; *Plym. Recs.* II, 38, 58–59, III, 127. It seems fair to call this family notorious. John Billington, father of Francis and John (who died a youth) was the first person hanged for murder in Plymouth. Bradford wrote of them, "He and some of his had been often punished for miscariags [*sic*] before, being one of ye profanest families amongst them." John Billington, indeed, was the first to be punished in Plymouth for any offence. In 1621 he had his neck and heels tied together for contempt and opprobrious speeches. *Bradford's History*, 329–330, 329 n.

53. MSS. Middlesex County Court, I, 89–90, 118.

54. *Ibid.*, 140–141 (1657).

55. *Essex County Court*, II, 261–2 (1660). For other cases see *Ibid.*, I, 113 (1647); E.I. *Colls.*, IX, 151 (1647), *Plym. Recs.*, III, 201 (1660).

56. *Mass. Recs.*, IV, ii, 394–395 (1668).

57. *Ibid.*, IV, ii, 395–396. Here, the court made explicit what it would accept as living under family government. Children under parents or masters, and apprentices , hired servants, or journeymen were acceptable "being subject to their com[m]ands and discipline. . . . " Professor Morgan found that this was an occasional and voluntary action taken by the various courts at random times, but the fact that the ruling came from the General Court, and that the county courts were required to send the notice would indicate that it was a concerted drive. See Morgan, *The Puritan Family* . . . , 86. In this same period, Plymouth Colony strengthened its laws by borrowing from Massachusetts. In 1669, the Plymouth Court enacted legislation against single persons not living in "well govrned families." Selectmen were to prohibit living singly and report offenders to the Court. Brigham, *Laws*, 156. In 1671, Plymouth enacted Massachusetts' legislation of 1642 concerning the education and

training of children and servants, providing, however, that only at the third warning should such dependents be bound out. *Ibid.,* 270–271.

58. MSS. Middlesex Court Files, file 49, no number (Nov., 1688); 88, no number (1688).

59. *Ibid.,* file 49, no number.

60. *Ibid.,* file 50, no number.

61. *Ibid ,* file 49, no number (Dec. 14, 1688).

62. *Ibid.,* no number (no date). A few individuals were turned into the court in the following years, but by 1680 there were none reported in Middlesex as living from under family government. See *ibid.,* files 51, no number (1669); 59, no number (1672); 61, no number (1672); Morgan, *The Puritan Family . . .* , 86. See also MSS. Middlesex County Court, III, 24 (1672).

63. *Mass. Recs.,* V, 240–241.

64. In that order: *Suffolk County Court,* I, 258 (1673); I, 442 (1674); II, 751 (1676); MSS. Middlesex County Court, III, 290 (1679); MSS. Suffolk County Court, I, 141 (1682); II, 324 (1686). See also *Plymouth Town Records,* I, 112 (1669, daughter disposed according to order); *Suffolk County Court,* I, 184 (1672, put out as a servant by selectmen for playing cards and keeping bad company); *Boston Records,* VI, 181 (1671/2, son put out at order of selectmen); *Essex County Court,* VIII, 295–6 (1682, boy ordered under care of selectmen for father's abusing of him). Others were treated even more severely. William Batt in 1683 and John Smith, in 1677, were ordered sold out of the country for idleness. *Boston Records,* VII, 162; *Suffolk County Court,* II, 844 and 870–71. Mary Smith, stranger from England, and infected with the "loathsome disease of *Moribus Gallicus . . .* " was ordered sold out of the country for four years because the doctor to whom she had been bound for payment of her cure found her of "ill conversation." MSS. Suffolk County Court, II, 265 (1685). In another case, the Widow Jefferies of South Suffield was ordered to service for being an idle and vagrant person. The selectmen complained to the court that she would not stay with anyone and that she denied the authority of the selectmen to bind her. The Court sentenced her to not more than ten stripes on her naked back plus daily work and. daily punishment in the prison (if she needed it) "til she shal be brought to some good order." MSS. Hampshire County Court, I, 112 (1686).

65. MSS. Middlesex County Court, III, 87–88 (1674).

66. *Ibid.,* 88.

67. *Ibid.,* 290–291 (1679).

68. *Boston Records,* VII, 67.

69. MSS. Hampshire County Court I, 36 (1680). For other cases of families losing their children see Suffolk County Court, II 599 (1675); 915 (1678); MSS. Hampshire County Court I, 84 (1684); MSS. Middlesex County Court, IV, 177, 194 (1685).

70. Suffolk County Court, II, 646–647 (1675).

71. *Mass. Recs.,* V, 373.
72. *Ibid.,* and *Boston Records,* VII, 157–158.
73. *Acts and Resolves,* I, 538–539 (1703); 587 (1706); II, 579 (1731); 1053 (1741). Even before the first enactment here listed, single persons were bound out in the provincial period. Hanna Sterling, age fifteen, employed at different times in two households and found to be without settled piece of abode, was ordered to live with Mr. William Corbot and wife for three years "in the manner & Condition of a Maid Servent. . . . " Like other poor "apprentices" she was to get meat, drink, lodging, clothing and washing. Her master was to teach her to read and provide her with "sufficient" clothing at the end of her term. MSS. Bristol Sessions, I, 55 (1700).
74. *Acts and Resolves,* I, 67 (1692); 378–381 (1699); 538–539 (1703); 587 (1706); 679–682 (1711/12); II, 579 (1731), 1053 (1741).
75. MSS. Suffolk Sessions, III, 209 (1723).
76. See above p. 86 ff.
77. *Acts and Resolves,* I, 654 (1710).
78. *Ibid.,* II, 242 (1722).
79. *Ibid.,* II, 756–758 (1735).
80. *Ibid.,* II, 758.
81. MSS Boston Indentures, I, *passim.*
82. Whitmore, *Laws,* 257 (1668). *Acts and Resolves,* I, 52 (1692). See chapter VI, below. Before 1668, bastards were sometimes dealt with in a similar manner. For example, in 1657, two persons and their five-weeks old child were put to service. MSS Middlesex County Court, I, 140–141. In 1672, a servant girl had a bastard, and she was ordered to serve three years after her time unless she paid six pounds to her master. In addition, the child was to be a servant of her master until age twenty-one unless the father redeemed it. A year later, the same girl accused one Teague Disco of getting her pregnant again. The court ordered that a forty-pound security and a mortgage on his land be taken until Disco answered the accusation against him. If he failed to offer such security, he was to be jailed. *Essex County Court,* V, 103, 240. See also MSS. Middlesex County Court, V, 36 (1690), 77 (1691).
83. MSS. Middlesex County Court, III, 255–256 (1678). See also, *Essex County Court,* V, 426–27 (1678); and MSS. Suffolk Sessions, III, 176 (1722).
84. MSS. Bristol Sessions, I, 2 (1697), 17 (1698), 20–21 (1698, although called an apprentice, no training provisions were incorporated in it). In 1672, the court approved the putting out of a bastard, provided the magistrates of Ipswich approved of the men. *Essex County Court,* V, 38 (1672). A half-century later, John Courser was relieved of the responsibility of care for his bastard, since one Sylvanus Plumer, "a substantial Man. . . . " had offered to take it. MSS. Essex Sessions, IV, 36 (1720). More casual was the advertisement by the sheriff of Suffolk County in 1748. He had a

white child lately born in jail to put out for eighteen years. Any person wanting it could apply. The taker was to have a sum of money with the child. *Evening-Post,* Nov. 21, 1748.

85. Whitmore, *Laws,* 51 (1641), 121 (1647). *Acts and Resolves,* I, 101 (1692/3). For examples of orphans bound out see *Essex County Court,* I, 72 (1644); V, 37 (1672); *Assistants,* II, 22 (1632, probable); E.I. *Colls.,* LVIII, 263–264 (two cases, 1694/5, 1696); MSS. Middlesex County Court, IV 120 (1684); MSS. Middlesex Court Files, file 58, no number (case of Thomas Hall, Apr. 19, 1671); MSS. Essex Sessions, I, n.p. (Sept. 27, 1692, children of woman executed for witchcraft); *Suffolk County Court,* I, 219 (1672/3); MSS. Hampshire County Court, I, 118 (1690); MSS. "City of Boston . . . 1695 . . . Indentures," numbers 5 (1679), and 14 (1679). For choosing guardians see *Essex County Court,* I–VIII, *passim; Suffolk County Court,* I, II, *passim;* MSS. Suffolk Sessions, *passim.* For two orphan servants choosing their masters as guardians see MSS. Middlesex County Court, V, 89 (1691). For masters appointed as guardians see Lechford, *Note-Book,* 153–154 (1639, estate good sized). For a case in which a child put out with a foster parent was subsequently bound to him as apprentice, see *Essex County Court,* III, 117 (1663). For orphans with estates see appendix A in Towner, "A Good Master Well Served . . . " (Ph.D. diss., Northwestern University, 1954). The Hampshire Court permitted two guardians to bind out the children for whom they were holding small estates in 1691. MSS. Hampshire County Court, I, 134, 135. In at least two cases, the court paid the persons to whom the children were put. *Plym. Recs.,* VI, 54 (1680, father slain by Indians); MSS. Middlesex County Court V, 75 (1691, father killcd in Canada expedition, daughter "apprenticed" to age eighteen).

86. *Plym. Recs.,* II, 86 (1645).

87. *Braintree Records,* 252–253 (1742).

88. *Plym. Recs.,* I 18–19 (1633). For another see *Plym. Recs.,* I, 36–37 (1635/6). He was twice transferred afterwards. *Plymouth Town Records,* I, 12 (1642/3). See also *Plym. Recs.,* I, 43 (1636); MSS. "City of Boston . . . 1695 . . . Indentures of Apprentices," numbers 6, 7 (1678).

89. MSS. Suffolk Sessions, III, 133–134 (1722).

90. *Ibid.,* III, 314 (1725). For a case where a widow objected to apprentice child's position see MSS. Suffolk Sessions, IV, 355 (1731).

91. For other fatherless or motherless children see E.I. *Colls.,* LVIII, 263 (1674); *Essex County Court,* I, 118 (1647); III, 309 (two cases, 1666); MSS. Middlesex County Court, I, 212 (1660); *Mass. Recs.,* III, 309–10 (1653); MSS, Bristol Sessions II, 62–3 (1704); III, 10 (1724); MSS. Plymouth Sessions, I, 38 (1668); MSS. Suffolk Sessions, IV, 176–177 (1728); *Winthrop Papers,* V, 77 (1646).

4. The Servant Lower Classes: Debtors, War Prisoners, Criminals, Indians and Negroes

Remaining to be considered among the roll of servants is a heterogeneous group of whites, serving involuntarily for one reason or another, and the colored servants, both Indians and Negroes. These, as a group, constitute the lower element among the servant population. In the case of the whites, they were criminals, debtors, or prisoners of war, none of whom had any control over the terms of their servitude, and in the case of the colored races, they were subject to a discrimination which automatically reduced them to the lowest place on any social scale. They are discussed, here, in the general order of their social status, although it must be kept in mind that the lines of distinction are blurred.

Servitude for debt was closely allied to servitude for crime, for debt was looked upon almost as a crime by the seventeenth and eighteenth-century English world. In criminal cases, however, the suit was brought by the crown, even though civil damages were awarded at the same time. In civil debt cases, suit was brought by the plaintiff, and damages were awarded according to the debt, not trebled as in theft and burglary cases.

With the above distinction in mind, servitude for debt, as separate from imprisonment for debt, was a minor phenomenon in Massachusetts and Plymouth, certainly not an "important source of bound labor. . . . "[1] Under Massachusetts law of 1641, a person in prison for debt, not having any estate, could be required to satisfy his debt by service to any English person if the creditor so demanded.[2] There were no cases of such servitude prior to the 1670s, although some fourteen appear in that and the following decade.[3]

Shortly before 1683, certain abuses crept into the system of servitude for debt, probably on the part of debtors as well as creditors. In that year, legislation was enacted to eliminate these abuses by both groups. The debtors apparently avoided prison or servitude to major creditors by becoming bound to minor creditors (or conspirators), who allowed them to pursue their own lives under the legal protection of servitude. The law read:

> For the prevention of deceite & cousenage by persons being taken by execution, or deliuering themselues ouer as servants vnto any, thereby to prevent their creditors taking hold on them, it is ordered & enacted by this Court & the authority thereof, that henceforth no person or persons shall be taken or deliuered ouer by execution, or shall deliuer vp themselues to any one or more of their creditors in way of service for sattisfaction of any debt or debts owing by him or them, vnless it be with the knowledge & approbation of the Court of that county where such debtor or creditor dwell, that they may receive satisfaction in the justness of the debt, & likewise sett the time that the debtor shall serve, and that it may be publickely declared that he is a servant, provided this order shall not be interpreted so as to obstruct the legall procedure of any other creditors against any person so disposed to service, either formerly or heereafter.[4]

During the provincial period, servitude for debt was even less important than it had been in the seventeenth century. In the first place, only certain persons were allowed to be made servants for the satisfaction of creditors. Heads of families were excluded, as were all married persons. In addition, a provision was made that those who were to serve must be of the laboring class, although this was later changed to include all who were of sound body.[5] Secondly, the debtor, like the poor, was subject more and more to institutional care. Debtor's prisons took their place alongside the poor house and work house.[6] Here, the lot of the prisoner for debt was unenviable, and at least one group sought relief by force as they cut a hole in their new prison in Boston, one night in 1736, and escaped.[7]

Servitude for crime was something else again. Although the English who migrated to New England's shores were not unfamiliar with criminal detention in institutions, and for that matter constructed their own jails and houses of correction, detention was primarily to secure a prisoner awaiting trial, or to hold one whose sentence was yet to be fulfilled. Punishment, on the other hand, consisted of the rare death penalty, branding, whipping, a fine, or such antiquarian delights as stocking, wearing signs, and standing on the gallows, a rope around one's neck, with one end over the gallows. Condemnation into servitude was rarely used as punishment per se, but sale or assignment of criminals occurred to those who would assume the prisoners' fines, fees, costs, and damages. Since the prisoner was responsible even for the cost of maintaining himself in jail, one without resources or friends would find it difficult to meet all his obligations. From the criminal class, as a consequence, a number of bound laborers were drawn who had originally been free, and a number of servants had years added to their term of service as they failed to pay the charges against them. In this way, society not only forced the criminal to pay for the economic costs of his behavior, but it put him under the supervision of family government whereby he might be reclaimed, or at least, utilized.

Theft (rarely robbery) was the most frequent crime for which hitherto free individuals found themselves performing as servants in the seventeenth and eighteenth centuries; the first recorded case occurred in April, 1633. Then, John Sayle was convicted before the Massachusetts Court of Assistants for theft of corn, fish, and clapboards. His sentence was whipping, the forfeiture of his estate (thereby paying double restitution to those from whom he stole), and binding out to a Mr. Coxeshall for three years at four pounds a year. For good measure, his daughter, left outside of family government, was bound for fourteen years in return for keep and a cow calf at the end of her term.[8]

Thereafter, the colonial courts ceased to provide wages for those they bound, and criminals became in effect temporary slaves, serving without wages or freedom dues. In the next few years, in fact, the courts recognized the servile status of servants for crime and called a slave a slave.[9] One woman thief, Elizabeth Sedgewick by name, was sentenced to be whipped severely and condemned to slavery until she made double restitution.[10]

Three other persons were committed to temporary slavery, for theft, two for unknown reasons, and another for sexual offenses. Only in the last case was there punishment for a non-property-offense.[11]

In the following years, the courts continued to place criminals out as servants, twice demanding double restitution, although it was not until 1645 and 1646 that Plymouth and Massachusetts enacted legislation whereby a person pilfering would be liable to restore not only the value of the goods stolen, but multiple damages, then set at threefold. Here was established by law what had already been obtained in practice: the personal liability of individuals for theft, destruction of property, as well as damages and costs arising from criminal action. Almost invariably criminal servitude followed such an accumulated obligation. Under this legislation, and similar laws in the provincial period,[12] more than one hundred cases appear in the court records down through 1750 in which free white individuals were declared liable to service to make satisfaction for crimes.[13]

The majority of those thus condemned were to serve between one and four years, the length of service depended upon the total amount of the financial obligation thus incurred, although there was no absolute value-to-time ratio holding for any period of years. Some were sentenced to serve as little as six months, others as much as ten and and even fourteen years. At the fall, 1745, session of the Hampshire Court of General Sessions, for example, John Morse and John Hiram were found guilty of stealing clothes to the value of two pounds, five shillings, from husbandman Samuel Bascom. Their fines were twenty shillings or five stripes each, while they were assessed nearly twelve pounds costs and treble damages. On default, Bascom was to be allowed to sell both to any of His Majesty's subjects for six months.[14] At the other extreme, a Boston scrivener named James Naplon, was ordered sold for ten years, after stealing £204. Thirty five stripes were laid on to further impress him with the enormity of his crime.[15] More extreme still was the case of Michael Pussee, a transient convicted in Plymouth on three counts of theft in 1745/46. His trebled damages came to £49:14:09, and his costs for the three actions were £14:16:09. In addition he was fined fifty shillings or twenty stripes. He paid fourteen years for his crime.[16]

In the seventeenth century, it should be noted, the courts frequently did not determine the number of years, but left it up to the master, or to the open market demand for convicted criminals, hoping to sell the prospective servant for sufficient cash to reimburse all concerned. Thus, in several instances the court simply ordered the individual to be put to service, or to be sold for satisfaction, and in one case at least, to serve the master until he was satisfied for the court costs and the fine.[17] By the provincial period, the practice had become more regularized, and the courts almost invariably determined the number of years of service owed.[18]

Crime added to the available labor supply in yet another way, for servants convicted of crimes of one sort or another quite frequently had time added to their terms of service; if their master refused to pay court costs and damsges, they were sold to the person damaged or to the highest bidder. The most persistent crime among servants was illegally absenting oneself from service, or running away.[19] Theft was a strong second, particularly when it is recognized that servants regularly stole money, clothes, or goods in the process of running. Larceny alone accounted for several extensions of service from a few weeks to seven years,[20] while excessive drinking, arson, assault, slander, receiving stolen goods, "gross misdeameanor and foul miscarriage," disobedience, stubbornness, fornication, attempted buggery, bastardy, concealing stolen goods, and other destruction of property resulted in penalties running from three weeks to twenty-one years.[21]

A few specific cases drawn from free and servant criminals will make clear the nature of the problem those accused of crimes were up against. When indicted, the suspect would ordinarily be incarcerated in the local jail or prison unless he could post a bond. The costs arising from this imprisonment were essentially his, as well as the charges of prosecution. This sometimes worked an injustice upon the prisoner, as can be seen in the case of Mary Fitz Patrick, servant to John Shippey of Boston in 1719. Arrested and jailed on suspicion of buggery with a spaniel dog, she was acquitted and released after her master paid her court costs. In return for this payment, the master was awarded three years beyond her indenture.[22]

When convicted, the prisoner faced a battery of charges against him: costs of apprehension, prison costs before conviction, costs of prosecution, court fees, a fine, and treble damages. The longer he delayed in settling, the more his total obligation amounted to, for jail charges piled up day by day. Look at manservant Christopher Thompson, arrested on suspicion of arson of a fence in 1704. His request of jury trial postponed the case to the next session of the court. Unable to raise the one hundred pound bond, he waited in prison. Worse luck, the jury found him guilty and the court awarded thirty shillings damages to the owner of the fence, costs of £2:17:09, and ten stripes on the naked body. Three months later, in December, Sheriff Samuel Gookin appeared in court to state that Thompson was in poor condition with regard to clothing, and that his prison costs had risen to where he owed nearly twenty pounds. Thompson was ordered sold to any person within the province for four years. The following January, Thompson still languished in prison, and it was allowed that he be sold to any neighboring colony. Having served for his crime, he blithely assumed, four years later, that he was free. However:

> The Court are of opinion, and It was their Intent when Christopher Thompson was ordered by the Court to be sold for his Crime he was convicted of, that the sd Tompson [*sic*] should make his Master Paige Saticfaction by Service, or otherwise for his loss of time in him & of his Service, during the time he was sold for pesuant to his Indenture to his Sd Master Paige, the said four years being accounted no part of his time he was to Serve by his Indenture.[23]

A final case involved bastardy. Thomas Hog of Haverhill, servant to John Sanders there, was jailed for more than six months because he could not raise surety for a judgment of being the reputed father of a bastard child. The jailkeeper complained that Hog was almost naked and "like to die this winter," whereupon the court ordered the local justice of the peace to make the best deal he could with the master and release the prisoner.[24] Such informal methods on the part of the courts were standard operating procedure. Fines, for example, were frequently satisfied by whippings, and not infrequently the prisoner was given a few hours or a few days to raise the fine if he could, in order to escape whipping. Similarly, the payment of damages and court costs was often postponed for a number of days in the hope that the money could be secured.[25]

Less fairly treated, because less guilty of crime, were the white prisoners of war (or political prisoners) sold in Massachusetts during the period of the English Commonwealth and Protectorate, particularly after 1650.

The defeat of the Scottish and Irish supporters of Charles II in the early 1650s made available a flood of prisoners, a small proportion of whom were sent to the Puritan commonwealth in America.[26] First to come were the Scots taken in the battles of Preston, Dunbar, snd Worcester.[27] Some 150 were sent in 1651 on the *Unity,* destined for Boston. About fourscore of them were consigned to John Gifford, covenant servant and master of the Saugus Iron Works. The others were sold to persons in the area for seven years' service.[28] A year later, an even larger consignment—between 240 and 272—arrived in Charlestown where Thomas Kimble took charge of their subsequent disposal in various New England towns.[29]

The Irish came to New England about the same time. One shipload on the *Good Fellow* of Boston arrived some time in 1653, and there is evidence to indicate some may have come in the year before.[30] That summer Amos Richardson wrote John Winthrop, Jr. from Boston that he had bought four servants, three of them for Winthrop. He would have taken more but none was left that he liked, and anyhow, other shipments were expected. In case Winthrop was hesitant, Richardson assured him, "Those which have had tryall of Irish Servants heare have found them to be good. . . ."[31]

In the years following, these Scotch and Irish political and military servants seem to have been treated as any other indentured individuals. John Gifford, at the Saugus Iron Works, employed them in farming, cutting wood, and on occasion rented them out or sold them.[32] Others appear in the court records as servants to persons in Boston, Braintree,

Salem, Ipswich, Woburn, Plymouth, Charlestown, Sudbury, and Sandwich.[33]

While Massachusetts law, in the famous *Body of Liberties* in 1641, was clearly permissive concerning the enslavement of prisoners made captive in just wars,[34] provincial legislation was nearly silent on the subject. French prisoners, for example, were prohibited in the province under an act of 1697,[35] although its enforcement was apparently lax. In 1704, all French persons in Massachusetts were ordered registered and kept under surveillance, and any who were Catholics were considered prisoners of war, but it is not known if they were sold into service.[36] Later wars provided still more, and in at least one instance they were let out on nominal wages, the master posting bond.[37] Otherwise, the eighteenth century made little servile use of whites in this way.

Negroes and Indians were a different story, of course, being regularly sold into servitude when captured in Indian wars in America, and when sold to shippers as captives of just wars on the coasts of Africa. As such, Negro slaves played an important part in the labor force of Massachusetts, particularly in the provincial period. Indian war captives, on the other hand, were of minor significance, for most were sold abroad. It was, instead, in the form of temporary servitude that Indians played their important labor role.

The Massachusetts Indians, a branch of the Algonquin family, had been nearly wiped out by a plague shortly before the investing of the coast by the English. In the Plymouth area, the branch of the Algonquins living there (the Wampanoags) had been weakened too, though not as severely. Consequently, neither set of colonists had immediate difficulty with their aboriginal neighbors. If a policy existed at all, it was to Christianize them if possible, settle them in a permanent agricultural way of life, and extinguish their titles to the land wanted by the whites legally, if not fairly.[38] As colonial experience with the American inhabitants grew, it became convincingly necessary to settle them in what today would be called Indian reservations, where they had a measure of self government, but were expected to adhere to the white man's laws and morality.[39] Living close to the whites as they did, friction between the two cultures was bound to develop, resulting in establishment of a definite ascendancy of the whites, enslavement of those Indians involved in warfare against them, and temporary servitude for individual infringement upon white man's law. In addition, the inferior position of the Indians made it possible to impose upon them an indentured servitude which the English found increasingly difficult to exact from their white compatriots.

The two major flare-ups of Indian hostility in the seventeenth century, the Pequot War and King Philip's War, resulted not only in the destruction of Indian power in southern New England, but in the mass deportation of some hundreds of Indian men and women as slaves. Massachusetts shared, with settlers in Connecticut, the Pequot Indians captured in the war against that branch of the Algonquins, the males being sent to Bermuda or the West Indies, and the women and girls disposed about the various towns, presumably into slavery.[40]

In the following decade Massachusetts experienced continuing Indian difficulty. From Salem came one evil suggestion made to Governor John Winthrop by Emanuel Downing that an Indian war be started against them in order to stamp out worship of the devil, and with the secondary purpose of swapping captives for Negroes, "for I doe not see how wee can thrive vntill wee gett into a stock of slaves suffitient to doe all our buisines. . . . "[41] It is to the Puritans' credit that the suggestion of this leading figure was not followed, although in principle, they were not averse to swapping uncooperative Indians in the West Indies for the less disruptive blacks.[42]

It was in the 1670s, however, when the frictions between the two races resulted in King Philip's War, that wholesale enslavement and transportation of Indians reached its highest peak. Both Plymouth and Massachusetts sold dozens of men, women and children abroad, only permitting those under fourteen to remain as slaves, and the children of those who voluntarily surrendered to be servants to age twenty-four.[43]

During the provincial period, hostile Indian activity centered in northern New England and was usually connected with the French in the epic struggle for control of North America. Apparently few found their way into slavery in Massachusetts, although an occasional instance appears in the records. For example, in 1722, one James Blin petitioned the General Court for permission to have two of the Indians he took prisoner, as compensation for service rendered. Two years later, Joseph Calef of Boston petitioned that he be allowed six Indian prisoners from the jail, offering to maintain them at his own expense for so long as he might have them.[44]

Temporary servitude was a more important device for utilizing Indian labor than was slavery, particularly in the eighteenth century. Apprenticeship, voluntary indenture of adults and children, criminal and debtor servitude, were all imposed by the whites in order to profit from their native neighbors.

In the early decades of settlement, few Indians found their way into English homes as servants. The Massachusetts Court of Assistants prohibited "entertaining" Indian help without the express permission of the court, rarely given.[45] Some settlers received the court's approval; and others took advantage of a smallpox epidemic in 1633 to take Indian orphans into their homes. In this way, a few, but very few, lived in with the English in Massachusetts, and few more in Plymouth.[46]

At the same time, however, both colonies were moving toward a reservation system whereby a population of settled abode would be maintained, where the Christian religion could be encouraged, and from where, incidentally, a number of servants could be drawn. Under the influence of John Eliot, five chiefs and their followers voluntarily settled themselves under Massachusetts' authority at Natick in 1645. By 1665 there were six or more of these settlements at such towns as Marlborough, Stoughton, Littleton, Grafton, and Hopkinton. Plymouth moved in the same direction, creating reservations at Sandwich, Eastham, Harwich, Yarmouth, Barnstable, Marshfield, Middleborough, and Wareham by 1675.[47]

Once settled, the Indians were subject to increasing pressure from the whites. Plymouth enacted a law in 1660 designed to encourage the natives to put their children to servitude by providing the payment of one coat yearly to the parents out of government stock or the master's for each year the child remained.[48] Eighteen years later Indian children were somewhat less exploited, because of a requirement that they be taught to read and be brought up as Christians although they were to be kept in service to age twenty-one.[49]

Under the above laws, and the enactment of 1646 in Massachusetts repealing the prohibition against taking Indian servants because there was "more use of incuragemt thereto than otherwise," some Indians came voluntarily into the English families Such a one was John French, who put himself under Captain Gilman's "tuition" at the beginning of the war.[50] Another was James, son of a deacon among the Christian Indians of Worcester County, who attended the Indian school in Cambridge. About 1659 he was apprenticed to Samuel Green, printer, where he learned his art and acted as pressman for Eliot's Indian Bible. James ran off during Philip's war before his time was out, but returned on offer of ammesty, staying as an employee or servant until at least 1709.[51]

Others ran afoul the criminal and debtor legislation, some of which was particularly enacted for the Indians. In 1674, Plymouth provided that idle debtors among the Indians should serve their creditors at twelve pence a day in summer and six pence a day in winter, plus diet, until their debts were paid. If they refused and ran away, they could be sold. Idle young Indians not in debt were liable to service upon complaint of their idleness. If they ran away, they could be forced to serve twice the time gone. Theft from the English was to be punished by fourfold restitution paid by serving the person damaged, or being sold for his benefit.[52]

Ordinarily thieves were whipped, fined, and sentenced to pay damages by working for the person from whom they stole, or by being sold as servants.[53] In some cases, they were condemned to be sold out of the country for a number of years, or for life.[54] Rape and bodily injury were more severely treated, although in the one case in which an English girl was involved, the man, an Indian and "therfore in an incapasity to know the horiblenes of the wickednes of this abominable act . . . ," was not put to death but sentenced to be shipped and sold out of the country.[55] For other rapes, similar treatment was accorded, ten years and banishment being the lightest sentence.[56] Bodily injury resulted in four years' servitude in one case and sale out of the country in two others.[57] Fornication with a white girl was punished by a twenty pound fine or sale in fourteen days for an undetermined time.[58] Debt resulted in one two-year sentence of service.[59] Indians already servants had time added to their terms for various crimes, including breaking and entering, and running away.[60]

Indian servitude, even including that of criminals, did not reach important numbers until the provincial period. Then, the entrapment of Indians in the legal tangles of white man's law so as to obtain service from them reached scandalous proportions. Cotton Mather exercised New England's conscience in 1710 as he damned those who took advantage of the ignorance and desire for drink of the Christianized Indians to get them in debt, and "then use Indirect and Oppressive wayes, to Exact an *Unreasonable Satisfaction* from them, and *Sell* them for Servants, or *Send* them out of their own Country. . . ."[61] This was some ten years after an act passed designed to prevent just that, whereby indentures for service had to be signed in the presence of two justices of the peace. They were ordered to take special care to see that the contract be just and reasonable.[62]

At the end of the decade a stronger act, whose preamble repeated the charges made by Cotton Mather, declared void any bill, bond, or contract made between white and Indian thereafter unless made in front of two justices. Indentures for service were similarly restricted.[63] Finally, in 1725, creditors of Indians were prohibited from suing for debts larger than forty shillings unless approval were first obtained from the Sessions Court.[64]

Most offenders were in the counties comprising Old Plymouth Colony. There, by far the greatest number of Indians were given sentences of servitude, or had their terms extended for crime—theft, bastardy, assault, and running away—almost six to one compared with the rest of present-day Massachusetts.[65] In fact, the legislation designed to regulate apprenticeship or indentured servitude of Indians was aimed right at the Old Colony and the heavy demand for servants in the fishing and whaling industry there. The first two acts were general, and were designed to prevent the illegal or unfair drawing of Indians and their children into servitude throughout the province, but the third came out of a joint committee set up in the General Court with particular reference to abuses in Barnstable County.[66]

This comprehensive act, premised on the fact that despite several previous acts "for the protection of the Indian natives, many oppressions, injuries and abuses are daily committed towards them . . . ," moved along a wide front. No married Indian could bind himself or herself for any number of years. No child could be apprenticed without the consent of both parents. No indenture was to be valid unless signed in the presence of two justices; one of them, or the clerk of session was to keep the Indian's copy of the indenture until the English part had been fulfilled and so certified. And since it was necessary at Nantucket, Martha's Vineyard, and several towns in Plymouth and Barnstable counties that Indians be employed on whaling and fishing voyages, it was allowed that the English might indent with Indians for a maximum of two years. These indentures were to be made under proper judicial supervision, and masters were required to assist in housing the Indians. Fuel and subsistence were to be supplied for their families. Indians of full age could hire themselves out to husbandry or any other shore work on reasonable wages for periods of not more than a year with the aporobation of two justices. No Indian was to be taken beyond the seas without order from the Courts, or upon security for his return by a bond of not exceeding £100. Finally, no indenture already made was to be good for more than a year unless examined and approved in open court.[67]

Limited in its application to three years, the act was nevertheless a catalogue of Indian grievances, and it suggests the frequency with which they found themselves in service to their white superiors.[68] From among these Indian servants, we may pause to note a few recorded in Josiah Cotton's Diary. Writing in 1730/31, Josiah was ruminating about the vagaries of fortune in his family. Two servants were lost on sailing vessels shortly before:

> I have been some what unhappy in my Male Servants, having with this, Lost two Indian Servants *before their time expired* (together with a bad prospect at this day Concerning a third). I

had also a Negro man who proved so disorderly that I was forced to part with him. O Lord pardon my Relative, as well as personal Evils & Neglects, & grant to us better success in our purchase made this year of Dutchess, & Quominuh two Negro's of our Daughter Phillips.[69]

A few pages later, his worst expectations were realized, for his Indian boy, James, died after oversetting a cart. "Those who are Servants for life are freed by Death, in ye Grave, the Servant is free from his master."[70]

Five years later he had again occasion to record that in the grave the "Servant is free from his master," for his Indian woman, Grace, married to his Negro and "bound to us for *two years longer,*" died shortly before her infant. "God forgive what has been amiss in our carriage toward our Servants. . . . "[71] Finally, in 1747/48, he noted the death of an old Indian serving woman, blind and deaf, living on his property in her old age.[72]

As in Josiah Cotton's family, Indian and Negro servitude were mixed throughout the period, but unlike the Indians, Negro slaves assumed an important role in the labor force of Massachusetts, by the eighteenth century.[73] Despite the early appearance of Negroes in Massachusetts Bay, somewhere between 1629 and 1638, and the equally early beginning as a slave trade of sorts with the trading of Pequot Indians for West Indian Negroes,[74] there were few blacks prior to the 1670s. To be sure, John Winthrop records in 1641 that a Boston church-woman lost some fine linen, because of the carelessness of an African maid; and he notes that yet another maid, servant to Mr Stoughton in Dorchester, was baptized "being well approved by divers years' experience, for sound knowledge and true godliness. . . . " Even so, few appear prior to the decade of Philip's War.[75]

By then, Massachusetts traders were already making the long trek to the East Coast of Africa,[76] and, moreover, had Indians to trade in the West Indies for surplus Negroes there.[77] However, it was not until the monopoly of the Royal African Company was broken in 1696, and the trade wrested from the Spanish in 1713, that Negroes came in large numbers to Massachusetts ports.[78] There, by the last three decades before 1750, the newspapers were filled with advertisements of slaves for sale, and in the last two decades, in particular, with runaways. Numerically, in that period Negroes were more important as a source of bound labor than any other type—apprentices, indentured servants, criminals, poor, or Indians.[79]

Slavery, like other forms of servitude, grew in Massachusetts and Plymouth colonies without any organized codes. Its only recognition in law was in *The Body of Liberties* which, while it deplored the Biblical crime of man-stealing, at the same time established slavery as a legitimate source of labor.[80] Negroes, like their white and Indian counterparts, of whatever status, were fitted into the family organization of Puritan and Pilgrim society, supped at the same table, worshipped in the same church, and sometimes, slept in the same bed.[81] They were seldom distinguished from their fellows by the term "slaves" but rather were called "perpetual servants," or more frequently "servants."[82]

As servants, Negroes shared a common experience with all others. They had a right to be clothed, fed, housed, and taken care of in sickness and in health.[83] Their masters were obliged to give them a Christian education, to supervise their morals, to keep them at work, and yet to give them fitting intervals of leisure.[84] They had access to the courts as plaintiffs, and their rights were protected as defendants.[85] They could be resold,[86] let out,[87] left by will,[88] and under certain circumstances, freed.[89] They had access to the church for worship, baptism, and communion,[90] while their marriages were recorded, and to a certain degree, protected.[91] Like their fellow servants they played, danced, sang, fornicated, committed bastardy, drank to excess, and ran away.[92] In their day-to-day activity they were almost indistinguishable from the whites who shared their servitude with them. Even their work was frequently the same.[93] In fact, their closest student has assessed their position as an "admixture of bondage and indentured servitude."[94]

Yet, they were slaves. That they were bought and sold, that their bastard children were taken from them, that they could be punished by a master, that they had to come and go as directed, that they were inferior to their masters, did not distinguish them from their fellow workers. But that they were servants for life most certainly did. And that they attained their status not through choice on the part of themselves or their parents as did apprentices and indentured servants, or even through poverty as did the poor, or crime as the criminals, or debt as the debtors or a conscious act of war as the Indians—but through the simple fact of being black and defenseless, distinguished them indeed. Like the occasional branded burglar or runaway, they carried their distinguishing mark of inferiority to the grave; but even worse, they passed it on to their children.[95]

The lower elements among the servant class were the debtor, criminal, or prisoner of war, and the colored races—Indian and Negro. None of them was in a position to determine the conditions of servitude in terms of years of service and remuneration, or to choose a master. Of the whites, criminals constituted the most numerous element, for debtors and war prisoners who were put to service were few. Indians served as temporary voluntary servants, and as slaves, but their numbers were few too. Negroes were by far the most important, numerically speaking, of this element of the servant class, and they became the largest single source of imported labor as well by the 1730s and 1740s.

NOTES

1. Morris, *Government and Labor* . . . , 354. Professor Morris is writing about all American Colonies here, but that it was intended to include Massachusetts and Plymouth is clear from the following pages, particularly page 357.
2. Whitmore, *Laws,* 123.
3. *Suffolk County Court,* II, 677–678 (1675/6); *Assistants,* I, 146 (1679); MSS. Suffolk County Court, I,182 (1683); *Essex County Court,* V, 23 (1672); 116 (1672); 264 (1674); VI, 394 (possible, 1678); VII, 333–334 (1680); VIII, 62 (1680). In the other two cases, the debtors were sold to satisfy prison costs, not creditors. MSS. Suffolk County Court, I, 170 (1683); 220 (1684). Two private agreements to serve for debt were made. *Essex County Court,* V, 50 (1672); VIII, 330–338 (1682), It seems worthwhile, at this point, to straighten out the confusion concerning Rawson's case misinterpreted in Morris, *Government and Labor* . . . , 357. In my opinion, the real point of it is missed—the connection wlth the legislation of 1683 quoted in the text, immediately below, and which, in my opinion, Morris also misinterprets. Wllliam Hukely confessed a judgment against himself for £40 for forfeiture of a bond, which made him debtor to William Rawson. Hukley agreed to serve Rawson or his assignes in order to pay the debt. While in his service, Hukely became obliged to one Abraham Briggs for £19:16 plus costs, whereupon Briggs had him (Hukely *not* Rawson) thrown in jail for debt for five weeks. Rawson sued Briggs for taking his servant from him, but the county court ruled against him. On appeal, Morris states accurately, the Court of Assistants confirmed the lower court's decision, but Rawson went on to the General Court. There the decision was reversed. The result of the highest court's appeal was to prohibit imprisonment for debt of another man's servant. *Suffolk County Court,* II, 677–678 (1675/6), 712–715 (1676); *Mass. Recs.,* V, 104–105, 121 (1676). The inference to be drawn from this, it seems to me, is that a debtor, fearing prison or servitude, could make a private agreement or contract to serve a friend or relative as a servant. He could not then be attached. Combined with the 1683 legislation, this seems quite plausible. Apparently Rawson and Briggs came to terms outside of court, for Rawson assigned Hukely to Briggs the following January after the

General Court's ruling. One proviso was made: Briggs would have to find his man for he'd run away. MSS. Mass. Archives, IX, 60 (1676/7).

4. *Mass. Recs.,* V, 415 (1683).

5. *Acts and Resolves,* I, 330 (1698, repealed, 1725, II, 363); II, 462 (1727, act good for two years); 658 (1732/3), act good for three years). In each act, the justices of the peace were to determine the number of years to be served.

6. *Acts and Resolves,* I–III, *passim.*

7. *Evening-Post,* Aug. 30, 1736. All was not on the debtor's back though, for creditors had a hard time too. In 1723 , for example, Thomas Beekster was in prison for debt of twenty-one pounds to a Mr. Johnson. He swore, according to the law, that he was not worth ten pounds although he owed some £120 to twenty-one other persons. His estate was listed as credits of forty to fifty shillings owed to him, one bed, two chairs, one small brass kettle, two or three pewter plates, two small tables, no real estate. Johnson and two others claimed he had sixty to seventy pounds in goods hidden by his wife, and they wanted assurance that he would pay, being willing to give him time. Apparently assurances were given, or else they were unwilling longer to maintain him in prison, for he was released, the county paying his fifty-one shillings jail fees. MSS. Essex Sessions, IV, 114 (1723), 123 (1723/4); MSS. Essex Files, drawer 1721–1724.

8. *Assistants,* II, 32. Sayle ran away in 1633/4 and was sentenced to be whipped severely. *Ibid.,* 40.

9. Except in one case, between 1633 and 1642 criminals put to servitude for crimes were called slaves. For the exception, see *ibid.,* II, 39 (1639).

10. *Ibid.,* II, 118 (1641/2).

11. *Ibid.,* II, 79 (1638, two cases), 94 (1640), 90 (1639), 97 (1640), 86 (1639, sex offense). It probably was not clear to the court at that time that a distinction was to be made between punishment for a crime and servitude for economic costs.

12. *Winthrop's Journal,* II, 169–170 (1644, two Harvard students sentenced to double restitution, or to service having stolen fifteen pounds). See also, *Assistants,* II, 132 (1643). For laws see Pulsifer, *Laws,* 47–48 (1645), Whitmore *Laws,* 127 (1646). Massachusetts distinguished between pilfering and larceny by a more severe punishment for the latter. *Ibid.* Provincial laws provided that criminals for theft and burglary be bound out if they could not pay fines, costs and treble damages (burglary, in addition, was punishable with branding for first offense, severe whipping and one hour on the gallows for the second, and death for the third). In 1702, a time limit of thirty days was placed on detention in jail for theft without the prosecutor's paying costs. If the prosecutor then failed, the jailor could sell for costs if prisoner could not pay. *Acts and Resolves,* I, 52

(1692), 504–505 (1702). By 1736/7, the death penalty wes required for the third theft if the first two were over forty shillings each, and the third over three pounds. *Ibid.,* II, 838. Receiving stolen goods was made a crime subject to the same service provisions in 1738. *Ibid.,* II, 300. In addition to theft and burglary, desertion of the frontiers by non-freeholders who could not pay their consequent fines made them liable to government service in 1694/5, and then to service for the towns in 1699/1700. This was, of course, a military measure. *Ibid.,* I, 195, 403. Desertion from the army and failure to pay the indemnification thereby required could result in service to any English subject in 1702, but in 1704 it was changed to service to the Crown. *Ibid.,* I, 499–500, 546. In 1705, white women having bastards of Negroes or mulattoes, and unable to maintain them, could be sold into service. *Ibid.,* I, 578. In 1698, illegal killing of deer could result in twenty to fifty days service, and in 1704, forgers of bills of credit could be put to work under the direction of the justices of the peace for prison charges and support. *Ibid.,* I, 556–557.

13. See appendix C in Towner, "A Good Master Well Served . . . " (Ph.D. diss., Northwestern University, 1954).
14. MSS. Hampshire County Court, IV, folio 204.
15. MSS. Suffolk Sessions, IX, 209–210, 212–213 (1729). For other ten-year cases see *Plym. Recs.,* IV, 33–34 (1662/3). This case involved children committing bodily injury. They were "apprenticed" to age twenty-one, one for ten years, the other for eight. See also, "Records of the Court of the General Sessions of the Peace For the County of Worcester, Massachusetts, From 1731 to 1737," Worcester Society of Antiquity, *Collections* (Worcester, 1877–), V, xviii, 111 (1734). Hereafter cited ss Worcester Sessions.
16. MSS. Plymouth Sessions, IV, 216–217.
17. *Assistants,* II, 132 (1643). See also *Suffolk County Court,* II, 889 (1677/8); MSS. Suffolk County Court, I, 97 (1681), 117–118, 131, 139 (1682), 151 (1682/3), 193 (1683/4), MSS. Hampshire County Court, I, 101 (1685); *Essex County Court,* IV, 126 (1699).
18. For exceptions, see MSS. Middlesex County Court, V, 153 (1691/2); MSS. Suffolk Sessions Miscellaneous Bundle (case of Ann Bissell, Nov, 6, 1738); MSS. Essex Sessions, VI, 65–67 (1746).
19. See chapter VIII, and appendix G in Towner, "A Good Master Well Served . . . " (Ph.D. diss., Northwestern University, 1954).
20. See appendix D in Towner, "A Good Master Well Served . . . " (Ph.D. diss., Northwestern University, 1954).
21. *Ibid.*
22. See the MSS. Records of the Superior Court of Judicature, 1715–1722, folio 49 (1719). For a not-guilty verdict in a murder case where the defendant was put to service for five years to pay costs of prosecution and imprisonment, see MSS. Essex Sessions, 142 (1724).

23. MSS. Middlesex Sessions, I, 151, 154, 156–157 (1704), 159, 236 (1709). In another case, that of Sarah Reed, convicted on two counts of burglary, the conditions were somewhat different. She owed thirty pounds damages minus goods returned, and costs of prosecution, besides getting fifteen stripes. The sheriff memorialized the court six months later to the effect that the whipping had been accomplished, and that Sarah had been committed to jail until the damages and costs were paid. The prosecutors had been notified that she had no estate to maintain her in jail, but they refused to pay her keep. The sheriff was given liberty to sell her for costs alone, but could not. Finally, the court ordered her keep paid by the county. She may be there yet. MSS. Essex Sessions, VI, 65–67, 82–83 (1746). In two instances, servants were sold into service for fees and costs, their old indentures to be void unless their masters paid the fees and costs within twenty days. MSS. Suffolk Sessions, II, 184–185 (1717/8). In 1724, Maurice Fitzgerald, in jail upon sentence and unable to pay £633 in damages, asked to be sent into military service. The house of representatives ordered him to serve his prosecutor seven years in satisfaction of claims, and if the prosecutor would not take him in thirty days, Maurice was to be allowed to go to war. *House Journals,* VI, 199.

24. MSS. Essex Sessions, IV, 114 (123). In one case, the court was even more generous. One Bullard, in jail because of unpaid fines and costs of prosecution, had his fine remitted by the Crown, and the prosecutor, a Dr. Jonathan Fairbanks, was warned the prisoner would go free in seven days unless Fairbanks would subsist him in jail. MSS. Suffolk Sessions, II, 219 (1718).

25. Usually ten to thirty days. MSS. Essex Sessions, I, n.p. (Sept. 29, 1702); MSS. Middlesex Sessions, II, 170–171, 172 (1728/9); III 337–338 (1743/4).

26. A.E. Smith, *Colonists in Bondage . . .* , chapter VIII, *passim.*

27. *Ibid.,* 153–157.

28. *Ibid.,* 157. Smith has sixty going to the Iron Works at Lynn, but see typescript "A Collection of Papers Relating to the Iron Works . . . ," 28. This is a letter dated London, 1652, asking Gifford what he did with the eighty-two Scots sent him four months after his arrival.

29. See *Suffolk Deeds,* I, 5–6, which gives a passenger list of 272, and typescrist, "A Collection of Papers Relating to the Iron Works . . . ," 28, which indicates 240 being sent to Gifford. Professor E. Neal Hartley, from his vast authoritative knowledge of the Iron Works, says that they were apparently not intended for labor at the Works, but as a side venture for sale. At any rate, they never reached the Works. Oral communication, Summer, 1953.

30. A.E. Smith, *Colonists In Bondsge . . .* , 166.

31. MSS. Winthrop Papers, W.17.102 (July 14, 1653). See also W.3.132 (July 28, 1653). A year earlier, Martha Brenton was given permission to have an Irish boy and girl. *Mass , Recs.,* III, 294.

32. Typescript, "A Collection Or Papers Relating to the Iron Works . . . ," *passim.*

33. In that order: *Boston Records,* IX, 37 (1652), and MSS. Winthrop Papers, W.14.60 (1657), *Braintree Records* 636 (1657); *Essex Probate,* I, 146–148 (1652), and *Essex County Court,* III, 264–265 (1665); II, 197–198 (1660); MSS. Middlesex County Court, I, 113–114 (1656); *Plym. Recs.,* III, 132 (1657/8); MSS. Middlesex County Court, I, 90 (1655), and I, 68 (1654); I, 84–85 (1655); *Plym, Recs.,* III, 91 (1655). For other Scots in Boston see *The Constitution and ByLaws of the Scots' Charitable Society of Boston with a list of members and officers, and many interesting extracts from the original records of the society* (Cambridge, 1878), 93 ff. Because of the "informal" method in which these war and political prisoners were garnered for shipment abroad, an occasional charge of kidnapping reached the colonial courts. Although illegal strong-arm or deceitful methods of obtaining servants for export to America were common in both centuries (A.E. Smith, *Colonists in Bondage . . . ,* 67–86), little evidence exists on this side of the Atlantic for their importation into the area of this study. Of five complaints to the courts in the seventeenth century, two servents were held illegally bound, one servant was satisfied with a two-year reduction in his term of service, one servant was declared free, and the last, a woman kidnapped from Scotland and separated from her husband, was ordered sent to her husband at her master's expense. In that order: *Essex County Court,* II, 293–296 (1661, two cases); *Plym. Recs.,* III, 220 (1661); *Suffolk County Court,* I, 18–20 (1671); and MSS. Suffolk County Court, I, 99 (1681). All but the last case were cited in Morris, *Government and Labor . . . ,* 341–343.

34. Whitmore, *Laws,* 53.

35. *Acts and Resolves,* I, 294–295 (1697). Those who escaped from neighboring governments were to be sent from constable to constable back to their places of confinement.

36. Isaac Addington to Fitz John Winthrop, Boston, 1704, in M.H.S., 6 *Colls.,* III, 191–192.

37. *News-Letter,* June 25, 1747. Here, Governor Shirley orders a listing of all French prisoners of war and the names of those with whom they lived. They had been offered for use three years earlier. *Evening-Post,* Nov. 11, 1744.

38. Herbert Levi Osgood, *The American Colonies in the Seventeenth Century* (New York, 1904–1907), I, 527 ff. But see Solomon Stoddard, "An Answer to Some Cases of Conscience," in Miller and Johnson, *The Puritans,* 457, for a short defense of the land policy.

39. Osgood, *loc. cit.* James Truslow Adams, *The Founding of New England* (Boston, 1921), 345–346. Brigham, *Laws,* 194
40. *Winthrop Papers,* III, 456–458 (1637). See also Hugh Peter to John Winthrop, Salem, 1637. M.H.S., 4 *Colls.,* VI, 95. "We have heard," he wrote, "of a dividence of women and children in the bay and would be glad of a share. . . ."
41. *Winthrop Papers,* V, 38–39 (ca. Aug. 1645). How secondary the labor problem was may be judged from the extract here quoted. "A warr with the Narraganset is verie considerable to this plantation. For I doubt whither yt be not synne in vs hauing power in our hands to suffer them to maynteyne the wo[rshi]p of the devill, which their Paw wawes often doe; 2lie, If vpon a Just warre the lord should deliver them into our hands, wee might easily haue men and woemen and Children enough to exchange for Moores, which wilbe more gaynefull pilladge for vs then wee conceive, for I doe not see how wee can thrive vntill wee gett into a stock of slaves suffitient to doe all our buisines, for our Childrens Children will hardly see this great Continent filled with people, soe that our servants will still desire freedome to plant for them selves, and not stay but for verie great wages. And I suppose you know verie well how wee shall maynteyne 20 Moores cheaper then one Englishe servant."

"The ships that shall bring Moores may come home laden with salt which may beare most of the chardge, if not all of yt."
42. For an instance where the commissioners of the United Colonies warned the residents of an Indian village that any who harbored a fugitive in an arson case would be given to the parties damaged or exchanged for Negroes, see David Pulsifer, *Records of The Colony of New Plymouth in New England. . . . Acts of the Commissioners of the United Colonies of New England* (Boston, 1859), I, 69–71 (1646).
43. George H. Moore, *Notes on the History of Slavery in Massachusetts* (New York, 1866),35 ff. Almon Wheeler Lauber, *Indian Slavery in Colonial Times within the Present Limits of the United States, Columbia University Studies,* LIV, iii (New York, 1913), 128.
44. *House Journals,* IV, 155; VI, 201. For other Indian slaves see: *News-Letter,* Nov. 6–13, 1704, Oct. 6–13, 1737; June 18–25, 1741, Nov. 3, 1748; *Evening-Post,* May 17, 1742; *Gazette,* Mar. 4–11, 1722/3; *Sibley's Harvard Graduates,* IV, 155 (ca. 1720), 436 (1708); Massschusetts Historical Society, *Proceedings* (Boston, 1879–), Third Series, IV, 656–657 (1728/9); E.I. *Colls.,* X, i, 79 (1708); MSS. Mass. Archives, VIII, 251–253 (1723, two cases). At least one Indian, an ex-servant, agreed to become a slave when she married a Negro slave. See Samuel & Joseph Moody, eds., *A Faithful Narrative of the Wicked Life and Remarkable Conversion of Patience Boston . . .* (Boston, 1738), 3. Some of these slaves may have been from the West Indies, because several "Spanish Indians" were sold in

Massachusetts. For examples see *N.E. Journal,* June 26, 1727, Aug.
30, 1731, Oct. 14, 1735; Aug. 10, 1736; *News-Letter,* Oct. 12–19,
1732 Mar. 2–9, 1732/3; *Gazette,* July 3, 1742; Cotton Mather,
"Diary" M.H.S., 7 *Colls.,* VII, 22 (1681); VIII, 549–550 (1718);
MSS. Suffolk County Court, I, 97 (1681); II, 232 (1684/5); MSS.
Plymouth Sessions, I, 180 (1701); E.I. *Colls.,* XXXV, 141 (1713).

45. *Assistants,* II, 11 (1630/1). It was revoked in 1646. *Mass. Recs.,* II,
    152. For enforcement see *Mass. Recs.,* I, 158 (1635); *Assistants,* II,
    49 (1634), 91 (1635).

46. *Winthrop's Journal,* I, 114–115 (1633); *Winthrop Papers,* IV, 46–47
    (1638), 139 (1639); *Assistants,* II, 100 (1640); *Essex County Court,*
    I, 11 (1639); II, 240–242 (1659/60, sold for five years by another
    Indian); MSS. Middlesex County Court, I, 73 (1655, a Pequot);
    M.H.S., 3 *Colls.,* I, 27 (1647/8, sold to Barbados); *Boston Records,*
    VI, 173 (1646). For Plymouth, see law against trading with Indians
    except men's servants. These may have been Pequot captives,
    however. Pulsifer, *Laws,* 33 (1639/40). See also, *ibid.,* 58–59, a 1651
    prohibition against selling guns and gunpowder to Indians, except
    those servants of whites for "divers years and . . . in good measure
    civilised. . . . " In 1658 a school Indian was disposed of, others to
    be taken by Massachusetts. Pulsifer, *Acts of the Commissioners of
    the United Colonies . . . ,* II, 207. See slso, *Plym. Recs.,* II, 69
    (1643/4); III, 4 (1650).

47. Osgood, *The American Colonies in The Seventeenth Century . . . ,*
    I, 537–539. Akagi, *The Town Proprietors of the New England
    Colonies . . . ,* 40–41. After Philip's war, the number of
    reservations was decreased, although the essential plan was kept. By
    1749, Massachusetts had Indian proprietors much like the English.
    Ibid , 41–42. See also, Brigham, *Laws,* 193–196 (1682).

48. Pulsifer, *Acts of the Commissioners of the United Colonies . . . ,*
    II, 251 (1660).

49. *Ibid.,* II, 397–398 (1678). In other words they were indentured
    servants.

50. *Essex County Court,* VI, 264–265 (1677). Here he was forced to return
    to service having run off when the war was over. For the revoked law,
    see *Mass. Recs.,* II, 152.

51. Isaiah Thomas, "The History of Printing in America . . . ," in
    American Antiquarian Society, *Archeologia Americana,* V–VI, 1, 95.
    Illustrative of the terms an Indian "apprentice" might get is the
    indenture of a ten year old Plymouth County Indian in 1694. His
    mother put him out as a "yearly servant or an apprentice" to Thomas
    Leonard of the Iron Works family in Taunton, for eleven years. Meat,
    drink, washing, lodging, and clothes were to be furnished "suitable &
    convenient for one of his degree." He was to be taught to read, and if
    possible, to write. After three years, the mother was to get a cow, one
    half of whose increase she could keep, the cow and the other half of

the increase to go to the boy. At the end of the time, another cow and two suits were to be freedom dues. Old Colony Historical Society miscellaneous MSS., "Documents Very Old," I, 135. For other posslble voluntary Indian servants see *Essex Probate*, III, 326–328 (1679); *Essex County Court*, III, 366 (1666); VII, 406 (1680); VIII, 15 (1680); MSS. Middlesex County Court, III 219–220 (1678), 238 (1678); IV, 80 (1683); MSS. Hampshire County Court, I, 60 (1682); MSS. Suffolk County Court, II, 353 (1689), 398 (1690/1); MSS. Plymouth Sessions, I, 38 (1688); *Boston Records,* VI, 182 (1678/9); M.H.S., 5 *Colls.,* VIII, 487–488 (1688); *Plym. Recs.,* VI, 178 (1685/6); VII, 309 (1690). Mather, *Magnalia . . .* , VII, 69–70 (ca. 1680).

52. Brigham, *Laws,* 172 (1674). In both colonies, of course, they were hedged about with protective-discriminatory legislation. See, *ibid.,* and Whitmore, *Laws, passim.*

53. *Suffolk County Court,* II, 778 (1676/7, service for theft of £12:19), MSS. Suffolk County Court, II, 255–256 (1685, branded, ear slit, four years); *Plym. Recs.,* IV, 112 (1665, satisfy by work or otherwise); VI 104 (1682/3, for several crimes including theft, one year); VII, 308–309 (1690, sit on gallows, branded on hand, pay damages etc., or be sold for them).

54. *Plym. Recs.,* V, 151–152 (1678); VI, 108 (1683), VI, 153 (1684/5, sold as perpetual servant); M.H.S., 2 *Proc.,* XIII, 250 (1686, transported for seven years); *Suffolk County Court,* I, 548–549 (1674/5, pay forty-two shillings costs, damages, or be sold to Barbados, branded).

55. *Plym. Recs.,* VI, 98 (1682).

56. *Assistants,* III, 216–217 (1671/2, sold for life to West Indies for rape of nine year old Indian girl); *Mass. Recs.,* V, 25 (1674, sold to West Indies for ten years).

57. MSS. Suffolk County Court, II, 263 (1685, four years' service for assaulting white man); *Assistants,* I, 295–296 (1685/6, cruelty to wife, who died, sold out of country); MSS. Superior Court of Judicature, I, folio 12 (Aug. 5, 1686), for wounding squaw, costs of cure and prosecution in twenty days or sold out of county for seven years).

58. MSS. Middlesex County Court, I, 218 (1660).

59. *Plym. Recs.,* VI, 32 (1679/80).

60. MSS. Suffolk County Court, II, 266 (1685, breaking, entering, and stealing on Lord's day. To be sold in two weeks); MSS. Middlesex County Court, V, 22 (1689/90, burglary, five years added); *Plym. Recs.,* VI, 152 (1684/5, running away, one year added).

61. Cotton Mather, *Theopolis Americana. An Essay on the Golden STREET of the holy City . . .* (Boston, 1710), 23.

62. *Acts and Resolves,* I, 435–436 (1700).

63. *Ibid.,* II, 104. "Whereas, notwithstanding the care taken and provided
    by [the previous act] . . . a great wrong and injury happens to said
    Indians, natives of this country, by reason of their being drawn in by
    small gifts, or [for] small debts, when they are in drink, and out of
    capacity to trade, to sign unreasonable bills or bonds for debt[s],
    which are soon sued, and great charge brought upon them, when they
    have no way to pay the same but by servitude. . . . "
64. *Ibid.,* II, 364 (1725/6). Reduced to ten shillings unless approved in
    1747. *Ibid.,* III, 306–307.
65. See appendix E in Towner, "A Good Master Well Served . . . "
    (Ph.D. diss., Northwestern University, 1954).
66. *House Journals,* VI, 349 (1725). A number of complaints emerged in
    the Old Colony of which Barnstable county was a part. See MSS.
    Bristol Sessions, I, 67 (1707, attempt to make slave of temporary
    servant), III, a, 55–56 (1718/9, complaint of Indian woman that she
    was being sold for unreasonable length of time, and her son being
    sold out of the province), 60 (1719, suit for freedom); III, 55 (1726,
    woman complained her daughter's indentures were delivered up without
    fulfillment on part of master), 202 (1733, complaint by boy's
    grandmother that he was abused and master threatened to sell), MSS.
    Suffolk Sessions, I, 204 (1710, two Indians being shipped as
    fishermen against their will from Martha's Vineyard), *Sibley's
    Harvard Graduates,* IV, 253 (1712, girl fired house of master), MSS.
    Plymouth Sessions, III, 67 (1726/7, appeal against white man's
    securing indentures on three children as security for performance of
    indenture by father), *House Journals,* I, 137–138 (1716, petition for
    guardians to be appointed to Indians of Nantucket, because of ill
    treatment by English), VI, 349 (1725, Barnstable Indians praying for
    relief in debt case); VII, 220 (1726, conflict over ownership of
    Nantucket debtor servent), II, 289 (1720, praying permission to
    appeal case against white Barnstable man), *Gazette,* Aug 11–18, 1729
    (two runaway Indians from Barnstable county). The loss of Barnstable
    county records in a fire in the court house undoubtedly destroyed many
    more cases of Indian difficulties.
67. *Acts and Resolves,* II, 363–365. One other provision, concerning
    debt, is discussed above The act was established for three years and
    was not re-enacted. How the pressures of the Indian war between
    1721–1725 influenced this action, can only be hazarded, but it is
    possible whites feared cooperation between the civilized Indians and
    the Indians to the north and west. At any rate, several Indians,
    including servants, were impressed into military service about that
    time, for fighting in Maine. *Sibley's Harvard. Graduates,* IV, 340 (ca.
    1725).
68. In addition to the cases already cited, a search of eighteenth century
    records yielded only seventy-five Indians who were servants down
    through 1750. There were undoubtedly many more. Sources yielding

results were: *News-Letter; Gazette; N.E. Journal; Evening-Post; Post-Boy;* MSS. Suffolk Sessions; MSS. Bristol Sensions; MSS. Essex Sessions; MSS Plymouth Sessions; MSS. Public Notary Books of Stephen Sewall and Mitchell Sewall; *Boston Records; Braintree Records; Sibley's Harvard Graduates;* E.I. *Colls.;* E.L. Motte, et.al., eds., *The Manifesto Church Records of the Church in Brattle Square Boston with Lists of Communicants, Baptisms, Marriages, and Funerals 1699–1872* (Boston, 1902); Stephen P. Sharples, ed., *Records of the Church of Christ at Cambridge in NeW England 1632–1830* (Boston, 1906); *passim.* MSS. Mass. Archives, IX, LXXXVIII, *passim.,* and indices, volumes I–III, VIII, CV.

69. MSS. Diary of Josiah Cotton, 1726–56, 202–203. Italics mine. 70. *Ibid.,* 211.

71. *Ibid.,* 266. Italics mine.

72. *Ibid.,* 376.

73. See Greene, *The Negro in Colonial New England . . . , passim.*

74. *Ibid.,* 16–17.

75. *Winthrop's Journal,* II, 30, 26. For others prior to 1670 see *Ibid.,* II, 253 (1645, a group sent back to Africa because they were victims of "manstealing." See *Mass. Recs.,* II, 168); *Assistants,* II, 118 (1641/2, admonished); MSS. Middlesex County Court, I, 59 (1654, two Negroes used as security for fine), 64 (1654, fornication with white woman), 189 (1659, fornication before marriage), 216 (1660, suit over a Negro); Middlesex Court Files, file 26, number 1628 (1661, Negro woman testifies), file 42, no number, Benjamin Crane's boy (1661, runaway), file 38, no number (Negro boy questioned, 1665); *Essex County Court,* II, 108 (1658, two Negroes, uncleanness), 183 (1659, freed Negroes sue), 247 (1660 fornication), 421 (1662, suicide), III, 55 (1663, mentioned), 99 (1663, mentioned), IV, 135 (1669, inquest over); *Boston Records,* VII, 5 (1661, prohibited employment as cooper), IX, 48 (1654, married), 72 (1659, married); *Suffolk Deeds,* I, 290 (1652/3, sold), IV, x–xi (1661, levied upon for execution in case against master); MSS. Suffolk Files, V, number 605, 1–7 (1663/4; fornication and bastardy); *Plym. Recs.,* III, 27 (1653, theft); *Mass. Recs.,* IV, i, 137 (1653, theft); *Winthrop Papers,* V, 284–5 (1648, errand boy).

76. Greene, *The Negro in Colonial New England . . . ,* 22. By 1676 they were trading with Madagascar, fearing to become involved in the dispute over West Coast slaving. Five years later, Greene notes, John Endicott and John Saffin were supplying slaves to Virginia. *Ibid.*

77. See above, p. 84.

78. Greene, *The Negro fn Colonial New England . . . ,* 22–23.

79. See appendix J in Towner, "A Good Master Well Served . . . " (Ph.D. diss., Northwestern University, 1954).

80. Whitmore, *Laws,* 53. For the conflict over interpretation of this law see Greene, *The Negro in Colonial New England . . . ,* 63–65. I

have two cases in support of the statement that servitude followed the mother. Both concern white mothers and Negro fathers. Neither resulted in slavery. *Suffolk County Court,* I, 259 (thirty years in 1673); MSS. Suffolk Sessions, III, 19–20 (1720, child supported by sale of mother).

81. See chapter VI. For the real concern Cotton Mather showed for the Negro servants in his family see his "Diary," M.H.S., 7 *Colls.,* VIII, 252, 369, 444, 477, 576. Ebenezer Parkman clearly thought of his slave, Maro, as part of the family. On December 5, 1729, he recorded that he, his wife, his children and Maro were all sick, "But especially Maro at ye Point of Death." And on the following day, "The Sun of Maro's LIfe Sat . . . The First Death in my Family." MSS. Diary of Ebenezer Parkman.

82. In the eighteenth century they were called slaves occasionally, but most of the time "Negro servant." For examples of use of "slave" see C. Mather, "Diary," M.H.S., 7 *Colls.,* VIII, 769 (1724); MSS. Suffolk Sessions II, 149 (1728); I, 116 (1705, "Servant or slave"). News-Letter, Mar. 11–18, 1742, *Gazette,* July 10–17, 1721.

83. *Suffolk County Court,* II, 648–9 (1675/6); MSS. Middlesex County Court, III, 134 (1675); *Boston Records,* XIII, 11 (1716); XIII, 81 (1721); XV, 277 (1740); MSS. Essex Sessions, II, 312 (1715/6); MSS. Middlesex Court Files, file 85, no number (case of Thomas Kine, ca. 1678); *House Journals,* VIII, 26 (1727); *N.E. Journal,* Apr. 20, 1730 (twelve cases); *Gazette,* July 10–17, 1721. See also chapter VII.

84. See chapters V and VI.

85. See chapter VII for action as plaintiffs. Defendants; for examples of cases where found innocent see MSS. Middlesex County Court, I, 64 (1654); MSS. Middlesex Court Files, flle 38, no number (1665); MSS. Suffolk Sessions, n.p. (case of Peter, Negro, Apr. 30, 1744).

86. *Suffolk Deeds,* I, 290 (1652/3); VI, 301 (1671/2); MSS. Robert Treat Paine Papers, June 2, 1715; M.H.S., 3 *Proc.,* XLIV, 335–6 (1729).

87. MSS. Mass. Archives, IX, 149 (1702); *Essex County Court,* VII, 394–5 (1680). M.H.S., 3 *Proc.,* IV 335–36 (1729); *Post-Boy,* Jan 25, 1748; *Gazette,* Mar. 24, 1747; Oct. 23 1750, *News-Letter,* Mar. 22, 1750; *Evening-Post,* July 30, 1744; Aug. 13, 1744.

88. *Suffolk County Court,* I, 159 (1672); Essex Probate, III, 5–9 (1675); *Sibley's Harvard Graduates,* IV, 243 (1721), 249 (1711), 520 (1703), V, 75 (1733), 84 (1709); *Publications of the Brookline Historical Publication Society,* First Series (Brookline, Mass. 1897), iv, 42 (1717), *Plym. Recs.,* VI, 134–137 (1676).

89. MSS. Mass. Archives, IX, 154–155 (1704); MSS. Middlesex Sessions, I, 171 (1705), 405 (1722); MSS. Suffolk Sessions, II, 147 (1716/7); *Plym. Recs.,* V, 216 (1676); *Boston Records,* XVII, 41 (1743); *Essex Probate,* III, 326–328 (1679); Kenneth B. Murdock, *Increase Mather The Foremost American Puritan* (Cambridge, 1925),

384 (1722); MSS. Public Notary Books of Stephen Sewall and Mitchell Sewall, I, 133 (1717); *House Journals,* I, 134 (1716).
90. See chapter VI.
91. MSS. Essex Sessione, IV, 16 (1719, charge of separating man and wife). See also chapter VI.
92. See chapters VI, VIII.
93. See chapter V.
94. Greene, *The Negro in Colonial New England . . . ,* 333–334.
95. A few Negroes did, however, serve as indentured servants or even apprentices. Undoubtedly these were manumitted Negroes, their children, or mulattoes whose mothers had been free. *Ibid.,* 126, 290–291. See alao *Suffolk Deeds,* XII, 376–7 (1683, mulatto binds self "apprentice" for four years); MSS. Middlesex County Court, IV, 116 (1684, Negro ordered to find a master as punishment for illegal sale of drink); *Essex Probate,* II, 405–407 (1674, "a Negro boy apprentice"); MSS. Essex Sessions, II 323 (1716, former servant); MSS. Suffolk Sessions, IV, 314–15 (1730/31, "Tony a Mollatto Covenant Servant. . . . "); MSS. Files, Essex County Inferiour Court of Common Pleas, Drawer March–July (1736) Indenture of Doney, Molatto (Jan., 1732, sold for two and one-half years).

5. The Servant at Work

Had Cotton Mather coined a phrase to be engraved upon the consciousness of every servant in the Massachusetts Bay, he could not have done better than to say, as he did, *"Come when you are called, and . . . Do what you are Bidden."*[1] The institution of servitude was designed for the doing of work at the order of a master. Those orders were frequent, for the Puritans disparaged idleness as they hated the devil. Here truly were the "hewers of wood" and the "drawers of water."

That the Puritans dissparaged idleness admits of no dispute. One scholar has well said that "few communities have legislated so frequently and minutely against idleness as the New England colonies, beginning with the first church covenant of Salem, whose signers promised to 'shun idleness as the bane of any state.'"[2] This ban against the easy life applied, of course, to those who "called" and "bade" as well as those who "came" and "did," but with this difference; the master worked for himself and his own, the servant for his master. Hence the pressures against the latter were greater, and more frequently brought to bear, requiring only the notice of the master that his man or maid was "misspending time."

The early settlers had ample opportunity to learn the dangers of idle servants, for more than one group had been sent to New England's shores to work and make a profit for absent masters—only to dissipate their time and their company's profits in careless living, and in sitting by the fireside when they should have been working.[3] Moreover, from early times they had the admonition of the Governor and Company of Massachusetts Bay before them, concerning its servants:

And wee hartely pray yow, that all bee kept to labor, as the only meanes to reduce them to civill, yea, a godly lyfe, and to keepe youth from falling into many enormities w[hi]ch by nature wee are all too much enclyned vnto.[4]

The laws which followed this experience and this admonition were as much the realization of the necessity of work in a frontier civilization, as they were the Puritan recognition of man's necessity to have two callings—secular and religious—and they were applied with a fine impartiality to free and bound alike, as we have seen.[5]

The eighteenth century, after the political domination of the Puritans was broken, saw no decline in the abhorrence of idleness, even if it saw an increase of the evil. The ministers and the government continued, as though with one breath, to damn those who would not work. Samuel Willard wrote and preached that man is by nature an active being who cannot be still. If he is not doing something active and productive he will be doing something evil and sinful. Therefore it behooves mankind, and mankind's rulers, to abhor idleness, "the Devil's Pillow, on which if he can gain Men to ly down, he hath them his own, to do what he pleaseth with them."[6] Workhouses were provided for those who lived idly and had no visible means of support as early as 1682; while a house of correction would suffice where no workhouse was, as one James Mead found out in Cambridge in 1737. The provincial legislature, following the example of the colonial general courts, legislated freely on the subject to the sorrow of those who preferred to misspend their time in taverns and other places of solace.[7] Work was indeed the common lot of man.

In those hardy times it was not only presumed, but ordered that free laborers should work the "whole day, alloweing convenient tyme for foode & rest," the eight hour day, indeed the ten hour day, being far, too far in the future.[8] Rare was the master who let his servant sleep later than he, or stop work earlier, and rare was the mistress who failed to rouse a sleepy maid from her bed in the attic before she stirred herself to get the day started. Indeed, since most servants worked along with their masters or mistresses on farm or in shop, in house or garden, they had a long supervised day of labor before them when the cock crowed. If they were among those who spent the night hours in dalliance or nightwalking, it must have been hard indeed to put on their crude "servant's shoes," leather or homespun working clothes, and appear lively and alert at breakfast time.[9]

Those servants who did not respond promptly to the cock's crow or the master's hallo, or who too frequently displayed a lack of diligence in their master's business were subject to discipline at the hands of their masters, and in more extreme cases to discipline at the hands of the courts. Moderate your stripes when whipping your refractory servants, urged Cotton Mather; and servants, "Let your obedience . . . be such, as will manifest that you are the Obedient Children of God." For, he continued, you

> are the *Animate, Separate, Active Instruments* of other men. Servants, your *Tongues,* your *Hands,* your *Feet,* are your *Masters,* and they should move according to the Will of your *Masters.*[10]

Probably most masters did punish with moderation, but the servant protests of the period indicate that all did not. For those too sunk in the sin of idleness to feel the moderate correction reasonable to give in the home, the courts provided punishments.[11]

It may be assumed, then, that so long as a master's eye was upon him, or near enough occasionally to supervise, so long as the master's good right arm was strong, or the courts were functioning, the servant put in a good day's work. Many would undoubtedly work without constant supervision, such as the Negro man advertised who was "a faithfull Fellow to Work without Inspection."[12] For those who would not, there was a ready word of reproof. "Be not those *Eye-Servants,* that will do their Masters Will, no longer then [sic] their Masters Eye is upon them. . . . "[13] Or, as Benjamin Wadsworth said, "Servants are very wicked, when they are LAZY and IDLE in their Masters Service. The *Slothful* Servant, is justly called Wicked. . . . "[14]

While a good day's work was long, and often arduous, a more leisurely pace was set than would today obtain in a modern factory. The master, who worked along with his servant, could see, and indeed feel, when his servant was working too hard, for he worked hard too. If the weather was hot, they probably took 'meete time' for rest at noon even though they did not perpetuate the ten-to-two respite masters and servants in Roger Conant's day in Salem took one hot summer.[15] An occasional drink of cider undoubtedly shortened the longest days: in winter, candle-lighting came early. Even when Massachusetts ordered children and servants to be employed at preparing and spinning wild hemp so that mornings, evenings, and "other seasons" would not be lost as formerly, masters were cautioned that it should be done without "abridging any such servants of their dewe times for foode & rest, or other needfull refreshings."[16] Generally speaking, servants were not worked as animals. Or if they were, it was worth advertising about, as was one lass in the eighteenth century: "The very best Negro in town, who has had the small pox & measles, is as hearty as a horse, as brisk as a bird and will work like a beaver."[17]

During the early period of settlement, roughly down to the end of the "Great Migration," most servants, and indeed most masters, were

engaged in what later economists would call capital formation—
bullding homes and barns, breaklng up the soil, clearing land, making
roads and building docks; or as a contemporary chronicler described it,
"much labour & servise . . . to be done aboute building & planting,
&c. . . . "[18] Indeed this activity was never to cease during the first
century of frontier life, even though the eastern coastlands were well
settled long before. Once broken, the land was kept in heavy use
providing the grain, cattle, and agricultural products of all kinds
necessary and profitable to sell to the seemingly endless stream of
immigrants who had fled the shores of England and the machinations of
the Stuarts. Illustrative, if not typical, of this investment of time,
money, and labor in land is the indenture between William Tyng,
merchant of Boston, and John Reade, Weymouth farmer, in 1639.
Reede was to farm Tyng's land at Mount Wollaston for ten years. Reade
provided forty-two head of cattle (ten milch cowe included), ten oxen,
four mares, one colt, twenty goats, one ram, twelve pigs, one cock and
ten hens, one turkey cock and two hens, one gander and four geese, one
drake and four ducks. He was to build a barn seventy-four feet by forty,
and to keep seven men-servante "able for their severall imployments,"
and two maid-servants. Tyng was to pay one half the wages of any
workmen or women hired at special times for planting, reaping,
mowing, and making hay.[19]

When the easily-cleared, or already-cleared, land of the eastern
shores was taken up, the colonists and their servants moved on to the
fertile clearings about the Connecticut River. Only when the cleared
land was gone did they fill in the gap between the two lines of
settlement, and then spread westward from the Connecticut. Indeed, as
late as 1739, the Reverend Mr. Ebenezer Parkman's servant was
clearing land of rocks or trees in Worcester.[20]

The lack of an exportable staple such as tobacco, rice, or cotton in
those days of staple products is likely to obscure the significance and
importance of agriculture in Massachusetts. Particularly is this so when
the more spectacular (and profitable) activities of fishing, ship-building,
and, above all, trade made it possible that the Bay should not be a mere
backwater of colonial settlement, but a vigorous leader in the economic
development of this new country. Nevertheless, it is wise not to
overlook the important fact that most residents of the colonies of
Plymouth and Massachusetts Bay, and later the Province of
Massachusetts were engaged in getting a living, a good living, from the
soil as late as the Revolution and after. Indeed, they exported
agricultural surplus in the form of horses and cattle, and even grains.

Without the trade they could never have prospered, but without the farmer they could not have lived.

This dependence on agriculture lends importance to the role of the servant on the farm, an area that should not be neglected. Since the farms were generally small, and since no staple was produced, heavy investment in laboring hands was neither possible, nor profitable. Moreover, the families of the colonists provided sons and daughters to do the work of the farm. Even so, many farmers of moderate means had at some time in their career a servant or two who worked shoulder to shoulder in the raising of food, or helped the overburdened mother in the multifarious household tasks of the day.

Look in on the farm of Robert Eames of Middlesex County in the 1670s, for example. Mr. Eames had a servant apprenticed to husbandry for ten years. This lad, not too well disciplined, it appears, nevertheless was diligently at work on the farm whenever one Isaac Richardson occasioned to be passing by. He plowed, loaded hay, took the cows to the salt marshes, went to the market for his master, and worked early and late and very hard. Moreover, this seventeenth-century farmer not only had the labor of himself and servant, but, on occasion, he hired others.[21] Or look in on the farm of Abraham Howe a few years earlier. Here a servant was making hay, husking corn, herding and feeding cattle, cutting wood, felling trees, and having charge of the farm work while his master was gone early in the spring.[22] A decade or so before this, in Essex County, the farm of Samuel Symonds is enlightening. Here was a farmer with two servants, both men, both capable of doing the heavy work of farming. Moreover, Farmer Symonds found it necessary to hire the son of a neighbor, Goodman Bragg, to help with the plowing.[23] Apparently, some of these one-man farms took more than one man.[24]

In addition to the above work, it is safe to assume that the servants on the farm, like the farmer himself, were jacks of all trades. It is certain that they milked the cows, planted corn, fetched water, tended cattle and sheep, drove hogs, carried bushels of corn, and threshed barley. In slack times they cleared land, fetched sand with a team and cart, carted mulch with a team of oxen, and spread dung.[25] Probably they gardened too, although that task was more likely the lot of the household servant than the man of heavy work.[26]

Illustrative of the relatively wide use of servants on New England farms, is the fact that servants of many types were to be found laboring there side by side with their respective masters. Zachary Edeth of Plymouth in 1646/47,[27] John Coggswell's son of Ipswich, in 1653,[28] and Alexander Perry of Boston in 1724,[29] for example, were apprenticed to farmers. Many others were simply white or Indian indentured servants bound out without training provisions,[30] and still others were Negroes, bound for life.

In fact, as early as 1661 (and probably earlier than that) Negroes were working on farms.[31] Despite the belief, fostered by some historians, that blacks were adaptable only to the mass production of the plantation economy, Negroes were apparently regularly used on farms even in the seventeenth century when such labor was scarce. One, rented along with a farm in 1678, was described as an able servant, despite the darkness of his skin.[32]

One needs only to turn to the newspapers to be convinced that Negroes in the eighteenth century were used on farms quite extensively. Scores of advertisements proclaimed that such and such a slave was "Fit for town or country."[33] If this seems too general and too vague, one who reads further will see Negroes specifically recommended for the country: a man, "fit for husbandry"; a young fellow, healthy and fit for town or country but "better for the Country"; a likely young man "completely fit for country business"; a man for "husbandry"; a young man about twenty-three fit for a "farmer"; a strong healthy man "fit for farming business"; a strong and lusty man "very suitable for husbandry work"; and a man about twenty-two "fit for any country Business."[34]

These men did not come from Africa trained to do New England farming, of course. They had to be taught. One diarist, in the late 1720s, shows this when he recorded that he could not perform many ministerial duties because his Negro boy, bought two weeks before, was new, and could not yet do his work.[35] But that the Negroes learned is shown in *The Weekly News-Letter* for March 182–25, 1742:

> If there be any Person qualified and disposed (with a proper Recommendation) to take Care of a large Farm not far distant from Boston, with Negroes and Stock thereon, he may meet with proper Encouragement, by applying to the Printer hereof.

The year before, *The Boston Gazette or Weekly Journal* offered three Negroes for sale from a farm in Cambridge plus a gardener's time for three years.[36] Others, more individual, show the ability of the Negro to accommodate himself to the diversified activity of the small farm. Offered for sale were: a man used to farming "an excellent fellow at driving a cart"; a man who could do "all sorts of husbandry well"; a man who was a "master of the farming business"; a man "bred up to husbandry"; a man "chiefly brought up to Country business"; a well-seasoned man who "understands Farming very well"; two men, one about twenty-six who could do "all sorts of farming business"; and one about twenty-five, "used to farming several years." The Negro farmed in Massachusetts too.[37]

Just as the servant population was engaged in farming and allied activities from the very beginnings of servitude in New England, so they were employed in domestic service. This term embraces much more than its present use would indicate, for the relatively low division of labor left to the household such duties as making yarn, butter, and clothes, milking cows, tending garden, and other diverse activities. Moreover, there was the business of being a gentleman's gentleman, a term few, if any, masters applied to their personal body servants, but one which expresses well the varied tasks of boys and men who attended their masters on travel days, performed as scribes, drivers, valets—in fact, did anything requested of them.

From the 1630s on, the well-to-do families of the Bay region employed servants in the house, and many a farm family or modest town dweller had at least one maid-of-all-work. Down to the late decades of the seventeenth century, such maids were usually young women of the neighborhood, afterwards Negroes, either male or female, frequently took the place of white indentured house labor. On occasion, Indian girls, slave or indentured, worked along with their darker or fairer sisters on the same menial tasks.[38] The nature of the work which these domestics did can well be imagined. At the risk of belaboring the obvious, however, it may be worth indicating what the colonists wanted, as shown in their newspaper advertisements. Quite common were notices such as the one offering for sale a strong Negro woman "well seasoned to the country who can do all sorts of Household work as Washing, Baking, Brewing and can sew very well . . . ," or a white maid, to be sold for a number of years, who "understands housework and can wash and Iron very well." Other advertisements specified, along with general household work, such activities as quilting, knitting, churning, dressing meats, waiting table, carding, making butter, dairying, gardening, dressing victuals, brewing, kitchen work, scouring, tending children, buying provisions, making shirts, and nursing babies at the breast.[39]

Negro men were used for some of the chores about the house, too. Several were advertised as being familiar with or fit for "all manner of Household work."[40] Others were specified as being good, and even excellent, cooks.[41]

In the better appointed homes, male house servants did the more specialized work of body servants for their masters. Several were advertised as being fit to serve a gentleman.[42] Thus, they shaved their masters, dressed wigs, waited table, ran errands, drove chaises or carriages, played the violin of an evening for the entertainment of master and guests, and performed that final service, carrying their late masters to the grave.[43] These house servants were not always black, although more frequently so, for it is rare that one finds whites being advertised as body servants, such as the two listed in the summer of 1738, one of whom could shave, dress wigs, and wait tables, while the other could "shave well and [was] used to attending a gentleman."[44] But that they were desirable is to be seen in a 1745 notice: "A Young Man inclin'd to wait on a Gentleman, may be informed of such a Place, inquiring of the Printer." Another requested a coachman, cook, and maid, while yet another was looking for a Jersey, English, or Irish boy who could shave or cook.[45]

Whether shaving or cooking, mending or baking, the young men and women were not born to the tasks they performed, nor did they always land on the shores of New England equipped to bear these responsibilities. If they were only "fit" to do all sorts of Household affairs rather than "used" to them, they had to be trained. While many whites learned their chores at home before being put to service, most Negroes had to be taught, either in New England, or in the West Indies, to do things the way their white masters desired. And even among the white population, it is interesting to note that it was not unusual for a young girl to be put "apprentice" to learn housewifery, to knit, and to sew. Thus (ae) early as 1643 the young daughter Of William Hoskins was put out to a Thomas Whitney and wife who were to instruct her in "learning and sewing in reasonable manner. . . ."[46] Four decades later a diarist recorded that

> This day came into our family Elizabeth Nevenson, daughter of Mr. Jno. Nevinson & Elizabeth his wife, who wilbe 13 yeares of age ye 22d. day of October next: the verbal Coven[ant] betweene my wife & Mrs. Nevenson is that she ye sd. Elizabeth shall dwell with my wife as a servt. six yeares, to be taught instructed & provided for as shalbe meet, & [tha]t she shall not depart from our family during ye said time without my wives [*sic*] consent.[47]

Many other young; girls were put out specifically as "apprentices" to learn "housewiferey" in the following decades.[48]

However they came to be trained, by the time they reached the newspaper columns, numbers were ready for service. We cannot fail to record a few: "an excellent waiting man for a gentleman"; a man about twenty-five, fourteen years in the country, who had had the smallpox, and was a "strong fellow for any outdoor work, excels in Household work ... washing, baking, dressing meats or rooms, waiting, etc ... "; a fine young Barbadian Negro fellow "fit for a gentleman's house"; and Luke Vardy's Negro man, Tom, "a compleat Fellow fit for any Gentleman. ... "[49]

Gentlemen to employ "compleat" fellows would have been few and far between if the decline in farm prices, and the fall in land values which accompanied the drying up of that seemingly endless stream of immigration in the 1640's had not speeded up the process already begun of looking to the sea for wealth. In the century or more which followed that first great depression, the people of the Bay region built an economy which would support an ever increasing division of labor.[50] The young men (and women) of the colonies, of England, Scotland, Ireland, and the Continent of Africa, and of the native Indian tribes were drawn by this division of labor into the artisan's shop, the rope maker's rope walk, the shipyard, the merchant's office, the distillery, and the blacksmith's shop as trainees or as common labor.

That economy was nurtured by the restless sea which pushed its way into the many rivers and harbors and on which floated ships of New England construction, carrying fish for the famous triangular trade, gold and slaves from the West Indies, horses, cattle and grain of New England growth, molasses and sugar for New England Rum, manufactures from England, coastwise shipping for other ports, and American-built ships to be sold at their destination.[51]

A modern writer has pointed out that the trade of Boston, a large and important town of the American scene in the eighteenth century, was more akin in volume to the business activities of the Middle Ages than to modern times. He has reminded us that the most important merchant house in Boston carried on a desultory trade amounting to but $4000 credit sales in a month (if lucky), and that its day was counted busy if three transactions were made.[52] Yet, this trade must be viewed against a frontier society and an artisan form of production, rather than being compared with modern-day economies. Then the export of such articles as "barreled beef and pork, hewn lumber and staves, bowls, buckets, brooms, ox-bows, axe-helves, and the like ... ,"[53] takes on greater significance. Then too the production, as early as 1676, of seven hundred vessels between six and one hundred tons and thirty vessels between one hundred and 250 tons, and the employment of thirty master shipwrights, seems important. By 1717, this trade was employing 3493 sailors and 492 ships, whose tonnage totaled 25,406; and in 1731, it kept six hundred ships totaling 38,000 tons active in European and coastwise trading.[54] Viewed against frontier society and artisan production, this trade seems vigorous.

Trade, combined with agriculture, supported, in the seventeenth century, more than thirty different occupations whose masters employed servants in their business (not including domestic or agricultural service), and by the middle of the next century enlarged the number of occupations which could support servants to nearly one hundred. There were probably many more whose records escape us, for one eighteenth-century writer pointed out that shipbuilding alone required about thirty different trades.[55] Thus, in that industry, records remain of men apprenticed to, or laboring with, ship joiners, sail makers, shipwrights, ship carpenters, rope makers, mast makers, and more.[56]

Once built, these ships employed still more servants, for we find many youths apprenticed to seamen or mariners to learn their "art, trade, or mystery" as well as the more complex navigation.[57] Others, not apprenticed, were employed in regular sailing voyages either with their masters or were rented out to the captain of a vessel.[58] Even privateers carried them, as in 1702, when John Halsey, commander of the brigantine, *Adventure,* hired Samuel Lynde's Negro to cook for him, guaranteeing Lynde one full share of any prizes and fifty-five shillings a month. In the next year he carried him to Barbados, London, and back again.[59]

Fishing and whaling took servants off to sea too, particularly Indians. In fact, the early whaling industry of the counties of old Plymouth Colony was built partly on the labors of Indian men and boys, many of whom were bound servants, serving specifically for that purpose.[60] White boys even became apprentices to learn the art of fishing.[61] Thus in one way or another, the sea accounted for the labor of many boys and men bound to service for a period of years, or for life.

Other servants were employed in various occupations, from the lowly chimney sweeps and porters through weavers, barbers, and periwigmakers, up to blacksmiths, and goldsmiths.[62] In fact, since almost every trade including merchanting[63] got its recruits from the ranks of its apprentices it would be safe to say that every occupation except teaching, preaching, and politics had its bound labor.

Of particular interest is the use of Negroes in skilled trades. Here, more than any other place, is shown the personal supervision, the sharing of common tasks and working hours, the variety of experience, which made Negro slavery approximate the workaday conditions of other forms of bound labor.

The employment of Negroes in varied trades, industries, and occupations, helped to raise the standard of living for the late seventeenth- and early eighteenth-century New Englanders, and contributed to the reservoir of skilled labor, thus belying those later historians who were to label them incapable of adaptation to a relatively complex civilization, whether in non-plantation agriculture or village and town artisanship.

That old fiction has long since been buried, and we need only to note in passing that the Negro, in Africa, was not unaccustomed to the handicrafts, and when willing, he was able to learn new trades in America and practice them with proficiency.[64] As early as 1661 a slave was employed by a Boston cooper in the making of barrels, and despite a Boston ordinance to the contrary,[65] Negroes appear more frequently in skilled occupations from that time on. They performed as carpenters, caulkers, shipwrights, mast makers, weavers, seamen, blacksmiths, whitesmiths, printers, painters, bakers, shoemakers, distillers, sailmakers, tailors, tallow chandlers, soapboilers, and others.[66]

Printing, alone, absorbed the labor of Negroes as well as Indians.[67] Thomas Fleet, for example, owned several Negroes, one of whom worked at the printing business both as a pressman and a typesetter. In addition, he made the wood cuts for Fleet's ballads and books, and left him two sons, who were raised to the same trade.[68] Isaiah Thomas remembered that Daniel Fowle, who formed the printing establishment of Rogers and Fowle in 1742, employed a slave in his business, too. "I well remember him"; he wrote, "he worked at press with or without an assistant until prevented by age. . . . "[69]

Help-wanted advertisements frequently specified skilled Negroes, thus indicating their general use. Among them were requests for ship and house carpenters, blacksmiths, and coopers. One specified, indeed, that they were to be "Masters of their business."[70]

Most servants, of course, were not "Masters of their business" but rather were in the process of acquiring skills; by indenture if apprentices, or in the case of the nonapprentices, at the master's discretion. They took care of the simple tasks, the sweeping, the fetching, the carrying—the menial work that went with every occupation, and whether they were servants to a village blacksmith or a town blacksmith probably made little difference in their working day. Most occupations were carried on in the family with the master employing at the most two or three members not of his own immediate family and using the same tools and the same techniques, wherever he lived. Thus most of these servants lived the same life six days a week from early morning until late in the afternoon—using the same tools and materials, working with the same people, in the same shop attached to the living quarters.[71]

Supposing, for a moment, that a servant served a shipwright: what sort of work might he have done? Up early in the morning, he probably hauled tools, tar, lumber, and poles from his master's sheds to the ship his master was currently engaged in repairing. In the course of those repairs he would be sent for water, or cider, or a forgotten tool. Then he might help with:

> calking up the portholes, recalking the deck placeing the Capstan as it should bee, a Ladder to Set to the Scuttle to go down between decks and placeing timbers to stow the Boate upon deck . . . recalking graving capstain windlice top mast top mast yards, tiller transome . . . mending and Setting the Boate sprite, Cheekes for the Chimneys fitting and setting the Mison mast, plaineing and Cleeting the maine yard maine top saile yard . . . and fore topmast, graveing two sides drawing and plaining . . . the mizon topsaile yard cross jack yard, mizon top mast calking between the wales fitting the sprittle yards and top mast, forelocking of bolts, the making the bulkehead in the Lazareta, the pump case the Loading port, the Setting of the pump and much other worke. . . .[72]

If he could write, he might find himself testifying some day in court that "I lived with Wm Holowell five yeares an Apprentice. . . ." During that time his master and other men carried on a partnership in shipbuilding and other carpenter work, while he "kep't the Accounts and was present at the time of their Reckonings. . . ."[73]

If he served a tanner he might find himself some bright morning enroute to pick up hides to take to his master's tanning yard. Upon his return he may have been put to work in the bark-grinding mill, or changing the liquor in the pits, or scraping the new hides which he had picked up by virtue of his master's acting as scavenger for the town.[74] If a tailor, he probably sat with folded legs sewing on a servant's coat or a shirt and drawers for another servant, while his master, sitting nearby, worked on a gentleman's "wastcote."[75] If a house carpenter he may have hauled tools and lumber for his master and helped him build a house

> Vizt to contain in Length thirty four foote more or less as the Land wil beare and in breadth twenty foote and Fifteen foote Stud with two jetts in the front next the Street, and a Leanto of ten foote wide joyning to the backside to reach throughout the Length of sd house, to Stone a Cellar underneath the sd main house throughout the whole Length and breadth thereof, to build a Stack of good brick Chimnys to the sd house to contain six fires one in the Cellar, three upon the first Floore

and two in the Chambers to inclose and cover the sides and Roofe with clapboards and shingles, to make and place Four great casemt frames in the front of sd building . . . to fill lath & plaister the walls . . . to lay a Floor of boards upon Sleepers in the Cellar, to make us all partitions, to make and hang all dores, Staires. . . . [76]

Whatever he did, it is safe to assume that the dirty, repetitious, simple, boring, tedious, and distasteful tasks were regularly assigned to him, and rightfully so, since a wise master would be unlikely to waste his own skilled time doing the tasks a servant could do. As Lucy Downing wrote to Margaret Winthrop in recommending a prospective serving maid, "she doth all the worst work in her mothers howes and is very servisable. . . . "[77]

The servant, then, fulfilled his function at work, to which he was driven by his society's fear of idleness and his master's need to make him worth his keep. No task was too menial, or too skilled, for him to undertake. His employment might be in the kitchen, the parlor, the office, the field, or the forecastle—wherever his master worked, or wherever his master sent him. Regardless of his status within the servant class, and regardless of race, he might be doing tasks which servants of another status or race did right along with him too. While he did not sssume the significance of the servant in staple-producing colonies, he lightened the loads of those for whom he worked, and he played a not insignificant role in the creation of a great economy. He was, moreover, the forerunner of that skilled worker for whom New England became so justly famous in the nineteenth century.

NOTES

1. Cotton Mather, *Tremenda* . . . (Boston, 1721), 27.
2. Samuel Eliot Morison, *Builders of the Bay Colony* (Boston, 1930), 166. "Surely they were much deceived, or else ill informed, that ventured thither in hope to live in plenty and idleness, both at a time;" wrote William Wood (early settler in Salem) against New England's slanderers, "and it is as much pity that he that can work and will not, should eat, as it is pity that he that would work and cannot, should fast." "New England's Prospect," in Alexander Young, *Chronicles of the First Planters of the Colony of Massachusetts Bay, from 1623 to 1636* . . . (Boston, 1846), 413.
3. C.K. Shipton, *Roger Conant, A Founder of Massachusetts* (Cambridge, 1945), 51–59, 49–50; Charles M, Andrews, *The Colonial Period of American History* (New Haven, 1934–1938), I,

329–334; *Bradford's History,* 154 ff; Frances Rose-Troup, *John White the Patriarch of Dorchester and the Founder of Massachusetts 1575–1648 with an account of the Early Settlements In Massachusetts 1620–1630* (New York, 1930), 71, 91, 104–105, 119, 143. John Josselyn, in his "An Account of Two Voyages to New England . . . ," M.H.S., 3 *Colls.,* III, 332, remarks "They have store of Children, and are well accomodated with Servants, many hands make light work, many hands make a full fraught, *but many mouths eat up all, as some old planters have experimented. . . . "* (1673). Italics mine.

4. *Mass. Recs.,* I, 397 (1629).
5. See above, chapter III.
6. *A Compleat Body of Divinity* . . . , 683.
7. Boston was given one hundred pounds in a bequest for the building of a workhouse for the relief of the poor. It burned, and in 1682 the town voted to raise one thousand pounds to build a new one to be used also for families and persons who "misspend" time in idleness and tippling. *Boston Records,* VII, 157–158. Earlier that same year the General Court had ordered the idle to be sent about their work or sent to the house of correction. *Mass. Recs.,* V, 373. Cotton Mather reminded his readers that a provincial law required the idle to be incarcerated in the workhouse. *A Faithful Monitor* . . . , 22. Mead's case is in MSS. Middlesex Sessions, III, 76 (1737). See also chapter III, above, *passim.*
8. *Mass. Recs.,* I, 109 (1633).
9. For examples of the night life of servants, see chapter VI. Young servants may have gone barefoot in the summer time but see the advertisement for "servent's shoes" in *Evening-Post,* Jan. 30, 1744.
10. *A Good Master Well-Served* . . . , 15–16, 38.
11. See chapters III, VII.
12. *Gazette,* June 5, 1750.
13. Cotton Mather, *A Family Well-Ordered* . . . , 68.
14. Benjamin Wadsworth, *The Well-Ordered Family* . . . , 118.
15. Shipton, *Roger Conant* . . . , 95–96. This long rest-hour was to avoid the effects of unaccustomed heat.
16. *Mass. Recs.,* I, 322 (1641). A shortage of clothlng was feared.
17. *Evening-Post,* Aug. 23, 1742.
18. *Bradford's History,* 476. Hutchinson, *History* . . . , I, 85. Even the ministers came prepared to farm. John Fisk arrived in 1637 "well stocked with Servants, and all sorts of Tools for Husbandry and carpentry. . . . " Mather, *Magnalia* . . . , iii, 142.
19. Lechford, *Note-Book,* 94–100.
20. MSS. Diary of Ebenezer Parkman, Mar, 3, 1739.
21. MSS. Middlesex County Court Files, file 58, no number (case of Thomas Hall, Apr. 19, 1671).
22. *Ibid.,* file 53, no number (case of Jerathmeel Bowers, May 18, 1669).

23. Morgan, *The Puritan Family* . . . , 70–71.
24. The Scotch servants of the Iron Works at Saugus, some thirty-five or more, were kept at farming. See the typescript, "A Collection of Papers Relating to the Iron Works . . . ," 9, 183 ff. For other farmers with large numbers of servants, see Lechford, *Note-Book,* 65–66, 94–100; *News-Letter,* Mar. 18–25, 1742.
25. Essex County Court, I, 137; *Plym. Recs.,* III, 91; *Winthrop Papers,* III, 247, 268–269; IV, 232–233, 236–237; *Suffolk County Court,* I, 196; *Evening-Post,* Jan. 19, 1736; *N.E. Journal,* Jan. 8, 1733; MSS. Diary of Ebenezer Parkman, Mar. 3–May 1, 1739; MSS. Middlesex Court Files, file 38, no number (case of William Clark, Nov. 1665); MSS. Middlesex Sessions, I, 44.
26. For general farming methods see Robert R. Walcott, "Husbandry in Colonial New England," *N.E.Q.,* IX (June, 1936), 218–252.
27. *Plym Recs.,* II, 112–113. The agreement specified husbandry or any business the master saw good for Zachary.
28. *Essex Probate,* I, 156.
29. MSS. "Edward Winslow Notary Public. Benjamin Drew 1741–1759," 4–5. Perry was to be taught husbandry or the "art or mistery of Ironwork. . . . " See also MSS. Middlesex Court Files, file 6, 200 (1653); MSS. Suffolk Sessions, III, 314 (1725); IV, 176–177 (1728); MSS. Boston Indentures, I, 1 (1740); 2 (1740); 7 (1740); 9 (1740); 12 (1741); 86 (1745); *Plym. Recs.,* I, 110 (1638); *Essex County Court,* I, 325–326 (1653)
30. For Indians see *News–Letter,* Oct. 6–13, 1737, "born in the country, and bred up to husbandry from his infancy." For Indians advertised as fit for the country, *ibid.,* Oct. 20–27, 1732; *Gazette,* Sept. 15–22, 1729. For Whites see MSS. Diary of Ebenezer Parkman, Dec. 5, 1738–June 22, 1739; MSS. Essex Sessions, IV, 106 (1723); *Gazette,* May 2–9, 1737; *Evening-Post,* Sept. 21, 1741; *Winthrop Papers,* III, 518–519 (1637); *Essex Probate,* II, 408–410 (1674). The newspapers advertised several men and women as fit for farming, or for town or country business. *News-Letter,* Aug. 5–12, 1717 (thirty men, tradesmen and farmers); Nov. 18–25, 1725; Dec. 9–16, 1725; *Gazette,* Mar. 21–28, 1719/20; Dec. 21–28, 1719; May 2–9, 1720; June 13–20, 1720; Dec. 6–13, 1736; Nov. 24, 1741 (several); *Courant,* Mar. 18–25, 1723; Apr. 1–8, 1723; *N.E. Journal,* May 31, 1737; *Evening-Post,* May 22, 1738; Feb. 19, 1739; Dec. 7, 1741; Mar. 8, 1742; Dec. 1, 1746; Mar. 23, 1747; May 14, 1750 (several Irish, male and female, fit for town or country); Oct. 15, 1750. In *ibid.,* Nov. 19, 1744, several French prisoners were offered for farm labor. In *ibid.,* for Feb. 11, 1745, and Apr. 11, 1748 were advertisements from people desirous of getting farm labor. The women were probably used in household, dairy, and garden.
31. MSS. Middlesex Court Files, file 42, no number (case of Benjamin Crane's Negro, June 14, 1661).

32. *Ibid.,* file 85, no nurnber (case of Thomas Kine, 1678).
33. One hundred and nine males plus a "parcel," and sixty females advertised as fit for town or country were noted in the files of the *Gazette, Evening-Post, Post-Boy, Courant,* and *N.E. Journal* between Mar. 1721 and Nov. 1750. For the period from 1731 to 1750 the *News-Letter* offered 230 slaves for sale, many of whom were listed as fit for either town or country. Duplicates have been checked in the first five papers. The women were probably used in household, dairy, and garden.
34. *Gazette,* Nov. 1–8, 1725; *Evening-Post,* Nov. 27, 1738 (advertisements following on Dec. 11, 1738, and Mar. 5, 1739, similar but not exact, may or may not be the same man); *Gazette,* Mar. 18–25, 1734; Sept 25–Oct. 2, 1732; Nov. 6, 1750; June 5, 1750; July 13, 1742; Nov. 3, 1741. For others recommended for the country see *N.E. Journal,* Aug. 11 1730; May 5, 1735; Nov. 6, 1739; Apr. 1740; Apr. 14, 1701; *Gazette,* Oct. 23–30, 1721; June 18–25, 1739; Nov. 3, 1741; Mar. 16, 1742; Sept. 25, 1744; July 4, 1749; *Evening-Post,* Sept. 8, 1735; May 1, 1738; Sept. 10, 1739; July 26, 1742; Apr. 22, 1745. Women recommended for the country can be seen in *N.E. Journal,* May 1, 1732; Nov. 27, 1732; Jan. 8, 1733; *Gazette,* Jan. 21–28, 1740; Evening-Post, Mar. 15, 1736; Oct. 24, 1737; Apr. 3, 1738; June 28, 1742; July 26, 1742; Mar. 4, 1745; Jan. 18, 1748. For a Negro farmer wanted, see *ibid.,* Aug. 5, 1743.
35. MSS. Diary of Ebenezer Parkman, Aug. 27, 1728.
36. Aug. 3–10, 1741.
37. *Evening-Post,* Dec. 15, 1735; Oct. 1, 1739; *Gazette,* Nov. 27, 1750; Nov. 22–29, 1736; Jan. 3–10, 1737; Dec. 9, 1746; *Evening-Post,* June 13, 1737; *Gazette,* Feb. 21, 1749; Apr. 11, 1749. For other Negroes trained to farming see *News-Letter,* July 7–14, 1707; *N.E. Journal,* May 14, 1733; Feb. 27, 1739; *Gazette,* Apr. 14, 1737; July 4–11, 1737 (A man and wife); Dec. 22, 1741; Mar. 24, 1747; Mar. 31, 1747; Apr. 28, 1747; May 3, 1748 Nov. 15, 1748; *Evening-Post,* Sept. 5, 1743; July 30, 1744; Aug. 13, 1744; July 28, 1746; Oct 13, 1746; Sept. 7, 1747; Feb. 15, 1748; July 10, 1749; *Post-Boy,* Mar. 31, 1746; June 19, 1749. Occasionally runaway slaves were listed as understanding farming. For examples see *Evening-Post,* June 26, 1749; Courant, June 8–15, 1724.
38. For Indians see M.H.S., 5 *Colls.,* VIII, 487–488 (1688); *Gazette,* Mar. 4–11 1722/3; July 27–Aug. 3, 1724; Nov. 15, 1748; Aug. 22, 1749; Dec. 12, 1749; *N.E. Journal,* Mar. 3, 1729; July 15, 1740; *Evening-Post,* May 17, 1742; *News-Letter,* Oct. 20–27, 1732; *Winthrop Papers,* IV, 139 (1639)
39. For the Negro woman see *N.E. Journal,* Feb. 20, 1739; for the white woman, *Evening-Post,* Mar. 23, 1747. Thirty-two Negro women, skills enumerated, were offered for sale between 1720 and 1750 in the *Gazette, Evening-Post, N.E. Journal, News-Letter,* and *Post-Boy.* In

addition, there were 112 Negro women, who were specified as household servants, offered for sale between 1711 and 1750 in the *Gazette, Post-Boy, Courant, Evening-Post, N.E. Journal,* and in the *News-Letter* to 1730. Between 1731 and 1750 the latter paper offered over two hundred slaves for sale. For skilled white servant women see MSS. Winthrop Papers W.3.132 (July 24, 1653); MSS. Suffolk Sessions, II, 14, 1713; *News-Letter,* Aug. 13–20, 1730; June 18–25 1716 (several); Feb. 19, 1739; Dec. 7, 1741; Mar. 8, 1742; May 17, 1742; Sept. 27, 1742; May 14, 1750; *Post-Boy,* Sept 18, 1749 (several); *N.E. Journal,* Mar. 29, 1731; Feb. 6, 1739; July 30, 1730; *Gazette,* Dec. 15–22, 1729; May 2–9, 1720; Sept. 26, 1749; Mar. 2, 1742; July 25, 1749; June 30–July 7, 1735; *Courant,* Dec. 17–24, 1722. For white female servants, skills not enumerated except as household see *Evening-Post,* Dec. 1, 1746; Dec. 22, 1746; Oct. 15, 1750; *Gazette,* Dec. 6–13, 1736; May 2–9, 1737; Nov 12, 1745; Aug. 30, 1748. It would, of course, be reasonable to assume that any woman, offered for sale, was for household purposes.

40. Thirty-seven Negroes were so advertised in the *Courant, N.E. Journal, Evening-Post, Gazette,* and *Post-Boy* between 1724 and 1750.

41. See the *Gazette,* Feb. 27, 1750; *N.E. Journal,* Dec. 10, 1733, Aug. 5, 1740; *Evening-Post,* Oct. 25, 1742, Jan. 10, 1743; Nov. 23, 1747; May 17, 1748; Dec. 12, 1748; *Weekly Rehearsal,* Apr. 17, 1732.

42. *Gazette,* Apr. 9–16, 1739; Dec. 1, 1747; Dec. 20, 1748; Dec. 12, 1749; Nov 6, 1750; Evening-Post, May 17, 1736; Dec. 5, 1737; Feb. 20, 1749; Post-Boy, Nov. 25, 1745.

43. For those and other general services see *Boston Records,* VIII, 225 (1728); XIV, 174; Pulsifer, *Laws,* 33 (1639/40); 255 (1682); *Winthrop Papers,* V, 284–285 (1648); M.H.S., 5 *Colls.,* V, 191 (1685); *Sibley's Harvard Graduates,* I, 597–598 (1697); IV, 626, 1719; MSS. Bristol Sessions, III, 300 (1737); *Post-Boy,* Mar. 5, 1750; *Evening-Post,* Oct. 25, 1742; Aug. 22, 1743; Feb. 9, 1741; Apr. 28, 1740; *Gazette,* July 29–Aug. 5, 1734; June 20–27 1737; Dec. 25, 1738–Jan. 1, 1739; Jan. 8–15, 1739; May 14–21, 1739; Feb. 1, 1743; Mar. 18, 1746; July 18, 1749; Oct. 23, 1750.

44. *Gazette,* May 1–8, 1738; Sent. 18–25, 1738. For another who could shave end "buckle wigs" see *ibid.,* June 13–20, 1720. For other white, male, household servants see *Winthrop's Journal,* II, 257–258 (1645); Hutchinson, *History . . . ,* I, 55 (1637); *Winthrop Papers,* III, 131–133 (1633); IV, 129–130 (1639); *Suffolk Deeds,* II, 51 (1654); XI, 1 (1677); XIII, 311–312 (1685); XIV, 202 (1684); 286–287 (1696/7); M.H S., 5 *Colls.,* V, 191 (1685); MSS. Hampshire County Court, I, 4–5 (1678); MSS. Suffolk Sessions, III, 304 (1724, the only gentleman's "gentleman" I found); *Evening-Post,* Aug. 22, 1743.

45. *Ibid.,* Nov. 26, 1745; Apr. 24–May 1, 1738; *N.E. Journal,* July 15, 1740.

46. *Plym. Recs.,* II, 67–68,
47. "Diary of Lawrence Hammond," in M.H.S., 2 *Proc.,* VII, 146 (1688).
48. MSS. "Clty of Boston . . . 1695 . . . Indentures," n.p., 2nd, 3rd, 4th, 5th, 8th (1679); 6th (1678); 13th and 16th (1680); 17th (1682); MSS. Boston Indentures, I, 3, 4, 5, 6 (1740); 11, 14, 15, 16, 18, 19, 20, 21 (1741); ff. Occasionally girls were apprenticed to "trades." For example, Mary Camden was apprenticed for seven years to Robert Patteshall of Boston, leather maker, to learn the trade or "mystery" of making gloves. MSS. Suffolk Sessions, II, 175 (1717). Others were apprenticed to become "Spinsters" or spinners. MSS. Boston Indentures, I, *passim.*
49. *Evening-Post,* Dec. 5, 1737; *N.E. Journal,* Jan. 1, 1728; *Gazette,* June 24–July 1, 1734; May 24–31, 1736. Alongside these young men entering on their "careers," it is impossible not to place this pathetic advertisement from the *Evening-Post,* Oct. 24, 1748, "A Negro fellow pretty well advanced in years but capable of doing service in a family . . . to be given away."
50. That is not to imply, however, that there was no division of labor in the period before 1641. The Governor and Company of Masschusetts Bay employed artisans to ply their trades and to train others to the same trades. Shipwrights, wheelwrights, coopers, cleavers of timber, and a man skilled in salt making and "well seene in mynes & mineralls . . . fortyfica[ti]ons . . . [and] well able to surveigh and sett forth lands," were among those sent over. Even a "chirurgion" was sent to keep the health and train up boys in his proression. See *Mass. Recs.,* I, 386–398. Quote from 391. In the same period, besides farming, private servants acted as messengers, carpenters, bricklayers, fishermen, sawyers, butchers, joiners, seamen, clerks, nailors, tailors, thatchers, hunters, carriage makers, and household servants. See *Winthrop Papers,* III, 131–133, 143–144, 222–223; IV, 27–29, 43, 129–130, 272–273; *Plym. Recs.,* I, 7, 16, 24, 37, 64, 110, 129–130; Hutchinson, *History,* I, 55; *Assistants,* II, 27, 88; *Mass. Recs.,* I, 137; Lechford, *Note-Book,* 210, 345349.
51. There is no single, up to date, economic history of New England in the Colonial period. I have used Willism B. Weeden, *Economic and Social History of New England 1620–1789* (Boston, 1890), I–II, *passim.* For maritime activities, see Samuel Eliot Morison, *The Maritime History of Massachusetts 1783–1860* (Boston, 1921), chapter I, *passim.*; Raymond McFarland, *A History of the New England Fisheries with maps* (University of Pennsylvania, 1911), particularly chapters IV and V; and for seventeenth-century data see George Francis Dow, "Shipping and Trade in Early New England," M.H.S., 6 *Proc.,* IV, 185–201. For shipbuilding and other trades see J. Leader Bishop, *A History of American Manufactures from 1608–1860 . . .* (Philadelpnia, 1864), I, passim., but particularly chapter III; and Victor S. Clark, *History of Manufactures in the United States*

(New York, 1929), I, chapters I–IX. For a general interpretation of economic life in colonial towns see Carl Bridenbaugh, *Cities* . . . , chapters II, VI, and X.

52. W.T. Baxter, *The House of Hancock: Business in Boston 1724–1775* (Cambridge, 1945), 294–295.

53. Morison, The Maritime History of *Massachusetts* . . . , 18.

54. Bishop, *American Manufactures* . . . , I, 46–47.

55. *Ibid.,* 48. The man cited was himself a shipbuilder.

56. See in that order MSS. Boston Indentures, I, 60 (1743); *Gazette,* Sept. 26, 1749 (three cases) *Evening-Post,* Jan. 8, 1739; MSS. Boston Indentures, I, 142 (1748); MSS. Suffolk Sessions, IV, 204–205 (1729); MSS. Boston Indentures, I, 74 (1744). For Negroes see footnote 66, below.

57. For apprentices to become mariners, or to learn navigation, see appendix A in Towner, "A Good Master Well Served . . . " (Ph.D. diss., Northwestern University, 1954). Some poor children were bound to the sea by the Boston Overseers, for example, MSS. Boston Indentures, I, 68 (1744).

58. Mather, *Magnalia* . . . , VI, 75 (1695); *Gazette,* May 10–17 1731, Aug. 14, 1750; *Suffolk County Court,* II, 635 (1675), 1092–1093 (1679); American Antiquarian Society, New Series, *Proc.,* VI, 191–195 (ca. 1700); MSS. Diary of Joseph Cotton, 1726–1756, 202–203 (ca. 1730). The demand for Negroes as sailors is illustrated in the case of John Mico's slave in 1703. Mico had been offered sixty-five to seventy shilllngs a month for his Negro's services aboard other ships, but he chose Samuel White's ship at fifty-five shillings. "I intreat [your] p[ar]ticular care of him, be he in health or sickness and that upon all accot you restraine, and keep him, wth in bounds as much as if he were your owne, I have brot him up from a Child and have a vallue for him. . . . " The wages were to be paid in gunpowder from London. MSS. Mass. Archives, IX, 151. Several servants were advertised as seamen in *N.E. Journal,* Jan. 18, 1731; July 14, 1735 (fit for sea); *Evening-Post,* May 22, 1738 (fit for coasting); Sept. 21, 1741 (willing to go to sea); Oct. 31, 1743; Jan. 4, 1748; *Gazette,* Feb. 13–20, 1737 (used to sea); Jan. 11, 1743 (three fit for sea); Oct. 17, 1749.

59. MSS. Mass. Archives, IX, 149–150.

60. Weeden, *New England* . . . , I, 430 ff. For Indians in particular, see *Acts and Resolves,* II, 364.

61. *Essex County Court,* I, 231 (1651). For another engaged in fishing, *Essex Probate,* III, 9–10 (1675).

62. In that order *Boston Records,* XVII, 5 (1742/3); VIII 173–175 (1723); MSS. Hampshire County Court, I, 12 (1678); *News-Letter,* Oct. 24–31, 1734; *Courant,* Jan. 7–14 1723; MSS. Boston Indentures, I, 34 (1742); Cotton Mather's "Diary," M.H.S., 7 *Colls.,* VIII, 53 (1711), and MSS. Suffolk Sessions, II, 5 (1712). For other representative

trades employing servants see MSS. Boston Indentures, I, *passim.* (shoemakers, cabinet makers, curriers, bricklayers, blockmakers, potters, joiners, turners, founders, shop keepers); MSS. Suffolk Sessions, II, 250 (1719, tailor); 88 (1715, victualer); III, 87 (1721, chair msker); MSS. Suffolk County Court, I, 140 (1682, taverner); *Essex County Court,* I, 111 (1647, locksmith); MSS. Middlesex County Court, III, 144 (1676, miller); *Essex County Court,* VIII, 249–50 (1682, felt and castor maker); *Gazette,* June 7, 1748 (nail maker); MSS. Suffolk Sessions, I, 244–5 (1712, two coopers). Clifford K. Shipton found servants offered for sale skilled in forty-one major trades. "Immigration to New Enaland, 1680–1740," *Jour. Pol. Econ.,* XLIV (April, 1936), 227.

63. MSS. Joshua Winslow Copy Book of Letters, Aug. 26, 1740; *Courant,* Nov. 12–19, 1722; *Gazette,* Dec. 26, 1720–Jan. 2, 1721.

64. See Melville J. Herskovits, *The Myth of the Negro Past* (New York, 1941), chapter III; John Hope Franklin, *From Slavery to Freedon, A History of American Negroes* (New York, 1947), chanters I–III. Leonard Price Stavisky, "Origins of Negro Craftsmanship in Colonial America," *The Journal of Negro History,* XXXII (Oct., 1947), 417–429, and by the same author, "Negro Craftmanship in Early America," *American Historical Review,* LIV (Jan., 1949), 315–325; Lorenzo Johnston Greene, "The New England Negro in Newspaper Advertisements," *The Journal of Negro History,* XXIX (Apr., 1944), 125–147, and *The Negro in Colonial New England . . . ,* 111–123.

65. Greene, *The Negro in Colonial New England . . . ,* 112. The Hat Act of 1732 forbade using Negroes in hat making, too. See *News-Letter,* Aug. 3–10, 1732 where the act was publicized.

66. See appendix M in Towner, "A Good Master Well Served . . . " (Ph.D. diss., Northwestern University, 1954).

67. James Printer, Indian, who helped Greene print Eliot's Bible, has already been mentioned above, chapter IV. He was important to Eliot, for he was the only one who could "compare the Sheets and correct the Prese with Understanding." Quoted in Isaiah Thomas, "The History of Printing in America . . . ," i, 95. In 1709, Greene printed an Indian psalter in Indian and English. It read, "by B. Greene and J. Printer." *Ibid.,* 98. For other skilled Indians see Pulsifer *Acts of the Commissioners of the United Colonies . . . ,* II, 204 (1660, carpenter); *N.E. Journal,* Nov. 26, 1733 (cooper); MSS. Mass. Archives, IX, 169 (1713, mason).

68. Isaiah Thomes, "The History of Printing in America . . . ," i, 99–104. Either this Negro or one of his sons did the woodcut reproduced in chapter VIII. Information received from Dr. Clifford K. Shipton. For his sons see C.S.M. *Pubs.,* XXV, 253–4 (1743).

69. Isaiah Thomas, "The History of Printing in America . . . ," i, 130 n.

70. Quote from *Post-Boy,* June 3, 1745. For others see *ibid.,* May 4, 1741; Jan. 26, 1747; *Evening-Post,* Aug. 15, 1743; June 10, 1745; June 2, 1746.

71. See Carl Bridenbaugh, *The Colonial Craftsman* (New York, 1950), particularly chapter V. See also the excellent illustrations of craftsmen at work throughout the book. Even in the trades such as shipbuilding, which required large numbers of workers, the work was split up among the different crafts, and each craftsman employed, housed, and fed his own servants. Jeremy Belknap, writing of slaves in the provincial period said, in 1795, "Excepting such tradesmen as rope-makers, anchor-smiths, and ship-carpenters, who employ a great many hands, scarcely any one family had more than two...." M.H.S., I *Colls.,* IV, 199,

72. *Suffolk County Court,* II, 903 (1678).

73. *Ibid.,* 1029–1030 (1680). For another servant who could keep accounts see *Courant,* Jan. 21–28, 1723.

74. *Suffolk County Court,* 1094 (1680); 740–741 (1676/7).

75. *Ibid.,* I, 104–105 (1667).

76. *Ibid.,* II, 1125–1126 (1678).

77. *Winthrop Papers,* IV, 64 (1638).

6. The Servant's Leisure Time

Despite the master's need to exact the maximum labor from his servants with the minimum outlay of goods in return, an attitude reinforced by the necessities of a frontier economy and the religious proscriptions against idleness, there were limitations—religious, social, and practical—to the extent which the servant's time could be exploited. Sleeping, eating, and other physical requirements placed obvious restrictions on the working day. Religious observance, enforced by society, made the Sabbath a day of rest if not of leisure. Obligations on the master to provide time for religious and secular education, whether prescribed by law, indenture, or a religious leader, reduced the working week. Fast, thanksgiving, and training days provided occasional relief from drudgery. Moreover, within the course of a normal week, only a rare master was able to account for every waking moment of his man. Thus the average serving man or wench counted on a few hours in the week for his own pleasure, while a crafty one carried on a surreptitious personal life even if at the risk of discovery and punishment.

In the seventeenth century in particular, when church attendance was seriously enforced, and when laws on the statute books required masters to catechize their children and servants at least once a week, we may be sure that servants spent part of their non-working time in religious activity.[1] As early as 1628/29 the Reverend Ministers Higginson, Bright, and. Skelton were sent by the New England Company to preach to and instruct the Company's servants, the "salvages," and the children of both.[2] Despite the complaint of John Winthrop in 1646 about some of the "young men who came over servants, and never had any show of religion in them . . . ," there is good evidence that the early servants took their religion seriously.[3]

The records of the first church in Roxbury, for example, show a number of white servants who became full members. Among them were Mary Hammond and Thomas Woodford, who joined some six months after their arrival in 1632,[4] and Elizabeth Ballard who joined soon after she came in 1633, and then married Robert Sever of the same church "where she led a godly conversation."[5] Another was Thomas Hills, who joined in 1633, and "lived among us in good esteeme & Godly [behavior]. . . . " Dying late in 1634, he was remembered as living in Mr. Eliot's family where he had been "a very faithfull & prudent servant, & a good christian. . . . "[6] Finally, we must note one who took his religion seriously enough to move to Rhode Island having been excommunicated for the heresy of "familisme."[7]

Occasional references in sermons, or elsewhere, further indicate that willing or no, servants attended church, as well as being members. The book, *A Good Master Well Served* . . . , for example, was originally "uttered" to its author's congregation, where he saw "many Hundreds of persons, which have been *Stated* in both of these two *Orders,* by the God of *Order.*"[8] " Three decades later, in 1740, the Great Awakening swept one servant lad to his death, if not to his salvation, as he was crushed in a meeting house where George Whitefield was preaching.[9]

Negroes and Indians, more easily identified in the records, were regular churchgoers too.[10] As early as 1641, a Negro woman was baptized and admitted to church membership.[11] Indeed, the *Body of Liberties* of that year stated that "these shall have all the liberties and Christian usages whIch the law of god estabiished in Israell concerning such persons doeth morally require."[12] In fact, the scarcity of Negroes rather than any reluctance to baptize them probably accounts for the few baptisms before 1700.[13] In the eighteenth century, as Negroes became more numerous, baptism was a regular thing. This was true even without legislation declaring the sacrament would make no difference in a slave's earthly status. This was true too before the notification by the King's Attorney and Solicitor General in 1730 that "Baptism doth not bestow Freedom on him, nor make any alteration in his temporal Condition in these Kingdoms."[14]

At least one Negro took his polity so seriously that he left the church where his master preached and attended the other Framingham house of worship. The point at issue was his master's failure to have ruling elders.[15] Enough colored persons, Indian and Negro, attended church to make segregation a problem. Separate pews, sometimes lofts, were maintained for them in many churches. A "Comical Accident" reported in *The Boston Weekly Post-Boy* in 1740, illustrates Negro attendance and segregation in church.

> as it is a general Rule for the Gentry to have Stoves brot them
> when at Meeting, to warm their Feet during the cold. Season,
> a Negro carried a Stove to her Mistress, who telling her she did

not want it, the Negro thinking to appear something like a Person of Quality, took the Stove to her self, and lending it to others of the Black Tribe in the same Seat, hapned [*sic*] among them to overset it, so that some of the Coals fell upon the Floor, and some got thro' one of the Cracks, which put the Sable Ladies into great Consternation, not knowing what the Consequences might be; but one of them having a quicker thought than her Companions, p__ss'd down the crack, and the others following the Example, put out the Fire effectually, so that no further Damage ensu'd.[16]

Formal churchgoing was only one aspect of religion to which the servants were exposed. Regular churchgoers or not, servants were supposed to participate in some religious worship in the family, during the seventeenth and eighteenth centuries, if only to study of the catechism.[17] Some of the Pequot Indians taken into the homes of the English as servants in the early years of settlement "attained to some acquaintance with the principles of religion, and seem to have been affected with what they had been taught. . . . "[18] That which was expected of masters in this way is perhaps better illustrated in a letter from Edward Howes to John Winthrop, Jr., in 1633, than in any law. Howes was sending four wolf dogs with

an Irish boy to tend them, for the doggs my mr hath writt sufficiently, but for the boye thus much. You heue bin in Ireland, knowe partlie the Irish condition. this ia a verie tractable fellowe, and yet of a hardie and stout corage; I am perswaded he is very honest especially he makes a great conscience of his promise, and vowe. I could wish . . . you would take him to be your seruant, although he be bound to your father for fiue yeare; At his first comminge ouer he would not goe to church; nor come to prayers; but first we gatt him vp to prayers and then on the lords day to catachise, and afterwards very willingly he hath bin at church 4 or 5 tymes; he as yet makes conscience of fridayes fast from flesh; and doth not loue to heare the Romish rel[igion] spoken against, but I hope with gods grace he will become a good convert.

• •

As for his fittnesse to be a member of your church; its well if the Lord worke it in 3 or 4 yeare, yet he can doe it sooner if he please; The fellow can reede and write reasonable well which is somewhat rare for one of his condition. . . . [19]

And this was to a layman.

Some servants were so smitten with religion, or the possibilities of living by their wits, that they set up as preachers after their period of servitude was over. Eleazer Kingsberry, for one, after having been freed of his apprenticeship to a tailor in Wrentham, because he was so "Vicious a Servant, that his Master could do no good with him," married, became a thief, and went westward, from where he wrote letters full of curses. In 1699, he appeared in Boston as a preacher but was arrested as a vagabond. Leaving again, he went to Cape May, where it was reported the people were very pleased with him.[20] Another about the same time, after learning the trade of a tanner, stole a pair of breeches and left hurriedly to earn his living preaching on Staten Island. Detected reading from a printed Scotch sermon while filling a sick minister's pulpit, he was allowed to depart "with Liberty to go as far as a New Pair of *Shooes* would carry him."[21] Yet a third, Dick Swayn, servant to a ship captain's widow, was given his time, for "she would not be troubled with so Thievish, Lying and Wicked a Villain." He left afterwards for Virginia having been detected in villainies "enough to fill a Volume." Around 1698, he worked his way back to Boston, preaching here and there, and developing a large following. In Boston he was successful leading prayers in private houses until his former mistress came to hear him. Her paraphrased remark on that occasion is sufficiently devastating to reproduce, even at the risk of destroying the thesis that some servants were religious, or that masters took care to teach them:

> the Gentlewoman could scarce believe her Eyes; and finding the Vagrant [could] not give her any Intelligent Account how he became a *Christian,* it was yet more Unintelligible to her how he became a Minister.[22]

Needless to say, she deprived the "populace of so *Charming* a *Preacher.* . . . " He left his mark on Boston, however, for some loose shillings left carelessly about stuck to his fingers as he departed.[23]

Even if all servants were not seriously religious, the Sabbath, thanksgiving, and fast days (which were not infrequent) placed leisure time in their hands, not, it is true, to use as they wished, but at least as a welcome relief from the drudgery of ordinary existence. Throughout the seventeenth and early eighteenth centuries, they were considered holy days, and the colonial governments sought, with partial success, to limit, activities to non-worldly pursuits.

That the attempt to limit holy-day activities was not entirely successful is attested to by the various enactments against such profanation, and the arrests occasioned by violations of sabbatarian regulations. The General Court of Massachusetts found in 1653 that second-generation Puritans were not as amenable to restriction as early migrants. It noted that information had been given concerning misdemeanors occurring on the Lord's day, and that children had been seen playing in the Streets. Moreover, these abuses were augmented "by Youths, Mayds, and other persons, both strangers and others, uncivilly walking in the streets and fields, travailing from town to town, going on Shipboard, frequenting common houses, and other places to drink [and] sport. . . . "[24] Such laws lend some credence to the slanderous invectives of Edward Ward that lecture days were called by some among the Puritans, "Whore Fair," because of the wanton behavior of some of the young people after devotions were over. They had, he continued, "recourse to the *Ordinaries,* where they plentifully wash away the remembrance of their Old Sins. . . . " And then they committed new ones for it was "*Uptails-all* and the Devils as busie under the Petticoat, as a *Juggler* at a *Fair,* or a *Whore at a Carnival.*"[25]

The eighteenth century saw no lessening of the problem as "Loose vain Persons negros &c . . . ," continued to profane the Lord's day, according to information given the Boston selectmen in 1732.[26] In the following decade it was frequently determined to set up guards at Boston Neck to keep such persons, including servants specifically, from walking to and from neighboring towns, bringing fruit and other commodities.[27] Thus, though they only infrequently worked on holy days, it is equally apparent that they frequently played.

Book learning as well as religion took some time away from the master and gave it to the servant. We have already met the seventeenth-century requirement of the Puritans that children and servants be taught so much as to be able "perfectly to read the english tongue . . . ,"[28] and the eighteenth century's watered-down version that no one was to be so barbarous as not to teach children the alphabet.[29] Perhaps these laws were only sporadically enforced; even so, there was opportunity to learn to read if the master could teach him and if the master would teach him.

Formal schooling, while generally available on an elementary level, was an advantage to few servants as servants.[30] Apprentices, for example, if they were to have institutional training, had it before the age of twelve to fourteen when they ordinarily went into service. Some servants, however, had formal schooling specified in their contracts, and others no doubt found their way through the good offices of generous masters, or vigilant selectmen.[31] Certainly the compulsory school law of 1647 recognized the possibility that masters might send their servants rather than teaching them at home,[32] and in the eighteenth century, at least one town, Braintree, recognized the same possibility when it provided that masters of servants going to school should deliver three feet of cord wood.[33]

Whether trained at home, at a grammar school, dame school, or in the home of the local minister, many servants were given a rudimentary education in reading, fewer in writing, and still fewer in ciphering. Most apprentices were to be taught reading and writing, and the children of the poor were universally required to be so educated; girls to read and write, boys the three Rs.[34] Some non-apprentices had educational provisions in their contracts,[35] while in the eighteenth century even a few Negroes were instructed at home or attended charity schools in Boston established for their race by Cotton Mather and others.[36]

With a rudimentary knowledge of reading, the industrious and bookishly inclined few could complete their education themselves if they lived where books were available, even if they could not become Harvard graduates. But most of them, it must be assumed, had other demands on their time and their interests, and proceeded to the grave nearly as unlettered as they had entered the world.[37]

Among the socially acceptable and sometimes required breaks in the workday routine, military training probably provided the most satisfactory opportunity for pleasure and relaxation. Both Massachusetts Bay and Plymouth Colony, in recognition of the essentially frontier nature of the early settlements, by the 1630s required nearly all males to have arms for themselves and servants.[38] Moreover, regular days were set aside when the males would foregather on the village common to shoot at the mark, and drill.[39] Except in special cases of undue hardship, or unusual importance of the master, such as his being a magistrate, all able servants were expected to participate.[40] Not fully, it is true, for in the seventeenth century they could not vote in the election of inferior officers of the train bands as could non-servants, but certainly fully enough to escape the surveillance of their masters for a time.[41]

Despite the fact that training days were a grim reminder of the ever present fear of hostile Indian or French forces, these interruptions in the normal working year, with their attendant crowds (in May, 1639, over a thousand participated in Boston), took on the atmosphere of a holiday.[42] The servant, as well as the free man, before the day was over, undoubtedly enjoyed himself with drink, planned escapades with his fellow servants, compared notes on masters' treatment, and possibly took advantage of the cover afforded by nightfall to carry on a casual courtship beneath the trees at the bottom of the common. Such at least is the impression given by the Plymouth Church in 1692, which reported some success after exhorting its young people to behave in a more Christian manner. At a meeting of the church it was observed, "that many were much affected at what was spoken," and the minister went on to point out that the young people did not "spend that training-day evening as formerly too many of them used to doe."[43] If Plymouth had an improvement in its training day morals, Boston did not, however, for Cotton Mather noted in 1696 that training days had become little more than drinking days and both Peter Thatcher and William Williams complained of excessive training-day drinking in election sermons in 1711 and 1719 respectively.[44]

Except for the days set aside by the society for rest, and the occasional training day, the servant had to steal time to lead a personal life. Either he stole it from his master when he was supposed to be working, or he stole it from himself when he was supposed to be sleeping. The only possible exception to this would be found in the case of that rare servant whose master permitted time off during the day or week for recreation. If there were such masters, no record remains of them. Indeed, a stolen hour here and there seems to have been the accepted pattern of servant life.

The varied nature of the work which a servant did made this surreptitious life possible. He was a house man, or "'prentice," or farm laborer, who worked at many things and variously performed as messenger, shopper, baby sitter, or jack-of-all-trades. In the presence of his master he probably worked diligently, or gave the appearance of doing so, but when sent on an errand, or left unsupervised, part of the time was his.

Moreover, some of the work the servant did was of a social nature. The raising of buildings is a case in point, and the vote of a Braintree church in 1731 gives a good indication of the relaxation attending such a project. Refreshments included "Bred Cheap Sugar Rum Sider and Bear [sic] &c. for the Raising of said Meeting House.... "[45] Maidservants probably attended quilting bees, and certainly both sexes were present at cornhusking. One servant committed fornication with her male companion on the way home from such a party in 1665,[46] and Edward Ward raised considerable smoke where there was doubtless some fire in his report on this activity. "Husking of Indian-Corn," he wrote,

> is as good sport for the Amorous Wag-tailes in *New England,*
> as Maying amongst us is for our forward Youths and Wenches.
> For 'tis observed, there are more *Bastards* got in that Season,
> than in all the Year beside; which Occasions some of the
> looser Saints to call it *Rutting Time.*[47]

Jacob Bailey, eighteenth-century New England versifier, recorded a cornhusking in Kingston, New Hampshire, which probably differed little from those in other parts of New England. Gayety and amour seemed to be the order of the day as kissing and liquor "set the virgins on flame. . . . " After a heavy supper;

> The chairs in wild order flew quite round the room;
> Some threatened with firebrands, some branished [sic] a broom,
> While others, resolved to increase the uproar,
> Lay tussling the girls in wide heaps on the floor.[48]

And there was always the night, whose uses John Tulley, almanac printer, well understood, for in Boston in 1688 he published his prognostication for February:

> The Nights are still cold and long, which May cause great Conjunction betwixt the Male and Female Planets of our sublunary Orb, the effects wherof may be seen about nine months after. . . . [49]

The prevalence of nocturnal activity among the servants suggests that Poor Richard's "Early to bed and early to rise . . . ," was to them less a reflection of a prevailing cultural attitude then an exhortation to reform. Indeed, the nighttime perambulations of the servant population were a constant problem for the master. Despite the almost universal prohibition in indentures against absenting oneself from one's master without leave, "night walking" was a persistent complaint leveled at the servants in the courts.[50] Indeed, both local and colony governments attempted to restrict these nocturnal habits,[51] but the advertisements of servants for sale who were recommended as not being night walkers indicate that such laws were without great success.[52]

The laws failed, because there were two attractions for the erring servant which often called him out of the immediate supervision of his master—the bed and the bottle—two forms of entertainment which even in the seventeenth century heyday of the Puritans were generally available. Transgression in the direction of the bed, or its equivalent, was more often brought to the attention of the courts for the simple reason that it was possible to have one drink and not get drunk, but one amorous bout could bring tangible results. Marriage was generally open only to those who were servants for life; but courting and illicit lovemaking were there for those with the courage, or lack of restraint (and many were the bastards to prove the point). For those without finesse or opportunity, rape, bestiality, and homosexuality gave release for unnaturally pent-up desire.[53]

Except in rare cases, temporary servants did not enter their servitude in a married state,[54] nor did they consummate marriage while bound. In the first place, apprentices, at least, were specifically prohibited marriage in their contracts. Moreover, unless both were bound to the same master, or had the unusual privilege of living from under their master's roof, they could have no home together. Children of such a union would have been the responsibility of the master until the servant or servants were free. The obstacles were almost universally insurmountable.[55] This was particularly true since the master's consent would be required. In Boston, for example, one Mathew Griffen filed his marriage intention in 1749, but his master forbade the match.[56]

Marriage of a servant girl to a free man was not as difficult to achieve as that of a serving man. However, marriage in this case meant the end of servitude for the wench in question. In the seventeenth century with the age of consent at sixteen, girls were sometimes less securely bound than in the eighteenth,[57] and it was sometimes specifically stated in their contracts that they were bound until a certain age or until married. In Plymouth, one Mary Moorecock bound herself for nine years until 1648, but if she wished to marry before that time, two indifferent men were to decide what she owed her master for raising her.[58] The daughters of Francis Billington were put out servants by the town until the age of twenty, *or* until married.[59] Masters in such cases had considerable control, however, for offer of marriage to a maid without consent of parent or master was prohibited on penalty of fine or punishment in Plymouth by 1638 and Massachusetts by 1647.[60] Even before this statutory provision such action was punishable, for in 1639 Thomas Sams spent an hour in the stocks after speaking of marriage to a servant without her master's consent.[61]

While marriage was thus prohibited among temporary servants, slaves were regularly allowed to marry. Most frequent were the marriages between Negro slaves, such marriages occurring as early as 1659 and regularly thereafter.[62] One fancy marriage between Negroes was well publicized in *The New-England Courant*. The master, a lawyer, had the happy couple taken to the ceremony in a sleigh. At the wedding he acted as father of the bride, and afterwards provided a dinner at which persons of "distinction" were present.[63] Marriage between servants of different masters involved some difficulty, but such could be resolved by agreement between the masters, by purchase of the mate, or by consent of the courts.[64]

In the eighteenth century, numerous marriages between persons of mixed status or race occurred, as well as between persons of the same status or race. Free Negroes married slaves,[65] Indians and Negroes married when one or the other was a servant,[66] and Indian servants married each other.[67] One Indian ex-serving woman settled down to married life with a Negro servant after carousing for a year. At the master's request, she bound herself during his lifetime.[68] Another Indian woman, to her regret, married a Negro slave, purchased his freedom, and was subsequently deserted.[69]

Whether restrained from marriage by law, indenture, master's wish, or personal disinclination, the servant found ample opportunity for "dalliance" with those of the opposite sex, and quite often with those of different status or race. A little of their pocket money, whether earned or stolen, went for the entertainment of the fair sex, as in the case of one enterprising young man who stole money from his master for cakes and wine for his lady friend.[70] Others came more directly to the point, such as the youth caught up for "lascivious carriages" towards his master's serving wenches,[71] or the even more indiscreet man of a Charlestown widow who was given twenty stripes for lascivious and wanton carriages toward "sundry women that brought grist to his mill. . . . "[72]

More than one servant promised or was promised marriage as an inducement to the loss of chastity, and some protested when the promise was not fulfilled. Jane Powell, serving maid, was hauled into court on a charge of fornication with David Ogillior, Irish servant, in 1655. The court recorded "shee saith shee was alured thervnto by him goeing for water one euening, hopeing to haue married him. . . . "[73] On the other hand, some, like Mary Mitchleson, bound to Thomas Gardner of Muddy River, apparently did not have to be promised anything in order to be gotten to bed. She first accused her master of being the father of her bastard, then decided it was someone else but held that Gardner had had too much familiarity with her.[74]

Familiarity like the above was made possible, in part, by the common practice of having one's servants living in. Numerous instances of sexual relations between members of the same household occurred. Two servants of Jonathan Wiman of Woburn admitted regular relations which took place after their master and dame were in bed.[75] Such relations cut across status lines as in the case of a Bristol servant who got his master's daughter pregnant, and the Milton master who was convicted of "uncivil carriages" toward his maid, "going to bed with her. . . . "[76] Apparently such cross fertilization was not always successful, for Elizabeth Dickerman got a new master after her old master offered "abuse to her body" and "sundry other vile and filthy carriages,"[77] while John Pecke's servant maid resisted Pecke's son's "vnchaste . . . attempting [of her] chastitie . . . many times for some yeares . . . . "[78]

Whether living in the same house or not, the servants showed a catholicity of taste in their choice of bed partners which denied the existence of sexually significant status or racial barriers. Negroes frequently cohabited without benefit of clergy, as Richard Dole's servant, Grace, who admitted fornication with another Negro and appeared in court four times on that charge in two years.[79] Negro and Indian servants found the same bed attractive as did couples of Indian ancestry.[80] More common than the latter, however, was temporary alliance between Negro and white, at least one of whom was a servant. While Negro women were often attracted by or susceptible to the wiles of white men, (as in the case of Bess, Negro servant to Captain Thomas Porter of Boston who admitted having two children by John Bernard of Boston, merchant),[81] white women seemed to be equally attracted to Negro men. For example, Ann Staples, servant of Samuel Eaton of Boston, slipped out of her master's house one night and crept into bed with Alexander, Negro servant of Simone Ramee, shopkeeper, of Boston.[82] Others like Stephen French's slave Marea, demonstrated indifference to race by sleeping with white and black alike, in this case, both servants of her master.[83] Indians both male and female also showed a fine tolerence by sleeping with whites of the opposite sex although fornication between black and white was more frequent.[84]

Whites, of course, cohabited freely. William Clark, for example, admitted in Cambridge that he had twice committed "misconduct" with Hannah Green, servant to Samuel Carter. The first time had been on the way home from cornhusking. The second was in her bed. Such boldness led to his downfall, for upon hearing a noise, he ran taking her petticoat and leaving his trousers by mistake.[85] Fornication between a servant and a free person was more frequently discovered, not to say more frequent in occurrence, than fornication between two servants. Occasionally servants were caught, however, as in the case of Nicholas Wallis, servant of a Mr. Long of Charlestown, and Jane Lindes, a maid of Lady Hopkins.[86] Many more were those who were of mixed status, perhaps because of the superior social prestige of a free man, or because it was easier to arrange a tryst when only one partner had to avoid a master. Take the case of the appropriately named Comfort Scott, Dedham servant, who welcomed a lover from Long Island to her arms. The New Yorker's status as a free man not only gave him access to Dedham, but to "comfort" as well.[87]

That so many servants found easy access to temporary "dalliance" may perhaps explain the remarkably few instances of rape committed by or upon servants. Two instances of rape of serving wenches occurred in so far as the existing records are concerned, one by her master and the other by her master's son.[88] Of eleven would-be rapists, three were whites and eight Negroes,[89] while of three successful rapes by servants two were whites.[90] One white and one Indian servant were convicted of abuse of a girl, and one serving maid suffered the indignity of a beating, of being forced to lie down, and of discovery of her "private parts."[91]

This remarkable restraint, as evidenced by the paucity of recorded rape, may be explained partly by the citizen reaction implied in the account of a would-be rapist published in *The Boston News-Letter*. To the westward of New London, the paper related:

> A very remarkable thing fell out . . . , A Negro Man met abroad an English Woman, which he accosted to lye with, stooping down, fearing none behind him, a Man observing his Design, took out his Knife, before the Negro was aware, cut off all his unruly parts smack and smooth, the Negro Jumpt up roaring and run for his Life; the Black new and Eunuch is alive and like to recover from his Wounds and doubtless cured from any such Wicked attempts.[92]

The persistence of illicit sexual relations (which were in no wise limited to the servant population), was accompanied by equally persistent opposition on legal, contractual, moral, and economic grounds. Such opposition tends to illustrate further the extent and significance of sexual relations as an outlet for the frustrating conditions of servitude as well as being the product of ordinary sexual drives.

Massachusetts Bay passed its first law against fornication in 1642, Plymouth Colony in 1636. Apparently the former law was ineffectual, for the General Court in 1665 exempted the crime from the limitation of a single punishment, finding that "shameful Sin much increasing amongst us, to the great dishonour of God, and our Profession of his Holy Name. . . . " In 1692 the law required a fine not exceeding five pounds or corporal punishment not exceeding ten stripes of both offenders. Fornication between whites and blacks was punished more severely, however, with the colored partner to be sold out of the province, whether man or woman, and with both partners to be whipped severely. If any children were born of mixed parentage, they were the responsibility of the white parent, who, if a woman, could be sold into service to pay costs of upbringing.[93]

In addition to the laws, which were regularly and severely enforced in the courts, contractual restraints were placed on the apprentice, if not on other temporary servants as well. Probably ineffective in individual cases, the indenture nevertheless prohibited illicit love making. Usually it had some such phrase as "Fornication in the house of his Master or elsewhere he shall not commit."[94]

Moral pressure was brought to bear upon the servant population in sermons, confessions of about-to-be-executed criminals, and in publications such as Cotton Mather's *A Good Master Well Served.* . . . Mather exhorted the servants to avoid wanton behavior, to renounce and forsake invisible masters, the world, the flesh, and the devil.[95] More pointedly, and less piously, he urged a group of Negroes to debar from their company for at least half a year any who committed fornication.[96]

Fornication of servants was opposed on economic grounds as well, for the resultant bastards occasioned considerable charge upon the masters before they could possibly be economically productive. Smallpox and other diseases, accidents and the high cost of living made such an investment risky.[97] Moreover the master was fundamentally responsible to the community that no charges should be added to the burden of the tax payers, as one Captain Pope learned to his sorrow. He not only had to pay forty shillings fine for his servant's bastardy, but was required to post a bond of forty pounds to save the town of Dartmouth "harmless" from any future charges arising in the care of the child.[98] Frequently, however, the master was able to pass on these charges to the servant responsible. Thus one William Cuthbert, a servant, having gotten his master's daughter pregnant, had to pay costs of the case, lying-in charges, and three shillings a week for the child's upkeep. His friends had to go bond for him a total of fifty pounds.[99] One luckless servant maid had to serve her master two years longer for his loss in caring for the bastard child.[100] Another child was to live with its mother's master until the age of twenty-one unless its father paid the costs, and the mother was to serve three years longer unless she paid six pounds.[101]

Similar economic grounds for opposing indiscriminate fornication applied to Negroes and Indians as well as whites. Despite Samuel Sewall's argument that Negro slaves were encouraged to commit fornication by their masters to avoid buying wives for them,[102] and the occasional suggestion of the breeding of slaves in Boston newspapers such as:

> A Certain Person in Town, hath a Negro *Wench of about* 19
> *or* 20 *Years of Age, who promises to be as good a Breeder, as
> any one can well desire, and to afford his Family a greater
> Stock than he cares for;* . . . [103]

It was not considered economical to encourage promiscuous breeding
among one's slaves any more than among one's indentured servants or
apprentices. The prospective slave-holder in Massachusetts was willing
to pay a premium for servants who were acclimated to the New World,
and even for those who had already had the smallpox.[104] Moreover,
frequent advertisements testified to the unwillingness of masters to
assume the risks in bringing up Negro children. Common were notices
such as "A Female Child, of an excellent Breed, to be given: Enquire of
the Printer."[105] Other advertisements told prospective owners that a
male child was to be given along with forty shillings, or a male child
of good servants in good health.[106] All told, some seventy-two children
of colored servile parentage were thus offered for disposal between the
years 1724 and 1750 via newspapers alone.[107]

Clearly the opposition to illicit love and the problem of bastardy
and unwanted children supplement the evidence which indicates how
frequently servents turned to sex for solace. Regularly denied access to
legitimate sexual expression, they turned to the illegitimate.
Undoubtedly sex played a quantitatively less important role in their
lives, than in the lives of free persons who could marry. Since servants
could not, their sexual expression took illegal form, and hence comes to
our attention. It may even have been a form of compensation.[108]

Of course, the servant did not spend all the leisure time he stole in
dalliance with maids; there were other modes of entertainment which
gave him relaxation and escape. Noteworthy among these were alcohol
and the places where it was dispensed—the tavern, ordinary, or place of
"Publick entertainment." It would have been bordering on the
miraculous indeed if the servant had not drunk, and at least exceedingly
remarkable, if the pressures under which he lived had not driven him on
occasion to excessive drink. Spirituous beverages were customary to the
early colonists who remembered and revered their consumption in old
England in preference to water, and although New England water was
good, small beer, cider and rum were preferred.[109] Moreover, the places
it was sold performed the function of the local club where gossip and
news were dispensed as freely as the liquors and foods. The serving man
found them as indispensable to his happiness as did the free man.

Places of "Publick entertainment," and homes which served as
retailers of liquor were common in Massachusetts and Plymouth

colonies. From early times they were subject to licensing and modest governmental control, and as soon as the importation and production of liquor became sufficient to permit excessive drink, the governments took action to prevent abuse. Drunkenness was, of course, considered a sin, because it reduced man to the level of the beast, thereby insulting God in whose image man was created. But dalliance in taverns was nearly as sinful, for it led to the waste of time, substance, and liquor.[110] Servants, in particular, not only wasted their masters' substance, but their masters' time as well. This could not be tolerated.

Massachusetts began the licensing of taverns in 1633, in an attempt to limit the number to one in each town, and three years later Plymouth Colony struck first at the selling of liquor to children and servants.[111] Massachusetts, in 1640, added a law prohibiting any play or game for anything of value, and added that dancing in taverns was illegal.[112] The "disorders" continued however, and six years later the Bay Colony banned games, shuffleboard, and bowling in and about houses of common entertainment, as they occasioned loss of precious time and the waste of wine and beer.[113] In 1658, the General Court of Massachusetts ordered, on penalty of forty shillings fine, ordinary keepers, taverners, victuallers and others, to discharge and hasten to their employments any "young people or persons whatsoever whether children, servants, apprentices, [or] schollers . . . ,"[114] wasting time there by night or day. Plymouth Colony, in 1663, strengthened her earlier laws banning the sale of liquors and wine to children and servants or any that were not housekeepers, without permission of their masters, and the next year Massachusatts, taking cognizance of the "younger sort" who met in places of public entertainment and dissipated with "wanton carriages, rudely singing and making noise . . . ," summarily banned such evil conduct.[115] Two decades later, Negroes and Indians were specifically barred from purchasing any strong drink "Beer, Wine, Cyder, Rum etc. . . . "[116]

By the 1670s the ubiquitous taverns led Cotton Mather to complain that they occupied every other house in Boston, a complaint underlined by his father's preaching two sermons against the "Sin of Drunkenness" in 1673.[117] A decade later the elder Mather complained that "Time was when in New England they durst not continue whole nights in Taverns, in drinking and gaming, and mispending Their precious Time . . . Time was when in this Boston men durst not be seen in Taverns after the Sabbath is begun. . . . "[118] His comments make Edward Ward's seem less a libel:

> *Rum,* alias *Kill Devil,* is as much ador'd by the *American English,* as a dram of *Brandy* is by an old *Billingsgate.* Tis held as the *Comforter* of their *Souls,* the *Preserver* of their *Bodys,* the *Remover* of their *Cares,* and *Promoter* of their *Mirth;* and is a Soveraign [*sic*] Remedy against the *Grumbling* of the *Guts,* a *Kibe-hell,* or a *Wounded Conscience.* . . .

The average New England farmer, Ward added, making his point ridiculous by overstatement, spent two hours in the ordinary for every hour in the field.[119]

In the provincial period, conditions did not improve, at least in the eyes of the elder Mather, for he lashed out again crying, "Is not that worse than Brutish Sin of Drunkenness, become a prevailing Iniquity all over the Country? How has Wine and Cyder, but most of all Rum, Debauched Multitudes of People Young and Old?"[120] Spurred to action, by the complaints of the Mathers and others, the General Court considered numerous regulations against drinking and abuse of the taverns. But the statutory enactments apparently had little effect.[121] In 1737, for example, a correspondent wrote the *Boston News-Letter* complaining about the excessive drinking and asked that extracts be printed from a recent London pamphlet entitled, *Distill'd Spirituous Liquors the Bane of the Nation. &c.*[122]

In that same year came a warning by one Hugh Henderson, who, about to be executed, confessed he got into this predicament by taking up drinking, stealing, cursing, swearing, lying, Sabbath breaking, gaming, whoring, and house breaking (for which he was about to die). He, as a man of experience, advised other conduct for children and servants.[123]

Had his admonition been followed by the servant population, they could have avoided considerable trouble, but unfortunately it came much too late. Drinking and taverning had indeed been a problem for masters of servants from the very beginning. John Winthrop wrote aboard the *Arbella* that one of the maid servants drank too much strong water and almost died. "We observed it a Com[mon] fault in our yonge people, that they gave themselues to drinke hott waters verye imoderately."[124]

On land, the servants continued to distress their masters and the court. One James Till, Plymouth servant, had to be whipped for alluring a fellow servant to drink. Once drinking he slandered his master's wife by saying he would go home and lie with her.[125] Tavernkeeper Stephen Hopkins, in the same Colony, was fined for allowing servants and others to sit drinking and playing shuffleboard in his place.[126] In Massachusetts, a servant lost control of his tongue as

well as his body in 1639, according to two witnesses who testified on
on oath that:

> Robert Wright servant to Mrs. Glover of Cambridge did
> overtake them beyond Charlston neck, and brake out into
> filthy and rayling speeches without any provocation, howling
> etc. and bidding 2 of the neighbors there kiss his ars, and
> calling this deponent Knopp bast theavish knave saying that
> all his Children were so, and calling him dogges-pricke slave,
> and other reviling speeches, and raylinge allso vpon this other
> deponent calling him rogue and raskall and iostling him divers
> tymes, so as they conceiued he was in drink for he was often
> ready to fall, and smelt of drink etc.[127]

Other cases in the seventeenth and eighteenth centuries indicate that
drinking was not an isolated phenomenon among the servant
population, any more than it was among the free although convictions
for drunkenness were remarkably few.[128]

Probably not all the excessive tipplers got to the courts, for, in
1693, Cotton Mather warned that same company of Negroes about
whose fornication he had been so concerned to suspend (but only for
two weeks against six months for the greater sin) those who sinned
with drunkenness.[129] And three years later he admonished all servants to
avoid alike ill haunts, wantonness, drunkenness and company
keeping.[130] Moreover, advertisements proclaiming teetotaling Negroes
for sale suggest strongly that this wss an important problem for
masters, who did not mind drinking their own liquor or wasting their
own time , but strongly disliked the habit in their servants.[131]

In 1750, a correspondent of *The Boston Gazette, or, Weekly
Journal* wns pleased to see an article reproaching the town for having so
many licensed houses. The writer was a sharer in the misfortune
because he had had a "good Servant *ruin'd* by one of the *Rum-sellers*
setting up near my-House." In his father's day, he recalled incorrectly, it
was considered a scandal for masters to drink but "Now the *Necessity* of
Nature calls for a large Draught even for the *Youngest* Apprentice."[132]

It would be a mistake to assume that all servants were drunkards,
just as it would be foolish to assume that only servants drank.
However, the pleasures of drinking, and the conviviality of drinking
with a friend or in a tavern were obviously available to the servant thus
disposed. Tavern keepers and other retailers of liquor seemed perfectly
willing to violate the laws, or else incapable of distinguishing between
money preferred by free men and that spent by servants. Richard
Cloughe, for example, had his strong water seized for selling "great

quantities" to other men's servants thereby causing drunkenness and misdemeanors.[133] Others were fined either specifically for selling liquor to servants, or for the less defined ill of entertaining them in their homes or place of business. Cormock Hasseldine of Ipswich fell under the latter category in 1658, as did James Habersham of Boston in 1728;[134] while Conungo, a free Negro, of Cambridge, was fined in 1684 for selling drink to and for entertainment of other men's Negroes. Mehitable Burgis, wife of a gentleman of Boston, was fined ten pounds and costs for selling liquor without a license and twenty shillings and costs for keeping a disorderly house where she entertained "idle and disorderly servants and Negroes...."[135] The problem was well enough recognized so that bonds were required of prospective retailers that they not allow children or servants to "lie tippling in the house."[136] And apprentices' contracts carried the almost universal prohibition: "Taverns or Alehouses he shall not haunt, Except it be about his Master's business there to be donne...."[137]

Despite the clandestine nature of much of their social life, servants were able to maintain some organized activities such as parties, and even clubs. Often these cooperative jollities involved not only stolen time but stolen refreshments as well. In 1712, Benjamin Wadsworth warned servants against stealing money, food, and drink to use in "Junkets and Merry Meetings...."[138] Occasionally a master, unwilling or unable to punish his charges for pilfering from his purse or cellar, brought them into court. Samuel Bacon, as early as 1643, was punished for stealing wine. Thomas Hall, in 1671, stole cider from his master's cellar. Two Indian servants in Cambridge one night cooperated in stealing cider and beer out of a master's cellar in 1685. Tulley, a Negro belonging to Christopher Pottle of Ipswich, stole a gallon of rum in 1692. Six Indian servants stole several bottles of wine in Boston in the early eighteenth century, and Patrick Madden, servant in Penbroke, made a false key to his master's cellar, where he garnered five quarts of rum.[139]

The use to which these stolen refreshments were put is well-illustrated in *The Weekly News-Letter,* which reported in 1738, a "Rendezvous" for a "Merry Frolick" among some Negroes in a warehouse. Some had brought bread, some fowl, some rum, and others sugar.[140] Three years later the same paper reported seven Negro servants on a frolic to Spectacle Island.[141] In 1740, a more detailed picture of a party emerges from the files of *The Boston Evening-Post.* A gentleman looking for his Negro woman one evening heard a noise in a Roxbury tavern. Entering he found about a dozen "black gentry, He's and She's, in a Room, in a very merry Humour, singing and dancing, having a

Violin, and Store of Wine and Punch before them." All of them belonged to gentlemen of Boston. The question of the convenience of taverners giving entertainment to slaves at that time of night, the story went , "we leave to the Consideretion of our betters."[142]

In dancing, as in other pastimes, the servants were emulating their masters, for from the 1680s on dancing gradually became accepted, at least in Boston.[143] Like Alexander Pope's "Vice," it was first hated, then endured, and then embraced. In the 1680's two dancing masters were forced to desist from their horrid practice, but without avail; for in 1700 and 1705 Cotton Mather, following his father's example, inveighed against the still existent evil.[144] By the 1720s, after one dancing school had been closed in 1717, this delightful amusement became accepted by those who dominated society, even though *The Weekly News-Letter* was still protesting in 1740.[145]

Group activity, of more serious purpose, began in seventeenth-century Boston among Scottish immigrants, some of whom had been sold as servants after being captured in the battle of Worcester. Arriving in 1652, six of them were among the twenty-seven members of the Scot's Charitable Society, the first year of its organization. This was in 1657, when they had yet a year or two to serve.[146] In 1684, at least one servant was on the roll of membership.[147] Primarily an immigrant aid society of the type which played so important a role in nineteenth-century immigrants' lives, it provided a focus for charitable, religious, and nationalist sentiment among its members, and undoubtedly helped the Scottish servants to feel more at home.[148] A similar organization, the Charitable Irish Society, begun in eighteenth-century Boston, undoubtedly played a like role among the many Irish who came as servants.[149]

This urge to get together for common entertainment sometimes resulted in more formal organization of clubs or gangs, among the Negroes too. Mather records in his *Diary* in 1693 that:

> a company of poor *Negroes,* of their own Accord, addressed mee, for my Countenance, to a Design which they had, of erecting such a *Meeting* for the Welfare of their miserable Nation that were Servants among us. I allowed their Design and went one Evening and pray'd and preach'd . . . with them; and gave them the following Orders. . . . [150]

There followed a list of eight rules, which when published as a broadside after 1706, were expanded to nine. They were to meet every Sunday evening between seven and nine, but only with the consent of their masters. They were to avoid wicked company and not only ask the minister to approve all members, but to have whites look in on their meetings from time to time. Those who sinned were to be reformed or barred, and they were not to help runaways. Servants were not to ask permission of masters to attend and then go elsewhere, and each meeting was to have the catechism.[151]

It is not known how long this society continued, nor how well it kept Mather's exhortation to do good, but, in 1716, Mather resolved to have the Negroes of his flock who formed a "religious society" as guests at his house.[152] And as late as June 10, 1744, Andrew Eliot spent the evening at the school house with a Society of Negroes.[153] That all such clubs were formed with high moral objectives is to be doubted, however, particularly in the light of one master's advertisement for a slave no longer wanted, because he had joined a "Rascally Club of Negroes. . . ."[154]

Noteworthy among the group activities of the colored servant population in provincial Boston was their celebration of funerals as social occasions, thereby emulating the master class whose wealthier members presented those who attended with rings or gloves and made funerals an excuse for opulent display. Free Negroes and slaves (with or without their masters' consent) attended the burials of their own kind, making of them significant occasions. Apparently in an effort to limit the numbers attending, Boston's selectmen in 1721 limited to one the number of bells that could be tolled for such funerals, and the length of tolling to six minutes per person. The funeral procession, instead of wending its way all over town, was to take the most direct route to the grave.[155] Two years later the provision was added that deceased colored persons were to be buried by one half hour before sunset and never on the Lord's day without permission of two selectmen. This was done because great numbers of Indians, Negroes, and mulattoes had been attending the burials, a practice conceived as one of "Ill tendancy [and perhaps of] great Inconveniency."[156]

Of equally "great Inconveniency" was the tendency of some servants to perform "riotous carriages" of one kind or other. It is likely that many of them were under the influence of liquor at the time, but they were probably getting rid, temporarily at least, of their frustrations in a society which seemed for now or forever to be keeping them standing still, when land or other opportunity was abundant. Many of these fracases involved the use of weapons, and ended in serious injury to one or more parties. A fighting Salem servant, for example, in 1658 beat another servant with a stick. In 1675, one Charles Fuller, servant, shot off the testicles of Jonathan Davenport's man, Thomas Barnes, who was "otherwaies greatly damnified by the sd Shott."[157]

More serious to the public at large were the occasional riots or disorders perpetrated by groups of servants and others. As early as 1662 in Charlestown, two men were fined for encouraging and abetting young people, including servants, to gather in crowds where they set fires, burned fences, shot guns, and tumbled one house into the Cove. This was on November fifth, Guy Fawkes' day, or Pope's day, as it came to be called in New England. Yearly this day was exploited by the populace much as Halloween has been in modern America. Called on this instance "a day of Thanksgiving," it seems more appropriate that the day after should have been so designated if the towns came through the night unscathed. One Pope's day was described in *The Boston Evening-Post:*

> Tuesday last being the anniversary of the *Gunpowder Plot,* two *Popes* were made and carried thro' the Streets in the Evening, one from the *North* and another from the *South* End of the Town, attended by a vast Number of Negroes and white Servants, armed with Clubs, Staves and Cutlashes, who were very abusive to the Inhabitants, insulting the Persons and breaking the Windows, &c. of such as did not given them Money to their Satisfaction, and even among those who had given them liberally; and the two *Popes* meeting in Cornhill, their Followers were so infatuated, as to fall upon each other with the utmost Rage and Fury: Several were sorely wounded and bruised, and some left for dead, and rendered incapable of any Business for a long Time, to the great Loss and Damage of their respective Masters."[158]

Such violence was by no means confined to Pope's Day, however. Four servants, in the fall of 1686, were charged with a riot, and with assaulting the Watch.[159] In the 1720s, three servants, under the spell of spring, went on a spree including "prophane Cursing and Swearing offering affronts and abuses to Women in the Street, breaking Glass windows and offering to break open . . . Doors &c."[160] These group activities, particularly of Negroes, Indians, and mulattoes, had long been a source of irritation to the residents of Boston who, since 1723, had been attempting to get a rigorous law passed regulating all such, free or in servitude, but with little success. The proposed law prohibited: entertainment of Indian, Negro or mulatto servants by free members of the same groups; their selling of liquor and food on training days; receiving stolen goods from such servants; stealing; servants going out of the house of their master within a certain time after sunset or before sunrise without permission of masters; their carrying arms; lurking together without permission; going to the common on training days or other public days and remaining after sunset; striking any of His Majesty's subjects; selling liquor to such servants; either bond or free, working as porters unless approved by the proper authorities; and leaving master's house at night in time of a fire.[161] In 1750/51, the town fathers were still looking for a more effectual method of keeping at a minimum disorders by Negroes in the night.[162]

Less destructive forms of entertainment were available to the average servant, and undoubtedly more widely participated in than such dubious pursuits as fornication, excessive tippling, and violence, but unfortunately servant participation in them rests greatly on assumption. The younger lads and wenches probably played such children's games as marbles, "Hoop and Hide," "Thread the Needle," "Blind Man's Buff," "Leap Frog," and "Hop Hat."[163] Football, throwing stones and snowballing were all common, so common, as a matter of fact, as to be banned in Boston's streets in 1701.[164] Playing in the streets with money, or paw paws was equally forbidden children and servants in Suffolk County in 1728.[165] Swimming, skating, fishing, and boating attracted the youth of the day, while the older servants probably took in an occasional horse race, pig run, bear baiting or horse fair.[166]

Gambling wasted some of the time and substance of servants, too. "Chuck Farthing," and "Peg Farthing," vied with various card games as ways to lose one's money.[167] Indentures generally forbade cards, dice, and other gambling, and Plymouth colony attempted to prohibit cards by banning their import and proscribing their being kept in the house. Servants were to be protected from being corrupted by cards or dice.[168] But still they played. One master was fined for twice playing cards with his man; a servant lost three pounds and eight shillings gambling; while a third, in eighteenth-century Bristol County was charged with playing cards on the Sabbath.[169] And there was always the lottery.[170]

Some servants spent their leisure time more wisely in productive labor of one kind or another, perhaps in hope of buying their freedom, or shortening their years of servitude. In a case which arose before the Essex Court, in 1670, one Edmund Ashby, servant, had worked a week for himself at harvest time.[171] He had to pay the master for that week, but presumably he had earned money above and beyond that payment. In Northampton a Negro, in 1686, was apparently trading with the Indians without his master's consent.[172] Early in the eighteenth century, Cotton Mather's Negro, Onesimus, gave his master a sum of money with which to purchase another slave. Onesimus was freed, but since he had earned the money at Mather's liberty in his service, he was to pay five pounds more in six months.[173] Other servants earned money by practicing "Negro-Mancey" (telling fortunes), stealing and selling their masters' goods, and doing odd jobs.[174]

The Reverend Samuel Willard, in a sermon, had warned servants that they broke the Fifth Commandment when they employed time for themselves,[175] but at least in Boston they paid him little heed, for it was a common practice among the colored servants, Indians, Negroes and mulattoes, to keep hogs. Since such practice tempted them to steal feed from their masters, occasioned loss of time, and gave them opportunities to meet together, it was forbidden in 1746. Their masters would be subject to a twenty-shilling fine, and any who rented a sty or pen to them would be equally subject to fine.[176] The law was at first disregarded, for eight months later the selectmen requested *The Weekly News-Letter* to print the law in their columns.[177] Thus, while idleness was rejected and diligence embraced, that diligence must be directed toward the economic welfare not of the servant, but of the master. Small wonder that servants used their leisure time ill, when its constructive use was denied them.

Despite the Puritan background and the necessity for constant attention to work, the servants of Plymouth and Massachusetts in the seventeenth century and the province of Massachusetts in the eighteenth century found considerable opportunity for enjoyment of what leisure time they could manage to achieve. The records suggest that bed and bottle were two important poles of their activity, but it was these which most often brought them to the attention of their superiors. Other activities, innocent in themselves, were probably taken for granted and were not ordinarily recorded. At best, the servant lived but half a life, for a good share of his waking time was demanded by his master, and this, no doubt, helps explain why many attempted to pack so much living into their own few hours. It is this also which explains, partly, why many servants protested so vigorously against their servitude. For protest they did.

NOTES

1. Whitmore, *Laws,* 136 (1642); Brigham, *Laws,* 270–271 (1671). Custom and what authority the ministry could wield were the only forces behind the religious training and worship of servants in the eighteenth century, although general Sabbatarian legislation prevailed throughout the period. See *Acts and Resolves,* I–III, *passim.* For sermons exhorting masters to take care of their servants' souls see C. Mather, *Family Religion Excited and Asserted*

(Boston, 1707), 2–3; *The Negro Christianized: An Essay to Excite and Assist that Good Work, the Instruction of Negro-Servants In Christianity* (Boston, 1706), 5, 30.

2. Frances Rose-Troup, *John White* . . . , 141 (1628/9).
3. *Winthrop's Journal*, II, 307–8 (1646).
4. *Boston Records*, VI, 75.
5. *Ibid.*, 78.
6. *Ibid.*, 79.
7. *Ibid.*, 81. For others see *ibid.*, 77 (1632); 78 (1633) 80 (ca. 1640, two cases), 82 (ca. 1640–59 five cases), 85 (1654–69, six cases), 86 (ca. 1644), 171 (1643, "She was a godly maide & was to have joyned to the Church, but the Lord P[re]vented her & tooke her to Heaven."), 199 (1662 brought before church where he confessed lying and stealing). John Cotton held that servants, like children, received church privileges because of their master's membership. Edmund S. Morgan disagrees. *The Puritan Family* . . . , 79–80.
8. Mather, *A Good Master Well-Served* . . . , 2, 6.
9. *News-Letter*, Sept. 18–25, 1740. For other occasions see *Essex County Court*, V, 141 (1673); VI, 236 (1676). Mather, *Magnalia* . . . , III, 5 (ca. 1640).
10. See Greene, *The Negro In Colonial New England* . . . , 257.
11. *Winthrop's Journal*, II, 26, cited in Greene, *The Negro in Colonial New England* . . . , 257.
12. Whitmore, *Laws*, 53.
13. For examples see *Records of the First Church at Dorchester 1636–1734* (Boston, 1891), 231 (1699/1700); Cotton Mather, "Diary," M.H.S., 7 *Colls*, 278 (1698, four cases).
14. *Gazette*, Aug. 31–Sept. 7, 1730. In reply to a query concerning (1) taking them to England or Ireland, and (2) baptism. For baptisms or recognized communicants before 1730 see Motte, *Records Brattle Square Church* . . . , 103–151 (fifteen cases); Sharples, *Records Church of Christ Cambridge* . . . , 59 (five cases); 108 (two Negroes, one Indian); *First Church Dorchester* . . . , 157 (sundry Negroes voted to be baptized); 234 (two cases); 243; L. Vernon Briggs, *Church and Cemetery Records of Hanover, Mass.* (Boston, 1895–1904), I, 118 (two cases); *Publications of the Brookline Historical Publication Society*, First Series, no. 8, p. 69 (three cases). For examples of Baptisms 1730–1750 see *Records of the Church in Brattle Square Boston* . . . , 109–177 (fifty-one cases); Briggs, *Church and Cemetery Records of Hanover, Mass.*, I, 124, 128, 181, 183; Sharples, *Records Church of Christ Cambridge* . . . , 108–159 (twenty-two cases); C.S.M. *Pubs.*, XXII, 295–297 (two cases), 441 (two cases), 442–446 (four cases); XXIII, 510–528 (twenty-two cases); *Publications of the Brookline Historical Publication Society*, First Series, no. 8, pp. 72–77 (nine cases); M.H.S., 3 *Proc.*, II, 198, 454 (four cases); 2 *Proc.*, VII, 488;

Boston Records, VI, 146 (five cases). Greene believes that the fear of Negroes being free if baptized was an important deterrent prior to 1730. *The Negro in Colonial New England...,* 260–261. See also, C. Mather, *The Negro Christianized...,* 26.

15. *Sibley's Harvard Graduates,* VI, 429 (ca. 1730).
16. *Post-Boy,* Apr. 7, 1740. For more serious, but hardly more enlightening information on the discriminatory attitude of whites towards Negroes and Indians in church see *Plymouth Town Records...,* II, 103–104 (1715/16); *Records of the Church in Brattle Square Boston...,* 21 (1723). See also Greene, *The Negro in Colonial New England...,* 282–284.
17. For examples of the various catechisms see Cotton Mather, *The Negro Christianized...,* 34–46; and American Antiquarian Society, New Series, *Proc.,* XII.
18. Hutchinson, *History...,* I, 137.
19. *Winthrop Papers,* III, 133–135 (1633). Ministers, of course, were more concerned than others. Even so, see Cotton Mather's intense concern with his servants, as reflected in his "Diary," M.H.S., 7 *Colls.,* VII, 579, wants to make his Negro slave a servant of Christ; VIII, 258, servant maid had become "disposed unto serious Religion...," since living with his family; 369, a new servant in family who must be "putt upon the Exercises of Piety."; 444, is to help his servant achieve communion; 562, chastises self for being remiss in bringing Negro servant to the Lord; 576, must speak to new servant maid about "our Saviour"; 603, his Negro servant seeks Baptism; 666, new servant maid, must give her books on piety; 698, a new servant, wants to be saved. Mather was not the only one so concerned. The Reverend Mr. Jonathan Burr made a covenant with the Lord after a recovery from smallpox, the fifth part of which read: "That I will set up *God,* more in my *Family,* more in *myself, Wife, Children,* and *Servants;* conversing with them in a more serious and constant manner...." Mather, *Magnalia...,* III, 80.
20. Mather, *Magnalia...,* VII, 34.
21. *Ibid.,* VII, 34–35.
22. *Ibid.,* VII, 32–34.
23. *Ibid.,* VII, 34.
24. Whitmore, *Laws,* 189–90. Admonishment, and fines of five and ten shillings were the penalties for first, second, and third offenses, respectively. Five years later (1658) it was noted that such behavior occurred on both Saturday and Sunday evenings and a five shilling fine or corporal punishment was provided. *Ibid.,* 190. Church attendance was required on the Lord's Day and fast and thanksgiving days. *Mass. Recs.,* II, 177–178 (1646). In 1739, Governor Belcher, to prevent disorders on the Lord's Day, warned all heads of families to keep children and servants from being unnecessarily abroad on the Sabbath and evenings before and after. *N.E. Journal,* Aug. 28, 1739.

General Laws prohibiting work and play on the Sabbath were enacted in the provincial period. See *Acts and Resolves,* I, 58–59 (1692); II, 58–59 (1716); 456–457 (1727); 1071 (1741); III, 270 (1746). For examples of court action against Sabbath-breakers see "Photoststic Copy of Records of County Court, Suffolk 1680–1692 " 2 parts (modern pagination used), I, 107 (1681/2); 170 (1683); 180 (1683); 193 (1683/4); 218 (1684); II, 242 (1684/5); 413 (1691).

25. George Parker Winship, ed., *Boston in 1682 and 1699: A Trip to New England by Edward Ward and A Letter from New England by J.W.* (Providence, 1905) 55 .

26. *Boston Records,* XIII, 223–224.

27. *Ibid.,* XVII, 30–31, 75–76, 116–117, 141–142, 200–201, 225–226, 246–247 .

28. Wthitmore, *Laws,* 136 (1642); Brigham, *Laws,* 270–271 (1671)

29. *Acts and Resolves,* II, 758 (1735).

30. See S.E. Morison's chapter on elementary schools in *The Puritan Pronaos: Studies in the Intellectual Life of New England in the Seventeenth Century* (New York, 1936), 54–82.

31. For example, in the will of Joshua Buffum it was provided that the children under his care were to be kept in school until the age of fourteen or so, and then to be bound out. MSS. Buffum Papers, Essex Institute, 1705. Franklin got his formal schooling prior to being bound. *Autobiography . . . ,* 11–12. For provisions for formal schooling in contracts see Lechford, *Note-Book,* 251–2 (1639); *Essex Probate,* I, 186–187 (1654); MSS. Public Notary Books of Stephen Sewall and Mitchell Sewall, II, 22 (1723), *Plym. Recs.,* I, 36–37

32. School attendance was not compulsory, the maintenance of schools was. Whitmore, *Laws,* 190–191.

33. *Braintree Records,* 86 (1715).

34. See appendix A in Towner, "A Good Master Well Served . . . " (Ph.D. diss., Northwestern University, 1954). See also MSS. Boston Indentures, I, *passim.*

35. *Essex County Court,* I, 57 (1643); MSS. Suffolk Sessions, I, 252 (1712); E.I. *Colls.,* I, 14 (1713).

36. *Sibley's Harvard Graduates,* IV, 128 (ca. 1717); C. Mather, "Diary," M.H.S., 7 *Colls,* VIII, 379, 500, 663 (1716–21). In 1728, another school for Negroes was begun with the note that any persons wishing to send their servants should do so. *N.E. Journal,* Apr. 1 and Apr. 18, 1728. This action of Mather's was taken despite his knowledge of the charge that education was dangerous for Negro slaves. See his *Tremenda . . . ,* 28, Where he wrote "Now, I lay the charges of God upon you, that the more you Know, the more you be careful to Do according to what you Know: And afford not the least shadow of any occasion, for that False complaint, that the worst

Servants are those that have had most Instruction bestow'd upon them."

37. One could hardly use Benjamin Franklin's remarkable achievement in self education as characteristic, but at least one other apprentice, this one bound out by overseers of the poor, attained a remarkable intellectual level. See C.K Shipton, *Isiah Thomas . . . , passim,* Information received from Dr. Clifford K. Shipton.

38. *Assistants,* II, 12 (1630/1) Magistrates and ministers were excepted. This law was still in force in 1658. See Whitmore, *Laws,* 177. For Plymouth see Pulsifer, *Laws,* 105 (1636). This provision was still in force in Plymouth in 1691. See *Plym. Recs.,* VI, 267.

39. Massachusetts set aside weekly training days in 1631, monthly in 1632, and eight times a year in 1637 and to the end of the century. *Mass. Recs.,* I, 85, 102, 124, 210. See also Whitmore, *Laws,* 177–178.

40. Magistrates, teaching elders, and the major general could hold back one servant each from training. Remote farmers were included among these. *Mass. Recs.,* I, 210. Whitmore, *Laws,* 177–178. Plymouth excepted Scotch and Irish servants in 1655, probably feeling that ex-prisoners of war were poor risks to be handling guns. Pulsifer, *Laws,* 65. Other evidence, besides statutory, places servants in military service. For example, Mathew Cradocke was fined four pounds for his man's being absent from training diverse times. *Assistants,* II, 29 (1632); permission for a servant to be absent was granted in 1653 in *Mass. Recs.,* III, 300. This is not the place to go into impressment and extended military service.

41. *Mass. Recs.,* I, 188 (1636/7).

42. George Francis Dow, *Every Day Life in the Massachusetts Bay Colony* (Boston, 1935), 114. Samuel Sewall indicated in his diary the festive nature of training days as he gave his troop money for a treat and drinks. M.H.S., 5 *Colls.,* V, 150 (1686), 360 (1692).

43. C.S.M. *Pubs.,* XXII, 169. People actually did fornicate at the "bottom of the common." MSS. Suffolk Sessions, I, 3 (1702).

44. Winship, *Boston in 1682 . . . ,* Introduction, xiii. C.S.M. *Pubs.,* I, 442–443. H. Telfer Mook's "Training Days in New England," *N.E.Q.,* XI (Dec.,1938), 675–697 holds, page 690, that seventeenth-century training and muster days were devoted exclusively to serious work, and that not until the second quarter of the eighteenth did they become social occasions. I would put him at least fifty years late in his estimate .

45. M.H.S., 2 *Proc.,* VI, 492 (1731).

46. MSS. Middlesex Court Files, file 38, no number (case of Samuel Carter, Nov., 1655).

47. Winship, *Boston in 1682 . . . ,* 55. Earlier (page 53) he made the delightful observation that "The women are very Fruitful, which shows the Men are *Industrious* in *Bed* tho' *Idle up.* Children and

Servants are there very Plenty; but *Honestmen* and *Virgins* as scarce
as in other places."

48. Dow, *Every Day Life* . . . , 117–119. He quotes it from Ray Palmer
    Baker, "The Poetry of Jacob Bailey, Loyalist," *N.E.Q.,* II (Jan.,
    1929) , 58–92. "A Description of a Husking Frolic Lately Celebreted
    by the Beaux and Belles of Kingston," is the title of the poem.

49. John Tulley, *Tulley 1688. An Almanack for the Year of Our Lord,
    MDCLXXXVIII. Being Bissextile or Leap-yeer, and from the
    Creation 5637* (Boston, 1688), 16.

50. For example, "Timothy Muphy [*sic*] Servant to James Green of
    Boston Cooper complained against and convicted of night walking,
    disturbing and affrighting . . . Susanna Gardiner his abusive
    Speeches to her, askeing her to let him come into her house in the
    night and to come to bed to her. . . . ," MSS. Suffolk County
    Court, I, 207 (1684). For other night-walking servants see *ibid.,* 40
    (1680); 194 (1683/4); 208 (1684); 230 (1684); *Suffolk County
    Court,* I, 265 (1673); 336 (1673); II, 1066 (1679). *Essex County
    Court,* VIII, 12, two cases (1680), 315–316 (1682). MSS. Middlesex
    County Court, III, 106 (1674). MSS. Suffolk Sessions, II, 10–11
    (1712/3).

51. Northampton, in 1678, made her tithing men responsible for seeing
    to it that servants were in their homes by nine P.M. MSS. Hampshire
    County Court, I, 9. A Suffolk court ordered Suffolk tithing men and
    constables to enforce the law of General Court regarding servants of
    color being abroad at night. *News-Letter,* Aug. 27–Sept. 3, 1705. An
    announcement in the *Gazette* underlines the failure to restrict
    nocturnal meanderings. "Whereas the due execution of that law
    [against Indians, Negroes, and mulatto servants being out at night]
    would much tend to promote good orders. We are desirous the Town
    may know . . . that some Gentlemen in Authority, with a
    considerable Number of well disposed Inhabitants [intend to enforce
    it] . . . " Apr. 3–10, 1738. In 1746, because "sundry houses" had
    been broken into at night, all masters were advised to take care that
    "their Servants and others under their Government keep in their
    Places of Residence in proper Hours. . . . " They were to take
    especial care that Negroes were not abroad after nine P.M. without
    certificates. *News-Letter,* Sept. 11, 1746.

52. *N.E. Journal,* Apr. 14, 1741. A Negro advertised as not going out
    nights. In 1733, an Indian, about to be hanged, warned servants
    against keeping late hours. *Ibid.,* Mar. 26, 1733.

53. For marriage and sex in New England see Greene, *The Negro in
    Colonial New England* . . . , ch. VIII; Morgan, *The Puritan
    Family* . . . , ch. I; by the same author, "The Puritans and Sex,"
    N.E.Q., XV (Dec. 1942), 591–607; Chilton L. Powell, "Marriage in
    Early New England," *N.E.Q.,* I (July, 1928), 323–334; Charles
    Francis Adams "Some Phases of Sexual Morality and Church

Discipline in Colonial New England," M.H.S., 2 *Proc.*, VI, 477–516; H.B. Parkes, "Sexual Morals and the Great Awakening," *N.E.Q.*, III (Jan. 1930) 133–135, which attacks Adams' position in above article; by the same author, "Morals and Law Enforcement in Colonial New England," *N.E.Q.*, V (July, 1932), 431–452; and an unpublished essay at Brown University by Malcolm Freiberg, "Boston, Sex, and the Great Awakening." For easily accessible raw materials (no double entendre) see indices to *Suffolk County Court* and *Essex County Court.*

54. For exceptions see *Winthrop Papers*, II, 88n.; 169n; IV, 105–106. Lechford, *Note-Book*, 307–308 (1640); *Essex County Court*, V, 23 (1672).

55. For exceptions see MSS. Suffolk Sessions, III, 303 (1724). In the 1650s, two servants were ordered to marry the mothers of their bastards. MSS. Middlesex County Court, I, 90, 125–126. See also *Winthrop Papers*, IV, 293–294, *Boston Records*, VI, 77. Massachusetts required marriage, or fine, or corporal punishment, or all three for fornication with a single woman. Whitmore, *Laws*, 153 (1642).

56. *Boston Records*, XXVIII, 292. For another example, see MSS Suffolk Sessions, II, 136–137 (1716).

57. Whitmore, *Laws*, 137. In the eighteenth century, the age of consent was twelve for females, fourteen for males. *Acts and Resolves*, I, 172 (1694). However, the largest single body of indentures extant makes no provisions for marriage prior to the end of the term of service. See MSS. Boston Indentures, 1734–1805, *passim*.

58. *Plym. Recs.*, I, 128–129. Actually she did not marry for ten years. *Ibid.*, VIII, 9.

59. *Records of the Town of Plymouth* (Plymouth, 1889–1903), I, 12.

60. Pulsifer, *Laws*, 29. Whitmore, *Laws*, 172. For a case of enforcement see *Mass. Recs.*, IV, ii, 66 (1662).

61. *Essex County Court*, I, 13.

62. *Boston Records*, IX, 72. For other seventeenth century examples see MSS. Middlesex County Court, I, 189; IV, 139; *Suffolk County Court*, II, 1153–1157; *Essex County Court*, VII, 327. For the eighteenth century see Motte, *Records Brattle Square Church*, 227 (two cases); 230 (two cases), 231, 234, 240, 241, 242, 245, 246 (three cases); *Braintree Records, 1640–1793*, 706, 750, 751, 752 (two cases); Sharples, *Records Church of Christ Cambridge . . .*, 110, 111; *Boston Records*, XXVIII, 102, 188, 255–257 (thirty cases); MSS. Massachusetts Archives, IX, 248; M.H.S., 3 *Proc.*, II, 463; Briggs, Hanover . . . , I, 90–93 (four csses); MSS. Essex Sessions, IV, 16. See again Greene, *The Negro in Colonial New England . . .*, for all phases of Negro marriage.

63. Dec. 18–25, 1721.

64. Greene, *The Negro in Colonial New England* . . . , 195–196. For consent of a court see MSS. Suffolk Sessions, I, 203 (1709/10).
65. *Boston Records,* XXVIII, 199; 255–257 (five cases), 283; M.H.S., 3 *Proc.,* II, 198; Motte, *Records Brattle Square Church* . . . , 233, 234, 236.
66. *Boston Records,* XXVIII, 256. *A Faithful Narrative of the Wicked Life and Remarkable Conversion of Patience Boston alias Samson* . . . (Boston, 1738), 3. M.H.S., 3 *Proc.,* II, 196.
67. *Boston Records,* XXVIII, 133.
68. *A Faithful Narrative* . . . , *loc. cit.*
69. M.H.S., 3 *Proc.,* II, 196.
70. MSS. Middlesex Court Files, file 56, no number (Mar. 8, 1671/2).
71. *Essex County Court,* III, 226 (1664).
72. MSS. Miidlesex County Court, III, 144 (1676),
73. *Plym. Recs.,* III, 91. For others see MSS. Middlesex Court Files, file 26, 1637 (1661); Mss. Middlesex County Court, IV, 224–225 (1686). Some servants apparently made good their promises, for they confessed to fornication before marriage: MSS. Middlesex County Court, I, 189 (1659); III, 176 (1677); MSS. Suffolk Sessions, III, 303 (1724). One couple was ordered to marry after committing fornication. MSS. Middlesex County Court, I, 90 (1655). This marriage was ordered under the 1642 law requiring fine and/or corporal punishment and/or marriage or all three . Whitmore, *Laws,* 153. For a brief discussion of this law see *Winthrop's Journal,* II, 38.
74. *Suffolk County Court,* II, 1099–1100 (1679). For other unparticular wenches see *ibid.,* 991 (1678/9); *Essex County Court,* IV, 199–200 (1669); MSS. Essex Sessions, I, n.p. (1705).
75. For the confession of Wiman's servants see MSS Middlesex Court Files, file 15, number 714 (1656); tried in MSS. Middlesx County Court, I, 113–114. For another case of two servants of the same master, see MSS. Suffolk County Court, II, 387 (1690).
76. MSS. Bristol Sessions, II, 96 (1706). MSS. Suffolk County Court, I, 182 (1683).
77. MSS. Middlesex County Court, IV, 13–14 (1681). For another who apparently resisted her master's "wanton and lascivious carriages. . . . " see *Suffoik County Court,* II, 807 (1677).
78. *Plym. Recs.,* III, 75 (1654). For other sexual relations between unmarried members of the same household in which at least one party was a servant, see *Assistants,* II, 107 (1641); *Essex County Court,* IV, 38–40 (1668); *Suffolk County Court,* II, 991 (1678/9); MSS. Middlesex County Court, III, 262–263 (1679); *Boston Records,* X, 58 (1681); *Plym. Recs.,* I, 15 (1633); *Mass. Recs.,* I, 298, 310 (1640); MSS. Bristol Sessions, II, 87 (1705); MSS. Middlesex County Court, I, 64 (l654); III, 4 (1671); 237–238 (1678); MSS. Essex Sessions, IV, 10–11 (1719).

79. *Essex County Court,* IV, 316; V, 411; VI, 73, 135, 137 (1674–1676). For others see *ibid.,* II, 108 (1658); VII, 94 (1678); 141 (1678); 411 (1680); MSS. Middlesex County Court, I, 189 (1659); III, 176 (three cases, 1677); IV, 209 (1685); MSS. Suffolk Court Files, V, 605 (1663/64); MSS. Hampshire County Court, I, 154 (1692); Mss. Suffolk Sessions, II, 173 (1717); III 319 (1725). MSS. Suffolk County Court, I, 208 (1684); 230 (1684).

80. Negro and Indian, *Suffolk County Court,* I, 233 (1672/3). Indians, MSS. Middlesex County Court, I, 73 (1685); *Assistants,* I, 115 (1677/8).

81. MSS. Suffolk Sessions, II, 133 (1716). For other mixed matings with black females see *Essex County Court* III, 99, 101 (1663); V, 409 (1674); VI, 23 (1675); VII, 183 (1679); *Suffolk County Court,* I, 185 (1672); II, 809 (1677); 991 (1678/9); 1164 (1679/80); MSS. Middlesex County Court, III, 237–238 (1678); 240 (1678); IV, 141 (1684); Essex MSS. "County Court 1679–1692 Salem," n.p. (26 June, 1683, case of John Besoon); MSS. Suffolk Sessions, I, 206 (1710).

82. MSS. Suffolk Sessions, II, 14 (1713). For other mixed matings with white females see *Essex County Court,* VI, 256 (1677); MSS. Middlesex County Court, I, 64 (1654); III, 262–263 (1679), V, 78 (1691); MSS. Hampshire County Court, I, 42 (1680); II, 54 (1729/30); MSS. fragment, Essex County, "Court of Pleas and Sessions 1688–1689," 10; *Plym. Recs.,* VI, 177 (1685); MSS. Plymouth Sessions, I, 146 (1703); MSS. Essex Sessions, IV, 10–11 (1719); VI, n.p. (case of Ann Connor, July 11, 1749); MSS. Suffolk Sessions, I, 6 (1702); 116 (1705); 144 (1706/7); 152–153 (1707); 160 (1707); 186 (1709); 212–213 (1710); II, 43 (1713/4).

83. *Suffolk County Court,* II, 991 (1678/9). For a white woman who fornicated with white and black see *Plym. Recs.,* VI, 177 (1685).

84. MSS. Essex Sessions, I, n.p. (27 Mar. 1705, csse of Wiltshire); *Plym. Recs.,* III, 180 (1659/60); *Essex County Court,* VII, 406, 410 (1680); MSS. Plymouth Sessions, I, 38 (1688); MSS. Suffolk County Court, II, 398 (1690/1).

85. MSS. Middlesex Court Files, file 38, no number (Nov., 1665).

86. MSS. Middlesex County Court, I, 90 (1655). For other servants caught see *ibid.,* V, 85 (1691); *Essex County Court,* V, 428 (1674); II, 151 (1659); MSS. Suffolk County Court, I, 194 (1683/4). See also note 73, above.

87. *Boston Records,* X, 60 (1684). For men servants fornicating with free women see MSS Winthrop Papers, M.H.S.W.14.60 (1657); MSS. Middlesex County Court, I, 125–126 (1657); MSS. Middlesex Court Files, file 28, number 1773 (1661); MSS. Suffolk County Court, I, 99 (1681); II, 398 (1690/1); MSS. Suffolk Sessions, I, 10 (1702); 240 (1711); III, 303 (1724); IV, 268 (1730); MSS. Essex Sessions, IV, 106 (1723); 114 (1725); MSS. Bristol Sessions, V, 28

(1748). For women servants fornicating with free men see *Essex County Court,* I, 250 (1652); V, 103 (1672); 155 (1673); 240 (1673); *Suffolk County Court,* I, 265 (1673); MSS. Suffolk County Court, I, 39 (1680); 129 (1682); 182 (1683); 205–206 (1684); MSS. Middlesex County Court, III, 90 (1674); MSS. Suffolk Sessions, II, 136–137 (1716); MSS. Bristol Sessions, III, 24 (1725). For other servants who fornicated but whose partner is undetermined bound or free see *Essex County Court,* I, 361 (female, 1654); II, 179 (male, 1659); III, 460 (female, 1667); IV, 243–244 (female, 1670); VI, 20 (female, 1675); VII, 406 (female, 1680); *Suffolk County Court,* II, 1063 (female, 1679); MSS. Suffolk County Court, I, 228 (female, 1684); II, 232 (female, 1684/5); *Assistants,* I, 125 (female, 1678); MSS. Bristol Sessions, III a, 65 (female, 1719); MSS. Suffolk Sessions, IV, 410 (female, 1732); *Courant,* Oct. 23–30, 1725 (female); *Evening Post,* Dec. 31, 1739 (female); *N.E. Journal,* June 19, 1727 (female); *Sibley's Harvard Graduates,* IV, 155 (female, ca. 1720).

88. *Assistants,* I, 199 (1681); MSS. Middlesex County Court, IV, 224–225 (1686). One master was convicted of "wanton and lascivious carriages. . . . " toward his servant girl. *Suffolk County Court,* II, 807 (1677).

89. Whites: although imprisoned for this and other crimes, one was released to his master on condition the girl declared her lack of fear for him. *Mass, Recs.,* I, 177, 193. A second attempted rape on three different girls. *Assistants,* II, 86. MSS. Suffolk Sessions, II, 84 (1715). Negroes: MSS. Suffolk County Court, I, 219 (1684); *Suffolk County Court,* II, 106–107 (1679); MSS. Essex Sessions, II, 229 (1710); MSS. Mass. Archives, IX, 166 (1712); 178 (1721); MSS. Plymouth Sessions, IV, 91 (1738); 131 (1739/40); MSS. Suffolk Sessions, IV, 149–150 (1728).

90. Whites: *Assistants,* II, 121 (two cases, 1642/3); Negro: *News-Letter,* Oct. 5–12, 1732.

91. *Mass. Recs.,* II, 46 (1643); MSS. Middlesex County Court, 62–63 (1654); MSS. Suffolk County Court, I, 97 (1681).

92. Feb. 23–Mar. 3, 1718.

93. Whitmore, *Laws,* 153; 231 (here disfranchisement was added to punishment of marriage, or fine, or corporal punishment or all three) *Acts and Resolves,* I, 52; 578–581 (1705). Plymouth's 1636 law allowed the magistrate to use his discretion in punishing fornication. In 1645, however, whipping, fine (not over ten pounds), and imprisonment (not more than three days) was specified. If the couple would marry, then the whipping would be eliminated. Pulsifer, *Laws,* 12 (1636), 46 (1645).

94. Indenture of Edmund Ashby, *Essex County Court,* IV, 256–258 (1670). For others see Morgan, *The Puritan Family . . . ,* 71–72; MSS. Volume "Inhabitants – 1695, List of & Indentures of

Apprentices." and MSS. Boston Indentures, *passim*. MSS. Indenture of Joseph Barber, Apr. 8, 1694, M.H.S. Miscellaneous Bound Manuscripts.

95. Cotton Mather, *A Good Master Well Served* . . . , 15–16, 22. Sermons and dying confessions are numerous. For examples see Samuel Danforth, *The Cry of Sodom Enquired into* . . . (Cambridge, 1674); John Rogers, *Death the Certain Wages of Sin to the Impenitent* . . . (Boston, 1701), Edward Ward, *Female Policy Detected, or the History of Lewd Women* (Boston, 1742); Cotton Mather, *Pillars of Salt* . . . (Boston, 1699). For others see Charles Evans, ed., *A m e r i c a n Bibliography* . . . (Chicago, 1903–1925) . Execution sermons and/or dying warnings: numbers 413 (1686), 417 (1686), 539 (1690), 655 (1693), 856 (1698), 1452 (1710), 1626 (1713), 1728 (1715), 1729 (1715), 1910 (1717), 3639 (1733), 3641 (1733), 3642 (1733), 3643 (1733), 3655 (1733), 3851 (1734), 4258 (1738), 4478 (1740), 4599 (1740). Hereafter cited as Evans, *American Bibliography.*

96. Cotton Mather, *Rules for the Society of Negroes, 1693* (New York, 1888), 7.

97. Seventy-seven cases of bastardy in which one or more of the parents was a servant were located before 1751. See appendix K in Towner, "A Good Master Well Served . . . " (Ph.D. diss., Northwestern University, 1954).

98. MSS. Bristol Sessions, III, a, 65 (1719).

99. *Ibid.,* II , 96 (1706).

100. *Essex Counyy Court,* VI, 20 (1675).

101. *Ibid.,* V, 103 (1672).

102. "The Selling of Joseph A Memorial," (Boston, 1700), in M.H.S., 1 *Proc., VII*, 161–165. See page 163.

103. *Gazette,* May 22–29, 1738. For other suggestions of deliberate breeding see *News-Letter,* Mar. 7, 1745, "A Very likely, healthy Negro Wench, a notable Breeder, under twenty years old, with a fine Male Child at her Breast. . . . " See also *Evening-Post,* Aug. 9, 1736, "She is an excellent Breeder, and is now big with Child." To cap the argument, read in *ibid.* Apr. 23, 1750, "A very likely healthy Negro Wench about 24 years old that breeds like a rabbit with a female child about five weeks old. Her only fault is she breeds too fast for her present master." In the county as opposed to the town, children may have been welcome, e.g., "To be sold in Town, A likely Negro Woman about eight and twenty years . . . but a very poor Breeder, therefore not fit for the Country. . . . " *Gazette,* Apr. 16, 1745.

104. See the files of Masssachusetts newspapers in the period, *passim.*

105. *News-Letter,* Apr. 22–29, 1742.

106. *Gazette,* Nov. 26, 1745; *Courant,* May 11–18, 1724; *Post-Boy,* July 14, 1746.

107. See appendix L in Towner, "A Good Master Well Served . . . " (Ph.D. diss., Northwestern University, 1954).

108. For those who found no solace in the opposite sex, by choice or circumstances, homosexuality and bestiality may have provided an outlet. I located two instances of homosexuality and four of bestiality. In Plymouth Colony in 1642 a servant named Thomas Roberts was committed with a friend for "often spendinge their seede one vpon another. . . . " *Plym. Recs.,* I, 64. The other homosexual charge was against two maid-servants in the same year. *Essex County Court,* I, 44. The first, and most remarkable, case of bestiality is recorded in *Plym. Recs.,* II, 44, and *Bradford's History,* 474–476. A youthful servant was executed for buggery with a mare, a cow, two goats, two calves, and a turkey! He claimed he'd learned his technique in Old England. One other was found guilty of buggery, a man with a heifer, and two were found not guilty, a woman and a dog, and a Negro with a cow. In that order, MSS. Bristol Sessions, I, 46–47 (1699/1700); MSS. Superior Court of Judicature, 1715–1721, folio 49 (1719); *Assistants,* I, 74 (1676).

109. Dean Albertson, "Puritan Liquor In the Planting of New England," *N.E.Q.,* XXIII (Dec., 1950), 477–479.

110. *Ibid.,* 485–486.

111. *Ibid.,* 483–484, 486–487.

112. Dow, *Every Day Life . . . ,* 111.

113. *Ibid.,* 110.

114. Whitmore, *Laws,* 137.

115. Pulsifer, *Laws,* 195. Whitmore, *Laws,* 228–229.

116. M.H.S., 2 *Proc.,* XIII, 252 (1686).

117. Samuel Adams Drake, *Old Boston Taverns and Tavern Clubs* (Boston, 1917), 14. Winship, *Boston in 1682 . . . ,* Introduction, xii.

118. Winship, *loc. cit.*

119. *Ibid.,* 52.

120. *Ibid.,* xiii.

121. See *Acts and Resolves,* I, 37, 51, 56 (1692); 122–123 (1693); 190–192 (1694/5); 223–224 (1695); 327–330 (1698); 679–682 (1711/12); II, 194–195 (1721); 700–701 (1734).

122. February 17–24, 1737. See also Benjamin Wadsworth, *An Essay to do Good . . .* (Boston, 1710); Cotton Mather, and others, *A Serious Address to those who unnecessarily frequent the Tavern . . .* (EoFton, 1726J.

123. John Campbell, *After Souls by Death are Separated from their Bodies . . .* (Boston, 1738), 34–36. See, for other warnings by dying men, footnote 95, above.

124. *Winthrop's Journal,* I, 38.

125. *Plym. Recs.,* I, 132.

126. *Ibid.,* 68.
127. *Winthrop Papers,* IV, 131.
128. *Essex County Court,* I, 3 (1636); 7 (1638); 10 (1638); 11 (1639); 57 (1643); II, 48 (1657); IV, 286 (1670); VII, 315–316 (1682); *Suffolk County Court,* I, 189 (1672); MSS. Suffolk County Court, I, 220 (1684); II, 245 (1685); 254 (1685); 256 (1685); *Plym. Recs.,* I, 118 (1638/9); II, 105 (1646); *Assistants,* II, 70 (1637); III, 63–66 (1657); M.H.S., 2 *Proc.,* VII, 168–171 (1678); MSS. Suffolk Sessions, III, 85–86 (1721, three cases); MSS. Essex Sessions, IV, 144 (1724/5); *N.E. Journal,* Jan. 1, 1728; Nov. 22, 1731; *Evening-Post,* Sept. 17, 1739; *Gazette,* June 2–9, 1740.
129. Cotton Mather, *Rules for the Society of Negroes, 1693. . . .,* 7. For other exhortations to temperance see Evans, *American Bibliography,* numbers 503 (1690), 778 (1697), 1364 (1708), 1452 (1710).
130. Cotton Mather, *A Good Master Well-Served . . . ,* 15–16.
131. *Gazette,* Sept. 6–13, 1736; *News-Letter,* Feb. 1, 1750.
132. July 17, 1750,
133. *Assistants,* II, 5 (1630).
134. *Essex County Court,* II, 116; MSS. Suffolk Sessions, IV, 128. One possible objection to such entertainment can be seen in the case of Hannah Goss who kept a bed and allowed two servants, John Linsey and Joanna Bishop, to go to bed together in her presence in "A Lascivious manner." MSS. Suffolk County Court, I, 194 (1683/4). For others see MSS. Middlesex County Court, III, 34 (1672); *Suffolk County Court,* I, 222–223 (1672/3); *Essex County Court,* II, 189 (1659); III, 251 (1665); IV, 275 (1670), V, 143 (1673); *Boston Records,* VI, 95 (1681); MSS. Suffolk Sessions, I, 133 (1706).
135. MSS. Middlesex County Court, IV, 116; Conungo was again convicted of the same offense in 1691, *ibid.,* V, 87; MSS. Suffolk Sessions, IV, 344–345 (1731). For others see *Mass. Recs.,* I, 262 (1639); *Plym. Recs.,* I, 118 (1638/9); *Essex County Court,* VIII, 46 (1680); *Suffolk County Court,* I, 336 (1673); II, 897 (1677/8); MSS. Plymouth Sessions, I, 139 (1698); MSS. Suffolk County Court, I, 130 (1682); 218 (1684); II, 243 (1684/5); 317 (1686).
136. *Essex County Court,* IV, 237 (1670).
137. *Essex County Court,* IV, 256–258 (1670).
138. *The Well-Ordered Family . . . ,* 118.
139. *Assistants,* II, 131; MSS. Middlesex Court Files, file 58, no number (Apr.–June, 1671); MSS. Middlesex County Court, IV, 158; MSS. Essex Sessions, I, n.p.; MSS. Suffolk Sessions, II, 130–131; MSS. Plymouth Sessions, III, 129–130. See also MSS. Middlesex Court Files, file 56, no number (Mar. 8, 1671/2). Nathaniel King, convicted of stealing money for liquor and food; and MSS. Suffolk County Court, II, 387 (1690/1). A Negro and an Indian, both servants, stole several bottles of brandy from the Negro's master.

140. Jan. 12–19, 1738.
141. July 9–16, 1741. On the return trip the boat overturned and only three survived.
142. Jan. 14, 1740. For another party involving servants' drinking, see MSS. Suffolk County Court, I, 218 (1684). For fiddle players see advertisements for Negroes, Indians, and mulattoes in *News-Letter,* Aug. 26–Sept. 2, 1736; *Gazette,* June 20–27, 1737; Oct. 2–9, 1738; June 2–9, 1740; July 9, 1745; Oct. 11, 1748; *Evening-Post,* Jan. 23, 1738; July 17, 1738, July 9, 1739; Feb, 9, 1741; Dec, 24, 1750; *Post-Boy,* May 4, 1741. At least one Negro of Massachusetts was an accomplished musician. Barzillai, oldest son of a Negro slave and mulatto ex-servant, was born Nov. 5, 1743. He became a famous musician and had children who were musicians. M.H.S., 3 *Proc.,* II, 198.
143. See Carl Bridenbaugh, *Cities . . . ,* 117–118, 277, 437–438.
144. *Ibid.,* 117–118; Evans, *American Bibliograrphy,* number 921 (1700); Winship, *Boston in 1682 . . . ,* Introduction, xvii.
145. Parkes, "Morals and Law Enforcement . . . ," *N.E.Q.,* V (July, 1932), 438–439; *Courant,* Mar, 4–11, 1723; News-Letter, Mar. 28–Apr. 5, 1740. Bridenbaugh, *Cities . . . ,* 437–438.
146. Compare the passenger list of the *John and Sarah* in *Suffolk Deeds,* I, 5–6 (1652), and the list of members for 1657 in *Scots Charitable Society.*
147. *Ibid.,* 94 (1684).
148. *Ibid.,* 25–46. See Oscar Handlin, *The Uprooted. The Epic Story of the Great Migration that Made the American People* (Boston, 1952), 172 ff.
149. Bridenbaugh, *Cities . . . ,* 134 (1737).
150. Cotton Mather, *Diary,* M.H.S., 7 *Colls.,* VII, 176.
151. *Ibid.,* 176–177, 177 n.
152. *Ibid.,* 364.
153. MSS. diary interleaved with *Nath'l Ames Almanac for 1744,* n.p. June 10. M.H S.
154. *Gazette,* June 10–17, 1734.
155. *Boston Records,* XIII, 87. For funeral practices see Samuel Sewall's *Diary,* M.H.S., 5 *Colls.,* V, 469–470; Justin Winsor, ed., *The Memorial History of Boston Including Suffolk County, Massachusetts. 1630–1680* (Boston, 1880–1881), II, 243n. (895 pounds subscribed for funeral of the Reverend Mr. William Cooper), 474n.; Bridenbaugh, *Cities . . . ,* 412. Other social habits of the master class were emulated as well. For example, four Negroes were arrested on Boston Commons for dueling with swords. *News-Letter,* Mar. 11–18, 1742.
156. *Boston Records,* VIII, 176–177.
157. *Essex County Court,* II, 107; *Suffolk County Court,* II, 644. In 1732 another castration was narrowly averted when an Indian servant cut

another Indian in his "private parts" greatly endangering his life "&c." MSS. Bristol Sessions, III, 193. For other belligerent servants see *Suffolk County Court,* I, 254 (1673); *Essex County Court,* VI, 193 (1676); MSS. Middlesex Court Files, file 51, no number (case of William West, Mar. 17, 1668/9); MSS. Suffolk Sessions, IV, 89–90 (1727); 135 (1727/8); 367 (1731); MSS, Essex Sessions, IV, 144 (1724/5); MSS. Suffolk County Court, I, 180 (1683); 183 (1683).

158. MSS. Middlesex County Court, I, 274 (Nov. 5, 1662). For other cases involving riots on Pope's day see MSS. Suffolk County Court, 1, 139 (1682) I, 180 (1683). In this case, a servant, and another young man were convicted of "riotous carriages" toward Benoni Eaton of Cambridge, riding on the highway from Dedham, pretending to be the watch, and swearing; MSS. Suffolk Sessions, VI, n.p. (Jan. 2, 1749/50). For the newspaper story see *Evening-Post,* Nov. 11, 1745. Following the quoted story is a letter from a "Gentleman of great Character. . . . " damning the riots and asking, "can our Children or Servants be *safe* in the Streets at such a Time, if such Rioters be permitted?" Other news items concerning Pope's day riots can be seen in *News-Letter,* Oct. 23, 1746; Nov. 3, 1748; Nov. 2, 1749; *Evening-Post,* Nov. 5, 1739. For a modern treatment of the subject see Esther Forbes, *Paul Revere and the World He Lived In* (Cambridge, 1943), 89–93.

159. MSS. Superior Court of Judicature, I, 2.

160. MSS. Suffolk Sessions, III, 85, 86 (1721). See also *ibid.,* III, 195 (1725), four Negroes rioting.

161. *Boston Records,* VIII, 173–175. *House Journals,* V, 18–19, 36, 43, 48, 114, 121, 138, 145, 258, 259, 264, 274, 286, 292, passed in the negative. However, there were isolated acts which regulated Negroes. See *Acts and Resolves,* I, 154, 327 (1693/4 and 1698, being at public house without consent of master); 578 (1705, striking a white man); 535–536 (1703, out at night without consent).

162. *Boston Records,* XIV, 193.

163. These games are illustrated and explained with short verses in *A Little Pretty Pocket-Book, Intended for the Instruction and Amusement of Little Master Tommy and Pretty Miss Polly . . .* (Facsimile of First Worcester Edition, 1787), 27–29, 31, 47, 51.

164. *Boston Records,* VIII, 12, 20.

165. MSS. Suffolk Sessions, IV, 165.

166. *N.E. Journal,* June 18, 1733 (a servant boy drowned while fishing in a canoe); *Gazette,* Aug. 28, 1750 (Negro servant drowned while in a canoe); *Post-Boy,* Apr. 5, 1736, post script (apprentice drowned at Dorchester Neck); MSS. Bristol Sessions, III, a 66 (1719), (Indian and Negro servants borrow a boat); "Extracts from the Diary of John Rowe," M.H.S., 2 *Proc.,* X, 48–52 (fishing in the 1760's); *A Little*

Pretty Pocket-Book . . . , 30, 42; *Sibley's Harvard Graduates,* VI, 266–277; Dow, *Every Day Llfe* . . . , 113–114.

167. *A Little Pretty Pocket-Book* . . . , 24, 34.
168. Pulsifer, *Laws,* 66 (1656).
169. *Plym. Recs.,* VI, 15–16 (1679); *Suffolk County Court,* II, 1162 (1679/80); MSS. Bristol Sessions, II, 215 (1713). For other card players (non-servant) see MSS. Suffolk County Court, I, 170 (1683); II, 301 (1686); *Sibley's Harvard Graduates,* VI, 402.
170. See C.S.M. *Pubs.,* XIII, 154, 156; M.H.S., 7 *Colls.,* VII, 202; R. Spofford Ainsworth, "Lotteries in American History," American Hirtorical Association, *Annual Report for the Year 1892* (Washington, 1893), 174.
171. *Essex County Court,* IV, 257.
172. MSS. Hampshire County Court, I, 106.
173. Cotton Mather, *Diary,* M.H.S., 7 *Colls.,* VIII, 363 n.
174. MSS. Bristol Sessions, II, 158 (1709), "pretending to discover lost or stolen goods and to find out ye persons that have them. . . . " See also *Evening-Post,* Jan. 8, 1739; *Post-Boy,* Apr. 11, 1743; *News-Letter,* Aug. 26–Sept. 2, 1736.
175. Samuel Willard, *A Compleat Body of Divinity* . . . , 649 (second pagination).
176. *Boston Records,* XIV, 96–97.
177. *News-Letter,* Jan. 1, 1747.

7. The Servant Protests

Inevitably, protests arose against a labor system restraining the individual worker for a few years or for a lifetime from taking advantage of the manifold opportunities existing in a new land for economic and social advancement. Particularly was this true of workers, who in many instances rejected, or at least did not completely accept, the underlying goals of the society in which they lived. Even the master class recognized this incompatibility and protested against the attempt to assimilate alien groups differing in race, religion, or social mores.[1] Frequently these protests did not represent complete rejection of the system, on the part of either master or servant, but were rather representations against excesses of individuals who were part of the system. Both classes protested then, but with one major difference. The master class reacted verbally, articulately: the servants, usually, though not always, reacted physically, running the gamut from minor disobedience to physical violence against their masters or members of the master class, and against themselves and their progeny. The master class was organized, however, and had fairly effective control of the courts and other means of discipline, whereas the servant, except in rare instances, acted alone or in conjunction with a friend or relative. Thus it was that minor protests against *excesses* were often successful in or out of court, but major protests against the *system* were unsuccessful and were followed with dire punishment.

A feeble thread of dissent on the part of the master class against various aspects of the system of servitude runs through the history of the period. Based at times on religious conviction, at times on economic considerations, patriotic motives, or a desire for racial purity, it never condemned all aspects of bound labor, for temporary servitude went unquestioned, even though slavery was opposed by some.

The first recorded protest against a part of the institution occurred in the *Body of Liberties,* which in 1641 set the death penalty for manstealing, and established the legality of slavery but placed

163

restrictions on the manner in which slaves were to be acquired. These, based on the Biblical injunction in Exodus 21:16, were undoubtedly placed within the *Body of Liberties* with serious intent,[2] for when the General Court became aware of the manner in which two slaves were acquired in Africa in 1645, they were ordered returned and the men involved were charged with manstealing. The disposition of the case is not known, except that the slaves were returned to Africa.[3] Three decades later the provision against manstealing was brought again into play in a case of Indian kidnapping. Two partners were indicted, along with their ship's master, for the stealing and transportation of seventeen Indian men, women, and children. The men were acquitted, although the Indians apparently regained their freedom.[4]

Judge Samuel Sewall, in his famous tract, *The Selling of Joseph,* cited the same Biblical injunction against manstealing and ranked it among the most atrocious of crimes, as did Elihu Coleman, Nantucket Quaker, whose antislavery tract equated it with murder.[5] Cotton Mather, slave owner, also proscribed manstealing, as distinct from the institution of slavery. In 1710, he published in Boston a tract entitled *Theopolis Americana . . . ,* in which he on the one hand damned the slave trade but on the other urged that if slaves must be had, they should be treated as Christians. "To go as Pirates, and Catch up poor Negroes . . . that have never forfeited Life, or Liberty, and to make them *Slaves* and sell them," he wrote,

> is One of the worst kinds of Theivery in the World; and such Persons are to be taken for the common enemies of Mankind: and they that buy them, and use them as Beasts, for their meer Commodity, and betray, or destroy, or neglect their Souls, are fitter to be called, *Incarnate Devils,* than *Christians,* tho' they be no *Christians* whom they so Abuse.[6]

Remonstrance against kidnapping by no means exhausted the protests of the class against certain aspects of servitude. Excessive physical abuse was proscribed, as well. The courts' frequent punishment or restraint of masters who were immoderate in their discipline is testimony to that effect, for after all, the courts were in the hands of those who gave the orders, not those who served. An early case was that of one Lewis who was enjoined not to strike his servant, John Lowe, in 1643.[7] Of greater significance was the reaction against William Franklin who caused the death of his "apprentice," Nathaniel Sewall, in 1644. In extenuation of his crime, it was admitted that the boy had the scurvy and "was withal very noisome, and otherwise ill disposed." Unlovely as he may have been, the court felt that Sewall had been used hardly. He was exposed to wet and wintry weather, and "divers acts of rigor [were used] toward him, as hanging him in the chimney, etc., and the boy being very poor and weak, he tied him upon an horse and so brought him (sometimes sitting and sometimes hanging down) to Boston, being five miles off. . . . " Franklin refused him water on the way, and the boy died a few hours after arriving in Boston. After much deliberation about intent, and one postponement, Franklin was hanged.[8] The members of Franklin's church felt as strongly as the court, for they excommunicated him.[9]

Not much later, John Winthrop received a letter from Thomas Jenner of Saco concerning a child of one Mrs. Allin who had been put out to Goodman Dexter of Lynne. The mother had heard that her son's conditions were bad, and "the truth is, the boy is used very hardly. . . . " Jenner knew whereof he spoke, for he continued

I saw the youth at Dexters owne house most miserable in clothing, neuer did I se any worse in New-Engld. I humbly intreat your worship to lay to heart the condition both of the mother, and the child, least it be some disparagement to our selues euen in London from whence they came, and were well known. The youth was not so firmly bound, but your worships (as I conceiue) may easily vnloose him.[10]

Thus did protests come from the master class.

Even higher than Winthrop, the protests came from the Crown as well, for in 1702, Queen Anne, in an order to Governor Joseph Dudley, required him to

endeavour to gett a Law passed, for the restraining of inhuman severities, which by ill Master or Overseers may be used towards their Christian Servants, and their Slaves, and that Provision be made therein, that the willfull killing of Indians and Negroes may be punished with Death, and that a fitt penalty be imposed for the maiming of them.[11]

Sermons and tracts published in Massachusetts in the late seventeenth and early eighteenth centuries carried out this theme. Cotton Mather, Benjamin Wadsworth, and Samuel Willard were among those who warned against immoderate punishment and urged masters to "Correct with Prudence and Humanity."[12] Other protests included the failure of masters to pay their servants their due,[13] failure to Christianize them,[14] denial of adequate food and clothing,[15] lack of care in time of sickness,[16] and the temptation to overwork them.[17]

More important in its outcome than peripheral complaints, however, was the thread of antislavery sentiment which can be remarked in the first half of the eighteenth century. Judge Sewall opposed slavery on racial and economic grounds. There were too many slaves in the province already, he felt, and "Few can endure to hear of a Negro's being made free . . . indeed they can seldom use their freedom well. . . . "

> And there is such a disparity in their Conditions, Colour & Hair, that they can never embody with us, and grow up into orderly Families, to the Peopling of the Land: but still remain in our Body Politick as a kind of extravasat Blood.

Moreover, economically, white servants were a much better investment for a few years, than Negroes for life.[18]

Echoing his sentiments, and indeed attributed to him, was an article in *The Boston News-Letter* published a few years after the *Selling of Joseph*. Negroes were likely to be thieves and liars, this argument ran, and they did not carry arms to defend the country, nor could they people the land with desirable subjects. White servants could be sent to war instead of the master's son, Negroes could not. White servants not only cost about one-third as much as slaves, but if the servant died, the loss was not so great.[19]

Ten years later, in 1716, patriotic motives were appealed to when Negro slaves were found to be a hindrance to the "Peopling and Improving the Country . . . ,"[20] And, in 1736, a local newspaper reprinted at length an article from the *Political State of Great Britain,* which reminded its readers that a sturdy yeomanry was the backbone of any English settlement. This backbone would be considerably weakened if Negro slaves were to be used rather than white indentured servants as the basic source of labor.[21] Such antislavery and anti-Negro sentiment received encouragement in the form of duties on Negroes (and Indians) imported into the province, and in bounties encouraging the importation of white servants.[22]

Religious convictions, too, led men to protest against the institution of slavery. Early among these was Judge Sewall's argument. All men, he thought, as sons of Adam were co-heirs and had an equal right to liberty. Originally and naturally, no such thing as slavery existed.[23] He not only demolished the argument that it was "a good" that Negroes should be enslaved so that they could become Christianized ("Evil must not be done, that good may come of it") but he flatly recognized the inconsistency between Christianity and perpetual bondage.[24] Later he had a tract, originally published in

London in 1704, reprinted in Boston. Taken from the *Athenian Oracle,* it answered affirmatively the question: "Whether trading for Negroes, i.e., carrying them out of their own Country into perpetual Slavery, be in itself Unlawful, and especially contrary to the great Law of Christianity?" The wars in which they were taken, the article asserted, were unjust, for they were started for that purpose. Even if Negroes were not stolen, buying them was as bad as stealing. One had no right to damn them because they were heathens, and once baptized they must be set free. How did one dare to disrupt God's ordering of humanity by making slaves of them?[25] A decade later an attack on the importation of slaves appeared in a pamphlet, which held that the "receiver is as bad as the Thief; and that if there were no Receivers, there would be no Thieves. . . . " It went on to ask,

> It those are true *Proverbs,* then are not we of this Country guilty of that Violence, Treachery and Bloodshed, that is daily made use of to obtain them; we rendering ourselves Partakers with them in that wickedness? (For 'tis not to be supposed, that these do voluntarily abandon themselves to be carried into a Foreign Country and there to be sold for Slaves.)[26]

Elihu Coleman's pamphlet, mentioned above, not only damned manstealing, but took the Quaker position on slavery as a whole. He distinguished between temporary servitude and perpetual bondage,[27] and went on to show that making one a slave was worse than killing in self defense.[28]

Finally, in 1737, *The New-England Weekly Journal* reprinted the argument from the *Athenian Oracle,* which had as its climax:

> If they come freely, what need a Cargo be carry'd to purchase them? What need of Chains and Bolts and Fetters? And why do many of thse [sic] poor Wretches endeavour to destroy themselves if so highly glad of being carried into perpetual Slavery? Or, if they find themselves happier under their Bondage than in their own Country, what is the Reason that when one of their fellow Slaves dies, all the rest sing and rejoyce and dance about him, as foolishly concluding he is happily return'd to his own country?[29]

The protests of the master class with regard to servitude, for the most part, dealt only with various abuses of the institution, not the institution itself. Only in the case of Negro slavery did they object to a fundamental part of the system, and even then it was generally on some other grounds than that of the equality of man. Those who genuinely objected to the slavery of man were few, and even those objected only to the permanent aspects of it, not to the temporary exploitation of a laboring person for a limited number of years. Such exploitation was part of the social and economic fabric of the times. Only the individual servants could protest against that, and only as individual protests were multiplied many times over did the individual reactions against specific abuse or abuses take on the appearance of rejection of the system.

To answer the question: "why did the servants react to servitude as they did," one could say it was because they were of an inferior sort, or that they were primitives who did not understand English civilization, or that they were lazy persons who would not have wqrked at all if it had not been for the discipline of a master and a society which backed up that master.[30] All of the above were true, in part. Certainly many servants were of an inferior sort. Some had been criminals in the colony, some Negroes and Indians were considered primitive, and still others were apparently just plain ne'er-do-wells. Yet it is not the entire answer. Outside of the main structure of society, held in an inferior position, restricted for years or for life from recognition by the society in whích they lived and from the acquisition of property, many servants naturally failed to see the point of full cooperation with their masters. Punishment or threat thereof was not enough to assure good behevior, and, except in the cases of apprenticeship, an adequate system of reward was not forthcoming.[31] In their protests, servants often opposed only minor infractions of the accepted rules of the institution, not the institution itself. However, all through the period certain protests in the form of one type of violence or another indicated rejection of the system. One servant, for example, condemned for the murder of his master, put his finger on the sore point when he said that:

> His *Pride* had been his *Bane;* For, he thought much of it, that such a one as *he,* should be a *Servant;* and he would sometimes utter such words as these, *I am Flesh and Blood as well as my Master and therefore I know no Reason why my Master should not obey me as well as I obey him.*[32]

Freedom was the answer, as it always has been.

Some were content to apply legally for relief against minor irritations as well as for freedom. One common protest was against physical abuse, or the threat of abuse, on the part of the master. They did not like to be beaten, but many were, and since moderate correction was considered perfectly normal, it is safe to assume that the life of the average servant was not free from blows of one kind or another.

Apparently the colonists took seriously the early injunction of the Governor and Company of Massachusetts Bay that "correccon is ordained for the fooles back. . . . "[33] Roger Glasse complained, when his master corrected him in a most "extreme and barbarous manner."[34] Welthian Richards' maid was afraid to go home after letting the cows escape. She admitted, however, that her mistress had not beaten her lately, just a blow or two on the ear.[35] In 1645, Daniel Kumble was fined for hitting his servant on the head with a hammer.[36] One John Bridges of Salem, petitioned for help in 1676 complaining that:

> he [his master] haveing shamefully abused and beaten me, soe
> that it is questionable wheather ever I shall be sound againe or
> not, he beate me so much one Saboath day after meeting
> which I counted an unfitt tyme for such discipline if I had
> deserved it that I was sick, and uncapable to doe any
> worke. . . . [37]

Isaac Richardson was fined in Charlestown for inhuman treatment of his apprentice in 1679, by "burneing of his breech at ye fire." The apprentice was given a new master and abated one year of his time for "recompense of his smart & payne endured . . . ,"[38] and in 1682 William Obbinson forfeited a ten pound bond he had posted against "any bad usage or beating of his Servant Dominick Dounough. . . . "[39]

Many other complaints against extreme punishment were made. Salem's Joan Suiflan, Irish maid, asserted, in 1681, that her master and mistress beat her with a horsewhip; Tobiah Taylor of Ipswich claimed that his master hung him by the wriste, tied his legs straddled so he could not wiggle, and then whipped him and struck him with a rake; James Taylor, in Salem in 1702/3, was immoderately beaten, without just cause, until he was in danger of life and health; Thomas Smith, of Boston, lost his apprentice after beating him until he was "black as a shoe all over his back and Shoulders . . . "; and Jaboz Henly's master was cautioned, in 1718, against using an improper instrument for purposes of correction.[40] A final example of rather unusual punishment against which servants protested is the case of Phillip Fowler, presented for abusing his servant, Richard Parker of Ipswich, in 1682. The court agreed that a misbehaving servant needed punishment but thought that Fowler should be cautioned against hanging up his servant by the heels as butchers do "beasts for the slaughter. . . . "[41]

Servants frequently objected not only to abuse but to the failure of their masters to live up to the terms of their agreements. Apprentices in particular, being in a strong position because of backing from parents or relatives who often lived in the same neighborhood, protested frequently the failure of their masters to teach a trade, or to comply with their indentures with regard to reading and writing. Such remonstrance was effective if it could be proven, for it was considered a breach of contract voiding the indenture.[42] As early as 1647, for example, an apprentice was freed becauee of his master's failure to teach him the trade of a locksmith.[43] In 1685, an apprentice who had lived nine years with Edward Hill, cordwainer of Boston, was freed for having not been taught a craft. The boy was not only ignorant of a trade, but was "very ragged & fil'd with vermin. . . . " His master, moreover, had encouraged him to steal and to do other "evil practices."[44]

Apprentices were sometimes employed at menial tasks unrelated to the training bargained for and this too led to protest. Such was the case of Mathias Smith, in 1672, who complained that he was employed constantly at common labor.[45] The following lonely petition illustrates both the plight of the indentured servant far from home and at the mercy of an unknown master, and the fact that his protests were heard and recorded.

> Intreatinge your honors to take the present condision of your poor Servant into consideration I hav'ge a desire to com into this land hoping I might have beane honestly dealt with: but I have found it far otherwayse; my passage was honestly paid by my friends; the man that had the care of me sold me for thirty shilinges to my master Thomas Peachey his family is so disordered as I can never expeckt to learn any good of him nither for soule nor body: he did ingage to teach me his traid of a Tailourr: but for his other Traides I hope god will give me more grace then to learn his humour is such that I am afraid of my life if I shold be forced to abid out my Tim with him; by Reson of the great abuces I have allreadi Reseeved at his hand Therfore I humbly intreat the faviour of this honored Court to helpe me beinge farr off and destitut of friends to stand by me that whatever becom of me I might not be forced into his hands anymore . . . if this honored Court will be pleased to direckt me to some honest master whereby I may afterward be abell to gett a poor livinge [in] the world: I shall be ever Bound to pray for your honors proscerity

> ### William Henwood[46]

Failure to teach a trade was not the only breach of the labor contract protested against. Inadequate food and clothing could be as important to the present health of a servant as the learning of a skill was to his future welfare. Moreover, to the many servants who were not taught a trade, the conditions of their servitude were all-important. All such charges were significant, because, if well founded, they too could lead to abrogation of the indenture.[47] Complaints were frequent, and the following cases illustrate the variety of actions to which they could lead. Sarah Harmon complained, in 1680, that Obadiah Emons was failing to provide suitable clothing and other necessaries for her son James Harmon. The son was freed and ordered apprenticed to another. Three years later, a master was given two weeks to change his custom of failing to provide convenient clothing and food, or lose his servant. Finally, John Cornish, master to Joseph Calef, after having shown that his servant was now better provided for than formerly, was dismissed promising to continue such provision.[48] Other protests about broken indentures included: being put to an unduly severe journeyman,[49] Sabbath work,[50] general neglect,[51] transfer without consent,[52] being locked out,[53] being locked out in midwinter while pregnant,[54] adding time to an illiterate servant's indenture,[55] neglect while in prison,[56] and putting a servant's children out without consent.[57]

A few complaints were made to the effect that masters refused to take servants into their service as agreed,[58] but many more were the servants who wished to get out of their uneasy servitude. Some used the excuse that their masters were leaving or had left the province,[59] while others just thought that their terms were too long. Such a one was John Eggon of Salem, who in 1664 complained he had been sold to several masters and had several years added to his term.[60] Another case appeared in the petition of Grace Pearson of Boston, who said her daughter had been bound out to age eighteen, that she had served seven years and had four to go. Grace decided, in 1732, that such terms amounted to slavery.[61] Another, one Stephen Mattock, petitioned to the Middlesex County court in 1653 that he not only had served long enough and should be free, but that he thought he should receive some recompense, because he had served beyond the age of twenty-one. His petition pointed out that he had been bound out to several different men without an indenture, that he had recently learned he owed a Mr. Treadaway of Watertown the coming summer, and that a Mr. Bunckar claimed his time for the following two years.[62]

Many suits for freedom arose over the legality of the indentures which bound the servant to his master. Some servants claimed that they had been tricked into signing. One, a Joseph Basker of Bristol, England, claimed he had intended to pay his own fare across the ocean, but had been forced to sign an indenture as security for his paying in New

England. When he arrived, the master of the ship refused his proffer of eight pounds and insisted upon his honoring his signature. The county court freed him, but the superior court of judicature reversed the decision.[63]

Another, hired out to a butcher by his grandfather, was persuaded to sign indentures in his guardian's absence, and without the latter's consent, a common complaint.[64] In Boston, two Indians were able to thwart the desire of their masters to send them to sea, in 1710, and at the same time, they obtained their freedom, since their indentures were found by the court to be improperly drawn, They were declared freemen and at their own disposal as any other Indians of the province.[65] The most extreme case of improper indentures occurred in the next decade in Plymouth County. Thankfull Wichett and her mother, Indians, complained that Quintin Crymble of Plymouth held indentures on three of her children as security for the performance of a three-year indenture by Thankfull's husband. Crymble attempted to enforce the contracts, but a court freed the children on the grounds that Crymble had a ninety pound bond in the name of the husband for a guarantee.[66]

Direct appeals for freedom were made by servants on other grounds as well. Adam, a Negro, appealed to the court in Suffolk County for his freedom, in 1703, claiming he had served his time, but the court ruled he was still a servant of his master.[67] Penelope, Negro and widow of a Charlestown slave, petitioned the Middlesex Court for her freedom on the grounds that, in 1691, her master had promised that she would be free after certain conditions were fulfilled. These conditions, she claimed, were fulfilled, yet she was kept as a slave. The case went to a jury which found her free.[68] Among Indian appeals for freedom was the case of Phebe of Bristol County, who claimed she was eighteen and should be free. Her master claimed her as a slave for life. The court determined on four more years of servitude.[69] Two white apprentices asked the court for their freedom after their master had died and their mistress had married another man, who assumed the direction of their activities. Their petition was denied, although both claimed they were not being properly instructed in their former master's trade of victualler.[70]

Protests to the courts thus covered a variety of complaints, and they were met with not indifferent success. Roughly fifty-five percent achieved some redress or modification of conditions of servitude. About half were made on behalf of or by apprentices, and the same proportion holds with regard to successful complaints.[71] That apprentices appealed to the courts more often than indentured servants, Indians, or Negroes, can be explained by a possibly higher literacy rate, the strong presumption that they had parents or interested relatives near by, and the fact that their rights were better defined.

Despite the regularity with which protests occur in the courts, illegal methods of dissent were far more frequent and hold a commanding position in the history of servant reaction to the institution of servitude. The costs of an unsuccessful suit would have to be borne by the servant or his friends. This alone must have forced many into non-legal methods of protest. Witness fees, court costs, constable fees were all borne by the loser. More important was the awareness that the courts were in the hands of the master class, and except in cases of clear neglect, abuse, or illegality, there was little chance of success. Most important of all, how could one tell the courts that he simply did not want to be a servant? How could one explain with any hope of success that servitude simply did not appeal to him? How could one demonstrate that the labor system "unjustifiably" kept him from taking up land or a trade or from working for wages as a free man? How could the inarticulate articulately explain to the master class that servitude was degrading and frustrating? How could one explain that the countless minor irritations of being at someone else's beck and call for seven years or a lifetime built up explosive forces that demanded release in recalcitrance, in violence, in absenteeism, in running away?[72]

The recalcitrant servant was a commonplace in seventeenth- and eighteenth-century Massachusetts. So commonplace was he, indeed, that a veritable thesaurus of abuse was necessary in order to describe him. He was, "stubborn," "disrespectful," "disorderly," "incorrigible," "self-willed," "rebellious," "sullen" "insulting," "abusive," "saucy" and "wicked." He was also "useless," "unfaithful," "lazy," "rude," "unmannerly," "desperate," "neglectful," and "untoward." Moreover, he was of a "wisked disposition," inclined toward "crossness," "disobedience," and worst of all, quite capable of "resisting authority." So predominant was this stubborn behavior in the seventeenth century that the General Court, in 1654, ordered magistrates or commissioners to sentence such individuals to not more than ten stripes.[73] In 1679, the court, in prescribing the duties of tythingmen, ordered that they report to the magistrates or commissioners the names of stubborn and disorderly children and servants.[74] Three decades later matters had not improved much, apparently, for Cotton Mather's *A Faithful Monitor* . . . reminded his readers that a house of correction was to be provided in each county for, among others, "Stubborn Servants and Children. . . . "[75] And, in 1735, a warning to servants was published in Boston under the lurid title of *The Confession Declaration, Dying Warning and Advice of Patience Sampson . . . , Who Was Executed*

at York July 24, 1735 for the Murder of Benjamin Trot. . . . In it
servants were cautioned to obey their masters and to beware rebellion
and stubbornness.[76] That servants were reformed by laws, punishment,
or warnings is to be doubted. In 1741, *The Weekly News-Letter*
advertised:

> Cesar Negro slave to Robert Auchmuty, Esq; is to be Sold on
> reasonable Terms, provided he is transported to North-Carolina
> and there sold, his Master having experienced that what with
> the Charge and Trouble of sending Negroes to the House of
> Correction, and the Lenity of the Laws, and Punishment
> when there, the Master has his Slave returned to him in a more
> confirmed wicked Disposition than at first.
>
> N.B. It is to be hoped that sordid Lucre will not be an obstacle
> to other Masters that have the like ill-minded slaves from
> following so good a Precedent, and that by publick
> Advertisements of this Nature. And that the Great and General
> Court now sitting, will immediately by some further Act
> correct the Licentious Behaviour of this black Crew, and
> timely avert what a neighbouring Government providentially
> escaped.[77]

Moreover, advertisers with Negroes for sale apparently felt that the lack
of stubbornness or sullen behavior was a good selling point. The
descriptions often carried the words, "good tempered," "good natured,"
"not sullen" or assurances that the Negro was not being sold because of
any "bad qualities."

These "bad qualitles" can be illustrated in numerous cases
throughout the period. John Pope was whipped for a rebellious and
stubborn carriage toward his master in 1640.[79] Richard Wilson got the
same treatment for "base reviling speeches" and refusal to obey his
master's lawful commands.[80] David Conway was whipped, in 1642, for
resisting his master.[81] In 1644, one James Thomas was sentenced to be
severely whipped for stubborness and disobedience to his master.[82] In
1648/9, one William Goodwin, servant to a John Hathorne of Essex
County, was whipped for maintaining a "lying and rebellious carriage"
toward his master.[83] In Cambridge, in 1653, one Joseph Shelton,
servant to Ensign Jonathan Carter, was "openly and severely" whipped
ten stripes for stubborness and rebellion. One month was added to his
time.[84] Twenty-five years later a Salem servant was charged with
abusive language and refusal to obey the commands of his master.[85] In
Northampton, a Negro named Cyrus, was charged with misspending his

master's time and violent and vehement carriage toward his master in 1686.[86] In 1700, a merchant sold his servant, because he had been saucy to the master's wife in his abeence.[87] The Reverend Mr. Ebenezer Parkman complained to his diary, in 1739, that his servant, John Kidney, had refused to put on old stockings and had been saucy.[88]

Many a servant got himself in trouble by protesting with a "saucy" tongue. In 1640, one Joseph Garlick was complained of for slander in repeating the complaints of John Hardy's servant, Benjamin Hammon. The "slanderous" remarks were: "if you see my mr you little think wt is in him for he is a very hasti man." Garlick deposed that Hammon complained of his master's swearing, cursing, and beating, and that he said, "it was wors with him now [tha]n when he lived with Lieft. howe for now he works night & day." The court had little sympathy for Hammon, finding hlm a "yong rash, unsetled & indiscreet yong man ready to run into divers enormities if Lett free." He had *indeed* been indiscreet, for he was sentenced to serve Hardy twelve months longer than his term.[89] Later indiscretion, disobeying his master, cost him a five pound fine and the posting of a bond for a year's good behavior.[90] If it seems strange that such mild dissent should receive so much attention, it is even stranger that a servant maid should be presented at court, as Elixabeth Iago was, for wishing that the "devil had Mary Lad and all the company, in which company was her master, John Attcason. . . . "[91]

More serious illegal protest than sauciness was refusal to serve or to sign an indenture indicating service due. In 1652, one Elline Wood refused to sign an indenture claiming he was only to serve a convenient time. Hailed before the court in Middlesex county he was ordered to serve for two years. He thereupon confessed that he was supposed to serve that length of time.[92] In another case, the indenture had been lost, and the servant refused to renew it even though he admitted he was bound for four years. He served his four years at court order.[93] A third case involved a William Perry of Boston in 1715 who had signed an indenture for two years in return for three pounds passage from Newfoundland. By mistake he was given the original copy of the contract and refused to return it. He also served according to his agreement. And he paid the costs of the complaint.[94]

Some sought freedom by altering, stealing, or destroying their indentures. Luke Perkins, for example, seventeenth-century Middlesex servant, attempted to cheat his master of a year's time by changing the dates on his contract. He failed.[95] A far-sighted (so he thought) servant named Nicholas Long, of Boston, destroyed his copy of the indenture, knowing that his master had lost the original and hoping to be free at his master's death. He also stole provisions from his owner's cellar. He needed to be free, for he had been many times too loose with his tongue, calling his master a rogue and his mistress a whore. He succeeded in getting two extra years, and his master was allowed to sell him to another.[96] In Essex County, an apprentice had the help of his father in destroying his indenture, while one servant girl stole hers apparently in preparation for running away.[97] This seemed to some a good thing to do, for several masters reported that servants had absconded taking their papers with them. Thus, William Bowden of Marblehead complained that his man was gone, his chest broken open, and the indenture gone too.[98]

Servant protests against living conditions or against servitude itself occasionally went beyond the bounds of reason. Probably nothing struck terror into the hearts of the master like the possibility of fire; deliberately to set fire to the buildings of one's master was protest indeed. In the days when most houses were built of wood, when fire fighting apparatus was simple and ineffective, a fire in the home quite often meant not only the destruction of property, but the loss of life as well. Arson, when detected, was therefore dealt with severely. The General Court, in 1652, taking cognizance of the fact that several dwelling houses had been set on fire, ordered the death penalty for persons of sixteen years of age and up who caused a dwelling house, meeting house, or storehouse to be burned, and a severe whipping plus double restitution for any other property destroyed by fire. Persons suspected of such crimes were to be held without bail until their trials.[99]

Indian, Negro, and white servants were convicted of arson during the period prior to 1750, with the majority of cases in the eighteenth century. Of those in the earlier period, the white arsonists outnumbered the Negroes,[100] but in the eighteenth century, as Negro slaves became more numerous, they accounted for most of the arson cases.[101]

Perhaps the most famous arsonists were Marja, Negro servant to Joshua Lambe of Roxbury, and Cheffaleer, Negro servant to Thomas Walker. In 1681, they were accused of joining together to fire two different homes, one the home of Marja's master. Marja confessed and was executed, but Cheffaleer, not being convicted, was merely sent out of the country. Marja's sentence, severe because a person died in the flames, included burning at the stake. It is this which has made her case famous. Some contend that she was burned to death, others that she was executed and her remains burned. More important for this study is the judgment of her contemporaries that she "in a discontent set her Mrs. house on fire in the dead of the night. . . . "[102] The white servants convicted of arson were not dealt with so severely as was Marja, although one was sentenced to twenty-one years' "slavery."[103]

In the eighteenth century, it was assumed that fires of undetermined origin, were set by Negroes. In the first place, several Negroes committed arson, such as the man who was to be executed in Boston in 1723 for firing one Powel's house at night. In the second place, Negroes were sometimes so foolish as to threaten or make known their intentions of burning down some one's house. Jeffry, Elizabeth Head's slave, advertised his intentions to set fire to his mistress' house, and he was promptly hailed into court, as was Caesar, servant to Thomas Fowler who threatened to burn Jobey Howland's dwelling, and Essex, Negro belonging to Ephraim Peabody, who was inclined toward arson at Phlllip Atwood's place.[104] Such actions through the years caused them to be immediately suspect at the first sign of arson. Thus two fires in Medway and Boston were attributed to unknown Negroes in the year 1749 by *The Boston Gazette or, Weekly Journal.*[105] Not only suspect, but tried, convicted, and sentenced by a newspaper, was the Negro whose story appeared in *The New-England Weekly Journal.*

> *Whereas on last Fryday night, between 10 and 11 o'clock, the Dwelling House, Barn, & Shop of Mr. Isaac Bemis was wholly consumed by Fire . . . ; and as its Probable he will also lose his Negro Man, who has been examined & committed, on Suspicion of being Guilty of said Fact. . . .*[106]

Violent protest was not limited to destruction of property, but included threats of violence against the master class, and acts of violence running from beatings to murder. The spleen of the dissatisfied servant was not always directed against those in authority, but instead was sometimes vented against others of the same status. Finally this form of protest was turned inwardly against the individual servant himself in the form of suicide.

Presumably most threats of violence on the part of servants toward the master class were taken care of by those who had responsibility for actions, but an occasional case appears in the court records where the master felt that legal steps were necessary. Usually some overt act, not necessarily connected with the threats, was charged as well, although this was not always the case. Captain Negro, slave of Captain John Ballentine of Boston, for example, was given twenty lashes and fined for threatening the blood of one Sarah Mason and her children in 1703. James Rosse, half a century earlier, had been given thirty-nine lashes for offering violence and shameful abuse to his master and fellow servants. Others, who combined action with threats, came more frequently into court. Thus, in 1654, one Andrew Tarras, servant to Lieutenant Appleton, was given twenty lashes and had thirteen weeks added to his service for threatening his master and his fellow servants, and for opposing his master's orders. Another, Thomas Queen, was convicted by confession in 1673/74 of cursing, and holding out his knife as if to cut his master. He was given thirty severe stripes and fined costs of court and prison.[107]

Cases of actual violence against the master class, more numerous than threats, follow a pattern similar to arson, for most involved white servants in the seventeenth century, and blacks in the eighteenth. These acts run all the way from the mere striking of blows up through assault and murder. Typical of minor blows struck were the cases of Mathew Boomer, William Hilton, William Johnson, and Sambo. They were charged with striking a master with a pitchfork, hitting a master, striking a constable, and striking a white man, respectively.[108]

Other acts of violence were more serious. William Simes, in 1654, had his servant, Scotsman Daniel Black, committed to prison after being assaulted and beaten by him. Charles Hill laid violent hands on his master, knocked him down twice, and brought blood to the surface. He only threatened to break his master's neck, but his master had had enough. In the eighteenth century, two violent servants brought blood and ran afoul of the law. The Reverend Mr. Ebenezer Parkman's Irish lad, John Kidney, attempted to assault the minister's daughter and cut her arms; the other, a Negro, affronted by the family to which he belonged, wounded two of its members with a cutlass, and blasted off the roof and one side of the house with a cask of gunpowder.[109] From this it was but one step to murder.

The first and most notorious case of murder of a master by a servant in Massachusetts Colony occurred in 1674, when Robert Driver and Nicholas Faevor were found guilty of murdering Robert Williams. In honor of the execution, Increase Mather preached and published a thirty-five page sermon, one of the first books printed in Boston. Titled *The Wicked Man's Portion or a Sermon (Preached at the Lecture in Boston in New-England the 18th day of the 1 Moneth 1674. when two men were executed who had murthered their Master.) Wherein is shewed That excess in wickedness doth bring untimely Death.*, it is a dull tome despite the fact that it was reprinted in 1685. If, as is quite probable, it was required that the servants listen to it before their execution, it was almost punishment enough. At least it is a classic illustration of adding insult to injury.[110]

Poison seems to have been a favorite means for would-be murderers. Easy to administer to one in the same household, and thought to be difficult to detect, it seemed the ideal way to rid one's self of an uneasy servitude, or at least of an unwanted master. Mark, servant of Captain John Codman of Boston, and involved with eleven other Negroes in the murder of his master, said he used poison, because he believed the Bible did not hold killing a sin if bloodshed were avoided. More probable he thought detection would be avoided.[111] At any rate, his trial along with Phillis and Phoebe, also servants to Codman is the most interesting of all cases involving poisoning. Before the murder, he had been successful in urging Phillis to burn down their master's workhouse hoping the Captain would be obliged to sell them for lack of work to do. Mark, who got the poison from a Doctor's slave (the second Doctor's slave he had approached) implicated Phoebe who, along with Phillis, cooked for Codman (part of his indictment of her throws light on the attitude of servants toward their masters, for she came into the shop one day and "got to dancing & mocking master & shaking herself & acting as master did in Bed"), However, the court found Mark and Phillis guilty of the murder and sentenced them to death, contenting itself with ordering Phoebe to be sold out of the country.[112]

Violent protest, on the part of individual servants, took one other form during the period—suicide.[113] The first known is recorded in *Winthrop's Journal*. A servant boy, who had stolen from his master and was threatened with court action, hanged himself. Winthrop wrote that the discontent of the boy arose from the long time he had yet to serve, "though he were well used." Fate played a cruel trick, for the day he died a letter arrived from his father with enough money to buy out his time.[114] Another case, about which there can be little doubt that it was protest against servitude, occurred in 1733, when a Negro woman of Salem cut her stomach open saying that she was going to her own country.[115] There were many others.

In 1662, Henry Bartholmew's Negro was found by a jury to have committed suicide. Ten years later, William Citterne, servant, was convicted of periodic drunkenness and attempting to poison himself. In 1682, a jury found that Joshua, Negro servant of Benj. Gaarfield, had cut his own throat. He had previously run away after burning down his master's barn and dwelling place. In 1733, a Negro man of Mr. John Walker clapped a pistol to his head and killed himself. Three years later, a Negro "wench" about sixteen years old belonging to Mr. Hardcastle of Boston was left at home while the family was at meeting. She locked all the doors and hanged herself. The girl had lived with her master about two or three months. A year later a "valuable" Negro man belonging to Mr. Peter Stone of Boston, tallow chandler was at work at Stone's farm in Roxbury, when "upon some Disgust [he] cut his

Throat with a Knife . . . he had sharpened for that Purpose. . . . "
To complete the job he then threw himself into a pond. In 1741, a
Negro boy succeeded in killing himself by jumping into a well. The
water was so cold he called for help, but even though he was pulled out
alive, he died of the cold. The same year, a Negro of Mr. Joseph
Goldthwaite of Boston, "being in a sullen Frame . . . ," hanged
himself. Stephen Williams, Minister at Longmeadow, lost two servants
by suicide. One, after being whipped for interrupting his master's
service, drowned himself in a well. The other slave accomplished the
same end in a mill pond. Finally, a Negro slave from Mendon
combined two forms of protest by attempting to murder his mistress
and her children, and by accomplishing his own self-destruction.[116]

While arson, murder, and suicide were ordinarily individual protests
directed against particular situations, an instance of group protest did
occur in Massachusetts prior to 1750. Slave revolts, and the less
common servant rebellions, were not unknown in other colonies,
especially where the numbers of servants were large,[117] but only one
organized revolt among the servant class, white or black, was attempted
in Massachusetts, and that in December of 1744. Its importance was
slight, viewed through colonial eyes, for only one of four Boston
newspapers carried the story; but viewed in the light of the many
instances of protest on the part of individual servants, it assumes greater
significance than would an isolated incident. As reported in *The Boston
Evening-Post,* a group of Irish servants and others joined in a "foolish
conspiracy to make an Insurrection in order to seize the Country with
an old Irish trooper at their head." Those who were captured (eight or
nine) were stood on the gallows until their faces were nipped with
frost.[118] Except for instances where servants organized in small numbers
for the purpose of running away, this group attempt was unique.

Although the institution of servitude was an unquestioned and
integral part of the every-day-life of the colonists, both the master class
and the servant class protested against certain aspects of it. Most master
protests were against abuse of the system, the essentials of which they
accepted, and only Negro slavery was held by some to be a violation of
the rights of manor of Christian principles. The servants, too, protested
against abuses within the system, only rarely against the system itself,
and even then only so far as it concerned themselves in particular. Legal
remedy was available for those who were abused or who thought they
were abused, so long as they did not reject the institution. To some,
however, servitude was intolerable, and these individuals found no form
of violence too great to commit in order to escape from it, or in order to
wreak vengeance upon society for having imposed it upon them. Except

in one instance, it did not occur to the servant class in Massachusetts to organize for resistance against that society. And since revolts were not unknown in other colonies, it can be assumed that the general conditions of bound labor were somewhat superior to those which existed in other areas. Abusive practices on the part of the master class existed, but they were particular, not general. Only in one form of protest—running away—was there sufficient evidence of fairly widespread unrest to indicate that servitude as a whole was an unsatisfactory labor system. This form of protest was significant enough to deserve separate treatment, and it is to running away that our attention is directed next.

NOTES

1. Governor William Bradford recognized this problem in 1642. Concerned with the number of "wicked" and "profane" persons who had already come to the New World, he wrote, "it is ever to be remembered that wher ye Lord begins to sow good seed, ther ye envious man will endeavor to sow tares. 2. Men being to come over into a wildernes, in which much labour & servise was to be done . . . such as wanted help in [tha]t respecte, when they could not have such as [th]ey would, were glad to take such as they could; and so, many untoward servants, sundry of them proved, that were thus brought over, both men & women kind; who, when their times were expired, became families of themselves, which gave increase hereunto. 3. An other and a maine reason hearof was, that men, finding so many godly disposed persons willing to come into these parts, some begane to make a trade of it, to transport passengers & their goods, and hired ships for that end; and then, to make up their fraight and advance their profite, cared not who ye persons were, so they had money to pay them." *Bradford's History,* 476–477. See also Parkes, "Morals and Law Enforcement . . . ," 436, who quotes Nathaniel Ward in 1635 "deploring the presence of 'multitudes of idle and profane young men, servants and others'. . . . "
2. Whitmore, *Laws,* 53, 55. Whitmore indexes the former as "Slavery prohibited," but George H. Moore, *History of Slavery . . . ,* 10–19, and Greene, *The Negro in Colonial New England . . . ,* 63–68 hold that the statement actually establishes slavery as a legal institution. There can be no doubt of their position.
3. For a discussion hostile to the sincerity of the injunction against manstealing see Greene, *The Negro in Colonial New England . . . ,* 67–68. For the case see *Mass. Recs.,* II, 168; III, 46, 49; *Winthrop's Journal,* II, 253. See also Moore, *History of Slavery . . . ,* 28–30.

4. *Assistants,* I, 86–88. For the manuscript of the indictment of the ship's captain, Jno. Houghton, see M.H.S. Miscellaneous Bound Manuscripts, Nov. 2, 1675. For a later case see MSS. Suffolk County Court, I, 99 (1681). Grizell Simerell complained she had been taken from Scotland against her will and separated from her husband, who was disposed of in Nevis. The court ordered her transported to Nevis and set on shore free.

5. Samuel Sewall, "The Selling of Joseph A Memorial," (Boston, 1700) in M.H.S., 1 *Proc.,* VII, 161–165. Elihu Coleman, *A Testimony Against that Anti-Christian Practice of Making Slaves of Men. Wherein it is Shewed to be Contrary to the Dispensation of the Law and Time of the Gospel, and very Opposite Both Grace and Nature* (n.p. 1733, reprinted in New Bedford, 1825), 19. Exodus 21:16 reads, "And he that stealeth a man, and selleth him, or if he be found in his hand, he shall surely be put to death."

6. *Theopolis Americana . . . ,* 21–22. Mather quotes from Richard and Baxter's *Christian Directory.*

7. Assistants, II, 133 (1643). In 1638, John Poole was fined £5 for abusing his servant. *Ibid.,* 80 (1638).

8. *Winthrop's Journal,* II, 187–189 (1644).

9. Morgan, *The Puritan Family . . . ,* 83.

10. *Winthrop Papers,* V, 77 (1646). For other protests by free persons against servants' abuse, see MSS. Suffolk Sessions, II, 25 (1713); E.I. *Colls.,* X, i, 91 (1711).

11. M.H.S., 2 *Proc.,* VIII, 93–105. Quote from 104.

12. Samuel Willard, A Compleat Body of Divinity . . . , 615 (second pagination). See also Cotton Mather, *A Good Master Well Served . . . ,* 15–16; BenJamin Wadsworth, *The Well-Ordered Family . . . ,* 105–106.

13. Wadsworth, *The Well–Ordered Family . . . ,* 107–108,

14. Cotton Mather, *Theopolis Americana . . . ,* 22–23; *A Good Master Well Served . . . ,* 16–18; Queen Anne to Governor Dudley, M.H.S., 2 *Proc.,* VIII, 93–105; Willard, *A Compleat Body of Divinity . . . ,* 16 (second pagination).

15. Cotton Mather, *A Good Master Well Served . . . ,* 13; Wadsworth, *The Well-Ordered Family . . . ,* 104.

16. Wadsworth, *loc. cit.*

17. *Ibid.,* 105.

18. Sewall, "The Selling of Joseph . . . ," 161–162.

19. June 3–10, 1706. Reprinted in Moore, *History of Slavery . . . ,* 107–108.

20. Quote from "Some Considerations upon the Several Sorts of Banks Propos'd as a Medium of Trade," C.S.M. *Pubs.,* VIII, 288 (Boston, 1716).

21. *Evening-Post,* Nov. 15, 1736.

22. *Acts and Resolves,* I, 578 (Dec. 5, 1705), a four pound per head import tax on Negroes; I, 634 (Feb. 26, 1708/9), extended the tax to Indians and provided forty shillings bounty for white servants between the ages of eight and twenty-five. See also *House Journals,* II, 25 (1718); VIII, 322 (1728); XI, 23 (1731). The latter is instructions from the Crown to Governor Belcher to prohibit duties on felons and Negroes.
23. Sewall, "The Selling of Joseph . . . ," 161–162.
24. *Ibid.,* 164–165.
25. Anonymous pamphlet, *The Athenian Oracle* . . . (Boston, 1705), 1–4. The copy at M.H.S. has a MSS. letter from Allyn Bailey Forbes attributing the reprinting of this pamphlet to Samuel Sewall.
26. "Some Considerations . . . ," 288 (1716).
27. Coleman, *A Testimony* . . . , 14.
28. *Ibid.,* 23.
29. *N.E. Journal,* June 21, 1737.
30. A case in point is to be seen in Samuel Danforth, *The Cry of Sodom Enquired Into* . . . , 8–9. While still a youth at home, Benjamin Goad, the subject of this tract, had "lived in Disobedience to his Parents. . . . " He had lied, stolen, broken the Sabbath, fled from the catechism, been slothful and idle, and committed buggery with an animal (after several unsuccessful attempts). Brought under the "Yoke of Government and Service, (which might have bridled and restrained him from such wickedness) . . . ," he violently broke away from his master and defiantly committed buggery in the middle of the day in an open field. For a master's complaint about lazy servants see *Winthrop Papers,* III, 176–178 (1634).
31. This is not universally true. Some masters promised rewards for faithful service, and others may well have been equally generous although little proof is extant. *Assistants,* II, 122 (1642/3, a servant promised two shillings eight pence at end of time for good behavior); *Plym. Recs.,* I, 119 (1638/9, promise to remit one year for good service); 121–122 (1639, promise to remit one or two years for faithful service); III, 133, and VIII, 88 (1658, given one yenr), III, 220 (two years cut if servant performs well); VI, 25 (one pound added to freedom dues if well behaved); *Mass. Recs.,* I, 206 (1637, two servants dismissed before time up, possibly for good behavior); 255 (1638/9, land granted for serving master well); *Essex Probate,* I, 141–142 (1651, left cow-calf in master's will); 227–228 (1655, freed and given yearling by mistress' will); MSS "City of Boston . . . Inhabitants–1695 List of and Indentures of Apprentices," n.p., 19th (1683, to be taught to read and write if he behaved himself).
32. Cotton Mather, *Pillars of Salt* . . . , 71.
33. *Mass. Recs.,* I, 397.
34. *Plym. Recs.,* I, 141–142 (1639/40).

35. *Winthrop Papers,* IV 232–233.
36. *Essex County Court,* I, 83.
37. *Ibid.,* VI, 236.
38. MSS. Middlesex County Court, III, 276–277.
39. MSS. Suffolk County Court, I, 131. Dominick was given one month off his time by indenture.
40. In that order: *Essex County Court,* VIII, 222–226; 315–316; MSS. Essex Sessions, I, n.p. (Jan. 19, 1702/3); MSS. Suffolk Sessions, II, 123–124; 203. The following summarized data on a case of abuse is both instructive and interesting. Petition of Thomas Hall: left an orphan and apprenticed to his master, Robert Eames, for nine years, of which he had one to go. His master beat him with anything handy, staves, stones, rods, etc, He worked hard and diligently and obeyed *lawful* commands. But Master made him load hay and take cows to salt water on Sabbath. Wanted to be freed or set to someone else. Testimony of Eames: he did strike Hall three or four times with an "iron S" on the head and shoulders whereby Hall was wounded, but Hall provoked him to it with his words. Testimony of John Till, youth: he was present at beating, but heard no provoking words. Thomas Webb: he heard Hall say "Strike me if you durst . . . ," when they were plowing. Hall took cider from Eames' cellar, and gave bread to a runaway. Isaac Richardson: he saw Hall diligently at work whenever he passed Eames' farm. T. Richardson: saw Eames throw a club at Hall in a rage. John Trowbridge: Hall kept back sometimes a shilling, sometimes less, when he went to market for Eames. Used money for drink. Stole cider from Eemes. Henry Means: saw Eames strike Hall several times with a great stick. Phebe Bolden: she saw Eames throw a stone at Hall. Joseph Richardson: Hall very diligent. John Richardson: Eames struck Hall with a whip many times and with a stick. Henry Totingham: Hall worked early and late and very hard, but Eames clubbed him. John Green: Hall dared Eames to strike him. MSS. Middlesex Court Files, file 58, no number (Apr. 19, 1671). For a record of testimony in a case in which a servant died see *Assistants,* III, 24–34 (1653). For other complaints against excessive punishment see *Assistants,* II, 103 (1640/1) cruel usage; *Winthrop's Journal,* II, 187–189 (1644), died of abuse including hanging in chimney; V, 154–155 (1647), abusive correction; *Plym. Recs.,* III, 51 (1654), misuse; 63–64 (1654), hardly used; *Mass. Recs.,* II, 20 (1642), beating; *Essex County Court,* I, 6 (1637), extreme correction; III, 365 (1666), abuse by master's children; IV, 37 (1668), abuse by master's son; VIII, 91–92 (1681), beat on head with stick, tied to bedpost, cradle foot, table leg, etc.; 295–296 (1682), abuse; *Suffolk County Court,* I, 149 (1672), abuse; II, 807 (1677), cruel beating; MSS. Plymouth Sessions, I, 38 (1688); unreasonably beaten; MSS. Bristol Sessions, II, 62–63 (1704), beating and unmerciful abuse, unreasonable stripes; 80 (1705),

violent beating; III, a, 55–56 (1718/9), abuse; III, 202 (1733), abuse; MSS. Suffolk Sessions, I, 214 (1710), cruel and unmerciful punishment; 255 (1712), abuse; II, 3 (1712), cruel usage; 12–13 (1713), immoderate beating, 42 (1713/4), evil "Intreating"; *ibid.*, severe and immoderate beating; 47 (1714), ill usage, cruel whipping; 173 (1717), cut off Negro servant's ears; 250 (1719), beatings; III, 184–185 (1722/3), beaten and cruelly treated generally; IV, 272 (1730), frequently beaten without cause; 309–310 (1730), constantly beaten; 355 (1731), ill use and mistreatment; 433 (1732), cruelly beaten, wounded and mistreated; MSS. Suffolk Court Files, Vol. 276, folio 40523 (1735), beaten, assaulted, and wounded. Lechford, *Note-Book,* 229–231 (1639), servant killed by master.

41. *Essex County Court,* VIII, 302–303. A few cases of sexual abuse of servants by masters occurred. See chapter VI. See also *Suffolk County Court,* II, 807 (1677); *Plym. Recs.,* III, 75 (1654); *Assistants,* I, 199 (1681); MSS. Middlesex County Court, IV, 13–14 (1681); 224–225 (1686).

42. Thomas Hill, *The Young Secretary's Guide: Or, A Speedy Help to Learning* (Boston, 1703), 122–123. There is no change in the fourth (1713), fifth (1718); or twenty-fourth (1750) editions in this respect.

43. *Essex County Court,* I, 111.

44. MSS. Suffolk County Court, II, 244. For other instances of failure to train properly see *Essex County Court,* II, 275–276 (1661); *Assitants,* I, 19 (1674); MSS. Middlesex County Court, I, 291 (1663); MSS Bristol Sessions, II, 62–63 (1704); MSS. Suffolk Sessions, I, 117 (1705); 161 (1707); II, 88 (1715, two cases); 175 (1717); 250 (1719); III, 57 (1720); 83–84 (1721); 87 (1721); 235 (1723); IV, 176–177 (1728); 259 (1729/30); 433 (1732).

45. *Suffolk County Court,* I, 155. For others see *Essex County Court,* VIII, 249–250 (1682); MSS. Suffolk Sessions, II, 175 (1717); 250 (1719); III, 83–84 (1721).

46. MSS. Middlesex Court Files, file 95, no number (Oct., 1681, case of William Henwood).

47. Thomas Hill, *The Young Secretary's Guide . . . ,* 122–123.

48. In that order: MSS. Suffolk County Court, I, 39 (1680); 182 (1683); II, 365 (1690). For other complaints about unsuitable food or clothing, or both, see: *Plym. Recs.,* III, 119 (1657); *Essex County Court,* I, 5 (1637); 57 (1643); 69 (1644); IV, 112 (1669); VI, 236 (1676); VIII, 91–92 (1681); MSS. Bristol Sessions, II, 172 (1709/10); MSS. Suffolk Sessions, II, 12–13 (1713); III, 187 (1721); 117 (1721/2); 132–133 (1722); IV, 101 (1727); 272 (1730); MSS. Bundle, Suffolk County Court of General Sessions of the Peace, 1738–1739, n.p. (Jan. 2, 1738/9, case of Nathaniel Harris).

49. MSS. Suffolk Sessions, II, 10–11 (1712/3).

50. MSS. Middlesex Court Files, file 58, no number (Apr. 19, 1671, case of Thomas Hall).
51. MSS. Middlesex County Court, I, 71 (1655).
52. *Winthrop Papers,* V, 154–155 (1647) MSS. Middlesex Court Files, file 28, number 1814 (1707); *Essex County Court,* I, 79 (1645); 181 (1649); III, 172 (1664); MSS. Suffolk Sessions, I, 18 (1703); 161 (1707); 242–243 (1711/2); MSS. Bristol Sessions, III, 202 (1733); MSS. Essex Sessions, IV, 165 (1725), this one a Negro slave.
53. See testimony of Samuel Mills, Ebenezer Ware and Benjamin Mills in the case of Joseph Barber v. Joseph Markes, M.H.S. Miscellaneous Bound Manuscripts, Apr. 15, 16, 1695. The master also threatened to beat his servant's brains out.
54. MSS. Suffolk Sessions, IV, 410 (1732). When the master learned his servant was pregnant, he talked her into giving him her indenture, which he then destroyed, and turned her out.
55. *Ibid.,* 113–115 (1727).
56. *Essex County Court,* VIII, 330–338 (1682). Which see for a graphic description of prison conditions in the seventeenth century. See also MSS. Suffolk Sessions, II, 198 (1718). Here two servants complain that they had been thrown into prison on their master's charges for abusing him and neglecting his business. They attested they had been kept on bread and water in the dungeon for several days.
57. MSS. Bristol Sessions, III, a, 55–56 (1718/9).
58. *Ibid.,* III, 55 (1726); MSS. Suffolk Sessions, I, 195 (1709), II, 58 (1714).
59. Leaving: MSS. Suffolk Sessions, IV, 113–115 (1727). Already left: *ibid.,* II, 122 (1716); 142 (1716/7); 261–262 (1719); IV, 436 (1732).
60. *Essex County Court,* III, 172.
61. MSS. Suffolk Sessions, IV, 433. For others see MSS. Bristol Sessions, III, a, 55–56 (1718/9); MSS. Suffolk Sessions, IV, 113–115 (1727); 176–177 (1728); *Essex County Court,* I, 25 (1641).
62. MSS. Middlesex Court Files, file 6, number 200. No disposition could be found except a note on the back of the petition to the effect that Mr. Bunker had some interest in the servant.
63. MSS. Suffolk Sessions, II, 102–103 (1715). MSS. Superior Court of Judicature, 1715–1721, folio 204 (1717).
64. MSS. Suffolk Sessions, III, 237–238 (1733). The indenture was held null and void. For others bound without consent of parent or guardian see *Essex County Court,* II, 357 (1662); III, 366 (1666, Indian); VI 18–19 (1675); MSS. Bristol Sessions, II, 161 (1709, Indian); MSS. Essex Sessions II, 314 (1716); MSS. Suffolk Sessions, III, 314 (1725); IV, 68–69 (1727).
65. MSS. Suffolk Sessions, I, 204 (1710).
66. MSS. Plymouth Sessions, III, 67 (1726/7). For a similar case see MSS. Essex Sessions, IV, 65. Here a Negro appealed to the court on

behalf of his Indian wife and three children who had been sold as
slaves. From March to December the court allowed the woman to be
kept in service adjacent to Essex County, but she was not to be sold
except day by day, week by week, or month by month. In December,
the court found them free. The owner appealed, but no record of the
case could be found. For other improperly bound Indians see Plym.
Recs., VI, 101 (1682/4 [*sic*]); MSS. Bristol Sessions, III, a, 60
(1719). Both found free. For another improperly bound servant see
MSS. Suffolk Sessions, V, 189 (1730/1).
67. MSS. Suffolk Sesslons, I, 17–18 (1703).
68. MSS. Middlesex Sessions, I, 171 (1705). For other Negro appeals
see MSS. Suffolk Sessions, I, 110 (1705); IV, 116–117 (1727);
House Journals, XIII, 215–216 (1735); XV, 172 (1737).
69. MSS. Bristol Sessions, I, 67 (1707).
70. MSS. Suffolk Sessions, II, 88–89 (1715). Other whites petitioned
for their freedom although their reasons are not given. See *Suffolk
County Court*, I, 411 (1673/4); MSS Middlesex Court Files, file 28,
number 1814 (1662), freed because he was not "legally made over" to
his master; MSS. Suffolk County Court, II, 274 (1685), servant freed
at death of his master after court read indenture and heard what his
master had said at his death; MSS. Suffolk Sessions, I, 18 (1703);
III, 127–128 (1722).
71. Compiled from the protests listed above, All figures are estimates
only, for roughly ten percent of the cases have no recorded
disposition, or if appealed, no appeal could be located. The
percentages with regards to apprentices, nonapprentice white
servants, Indians, and Negroes are roughly fifty, thirty-four, nine,
and two percent respectively.
72. As an example of this explosive force, take the case of John Moody
who came to New England in 1633. He had two menservants who
were "ungodly, especially one of them; who in his passion would
wish himselfe in hell; & use desperate words. yet had a good measure
of knowledge. . . . " Both went to the oyster beds against the
counsel of their master and were drowned, giving "a dreadfull
example of God's displeasure against obstinate serva[n]ts." *Boston
Records*, VI, 78. Winthrop agreed that this was God's judgement
upon them. "One of them," he wrote, "a little before, being reproved
for his lewdness, and put in mind of hell, answered, that if hell were
ten times hotter, he had rather be there than he would serve his
master, etc. The occasion was, because he had bound himself for
divers years, and saw that, if he had been at liberty, he might have
had greater wages, Though otherwise his master used him very well."
Winthrop's Journal, I, 103–104 (1643).
73. Mass. Recs., III, 355 (Aug. 22, 1654). The preamble begins,
"Forasmuch as it appeares by too much experience that diuers

children & servants doe behaue themselues too disrespectively [*sic*], disobediently, & disorderly. . . ."

74. *Ibid.*, V, 240–241 (Oct. 15, 1679). In 1699, Cotton Mather generalized on the evil beginnings which led about-to-be-executed malefactors to crime. Most often lamented by them was "Oh! my Disobedience to my Parents, my Disobedience to my Parents, and my Ungovernableness, under such Parents, and Masters, as God had given me!". *Pillars of Salt* . . . , 55. He quoted one Hugh Stone, wife murderer, as saying, "'*Young Men and Maids;* observe the Rule of Obedience to your Parents, and Servants to your Masters, according to the will of God, and [observe the rule] to do the will of your Masters. . . .'" *Ibid.*, 93.

75. Cotton Mather, *A Faithful Monitor* . . . , 20–21. The servants were listed with a motley crowd of "Rogues, Vagabonds, Common Beggars, and other Lewd, Idle, and Disorderly Persons; Pretenders to any Subtil Craft, Juggling, or Unlawful Games or Playes; Pretenders to skill in Physiognomy, Palmestry, Fortune-telling, &c. Common Pipers, Fidlers, Runawayes . . . Common Drunkards, Common Night-Walkers, Wanton Persons, Common Railers and Brawlers, and such as Neglect their Families."

76. Page 4.

77. *News-Letter*, July 9–16, 1741. The reference to the "neighboring Government" undoubtedly means New York. The city of New York had uncovered a "conspiracy" among Negroes to burn the city. *Ibid.*, June 18–25, 1741.

78. *Courant*, Nov. 16–23, 1724; *Evening-Post*, May 17, 1736; Sept. 24, 1739; June 19, 1738; Mar. 8, 1742; *Gazette*, Feb. 25–Mar. 3, 1740; Feb. 13, 1750; *Post-Boy*, Mar. 31, 1746; June 19, 1749.

79. *Assistants*, II, 92.

80. *Ibid.*, 104 (1641).

81. *Ibid.*, 127.

82. *Essex County Court*, I, 68 (1644).

83. *Ibid.*, 156–157.

84. MSS. Middlesex County Court, I, 45.

85. *Essex County Court*, VII, 74 (1678).

86. MSS. Hampshire County Court, I, 106.

87. *Sibley's Harvard Graduates*, IV, 405.

88. MSS. "Diary of Ebenezer Parkman," June 16, 1739. For other examples of untoward behavior see *Essex County Court*, II, 197–198 (1660); III, 226 (1664); *Plym. Recs.*, III, 201 (1660); MSS. Middlesex County Court, I, 176 (1659), MSS. Suffolk County Court, I, 85 (1681); 97 (1681); II, 254 (1685); 256 (1685); MSS. Bristol Sessions, III, a, 2–3 (1714).

89. *Essex County Court*, I, 23.

90. *Ibid.*, 35 (1641/2). For others who could not curb their tongues see *ibid.*, 20 (1640); 34 (1641/2); VII, 74 (1678); *Suffolk County Court*,

I, 222 (1672/3); 412 (1673/4); *Assistants,* II 104 (1641); MSS. Suffolk County Court, II, 275 (1685); MSS. Suffolk Sessions, II, 11 (1712/3); MSS. Essex Sessions, IV, 16 (1719); MSS. Bristol Sessions, III, a, 2–3 (1714); *Plym. Recs.,* I, 159 (1640).
91. *Essex County Court,* VI, 138 (1676).
92. MSS. Middlesex County Court, I, 29.
93. MSS. Suffolk Sessions, II, 222 (1718/9).
94. *Ibid.,* 90.
95. MSS. Middlesex County Court, I, 232 (1661). The year was restored and a fine of forty shillings plus punishment with ten stripes was given.
96. MSS. Suffolk County Court, II, 289 (1685/6).
97. *Essex County Court,* II 403–404 (1662); MSS. Suffolk Sessions, III, 184 (1722/3). The master had purchased four years of this Irish girl's time for eighteen pounds. His petition pointed out that her indenture had disappeared and he was afraid she would abscond He wanted the court to order her to serve out her time, which it did after hearing her.
98. MSS. Essex Session, V, 258 (1732). For other servants who stole indentures and ran see *ibid.,* V, 58–59 (1727/8); MSS. Suffolk Sessions, I, 178 (1708); III, 132–133 (1722); *N.E. Journal,* Nov. 4, 1734. For other stolen indentures see MSS. Suffolk Sessions, II, 98 (1715); 135 (two cases, 1716); III, 124 (1722); IV, 45 (1726); 373–375 (1731); MSS. Plymouth Sessions, I, 5 (1686); IV, 1–2 (1730); *Plym. Recs.,* IV, 154 (1663). MSS. fragment, Bristol County General Sessions of the Peace, 1720–1721, n.p. (case of James Bryant, July, 1721).
99. Whitmore, *Laws,* 152. For a discussion of the problem of fire in Boston see Bridenbaugh, *Cities . . . ,* passim.
100. Negroes: C.S.M. *Pubs.,* VI, 323–335 (1681); MSS. Middlesex Court Files, file 99, no number (Mar. 30, 1682, case of Joshua, Negro); MSS. Suffolk County Court, I, 74 (1681) Whites: *Essex County Court,* VI, 223 (1676); 249 (1677); MSS. Middlesex County Court, III, 218 (1678); *Assistants,* II, 11 (1630/1); 100 (1640); Indictment of Jude Shepherd, M.H.S. Miscellaneous Bound Manuscripts, July 30, 1695; and a possible arson case against two servants, MSS. Suffolk County Court, II, 245 (1685).
101. Not all, however, for three Indians and one white committed arson between 1700–1750. Indians: MSS. Bristol Sessions, II, 100 (1706); *Sibley's Harvard Graduates,* IV, 253 (1712); *N.E. Journal,* Feb. 26, 1733. White: *Evening-Post,* Apr 1, 1745.102. Quote from *Boston Records,* VI, 95 (1681). See also C.S.M. *Pubs.,* VI, 323–335; *Assistants,* I, 197–198.
103. *Assistants,* II, 100 (1640).
104. Cotton Mather, "Diary," M.H.S., 7 *Colls.,* VIII, 686–688. Mather wrote Thomas Prince about the Negro involved at Powel's. He urged Prince to preach a sermon on the subject, and wondered if "Burning

for Burning, was required by the Word of the glorious GOD." He doubted that Negroes were always treated as Christians should be, but felt that the Negro population would profit from the execution. It is interesting to follow the story of the Powel arsonist in the *Courant* in 1723: Apr. 1–8, a Negro man admits setting fire to Mr. Powel's house, and admits trying it once before; Apr. 8–15, several fires started in Boston, supposedly by Negro servants, the one committed for Powel's place accused five others who were then jailed, two Negroes were taken up on suspicion of starting a fire in a tanning yard; Apr. 15–22, proclamation issued by the Governor offering fifty pounds reward for discovering the fire bugs, and a promise of pardon for the informer be he Negro or white; A Negro seen setting fire to house on Newbury street, but escaped; June 10–17, all Negores except Powel's arsonist acquitted, the latter under sentence of death; July 1–8, Powel arsonist hanged. For other Negro arsonists in the eighteenth century see *Gazette,* Jan, 3–10, 1737; June 20, 1749: *News-Letter,* Feb. 4–11, 1731; *N.E. Journal,* Aug. 26, 1734; *Evening-Post,* Sept. 5, 1734 (possible). For those who threatened arson see MSS. Bristol Sessions, III, a, 61 (1719); III, 116 (1729); MSS. Essex Sessions, IV, 16 (1719).

105. Feb. 14, 1749 and Aug. 8, 1749. The Medway story was also carried in the *Evening-Post,* Feb. 13, 1749.

106. Oct. 14, 1734.

107. MSS. Suffolk Sessions, I, 14; MSS. Middlesex County Court, I, 84–85 (1655); *Essex County Court,* I, 356; *Suffolk County Court,* I, 412. For others see *Suffolk County Court,* I, 560–561 (servant accused of having gotten his freedom by threats of force, 1674/5); *Essex County Court,* I, 97 (servant fined for threats to kill master and for running away, 1646); MSS. Suffolk Sessions, III, 11 (returned runaway who threatened his master's life, 1719/20); MSS. Bristol Sessions, III, a, 2–3 (ten lashes for threats and striking a person, 1714).

108. *Essex County Court,* I, 132–133 n. (1647); *Suffolk County Court,* II, 884 (1677/8); MSS. Suffolk Sessions, I, 125 (1705/6). For others see MSS. Suffolk Sessions, III, 195 (four Negroes threw dirt in white woman's face, 1723); MSS. Bristol Sessions, III, 116 (Negro slave struck white man, 1729); *Assistants,* II, 134 (servant imprisoned for striking his master, 1643).

109. MSS. Middlesex County Court, I, 68; *Essex County Court,* IV, 200 (1669); MSS. "Diary of Ebenezer Parkman," June 2, 1739; *Evening-Post,* Apr. 27, 1747. For other cases of assault see MSS. Suffolk Sessions, I, 131–32 (Negro struck and assaulted white man, 1706); MSS. Hampshire County Court, III, 295 (Negro struck white man with fist and stick, 1738); IV, 165 (Negro beat white man, 1744); *Suffolk County Court,* II, 884 (Negro aimed gun at master and wounded him with a knife, 1677/8); *Evening-Post,* Jan. 13, 1746

(Negro threatened to kill all the family he served. Watch sent for and Negro wounded one with a knife. While Watch was securing him, he died, "as is supposed, of passion.")

110. *Assistants,* I, 30, 32. The sermon was printed in Boston in 1675. See also Kenneth Ballard Murdock, *Increase Mather The Foremost American Puritan* (Cambridge, 1925), 131.

111. For other servants who used or would have used poison, see MSS. Suffolk Sessions, I, 165 (Margaret Mitchell, Negro servant, put poison in Mistress' tea, 1707); MSS. Essex Sessions, I, n.p. (Caesar, confessed poisoning a white maid servant whom he feared would complain to his master about his stealing money from her. He put rat poison in her milk, June 25, 1695); MSS Middlesex County Court, III, 218 (white servant convicted of contemplating poisoning fellow servant, 1678); *Gazette,* July 28–Aug. 4, 1735 (attempt to poison master with ratsbane); *Evening-Post,* Sept. 1, 1735 (two Negroes put arsenic in master's chocolate); Apr. 9, 1744 (apprentice attempted to poison his master) Sept. 3, 1744 (Negro attempted to poison his master); Feb. 4, 1746 (Negro woman of Portsmouth, N.H., attempted to poison nine persons by putting ratsbane in cider).

112. Mark was sentenced to hang, Phillis to be burned. Both confessed. M.H.S., 1 *Proc.,* XX, 122–157 Quote from page 136. For other murders by servants see C.S.M. *Pubs.,* VI, 323–325 (Marja again, who besides committing arson, killed one person in the fire); *Sibley's Harvard Graduates,* I, 318 n. (White servant women killed her master, 1679); *News-Letter,* Sept. 7–14, 1732 (runaway Indian stabbed to death a man who tried to stop him); Sept. 20, 1745 (Negro split skull of mistress with an axe); *Evening-Post* (Sept. 12, 1743) (Negro shot youth in a tussle over a gun, reported as accident); Aug. 31, 1747 (Negro murdered Negro); Dec. 10, 1750 (Negro killed another in fight); *The American Magazine and Historical Chronicle* (May, 1746), 240 (servant on ship found guilty of murder); M.H.S., 2 *Proc.,* VII, 169 (1677, Indian killed master).

113. There is some doubt in my mind as to whether infanticide by servants should be included under protests. Greene, *The Negro in Colonial New England . . . ,* 113–114, was unable to determine the issue although he raises the question. The evidence is all circumstantial, and the only positive evidence indicates otherwise. In the case of white servants, bound only for a term, it seems to be an obvious effort to escape punishment and a possible extension to their term to pay for the costs of raising the child. In the case of Esther Rodgers, executed in 1701, for example, the reason seems to be to avoid punishment. After describing her youth, her conception, and the murder of the newborn infant, she went on to say, "All this was done in Secret, no person living whatsoever, no not so much as the Father of the Child himself was privy to my disposal of it, or knew that I

ever had such a Child." She later disposed of another, for which she was caught. John Rogers, *Death the Certain Wages of Sin . . .* , 123–124. For other white servants who killed their bastards see *Winthrop's Journal,* II, 317–318 (1647); *Assistants,* I, 125 (1678); Cotton Mather, *Pillars of Salt . . .* , 60–62 (1646); 99 (1693, non-servant?), 103 (1698, non-servant?); 104–105 (1698, non-servant); *Evening-Post,* Dec. 31, 1739. For Indians see *Sibley's Harvard Graduates,* IV, 155 (ca. 1720); *Evening-Post,* Apr. 11, 1743 (possibly a servant). In the case of Negro mothers, circumstantial evidence points the other way. Already at the bottom of society, and already bound for life, they had little to lose in admitting bastardy. Punishment for fornication was brutal indeed, but not as bad as death for discovery of infanticide. Occasionally forced to breed, they would have little tenderness for such offspring. Moreover, it was quite likely that their children would be separated from them anyhow, and given away. See chapter VI. However, until stronger evidence is obtained, it must remain a moot question. For Negro servant infanticides, see MSS. Suffolk Court Files, V, 605 (1663/4); Briggs, *Hanover . . .* , I, 128 (1748); *Assistants,* I, 29–30 (1674/5); Cotton Mather, *Pillars of Salt . . .* , 99 (1693); *N.E. Journal,* June 19, 1727; Dec. 25, 1732; *Gazette,* May 12, 1747; *Post-Boy,* Aug. 14, 1749.

114. *Winthrop's Journal,* I, 175.
115. *Gazette,* May 21–28, 1733. Both Increase Mather and Samuel Willard preached and wrote against suicide. The former's *A Call to the Tempted. A SERMON on the Horrid Crime of Self-Murder, Preached on a Remarkable Occasion, by the Memorable Dr. Increase Mather. And now published from his notes, for a charitable stop to suicides* (Boeton, 1723/4) was first preached in 1682 after there had been five suicides in as many weeks. Samuel Willard's *A Compleat Body of Divinity . . .* , 663 (second pagination), notes that it was "a too frequent Temptation, which some are hurried by, when under Discontents; and Apt to hope there is not so great a Sin in it." It was delivered in 1704.
116. *Essex County Ccurt,* II, 421; *Suffolk County Court,* I, 189; MSS. Middlesex Court Files, file 99, no number (Mar. 30, 1682, Apr. 25, 1682); *N.E. Journal,* Nov. 19, 1733; *Evening-Post,* Oct. 4, 1736; Sept. 19, 1737; Feb. 16, 1741; July 27, 1741; *Sibley's Harvard Graduates,* VI, 31; *N.E. Journal,* Oct. 27, 1729. For other suicides see *Evening-Post,* June 6, 1743 (Indian men found hanged in Weymouth); Mar. 26, 1744 (journeyman hanged self in Boston); Sept. 8, 1746 (Negro slave found drowned in Boston, possible suicide). For confirmation of suicide's being a form of protest see Melville J. Herskovits, *The Myth of the Negro Past,* 102–103. Franklin, *From Slavery to Freedom . . .* , 206–207; Smith, *Colonists in Bondage . . .* , 253; Morris, *Government and Labor . . .* , 487.

117. Smith, *Colonists in Bondage* . . . , 260 ff. Herbert Aptheker, *Negro Slave Revolts in the United States 1520–1860* (New York, 1939), 16–23.
118. *Evening-Post,* Jan. 7, 1745.

8. The Runaway Servant

The nearly seven hundred servants who decided to risk the known and unknown hazards of running away between 1620 and 1750 made of this practice an institution of protest against all forms of unfree labor.[1] No category of servitude was without its runaways, whether apprentice or slave, and although the numbers are relatively insignificant in terms of the total servant population, the persistence of the phenomenon, regardless of punishment, is testament to the servants' devotion to personal freedom and to their rejection of the system. Similarly, the energy which the master class expended to limit the effectiveness of this form of protest, belies the seeming infrequency of these individual revolts. To the master, as to the servant, one successful attempt to run away was important.

The permanent escape of a servant involved considerable economic loss to the owner, not only in terms of the original investment, but for the clothes the escaping servant wore, the victuals and other goods which he frequently stole to aid him on his flight, the loss of the servant's labor(worth more than the original investment), and the expense of a search for the runaway. Even a temporary absence, say at harvest time, could be costly when other labor was not available. It is not surprising then, that the colonists early moved to protect themselves against this bleeding away of their property and welfare.

Governmental protection against loss from runaways took two forms: legislation to provide punishment or facilitate capture and return, and treaties or agreements with other colonial governments for the return of fugitives. As early as 1634, the Massachusetts Court of Assistants ruled

> if any boy (that hath bene whipt for runing fro[m] his maister) be taken in any other planta[ti]on, not haueing a note from his maister to testifie his business there, it sh[albe] lawfull for the

Constable of the said planta[ti]on to whip him a[nd] send him home.[2]

Provision for return and punishment, then were established in the first law relating to running away; and a pass system to cut down its incidence was implicit if not formally made explicit by law.[3]

A year later, the Bay Colony assumed public responsibility for the protection of this form of property. Significantly this was two decades before the town of Boston assumed public responsibility for protection against fire. Thus in 1635:

It is ordered, that whensoeuer any serv[an]ts shall run from their maist[e]rs . . . it shalbe lawfull for the nexte magistrate, or the constable & two of the cheife inhabitants, where noe magistrate is, to presse men & boates, or pynaces, att the publ[ic] charge, to pursue such p[er]sons by sea or land, & bring them back by force of armes.[4]

Soon, magistrates in Massachusetts were given the power to commit runaways to the house of correction, a power renewed in 1655, 1657, and under the Provincial Charter in 1699.[5] And then, having provided what was considered adequate punishment and pursuit, the Puritans moved to cut off one avenue of escape for the wayward and footloose servant, the sea. In 1680 the General Court, cognizant that unscrupulous or careless shippers might aid runaways, imposed a fine of twenty pounds for the "entertaining" of servants aboard ship without the consent of their masters.[6] In the next century, this fine was increased to fifty pounds for those who transported unfree workers out of the province against their owners' wishes or without their owners' knowledge.[7]

Before incorporating with Massachusetts, Plymouth Colony attempted to cut down her loss from runaways by providing that Indians at service for debt, who fled their masters and were recovered, could be sold for the debt and charges in recovering them at the discretion of any two magistrates or selectmen. Eight years later, in 1682, they instituted a procedure whereby Indian runaways who fled to their fellow natives were to be apprehended by the Indian constables and returned to an overseer or magistrate.[8]

The second form of legal action to protect property in servants was inaugurated by intergovernmental agreement in 1631/2 between Plymouth Colony and Massachusetts Bay for the return of servants who had left without permission.[9] Five years later the Puritans reached a similar agreement with the Sachem of the Narragansetts, whereby the Indians were to return any fugitives who fled to them.[10]

A more extensive measure was taken in 1643 by the members of the New England Confederation, who mutually agreed on extradition of runaway servants upon the submission of due proof of ownership. The fugitives were to be held and delivered over to the master or any other bearing said proof.[11] Similar provisions, such as the one negotiated in 1653 between the United Colonies and New Netherlands,[12] were common all along the colonial seaboard, and they were apparently honored. Although few records of actual extradition have survived in Massachusetts, one is illustrated in a letter from Roger Williams to John Winthrop, Jr., in April, 1655:

> Sir, a hue and crie came to my hand lately from the Gov'r at Boston, after 2 youths one runn from Cap: Oliver whome I lighted on and have returned, another from James Bill of Boston who I heare past through our Towne and said he was bound for Pequt. his name is James Pitnie.[13]

Arrangements for apprehending runaways went far beyond statutory and intergovernmental agreements. Indeed the masters were extremely active and cooperative in upholding their own and each other's interests in this mobile frame of property. The old English custom of hue and cry, as well as pursuit, broadsides, newspaper advertisements, and the detention of likely suspects, were all used extensively to prevent the permanent escape of fugitives. Illustrative of these efforts is the bill of charges in the case of Robert Crose against his servant Nicholas Varden in 1668:

> Riding to town, horse & man to give nottis of his Ronen away, 3s; for senden three men & three horses with three hew and Crise, 9s.; for too men & 2 horses to search & inquier of Salem farmes & out houses, 6s.; giting of him Cried at Salem on a Lecttor day, 2s.; too menn & too horses one day more, 6s.; expenses in our travelles, 5s.; damidg in my buisnes about my haye, Loss & spoyll, 21i.; for what he stole & spoylde, 101i.; . . . my sonn was at bass river when the hew & Crie came there which yet hath not binn reckoned which rid about by mackrell Cove & mantchestor to stop the pasedg & an other mesenger to gloster, 5s. . . . [14]

While only one broadside could be located, that of Hannah Bosworth of Hull in 1683/4, other evidence suggests the use of broadsides in apprehending runaways was common even after the advent of the newspaper. Thus the *New-England Weekly Journal* for April 21, 1735, advertised a correction in name for one of two servants who had run away and who had been publicized by means of "printed advertisements."[15] However, the paucity of broadsides preserved and the wide use of newspapers for notices of runaways suggest that the latter were used more extensively after 1704, when Boston's first successful newspaper appeared. In the eighteenth century, all papers, although not every issue, had some notices each year.

These notices generally gave a brief description of the runaway, often warned persons against helping him, and usually guaranteed costs and a reward. The following, from *The Boston Evening-Post,* is typical.

> Ran away from his Master Captain John Avee of Boston on the 5th of this Instant August, a Negro man named Phillip, about 28 years old, much pitted with the small pox, and speaks pretty good English and Portuguese. He is used to the sea, and 'tis supposed will endeavor to get off in some Vessel, having carried away his sea Bedding and all his other Cloathes; therefore all Masters of Vessels and other persons are hereby cautioned against concealing or carrying him off, as they will avoid the Penalty of the law. And whoever shall take up the said Negro and bring him to his abovesaid Master living near Dr. Cutlers Church at the North End of town shall have five pounds . . . and all necessary charges paid.

Not infrequently such advertisements were repeated in later issues or the same paper, or in current issues of different papers. Mr. Richard Billings, tailor of Boston, for example, advertised for his runaway Negro, Exeter, in five different newspapers in 1741. Most interesting of all, however, is the fact that some advertisements were directed at the runaways themselves, promising that all would be forgiven.[16]

Other advertisements published in the newspapers indicate that the masters continued in the eighteenth century the cooperation they began in the seventeenth. Frequently a "suspicious" person would be stopped and held while an unknown owner was sought. Mr. Joseph Gold of Rumney-Marsh gave notice that he had "picked up a Portuguese or Spanish Lad about 15 or 16 on suspicion of his being a runaway." The owner could have him back by paying charges.[17] More often than not, these suspects were Negroes, who were more easily identified as servants than were whites or Indians who could as well be free as bound. Such captures were reported in *The New-England Weekly Journal,*[18] *The Boston Post-Boy,*[19] *The Boston News-Letter,*[20] and *The*

Boston Gazette.[21] Occasionally the newspaper columns advertised the capture of a servant for whom there had previously been a reward posted. Thus one Philemon Dane indicated his cooperation concerning the Indian servants of Shubal Jones and Joseph Burdley of Barnstable by saying, "I have taken up . . . Solomon Wampum and Joseph Wampum . . . [now] in his Majesty's Goal in Salem. . . . " They would be delivered on the conditions which their masters had promised.[22]

Once recovered, the wayward one could expect some kind of chastisement. Heavy corporal punishment, fines, assessments for damages, and the addition of extra time were all common. In the seventeenth century, corporal punishment, generally a whipping, was the usual mode of correction. Runaways thus maltreated would receive ten or fifteen stripes (rarely as many as twenty or thirty) "severely laid on."[23] Only in extraordinary circumstances was a servant branded with an "R" for "Runaway," although since he often stole to survive he could be given "B" for "Burglar," and was.[24] Less permanent, but no less noticeable, was the occasional chaining of a servant, or the encirclement of his neck with an iron collar for incorrigible "absconders." George Fairfax, for example, apprentice to Thomas Raynam of Salem, convicted of theft and of running away nine times, was ordered, among other things, to wear about his neck an iron collar protruding eighteen inches before and behind. And *The Boston Evening-Post* recorded that grim accessory to involuntary servitude when it advertised for an absent Negro who had an "Iron collar about his neck with the name of his master on it in capital letters. . . . "[25]

To their credit, some masters preferred to pay an alternative fine rather than see their men whipped.[26] While this may have been as attributable to their cupidity (in that they sometimes received extra time for the fine) as to their humanitarian instincts, for the servant the result was the same; no whipping. At any rate, corporal punishment for running away, as administered by the courts, was gradually supplanted by another deterrent, the adding of extra time. By the latter decades of the seventeenth century this was becoming general practice, perhaps in the long run more annoying to the servant, but certainly less painful, This is not to say, of course, that extra time was not added earlier, or that runaways did not sometimes get both forms of punishment. Indeed, one of the earliest cases of running away resulted in several servants being whipped and having their times of absence doubled and added to their periods of service.[27] Thus, in the early period before 1670, about forty-five percent of the runaways had either to make up the time they were gone, or had extra time added. In the following decades, this increased in incidence to about sixty-five percent. Complicated by theft, damages, and court costs, most of those so treated had extra time imposed.[28]

It appears in the case above, that justification for the addition of *extra* time rested as much upon the financial loss occasioned by theft, court costs, and recovery costs, as it did upon mere running away.[29] In all fairness to the New Englanders, who appear to have been far less rapacious and far more considerate of their charges than their southern contemporaries, it must be stated that this was frequently the case. The assessment of treble damages for theft was not exclusively applied to servants, and since the unfree was almost universally unable to pay for his dereliction, he was caught in a system, as was the master.[30]

Laws and punishment were not the only deterrents to the servant who thought he could not take twenty-four hours more under another's jurisdiction. Indeed, considerable social pressure was brought to bear against this instinct for freedom. Those who were temporarily bound could remember signing, if not reading, a contract or indenture which flatly stated, "He shall not absent himself day or night from his Master's service without his leave. . . . " One servant, indeed, went so far as to incorporate within his contract the agreement that he would serve two years for *each* time he ran away.[31]

Moreover, the masters, through their ministers, exhorted the servant population to be content with their lot and to avoid that evil day of absconding as they would the fires of hell. Cotton Mather, who did not disdain to pronounce on any subject, not only canvassed the totality of master servant relations as he saw them, in his *A Good Master Well Served* . . . , but proclaimed that a "Run Away Servant is a Dishonest, and Disgraced sort of a Creature, among all the Sober part of mankind."[32] Earlier he had advised a religiously-inclined group of Negroes to refrain from attending the meetings of the group without their master's consent and, more importantly, to "do good" to their fellow servants by not giving them shelter if they were running away.[33] Shortly thereafter, the angels and apostles on the one hand, and the Fifth Commandment on the other, were invoked against this practice by Benjamin Wadsworth and Samuel Willard, respectively. Wadsworth quite mildly stated that wayward souls "do very wickedly when they run away from their masters," but to clinch his argument he reminded his readers that the aforementioned angels and apostles had played the part of eighteenth-century constables in returning absconding servants.[34]

Moreover, the master class discouraged the footloose servant from attempting to overthrow his obligations by playing upon him the hot breath from the fires of hell. Many a dying malefactor received temporary notoriety in this way by confessing his dark deeds and warning all and sundry not to do *anything*. These confessions and dying warnings make some of the choicest reading in the literature of the period, and they invariably warn servants to behave, if they do not always focus on the problem of running away. Appended to a sermon, or published as broadside in verse or prose, they reflected exactly what the religious or secular authorities wanted said, if not always, one suspects, what the dying malefactor sincerely believed (although he indeed had cause to repent). Started in the seventeenth century, this practice reached an early peak in Cotton Mather's collection of twelve condemned murderers, *Pillars of Salt . . .*, and another height in 1733 when "Poor Julian," an Indian servant, was convicted of murder and arson. Before being "turned off into an awful Eternity," he was prayed for, preached at, and at the gallows he, himself, warned all servants against absconding from their masters' service. Three separate broadsides commemorated the occasion.[35]

The masters, then, had government and law on their side, both the ministry and the tremendous might of custom endorsing the institution of bound labor, whether the individual was voluntarily or involuntarily a partner to an enforceable labor contract. They could point at punishments on earth and warn of everlasting punishments in a vividly-conceived elsewhere—all for running away—and yet the servants ran.

That the servants ran is eloquently attested to in a deposition concerning one William Warrener whose sale to Richard Brabrook was like the phrase in a marriage contract "for better or for worse," for he was sold "living or dying, staying or running . . . "[36] And just as the masters developed legal and social techniques to cut down the incidence of running away, or its cost to the owners, the servants developed techniques to increase their chances of obtaining and maintaining freedom—avenues of escape, means of obtaining sustenance, clothes, transportation, and ways to disguise their status as servants, if apparent.

To those living near the sea, or to whom the sea was accessible, there was a convenient route of escape. From the earliest times it beckoned to those who wished to be relieved from oppressive masters or unbearable restraint. As early as 1635, six servants achieved temporary escape by fleeing from the Bay Colony in a stolen shallop.[37] Others got aboard ships in harbor, having hopes of escape or promises of employment.[38] To these hardy souls, the newspapers of the day give eloquent testimony in one advertisement after another. *The New England Courant,* in listing a runaway, told its readers that the servant in question was inclined to hide on ships unknown to their captains in hopes of stowing away. Another warned that an absconding servant was

familiar with the ways of the sailing-men and might try to "get off by
sea." A third resignedly reported that "Tis supposed some ill-minded
person has enticed him [aboard] to be carry'd off. . . . "[39] After 1718,
when the law against transporting servants out of the province was
strengthened, it became general practice to append to these
advertisements a word to "All Masters of Vessels" cautioning them to
avoid the penalty of the law in such cases.

Apparently the penalty of the law did not encourage masters of
vessels to enquire too carefully into the background of prospective
passengers or employees. Frequently short on labor, always willing to
pick up an honest shilling or two for passengers, and not above selling
someone else's servant in another port, the occasional captain who
willy-nilly aided a fugitive to escape must not have had to search his
soul too deeply to find the answer "yes" within it. That most famous
runaway of all, Benjamin Franklin, relates that his brother, aware that
Benjamin was about to leave him, had warned all printers in town not
to employ the youth. The father, siding with the elder Franklin boy,
would have stopped Benjamin's leaving had he left openly.

> My friend Collins, therefore, undertook to manage a little for
> me. He agreed with the captain of a New York sloop for my
> passage, under the notion of my being a young acquaintance of
> his, that had got a naughty girl with child, whose friends
> would compel me to marry her, and therefore I could not
> appear or come away publicly. So I sold some of my books to
> raise a little money, was taken on board privately, and as we
> had a fair wind, in three days I found myself in New
> York. . . .[40]

Even without the captain's assent, acquired by some such simple
and plausible subterfuge, the sea beckoned. All the way from
Marblehead to Plymouth came Pompey, Negro servant on the run,
looking for a friendly forecastle to hide in. For some reason the good
ship *More-Hampton* in Plymouth Harbor appealed to him and there he
remained undetected when the ship was searched. Not until the second
day at sea was he discovered, and while he was not taken back,
presumably he did not ride as a free passenger to Oporto, Portugal, the
ship's destination. The captain, an honest man, hoped to ship him back
from there, but failing to find a vessel homeward bound, kept him
aboard until the shores of England were reached. There Pompey eluded
his captors, shipped before the mast as a free man, but was recognized
and recaptured in Cadiz by a Captain John Hastie, who returned him to

his master. His private saga ended with his sale, quite probably to a less happy clime in the West Indies.[41]

Whether he fled by sea or land, the runaway had to have clothes, and food, or goods or money which he could exchange for these basic necessities, and if possible, some means of transportation better than his own two legs. This took some planning as well as some stealing. Consequently he often deliberately became a thief, as well as a runaway. He stole food, clothes, cash, silverware—almost anything he could get his hands on and carry; and he stole canoes, boats, and horses—almost anything he could get onto or into.[42]

Such behavior did not endear him to his master or to those along his route from whom he stole or might steal, and when captured, he paid dearly for it; treble damages, frequently worked out in long months of planning for his next escape. Certainly some absconders were confirmed thieves who fled to escape punishment for their misdeeds, but the majority of them probably made a temporary virtue of necessity without becoming or having been addicted to the light-fingered habit.

Some did become addicted, however, but to running away rather than to thievery, for if they failed to obtain freedom the first or second time, they would try a third or fourth. It is difficult to determine in every case of a repeater whether the charge of absconding should have been reduced to mere temporary absence for an evening or day without intent of leaving service. This is particularly true in light of the evidence from other colonies where masters would charge running away for the briefest unauthorized absence in order to obtain extensions of their servant's time.[43] Thus one *suspects* that the misdeeds of Edward Stone, in 1672, of running away fourteen or fifteen times, and William Cheeney in 1680 of more than twenty attempts in eighteen months, were more likely brief periods of absence without permission rather than a sustained series of attempts to achieve freedom.[44] Nevertheless, frequent cases of repeaters who made definite attempts to strike out on their own indicate that the fear of punishment and the now known hazards would not down the desire to be one's own man. The punishment for such repeated misbehavior was, of course, more severe; but even that knowledge failed to keep some from running a second and a third time.[45] In repeatedly running, they learned to disguise themselves as free persons, to change their appearance so as not to conform to their description in advertisements, to hide by day and run by night; and this knowledge passed on to others who intended to abscond. They cut off their hair if it was distinctive, wore men's clothes if they were women, changed their names, brazenly assumed the status of free persons. For example, Caesar, Negro of Samuel Bass of Boston, pretended he was named John Mallott, free-born son of a Jamaican Negro sent to Boston for his education. Another, English servant lad, John Kirby, raised money for his keep by pretending to be the servant of several masters and thereby taking up money and goods in Boston in their names. A third was advertised as:

> A Negro Man named *Cato,* a tall well set Fellow, Aged about 25 Years, speaks English pretty well, has lost all his toes by the Frost in *Maryland,* where he practiced runing away for some Years, his Way is to hide in the Day Time, and travel in the Night in the Woods, and kill Fowls, Shoats &c. for his support.[46]

In viewing the problem of the runaway, it would be a mistake to think of him as always alone, unbefriended, making a lonely decision to run, and once run, huddling in a cave, or wallowing in a swampy mosquito land while the master and his neighbors cried the countryside for him; or as eating rats in a ship's hold while stale seepage sloshed about his frostbitten toes. Such a picture would certainly evoke sympathy from the flintiest heart; but in actual practice, the servant may as well have embarked upon his adventure with the advice of a friend still sounding in his ear, worn clothes provided by a kindly farmer or artisan, warmed his toes at the hearth of a relative, a countryman equally hostile to the English, or a gullible rustic, while his host helped him remove the marks of this servitude.

Henry Spencer, for example, admitted staying all night at one John Upton's house, intending to leave the next day. However, getting as far as Wenham, he heard a hue and cry out for him, and he returned to Upton's house. He told his host then that he was a runaway. That evening they made him a new pair of trousers out of linen, and Upton started him off the next day toward Andover. Thus many a servant was advised to abscond, was helped in his planning, was given transportation, concealed in flight, fed and clothed, or helped in some unspecified manner.[47]

Even if he did not find friends on his way, he may have started with some, for running away together was one of the earliest forms of joint action developed by the American worker. It precedes any form of collective action on the part of artisans in Massachusetts, and is a persistent phenomenon throughout the period, involving almost one-fifth of those who ran.

For example, Thomas Jackson, Richard Stinnings, and Daniel Crose, along with a non-servant, Arthur Peach, gained notoriety and a small niche in history when they were described by Governor Bradford as running away together.

> This Arthur Peach was ye cheefe of them, and ye ring leader of all ye rest. He was lustie and a desperate yonge man, and had been one of ye souldiers in ye Pequente warr, and had done as good servise as ye most ther, and one of ye forwardest in any attempte. And being now out of means, and loath to worke, and falling to idle courses & company, he intended to goe to ye Dutch plantation; and had alured these 3., being other mens servants and apprentices, to goe with him. But another cause ther was allso of his secret going away in this maner; he was not only rune into debte, but he had gott a maid with child . . . a mans servante in ye towne. . . . The other 3. complotting with him, rane away from their maisters in the night, and could not be heard of, for they went not ye ordinarie way, but shaped such a course as they thought to avoyd ye pursute of any.[48]

More than thirty-five servants sought to emulate this group in the seventeenth century,[49] while in the next half century, forty-one instances of joint action involved more than eighty servants. Most of the latter were twosomes,[50] but six included three or more. The most spectacular of those occurred in 1741 when several "Black slaves," captured on a Spanish prize, escaped from Boston Harbor with several Massachusetts Negroes in a stolen longboat. Unfortunately for them, they were recovered in Barnstable Bay.[51]

The psychological advantage of having a companion on one's strike for freedom must have been considerable, for servants not only were willing to take members of the opposite sex with them despite the possibility of being slowed down,[52] but were willing to ignore the racial barriers, as Negroes, whites, and Indians ran away together. For a white to do this was quite risky: being with a Negro or Indian made him liable to be stopped wherever he went. Nevertheless, the real or imagined desperateness of their situation made several willing to run the risk. For example, in 1724, an Irishman, a Negro woman, and two Negro men, had run away in a stolen shallop. Pursued, they ran aground and were captured by a boat from a man of war.[53] Apparently the desire for freedom proved stronger than racial bars.

It is certain that the desire for freedom was not restricted to any one race. Out of the 669 runaway servants located before 1751, 391 were whites, 191 were Negroes, seventy-two were Indians, and fifteen were Negro or Indian mulattoes. Nor was it confined to the male sex, for fifty-four of the 669 were women or girls. In the seventeenth century, an overwhelming majority was white, but towards the middle of the next century, Negroes began to outnumber them. Thus in seven of the years between 1738 and 1749 the blacks took first place.[54]

It is unfortunate that no conclusions can be reached concerning the effective achievement of freedom by the runaways. As far as white servants are concerned in the eighteenth century, the majority *probably* got away.[55] Certainly the number of advertisements far exceeded the number of cases brought up in the courts. While this should be moderated somewhat by the possibility that masters forgave and forgot when a servant was returned, or that the case was handled by a local justice whose records are lost, it stands substantially. In the case of Negroes, however, circumstantial evidence points the other way.

Negroes, in the first place, would be far easier to detect, despite the existence of free Negroes in the larger towns. The frequent repetition of advertisements for an individual slave suggests that running a notice in the newspaper was not an idle gesture, but one productive of results. Finally, there were few places that a Negro could go and live in assurance that he would not be molested,[56] unless he had papers of manumission, and quite likely, some friend to post a bond to the town he entered that he would not become a charge. This must be weighed against the rare appearance of a Negro in court on runaway charges. While he too may have been punished by a justice of the peace, it is more likely that his master, himself, handed out a whipping. Moreover, since Negroes were already slaves, having no property or financially responsible friends, the master had nothing to gain from taking them to court. Thus if the Negro had not damaged another person's property, his master would be wise to avoid the expense of a court suit.[57] Whatever the answer, the significant thing is that escape was tried, sometimes with success, and that to some servants, every road looked like freedom road.

It remains to be asked, why did servants run away? The answer, like that to any question concerning a complex social problem, is many sided. Specifically, there were probably as many answers as there were servants who absconded; and these answers lie within the context of a wider problem—the totality of servant protest against the system.

Obviously, some servants like Thomas Starbuck and Jerathmeel Bowers of Middlesex County, were lazy, indifferent, and irresponsible by our standards as well as the standards of their own day. Starbuck, for example, could give no reason for running away. Upon examination, the court found him to be idle. His coworkers, on the farm of Benjamin Crane, testified that he had no cause for desertion but was a "runaway lying boy. . . ."[58] Bowers was even more irresponsible. He went riding on a neighbor's horse during haying, and was out all night without leave during husking time. Admonished by the selectmen, he pled ignorance of the law, and was let go. Instead of reforming, he immediately celebrated the leniency of the authorities by drinking in an ordinary the rest of the day and by staying out all night. Subsequently he ignored his chores, threatened to knock a hole in his master's head, frightened his mistress (whom he called an "[ordin]ary whore, burnt-taile Bitch & hopping toad . . . "), so that she would not stay alone with him, took the house door off its hinges, and finally ran away stealing a pair of shoes and a horse from a neighbor to help him on his way.[59] Such intransigence, reprehensible as it was, must still be recognized as unwillingness to be forever at some one else's business, even if the "forever" was only a few years. Other servants ran away simply to escape what they considered to be excessive punishment for something their masters considered as "evil doings." With these, there may have been no conscious awareness of a general desire for freedom, but only a particular desire for freedom from the particular situations in which they found themselvee. Even so, the fear of punishment may well have been the decisive factor in making them come to the conclusion that independence at any cost was better than being another's servant for whatever length of time.[60]

Certainly relatively trivial things, compared with the known hazards of flight, were magnified beyond the endurance point by the built-up pressures of being constantly at another's beck and call, until the walk down the road seemed the next logical move to make.[61] Others left because they felt they were inadequately clothed, or fed, or because they could no longer face the probability or possibility of excessive physical abuse by their masters.[62]

Not the least attraction for wayward servants was the search for adventure, which often culminated in a trip to sea, or less often in going to war. For example, the authorities had considerable difficulty in restraining servants (including apprentices) from joining their fellows who had already shipped aboard the man-of-war *Boston* in the Boston harbor in 1748 without the permission of their masters. From the vantage point of an enlisted person in His Majesty's Navy, they enjoyed and exercised the privilege of insulting their former masters.[63]

Whatever the specific reasons for absconding from their masters, and there were many, behind them lay the belief that they could in some way better themselves. Perhaps they could take up cheap land in the West. Perhaps, like Franklin, they could find an opportunity to ply their skill or their strength alone to better advantage than in the normal course of servitude.[64] Slaves, of course, had little to lose. Physical punishment they could receive, they could be sold into a harsher environment, but they could hardly have their period of service extended. Not to be overlooked, in the assessing of motivation, is the problem of assimilating peoples of alien ancestry. The unwillingness to adjust to a transplanted English culture on the part of Negroes cannot have failed to produce restlessness. Awareness of being alien must have made the ties which bound one to a master weaker than they would have been had the servant wholeheartedly accepted his master's culture and mores. This factor takes on greater significance when one considers the fact that Negroes, Indians, mulattoes, and whites of non-English origin account for more than half of those who ran.

Unfortunately, few runaways speak for themselves, and we have to rely heavily upon the words of their masters. The latter saw no petty grievance which would cause their "well treated" help to run away. Yet, the desire for freedom had a solid foundation; particularly so if the younger John Winthrop's conception of perfection in a servant was widespread. "You will find her," he wrote his mother about a servant girl, "as absolutely and humbly at your command as any that ever you could have."[65]

Masters recognized the significance of freedom to the servants. Samuel Sewall centered one of his arguments against the importation of Negroes on that very subject, when he wrote:

> Few can endure to hear of a Negro's being made free; and indeed they can seldom use their freedom well; yet *their continual aspiring after their forbidden Liberty, renders them Unwilling Servants.*[66]

Benjamin Wadsworth analyzed the problem more comprehensively when he wrote, "Possibly some Servants are very high, proud, stout, they'll scarce bear to be commanded or restrained: they are much for liberty." And then he spelled out that liberty the servants found wanting under servitude:

> They must have liberty for their tongues to speak almost what and when they please; liberty to give or receive visits of their own accord, and when they will; liberty to keep what company they please; liberty to be out late on nights to go & come almost when they will, without telling why or wherefore; such liberty they contend for, they wont be rul'd, govern'd, restrain'd; or it may be the work they are set about, they reckon 'tis beneath and below them, they wont stoop to do it,

but will rather disobey Masters or Mistresses; such Servants
are very wicked. They are daring in their plain disobedience to
God, their abominable rebellion against him; they trample
God's law, his Authority, under their feet.[67]

Cotton Mather noticed this pride too and the discontent it
engendered, equating it with the pride of the fallen angels.[68] But in a
sermon directed ostensibly at Negro slaves, although manifestly
applicable to other servants as well, he seems to have touched this
major cause of running away better than any other:

> There is a *Fondness* for *Freedom* in many of you who live
> comfortably in a very easy servitude.[69]

And it was true. Compared with other sections of the colonial
seaboard, this was an "easy servitude." What Cotton Mather did not
recognize is that for those who had a "Fondness for Freedom" no
servitude was easy.

NOTES

1. Prior to the advent of the newspaper, these cases were most commonly
   found in the published and manuscript court records for the counties,
   in *Mass. Recs.,* Plym. Recs., and in *Assistants.* While the courts
   continue to have such records in the eighteenth century, the
   newspaper files of the period are the most prolific source for
   runaways. A complete search was made of both for the period down to
   and including 1750.
2. *Assistants,* II, 43.
3. Apparently a pass system was general in the other colonies. See
   Smith, *Colonists in Bondage . . . ,* 265. However, other than the
   law cited above, and a reference to certificates of dismissal in
   Winthrop Papers, III, 64–65, there is no support for the existence of a
   pass system in Massachusetts or Plymouth. The latter reference is in a
   letter from the Governor of Plymouth to the Governor of
   Massachusetts Bay in Feb. 1631/2 replying to a request that any
   person leaving the Bay Colony without consent of the authorities be
   returned. That this did not apply simply to servants can be seen in the
   law of June 14, 1631, prohibiting such travel. *Mass. Recs.,* I, 88. In
   the eighteenth century, at the request of Boston, the General Court
   enacted a law for Boston only, requiring Negro, Indian, and Mulatto
   servants out after nine P.M. to have an "order" from their masters. This
   was not a runaway measure, but an attempt to avert disturbances.
   Boston Records, VIII, 173–175; *Acts and Resolves,* I, 535–536. The
   preamble gives the key, "Whereas great disorders, insolencies and

burglaries are ofttimes raised and committed in the night time. ... " Further evidence for this "disorders" interpretation is in the *News-Letter* for Sept. 11, 1746. Several houses had been burglarized at night and the provincial justices ordered all masters of families to keep servants, and others under their government, in homes at night. Special care was to be taken that Negroes be not abroad after nine P.M. without "Certificates."

4. *Mass. Recs.,* I, 157 (Sept. 1635). In that same month, under the authority thus granted, or possibly before it was granted, some servants were captured who attempted to flee by boat. *Winthrop's Journal,* I, 158; *Assistants,* II, 59–60. It was the "Great Fire" of 1653 which brought the enactment of the first fire code in Boston. Bridenbaugh, *Cities . . . ,* 58.

5. Whitmore, *Laws,* 186–187; *Acts and Resolves,* I, 378. The first law came in 1646.

6. *Mass. Recs.,* V, 290. Eight years earlier a court had fined one Joseph Harris five pounds for "entertaining" a servant aboard his vessel and agreeing to take him to Barbados. Thus the courts went beyond the law in protecting property in servants. *Suffolk County Court,* I, 176. For similar cases see *ibid.,* 139 (1672); 265 (1673); II, 822 (1677); and *Essex County Court,* IV, 151 (1669).

7. *Acts and Resolves,* II, 119. Even before this law was broadened, the act of helping servants escape other than by ship did not go unpunished. In 1690, one John Loucklin was fined five pounds, and assessed twenty shillings damages for each of two servants whom he enticed to desert their master's service "designing to convey them away" by canoe. MSS. Suffolk County Court, II, 376. For other cases see *ibid.,* I, 99 (1681); Mass. Archives MSS. Vol. IX, 158–159 (1707). A curious case arose over this provision of the law. A mulatto servant named Doney had fled from his master and was captured. His master refused to pay prison charges, and Doney was sold for two years and six months. Subsequently one James Collins was indicted for taking Doney out of the province without his new master's consent. The plaintiff lost the case, appealed, and lost again on the grounds that the county court had illegally bound Doney for the prison costs, an unusual decision. Part of the owner's costs were reimbursed by the lower court which had originally sold the mulatto. See MSS. Essex Sessions, V, 264, 838–840; MSS. Essex County Inferior Court of Common Pleas, 1736–1740, n.p. (July 13, 1736); MSS. Essex County Inferior Court of Common Pleas, Files, drawer, March–July, 1736; MSS. Essex and York, Superior Court of Judicature Minute Book, 1732–1736, n.p. (Oct. 6, 1736); MSS. Essex Superior Court of Judicature, 1736–1738, 81–82 (May 10, 1737).

8. Pulsifer, *Laws,* 237, 255.

9. *Winthrop Papers,* III, 64–65.

10. *Winthrop's Journal,* I, 193.

11. David Pulsifer, ed., *Acts of the Commissioners of the United Colonies* . . . , I, 6–7. Renewed in 1672, *ibid.*, II, 20.
12. *Ibid.*, II, 20.
13. MSS. Winthrop Papers, W.20.43. For others see *Winthrop Papers* IV, 278–279 (1640); 463–464 (1644); Morris, *Government and Labor* . . . , 436. For a general discussion see Smith, *Colonists in Bondage* . . . , 270. See also MSS. Suffolk County Court, I, 220 (1684). In *ibid.*, I, 80, a Rhode Island servant was not only extradited, but was given fifteen stripes to speed him on his way. In MSS. Suffolk Sessions, II, 99–100 (1715), a servant was extradited from Msssachusetts back to London. *Ibid.*, II, 242, returned to New York (1684/5); MSS Bristol Sessions, II, 2 (1702), returned to Rhode Island.
14. *Essex County Court,* III, 351–352. A similar bill of charges is in MSS. Middlesex Court Files, file 70, no number (case of Henery Hall, May 3, 1674): constable charges, eight shillings; recording complaint, four shillings; time lost, twelve shillings; hue and cry and messenger, fourteen shillings, prison keeper, four shillings, three pence. In 1692/3, justices of the peace were empowered to make out "hue and crys after runaway servants, thiefs and other criminals." *Acts and Resolves,* I, 52–53.
15. See also the issue of Jan. 2, 1739, in which was advertised a lost pocket case containing "one or two printed Advertisements after a Runaway Negro Man. . . . "
16. Quote from *Evening-Post,* Oct. 11, 1742. The following advertisement is a model of the art of description. Who could fail to recognize the runaway who fled "from his Master Edward Carter of Boston, Silk Dyer, an Irish Man Servant, named Thomas Manning, alias Carter, he is a lusty well set Fellow; had on when he went away, a black cloth Jacket, blue Kersey Breeches Trim'd with black, suppos'd to have Trousers, yarn Stockings, good Shoes, cotton and linnen Shirt, new Beaver Hat, dark colour'd natural Wigg or Cap; he speaks thick, rolls his eyes, stoops a little, treads firm, speak smartly to him and he'll repeat your Words again. His Nails somewhat stain'd, if not scrap'd. He is a Sheerman, Preseer, &c. at the Cloathers Business." *Post-Boy,* June 11, 1739. Multiple ads in *N.E. Journal,* Aug. 11, 1741; *Evening-Post,* Aug. 31, 1741; *News-Letter,* Aug. 20–27, 1741; *Gazette,* Aug. 24, 1741; *Post-Boy,* Aug. 31, 1741. For promises of forgivness see *Gazette,* May 17–24, 1731; *Evening-Post,* Jan, 4, 1748 and *Post-Boy,* Dec. 21, 1747.
17. The *Gazette* for Aug. 4–11, 1735, carried an advertisement by the lad's master asking for his return.
18. Aug. 24, 1738.
19. Jan 21, 1740, and Nov. 3, 1740.
20. Nov. 19–26, 1741, Sept. 1, 1743, Mar. 16, 1750, Feb. 4–11, 1731.

21. Aug. 11–18, 1729, Oct. 30, 1750. For another Negro stopped on suspicion, see MSS. (unbound) Minute Book Suffolk General Sessions, Oct. 1738.

22. *Gazette,* Aug. 11–18, 1729. See also *N.E. Journal,* Aug. 24, 1736. In the same paper for Sept. 18, 1732, is the story of an Indian taken up as a runaway. He killed the man who stopped him. Later he hanged for murder. *Ibid.,* Mar. 26, 1733. For a court case involving a Negro stopped on suspicion of being a runaway see MSS. Suffolk Sessions Miscellaneous Bundle for 1738 (case of Thomas, Negro, Oct. 31, 1738). He was freed the following January, but no record of damages accorded him was found, despite the assumption of any possible damages by the men who found him. Apparently this was one of the hazards of being a free Negro.

23. Out of 112 seventeenth-century court cases, seventy-two received whippings. See appendix G in Towner, "A Good Master Well Served . . . " (Ph.D. diss., Northwestern University, 1954), Servants getting twenty stripes: *Suffolk County Court,* I, 184 (1672); MSS. Plymouth Sessions, III, 70 (1727); thirty: *Assistants,* I, 200 (1681).

24. Branded with an "R": *Essex County Court,* IV, 234 (1670) Runaways given a brand of "B" for burglar: *ibid.,* III, 254 (1665); *Assistants,* I, 200 (1681).

25. MSS. Suffolk County Court, I, 84 (1681); Oct. 4, 1736. For other chainings see *Essex County Court,* I, 8 (1638); V, 230–231 (1673); VIII 142–143 (1681); MSS, Suffolk County Court, I, 84 (1681); *Assistants,* II, 86 (1639).

26. For examples see *Essex County Court,* VIII, 301–302; MSS. Suffolk County Court, I, 99 (1681).

27. *Assistants,* II, 59–60 (1635). Another had only to make up half the time he was gone. *Plym. Recs.,* I, 128 (1639).

28. See appendix C in Towner, "A Good Master Well Served . . . " (Ph.D. diss., Northwestern University, 1954). For a detailed example see MSS. Plymouth Sessions, I, 93 (1716). Jacob, Indian servant of Samuel Seabury of Duxbury, ran away for four months. He stole sixteen shillings in goods from his Master and one other person. He was assessed treble damages, fined sixteen shillings, and assessed two pounds, eleven shillings costs of court. Seabury paid damages and costs. Jacob took ten stripes instead of the fine, and Mr. Seabury was awarded twelve months extra service.

29. Presumably not only runaways but others who had unfaithfully served their masters, could be forced to serve extra time for compensation for their misdeeds. Such were not to be "dismissed till they have made satisfaction according to the Judgement of Authoritie." Whitmore, *Laws,* 53 (1641). However, I have not found any who had time added unless they had in some way damaged their masters by running away,

stealing, damaging property, or becoming pregnant, whereby the master was out both time and money.
30. See appendix G in Towner, "A Good Master Well Served ... " (Ph.D. diss., Northwestern University, 1954). For comparison with masters in other colonies see Morris, *Government and Labor ...* , 434 ff. See also Smith, *Colonists in Bondage ...* , 265–269. The data in Morris should be handled carefully for he does not always differentiate between true runaways and temporary absenteeism. See note 43 below.
31. The quote is from Morgan, *The Puritan Family ...* , 71. For others see MSS. indenture of Joseph Barber, M.H.S. Miscellaneous Bound Manuscripts, Apr. 8, 1694; MSS. volume "Inhabitants—1695, List of & Indentures of Apprentices," and MSS. Boston Indentures, *passim*. For the unusual provision of two years for each running-away see *Plym. Recs.,* I, 129 (1657/8).
32. Page 23.
33. Cotton Mather, Rules for the Society of Negroes ... , 6, 8,
34. Wadsworth, The Well-Ordered Family ... , 119. Willard, *A Compleat Body of Divinity ...* , 649 (second pagination).
35. The earliest of these is Increase Mather's *A Wicked Man's Portion.* ... First printed in 1675, it was reprinted in 1685, and was summarized in Cotton Mather's collection, *Pillars of Salt ...* Others include *The Confession Declaration, Dying Warning and Advice of Patience Sampson ... Alias Patience Boston Who Was Executed at York July 24, 1735 for the Murder of Benjamin Trot.* ... (Boston, 1735), which warned servants to beware of rebellion and stubbornness on page 4; *A Faithful Narrative of the Wicked Life and Remarkable Conversion of Patience Boston.* ... (Boston, 1738); John Campbell's *After Souls by Death are Separated From their Bodies, They come to Judgement Asserted in a Sermon Deliver'd At ... the Day of the Execution of John Hamilton ... [with his Confession and Dying Warning]* (Boston, 1738); *Declaration and Confession of Jeffrey, A Negro, who was executed at Worcester, Oct 17, 1745 for the Murder of Mrs. Tabetha Sanford, as Mendon.* ... (Boston, 1745). Michael Wigglesworth's *Day of Doom* had a place for runaways in hell, right amongst the other goats. Perry Miller and Thomas H. Johnson, eds, *The Puritans,* 593, verse 28.
36. *Essex County Court,* III, 28 (1681).
37. *Winthrop's Journal,* I, 158. For other attempts to escape by sea in a small boat see *Suffolk County Court,* I, 184 (1672); *Courant,* May 4–11, 1724; *Gazette,* Sept. 28–Oct. 5, 1741.
38. *Essex County Court,* VIII, 205 (1679); MSS. Essex Sessions, I, n.p.(June 27, 1704, case of John Monant); *Suffolk County Court,* I, 176 (1672).

39. In that order July 6–13, 1724; *N.E. Journal,* June 12, 1732; Feb. 14, 1732. For othere see *Evening-Post,* Aug. 8, 1743, Apr. 28, 1746; Feb. 24, 1746; Apr. 6, 1747.
40. Franklin, Autobiography . . . , 25–26.
41. MSS. Mass. Archives, IX, 182–185 (1724–1727); *House Journals,* VI, 277; VII, 290–291; IX, 9–19. Greene, *The Negro in Colonial New England* . . . , 164–165, treats this as a case of abduction. He used only the Archives, but the *House Journals* show clearly that it was more likely a case of a runaway. The original Captain was fined and assessed damages. He attempted to get the General Court to distinguish in the law between those who deliberately aided a runaway and those who unwittingly did so. The General Court refused, but remitted his fine.
42. A case in 1673 illustrates this very well. Five servants (one a Negro) spent a month in planning their escape. One stole two horses with saddles and bridles, another stole several articles of clothing from his master's son. *Suffolk County Court,* I, 249–250 (1673). About one-third of the cases of running away brought before the courts involve theft as well. See appendix G in Towner, "A Good Master Well Served . . . " (Ph.D. diss., Northwestern University, 1954). Frequently the newspaper advertisements list goods stolen by runaways as well as the runaway himself. For examples see *News-Letter,* Sept. 2–9, 1725; Aug. 14–21, 1740; *Gazette,* Nov. 2–9, 1720; Nov. 2–9, 1730; *N.E. Journal,* Dec. 2, 1728; May 18, 1736; *Courant,* May 17–24, 1725. For servants who stole boats or horses see *Plym. Recs.,* II, 204 (1660/1); MSS. Middlesex Court Files, file 53, no number (Case o f Jerathmeel Bowers, May 18, 1669); *Suffolk County Court,* 1, 249–250 (1673); MSS. Suffolk County Court, I, 228 (1684); *Essex County Court,* II, 254 (1665); *Post-Boy,* Nov, 25, 1745; *Gazette,* Sept. 20, 1748; *N.E. Journal,* Aug. 12, 1732; Feb. 26, 1733; and footnote 37.
43. See Smith, *Colonists in Bondage* . . . , 268–269; Morris, *Government and Labor* . . . , 434 ff. Many servants were charged with temporary absenteeism, and, apparently, had no intention of running away. Others quit, not to run but to work for another master. See MSS. Suffolk Sessions, I, 4 (1702); 177 (1708); III, 69–70 (1720/1); 267 (1723). No time was added. In at least one case, a servant who left without leave to visit relatives and returned nine days later, time was threatened to be added for an obvious absence without leave rather than for running away. See MSS. Middlesex Court Files, file 29, number 1901 (1662). No disposition by the court could be found.
44. *Essex County Court,* V, 23; MSS. Suffolk County Court, I, 37 (1680). In the latter case, Cheeney was allowed to be sold out of the country since "no means used" could reclaim him from his evil ways. The earliest case of repeated running was in 1636, when one William

Dodg's boy was shipped for such behavior. *Essex County Court,* I, 4. In the following year another servant, Marmaduke Barton or Barneston, began a career of desertion which brought him into court three times in four years. *Ibid.,* 1, 6, 8, 20. For other repeaters see MSS. Indenture of John Humphreys (1679) in "Inhabitants—1695— List of & Indentures of Apprentices"; *N.E. Journal,* Aug. 24, 1736; May 18, 1736; Nov. 11, 1740; *News-Letter,* Aug. 26–Sept. 2, 1736; Oct. 11, 1739; Aug 15–22, 1734; *Evening-Post,* Mar. 10, 1740 and June 2, 1740; Oct. 25, 1742; *Gazette,* Sept. 20, 1748; Apr. 4, 1749. For court cases see Appendix G in Towner, "A Good Master Well Served . . ." (Ph.D. diss., Northwestern University, 1954).

45. Three of the servants who were chained or collared were repeaters, as were two of those who were branded. MSS. Suffolk County Court, I, 84 (1681); *Essex County Court,* I, 8 (1638); V, 230–231 (1673); IV, 234 (1670); *Assistants,* I, 200 (1681).

46. Cut off hair, or suspected of doing so: *Evening-Post,* Sept. 19, 1737; July 23, 1750; *N.E. Journal,* Aug. 5, 1734. Wore Men's clothes: *Suffolk County Court,* II, 1063 (1679); *Evening-Post,* Oct. 8, 1743. Changed names: *Evening-Post,* Oct. 25, 1742; Feb. 24, 1746; *N.E. Journal,* Mar. 24, 1729; *Courant,* Nov. 5–12, 1722 Caesar: *N.E. Journal,* Mar. 24, 1729. Kirby: *Courant,* Dec. 17–24, 1722. Quotation: *Gazette,* Apr. 4, 1749. For another Negro advertised as running by night, hiding by day, see *ibid.,* Sept. 20, 1748. This man took a halter with him in hopes of stealing a horse.

47. *Essex County Court,* III 264–265 (1665). Advice in planning escape: *ibid.,* I, 6 (1637); III, 278 (1665); MSS. Middlesex Court Files, file 74, no number (Jan. 24, 1670/1, case of Richard Hancock): *Suffolk County Court,* I, 186 (1672); II, 1158 (1679/80); MSS. Hampshire County Court, I, 68 (1683). Transportation: M.H.S., 4 *Colls.,* VI, 135–136 (1635); *Suffolk County Court,* I, 176 (1672); *Essex County Court,* VII, 205 (1679). Concealed in flight: *Assistants,* II, 122 (1642/3); MSS. Plymouth Sessions, IV, 149 (1741/2). Miscellaneous help: *Essex County Court,* VIII, 142–143 (1681); *Plym. Recs.,* VI, 104 (1682/3); *Sibley's Harvard Graduates,* IV, 340 (circa 1725) MSS Middlesex Court Files, flie 58, no number (case of Henery Hall, June 20, 1671). Hall, a servant, gave food to a runaway.

48. *Bradford's History,* 432–433 (1638). One servant escaped. The others were executed for murder of an Indian, whom they stopped while resting on their journey.

49. *Assistants,* II, 97 (1640); *Suffolk County Court,* I, 249–250 (1673); MSS. Middlesex Court Flles, file 16, number 740 (1660/1); file 70, no number (case of Henery Hall and Caleb Blease, May 3, 1674); file 74, no number (case of Richard Hancock, Jan. 24, 1670/1); MSS. Middlesex County Court, I, 190–191 (1659); MSS. Suffolk County Court, I, 74–75 (1681); 141 (1682); 143 (1682/3); 64 (1680/1); II, 376 (1690). One group of undetermined size plus one group of six

preceded the Peach gang. See *Assistants,* II, 51 (1636/5); and
Winthrop's Journal, I, 158 (1635).
50. MSS Bristol Sessions, II, 87 (1705); *N.E. Journal,* Dec. 2, 1728; Oct.
11 1731; Oct. 18, 1731; Aug. 21, 1732; Apr. 21, 1735; Apr. 24,
1739; Apr. 22, 1740; Sept. 16, 1740; June 23, 1741; *News-Letter,*
June 20–27, 1715; Nov. 19–26, 1730; Dec. 18–25, 1735; Sept. 22–
29, 1737; Aug. 10, 1749; *Gazette,* Oct. 19–26, 1730; Oct. 1734;
Sept. 26–Oct. 3, 1737; Oct. 17–24, 1737; July 2–9, 1739; Sept. 25,
1744; Dec. 22, 1747; Jan. 26, 1748; Oct. 17, 1749; Nov. 14, 1749;
Evening-Post, Oct. 20, 1735; Oct. 3, 1737; July 17, 1738; Mar. 18,
1742; Feb. 7, 1743; May 2, 1743; Dec. 29, 1746; Jan. 4, 1748.
51. *Gazette,* Sept. 28–Oct. 5, 1741; and *News-Letter,* Sept. 24–Oct. 1,
1741. They had already been sold. For other cases involving three or
more servants see *Courant,* May 4–11, 1724 (four); *N.E. Journal,* Jan.
2, 1739 (six); *Evening-Post,* May 9, 1743 (four); *Gazette,* Apr. 12,
1748 (three); Sept. 26, 1749 (three).
52. *Gazette,* Sept. 25, 1744; *Evening-Post,* Oct. 20, 1735.
53. *Courant,* May 4–11, 1724. For others see *Suffolk County Court,* I,
249–250 (1673, four whites and a Negro); *N.E. Journal,* Dec. 2, 1728
(Indian and white); *News-Letter,* Dec. 18–25, 1735 (Indian and white);
Sept. 22–29, 1737 (Negro and white); Aug. 10, 1749 (Negro and
white); *Gazette,* Sept. 26–Oct. 3, 1737 (white and Negro); *Evening-
Post,* Oct. 3, 1737 (Negro and white).
54. The years are 1738, 1740, 1742, 1745, 1746, 1747 and 1749. Blacks
also outnumbered the whites in 1693, 1719, and 1727.
55. See Smith, Colonists in Bondage . . . , 269–270.
56. One exception was that Negroes (and perhaps whites and Indians)
camped out in the woods for varying lengths of time. The *N.E. Journal*
for Dec. 2, 1740 reports a Negro running away and suggests that he
has joined the Negroes in Needham woods. Another possible hiding
place would be with the Indians or the French. It may have been
difficult to locate a runaway Negro even in Boston, however. Thus one
advertisement states that the runaway in question was well known in
town and had been seen there as well as in New Town "going to his
Whore. . . . " *Post-Boy,* Apr. 26, 1742.
57. For a Negro posting a bond with the town of Boston to save the town
any expense if he should become destitute, see MSS. Boston Public
Welfare Department, 1747 File, January 13, 1747 (Ebenezer Prince).
Such posting of bonds was a common practice. The authority on the
New-England Negro, Lorenzo Johnston Greene, does not venture to
guess what percentage of them escaped permanently. Greene, *The
Negro in Colonial New England . . . ,* 149.
58. MSS. Middlesex Court Files, file 53, no number (case of Thomss
Starbuck, June, 1669).
59. *Ibid.,* no number (case of Jerathmeel Bowers, May, June, 1669). Cited
in Morgan, *The Puritan Family . . . ,* 75.

60. For examples see *Winthrop Papers,* IV, 232–233 (1640/1); MSS. Middlesex County Court, III, 47 (1672); *Evening-Post,* Feb. 13, 1749; *Post-Boy,* Jan. 21, 1740; *News-Letter,* Aug. 15–22, 1734.

61. An example of subsurface discontent brought to the surface by a seemingly trivial incident is the case of one Charles Attwood, apprentice to William Baker, glover, of Essex County. Attwood's father had apprenticed him for thirteen years from 1687 to 1699. In the writing of the indenture, Thomas Lovell, apparently a justice or notary, had inadvertently failed to write "nine" after sixteen hundred and ninety. In 1696 the boy's father died, and while he and his mother were going through the father's papers, the indenture was discovered and read. This made young Attwood greatly discontented, although the indenture clearly said for thirteen years, and he ran away. His master pursued and caught him in Rhode Island and brought him back for trial. The court agreed with the mother (despite several testimonies) and freed the boy holding that what was written must stand. E.I. *Colls.,* XI, 74–80.

62. MSS. Suffolk Sessions, III, 132–133 (1722); *Essex County Court,* VII, 74 (1678); VIII, 91–92 (1681); *Mass. Recs.,* II, 20 (1642); MSS. Middlesex County Court, I, 119 and MSS. Middlesex Court Files, file 11, number 441 (1656); file 42, no number (case of Benjamin Crane's Negro, June 14, 1666). This Negro boy was described by witnesses as a very bad character, "as full of Bad qualitie almost as is posable for a boy to bee. . . . " The constable who caught him testified the boy said he ran because his master beat him so often. He saw his back, raw with welts, some healing, others healed. When he delivered the Negro to his master, Crane, he was beaten again with a small walnut rod and the constable could hear the cry one quarter mile away.

63. *Evening-Post,* July 25, 1748. See also Apr. 28, 1746; *House Journals,* II, 293 (1720).

64. Many years after Franklin, another printer's apprentice whistled at his indenture and absconded. Isaiah Thomas, after an argument with his master, in 1765, ran away to London where he thought he would "become really competent in his trade." Clifford K. Shipton, *Isaiah Thomas . . . ,* 8–9. Advertisements such as that in the *Evening-Post* for Nov. 22, 1742 offering high pay for shipwrights, caulkers, and smiths in Jamaica (servant or free) in His Majesty's service must have stimulated servant imaginations.

65. *Winthrop Papers,* IV, 68–69.

66. In M.H.S., 1 *Proc.,* VII, 162. Italics mine.

67. *The Well-Ordered Family . . . ,* 117–118.

68. *A Family Well-Ordered . . . ,* 66–67.

69. *Tremenda . . . ,* 27.

9. Conclusion

The English Puritans and Pilgrims, who successfully built seventeenth-century Zions on the shores of the present state of Massachusetts, built them in part on a system of unfree labor. The "Bible Commonwealths" passed out of existence before the end of the century, but the institution of servitude, which had assured the colonists that their worldly work would be done, was handed on intact to the eighteenth-century residents of the province of Massachusetts Bay. By 1750, servitude was still firmly established, and, by that date, it had played an important part in the economic development of the area. In addition, it had provided a means of regulating dangerous elements in the society, and it had proved successful as an institution for the care of dependent individuals. In the years intervening between its establishment, and 1750, many changes occurred: for example, in the sources and types of bound labor, and in the use of the system as a method of social control. Meanwhile, a servant class had been created whose members were relatively unimportant as individuals, but who, as a group, made a significant contribution to their society, and left their imprint upon the community as a whole.

The institution of servitude had its origin in Massachusetts with the beginnings of colonization—coming with the Pilgrims in 1620, being immeasurably strengthened by the heavy invasion of Puritans down to 1641—and it touched on the lives of many individuals, free and unfree alike. Before the seventeenth century was half over, all of the variant types of servitude had appeared; some of them, like the company-owned servants, emerging only to disappear again within the lifetime of the first comers. Apprentices, indentured servants of one kind or another, poor apprentices, idlers, bastards and orphans, debtors, criminals, war prisoners, Indians and Negroes—all alike heard the call of the master's voice in the seventeenth century, and most of them responded to that call in the eighteenth century, too.

During the first decades of settlement, English servants, transported individually and in small groups, were the most important source of bound labor, whether serving for transportation and keep, or for wages as well. But as the heavy stream of immigration was reduced to a trickle, the colonists on New England's labor-hungry shores sought to meet their manpower needs by any means consistent with their consciences and their social mores. London was scoured for orphans and bastards, and the prison camps of the Irish and Scottish were searched for victims of internecine warfare—likely candidates to drive the plow, swing the axe, carry the water bucket, and milk the cow. Indians and Negroes became fair game, though in small numbers; and, at the same time, the settlers of the "New English Caanan" found themselves willing to risk a hazardous choice of servants sold off the ships of entrepreneurs engaged in a new business—the transportation and sale of indentured servants. All this occurred within the first thirty years of settlement.

Meanwhile, the colonists did not neglect their home-grown crop of boys and girls, men and women. Wage ceilings were imposed upon free artisans and workers, while restrictions were placed on bound servants to keep them bound to the last moment of their contracts. Those who were about to become servants were encouraged to sign long-term contracts, as terms of less than six months in Plymouth or a year in Massachusetts were prohibited. At the same time, boys became 'prentice lads, and the socially undesirable elements were made socially useful under the particular care of determined masters.

In the closing decades of the seventeenth century and in the early decades of the eighteenth century, certain changes occurred in the general composition of the servant class. Except for apprenticeship (whose rewards were sufficient to encourage enrollment) and poor apprenticeship (which drew on a large class of legally defenseless poor), servanthood had less and less attraction for the white population, and most native American workers retained their status of free labor. At the same time, certain types of social deviants—debtors, adult idlers, and the adult poor—usually received institutional care instead of being put to service. To fill the already existent gap between labor demand and labor supply, white servants of non-English stock from the Continent and from Ireland were imported in increasing numbers. Even these sources did not fulfill the colonists' needs, and it was left to the Negro to meet the remaining requirements for bound labor. In fact, except for the decade of heaviest importation of whites, 1710–1720, Negroes appear to have dominated the bound labor scene in the first half of the eighteenth century.[1]

The primary factor influencing the development of the institution of servitude was the great need for workers of all kinds in a frontier society, and, as the frontier life gave way to settled habitation, the need for workers to provide manpower for an expanding agricultural, manufacturing, and seafaring economy. At the same time, there was a persistent demand for labor to ameliorate the conditions of life for those who could afford domestic help. However, the need for labor was only the primary, not the exclusive factor in shaping the institution. Other important forces were: the land system; custom; a desire to maintain religious, racial, and social homogeneity; and religion.

The land system, for example, tended to limit the demand for servile labor. Most Massachusetts and Plymouth farms were small and required the diversified and intensive application of few hands rather than the extensive and repetitious labor of many. Without a staple crop in demand in England or on the Continent, those farms could not support, as they could not use, large numbers of laborers. In addition, the distribution of land to communities, and then from the communities to the individual resident therein, limited the use of land as an inducement both to prospective servants and to prospective importers of servants.

Custom provided the molds into which the early institution of servitude was poured, end even though the system overflowed to create different sets of relationships between masters and servants, much that was old persisted. Apprenticeship, for example, was patterned after the traditional English model, and poor apprenticeship had much in common with the legal provision for the poor with which the colonists were familiar before emigrating. Even where innovation was called for, as in indentured servitude, the apprentice contract and the system of the long-hire provided partial answers to serious questions of organization and procedure, such as how to bind a transported servant securely. Thus, in their labor system, as in other aspects of life, the colonists were not stripped bare of all inheritance by the harsh facts of frontier life.

Almost as effective as custom in shaping the institution of servitude, was the desire to maintain religious, social, and racial homogeneity. To the Puritan or Pilgrim colonist, the ideal servant was a white Englishman from a sober and religious family of modest, but not lowly means. This factor restricted the effectiveness of the purely economic demand for labor: it prohibited the wholesale importation of English criminals, for example, and it sought, with only partial success, to curtail the use of Negroes in favor of white servants.

Religion, the last major factor influencing servitude, justified it as a legitimate, and indeed, as a divine institution. The ministers of the gospel emphasized and encouraged the fundamental role of the family in society, and they insisted that the divine souls of all men made it necessary for masters to consider their servants as parts of their families. In fact, religion emphasized family government so strongly that individuals found themselves made servants merely because they had not been living under proper family government or because they had lived "extravagant" lives contrary to the mores of the community. Moreover, religion was undoubtedly an ameliorating force in the servants' lives, for it proscribed, on the part of the masters, excessive and cruel punishments, neglect (whether spiritual or physical), and unfeeling exploitation.

The servant class, which emerged as a consequence of the above forces and which was shaped by them, included several categories from the apprentices down to the slaves. These differences in status were not lost upon the master class, even though in practice rigid stratification of status and function were not always preserved. In the eighteenth century, Samuel Willard explained the nature and origin of the differences between the various classifications. "We know by Experience," he wrote, "that these [servants] are not all of a sort, or come under the same degree of Servitude; some are more Free, and others more in Bondage. . . . "[2]

There were four primary divisions: those who became servants by compact or agreement, by self-alienation, by captivity, and by natural generation.[3] The first category, Willard said, embraced the "most *honourable* sort of Servants. . . ." The reason was that:

> these are such as are originally Free, and either by themselves or by their Parents or Overseers Indent with their Masters, between whom there are mutual Obligations, such as Apprentices bound to Trades, or hired Servants for a shorter or longer Time; of this sort of Service there are few that make any dispute against the Lawfulness of it, being apparently necessary.[4]

The second degree, those who became servants "By *Self Alienation through Poverty or Forfeiture,*" included those who were reduced to

> such Exigence, as they either Sell themselves or Children to their Neighbors; or run themselves in Debt and have nothing to Pay; or for some pecuniary Crimes are Sold. . . .[5]

Still further down the scale were those who were taken as captives in warfare. Since they might have been slain, keeping them as servants was to be "accounted Indulgence"[6] And at the bottom, the least honorable of all, were the slaves: those who were servants by "Natural Generation. For, though Men are not naturally Servants as they are Men; Yet Men may be born Servants, being descended of such Parents as are so."[7]

Depending upon their position on this scale, servants received greater or less compensation for their labors, served shorter or longer terms (or at least had a voice in determining the length of their terms), and either moved into the skilled artisan class, the unskilled labor market, or remained in servitude for life. Thus, apprentices received training, keep, and freedom dues, while indentured servants received transportation (and/or wages), keep, and freedom dues. Generally speaking, other servants served only for their keep. In addition, the terms of service of the servant elite—apprentices and indentured servants—were determined in part by their own decisions, in part by custom; but other servant categories had no control over the duration of their servitude, and Negro or Indian slaves could look forward only to a lifetime of service.

Despite these very real differences between the categories, the servants were recognized as belonging to a distinguishable group, the servant class. Willard recognized this similarity, which was imposed upon them by their status, when he wrote that the term, servant, "is applied to all such in a Family as are under the Command of a Master, and owe to him Subjection. . . . "[8] Underlining this similarity—this identification as a class—was the fact that the servants, as servants, lived a common life. Indeed no day's work or night's play, no religious experience or untoward protest could serve positively to distinguish one type of servant from another.

In their workaday world, servants were not necessarily distinguished one from another merely by the nature of their tasks. Apprentices, it is true, generally worked at their skills, but they frequently did menial jobs unconnected with the learning of a trade. Conversely, the lowly Negro slave was often put to work as an artisan alongside his white fellow servants instead of doing exclusively lowly tasks. As a part of the labor force, the servants performed a variety of work: from printing to sailing, from farming to valeting, from rope-making to whaling, from washing pots and pans to keeping accounts. These things they did for someone else's profit, or they did them simply to make life easier for their masters. They were always at the command of others, whether the servants were black, white, or red; apprentice, criminal, or slave.

Not only did their workaday world tend to blur the distinctions between the various categories of servants, but so too did the pleasures they sought, and the religious and educational experiences that were made available to them, or foisted upon them, during their leisure hours. Since servants were apparently not invited to partake of the social functions of their masters, except in church-going and on military training days, they sought diversion among themselves. These diversions were carried on regardless of status within the class. Among the socially acceptable recreations were fishing, swimming, boating, and games of various sorts, as well as merrymaking connected with productive tasks like corn husking or the raising of a church. Less socially acceptable behavior illustrated the frequency with which racial and status lines were crossed in such pastimes as fornication, tippling, gambling, dancing, and occasional rioting—during Pope's day celebrations in Boston, for example.

As in their work and play, so too in their protests, the servants may be considered as a group. All categories had reasons for protest. For the most part, both masters and servants accepted the institution of servitude as an institution, even though they both protested about certain aspects of it, or certain abuses within it. Servants found the courts open to them when physical abuse, violations of contract, or violation of the mores of the community were involved. When real evidence of maltreatment was established, justice was meted out to the complainant fairly consistently. However, protests against the system, as distinguished from protests against abuse within the system, were rarely made articulate and almost never came to court at the behest of the servant. Instead be took extra-legal action.

Extra-legal protest was of three different sorts. The first was idleness, negligence or generally intractable behavior. For this, the master had an answer: physical punishment meted out at his own discretion or at the order of the courts. Even so, the recalcitrant servant was common throughout the period. The second was violence. This took several shapes: violence against the master's property, against the master or his family, and, occasionally, against self. Arson, assault, murder, and suicide were the strong weapons of those servants who wanted to protest violently and directly against the persons involved in their servitude. The third sort of extra-legal protest was running away— the most persistently recorded form of protest throughout the period. It was in running away that individual servants registered their distinct rejection of the system of servitude. As was the case in other protests, running away attracted all types of servants regardless of race, status, or sex; and, in running away, the servants developed the first form of cooperative action against what must have seemed to them to be oppression.

The socially irresponsible or socially reprehensible behavior illustrated in some of the servants' recreation, and in their protests was perhaps inevitable among those whose lives were not their own but another's, and particularly inevitable among the many servants who did not accept the cultural patterns of the dominant social groups—cultural patterns which were alien to imported Negroes, to Indians, and partly so to many imported whites. Since the servant class was, to a considerable extent, made up of outsiders and of those who ran afoul the law as criminals, poor, or idlers, it is remarkable that there was so much conformity, rather than that there was so much socially unacceptable behavior.

The social or cultural incompatibility reflected in servant behavior was noted by the masters: the English servants who slept in their bedrooms or lofts were not always local farmers' sons, but often paupers, idle wastrels, or worse yet, thieves, fornicators, arsonists, or other addicts to violence, who might corrupt their children, defile their beds, blaspheme their God, or burn down the houses over their heads. The incompatibility was still greater in the case of non-English whites, Negroes or Indians alien in culture or race. There was always the worry that they might resent strongly the commands of the strangers who imposed different customs upon them. The recognition by the master class of this incompatibility may be seen, for example, in the reaction to the eighteenth-century's large influx of Negroes and non-English whites which aroused real fears over the presence of the "extravasat blood"[9] of the Negroes, and the "vermin" and "corrupting influence" of the Irish and continental whites.[10]

Nor was this the only protest from the ranks of the free. American-born labor—by the eighteenth century, almost universally free (excepting apprentices)—began its protests too. Negroes were discriminated against, at least in the skilled trades, and the occasional beating of them, or riot against them, may have reflected the workingman's discontent with their presence, for Negroes were thought to degrade white men's tasks.[11] In fact, the protest of James Franklin's *Courant* against the "verminous" Irish may have reflected the attitude of the artisan class of which Franklin was a part rather than the feelings of the upper class to which he did not belong. It could easily have been reaction against cheap labor as much as an over-developed fastidiousness about lice and nasty habits.[12]

Viewed with seventeenth- or eighteenth-century eyes, the servitude in which the servants lived should not be entirely condemned any more than it should be entirely condoned. Those domestically bound servants, after all, were either bound by their own or their parents' choice, or, in the case of social deviates, were put to service in homes instead of being incarcerated in penal or charitable institutions (establishments between which there was little to choose).

As for imported white servants, they may have found an easier adjustment in service to a going concern, the family, where their physical wants were supplied than did the later free immigrants of the nineteenth century for whom no one—master or corporation—took full responsibility. The two to six years with keep and protection, along with a small amount of freedom dues, may have prepared them more adequately to face the new, but no longer completely unfamiliar, world than did residence in a ghetto for nineteenth-century expatriates with only their own resources to draw upon in case of unemployment, sickness, or death.

Indian servitude, though obviously exploitation of another culture, would, if continued, perhaps have resulted in amalgamation and a happier solution than the reservation system begun in seventeenth-century Plymouth and Massachusetts. Separated from the whites enough to preserve independent cultures, but thrown together with the whites enough to retain the superior-inferior relationship, the Indian was bound to suffer, whether he was forced into servitude, or lived with his own people as a lower-caste resident of the encircling white community. Negro slavery, even in the relatively mild form prevalent in the province of Massachusetts Bay, had no excuse. The colonists knew better, and they knew they knew better. It was a case of rationalizing a need for labor into the right to have that labor. If sins there be, it was a sin, unmitigated by kind treatment, Christianization, education, or manumission.

Since the labor needs of a raw community and the morality of the times made a virtue of necessity, servitude was adopted and developed into a thriving institution which touched the lives of thousands of individuals, whether masters or servants, in the present area of Massachusetts before 1750. The servants, perforce, made their mark on the society in which they lived. They required legislation for their control, the use of the law courts for its enforcement, newspapers to advertise them or to note their illegal absence, special pews in church, and special sermons to define their relations to their masters and to society. They became articles of commerce, and they helped create other articles of commerce, as well as the ships in which those articles were carried. They even manned the ships. Wherever one turns in the social and economic history of the colony, one finds the servants there. Whatever their lives, hopes, hates, fears, the servants were among the unsung many who helped to make it possible (and sometimes difficult)

for the well-known few to accomplish those things for which they
became famous.

NOTES

1. For the changes in composition of the servant class see appendix J in
   Towner, "A Good Master Well Served . . . " (Ph.D. diss.,
   Northwestern University, 1954).
2. Willard, *A Compleat Body of Divinity* . . . 614 (second pagination).
3. *Ibid.*
4. *Ibid.*
5. *Ibid.*
6. *Ibid.*
7. *Ibid.*
8. *Ibid.*
9. The term is Sewall's, "The Selling of Joseph . . . ," 161–162.
10. *Courant,* Jan. 4–11, 1725.
11. This was true even in the seventeenth century. See *Boston Records,*
    VII, 5 (1661). Later, more than forty coopers, shipwrights, and
    mariners were charged with mistreating Negroes by pushing them off
    the causeways (leading to the Charlestown Ferry) and into the water.
    John Harris, boat builder, was threatened by them also. Two of the
    four individuals brought to trial were fined. MSS. Suffolk Sessions, V,
    n.p. (July 27, 1747). In 1744, four caulkers assaulted a Negro in
    Boston. *Ibid.,* V, n.p. (July 30, 1744).
12. *Courant,* Jan. 4–11, 1725.

Bibliography

Primary Sources

Legislative Records

Published Materials

Acts and Resolves, Public and Private of the Province of the Massachusetts Bay to which are prefixed The Charters of the Province. With Historical and Explanatory Notes, And an Appendix, 21 vols. (Boston, 1869–1922), Volumes I–III, 1692–1756.

Brigham, William, ed. *The Compact with the Charter and Laws of the Colony of New Plymouth: with the charter of the Council at Plymouth, and an appendix, containing the Articles of the United Colonies of New England, and Other Valuable Documents.* (Boston, 1836).

Journals of the House of Representatives of Massachusetts (Boston, 1919–in progress), Volumes 1–28, 1715–1751.

Shurtleff, Nathaniel B., ed. *Records of the Governor and Company of the Massachusetts Bay in New England. Printed by order of the Legislature,* 5 vols. in 6 (Boston, 1853–1854), 1628–1686.

_____., ed. *Records of the Colony of New Plymouth in New England. Printed by order of the Commonwealth of Massachusetts.* 8 vols. (Boston, 1855–1857), 1633–1692.

Pulsifer, David, ed. *Records of the Colony of New Plymouth in New England. Printed by order of the Commonwealth of Massachusetts.* 4 volumes, a continuation of Shurtleff, above (Boston, 1859–1861). Volumes I (IX) and II (X), *Acts of the Commissioners of the United Colonies of New England, 1643–1679.* Volume III (XI), Laws, 1623–1682. Volume IV (XII), *Deeds, 1620–1651.*

Whitmore, William H., ed. *The Colonial Laws of Massachusetts. Reprinted from the Edition of 1660, with the Supplements to 1672. Containing also, the Body of Liberties of 1641.* (Boston, 1889).

Judicial Records

Published Materials

Dow, George F., ed. *Records and Files of the Quarterly Courts of Essex County Massachusetts,* 8 vols. (Salem, 1911–1921), 1636–1683.

Noble, John, ed. *Records of the Court of Assistants of the Colony of the Massachusetts Bay 1630–1692,* 3 vols. (Boston, 1901–1928). Volume Three edited by John F. Cronin.

Rice, Franklin P., ed. "Records of the Court of the General Sessions of the Peace for the County of Worcester, Massachusetts, From 1731 to 1737," Worcester Society of Antiquity, *Collections* V (Worcester, 1883), xviii.

Records of the Suffolk County Court 1671–1680, 2 parts, in The Colonial Society of Massachusetts, *Publications* XXIX–XXX (Boston, 1933).

Shurtleff, Nathaniel B. *Records of the Colony of New Plymouth in New England, Printed by order of the Legislature of the Commonwealth of Massachusetts.* 8 vols. (Boston, 1855–1857), 1633–1692.

Shurtleff, Nathaniel B., ed. *Records of the Governor and Company of the Massachusetts Bay in New England. Printed by Order of the Legislature,* 5 vols. in 6 (Boston, 1853–1854), 1628–1686.

Trask, William B., ed. *Suffolk Deeds,* 14 vols. (Boston, 1880–1906).

The Probate Records of Essex County Massachusetts, 3 vols. (Salem, 1916–1920), 1639–1681.

Manuscript Materials

Bristol County. Records of the Court of General Sessions of the Peace, Bristol County Court House, office of the Clerk of Courts.

I. "Sessions 1697–1701"

II. "General Sessions 1702–1714"

III. "Sessions 1724–1738" (Contains also Sessions for 1715–1719 in rear of volume. Cited as IIIa).

IV. "Common Pleas 1740–1744 Sessions 1738–1746" Sessions begin page 344. Writs included pp. 123–173 running from 1740–1768.

V. Untitled Volume, Sessions Records 1746–1768

Unbound Fragment, sessions Records 1720–1721

Miscellaneous Records, 1685–1727

Essex County. Records of the County Court, Records of the Court of General Sessions of the Peace Essex County Court House, office of the Clerk of Courts.

"County Court Ipswich Sept. 1682 to Apr. 1686"

"County Court 1682 to 1692 Ipswich"

"County Court 1679–1692 Salem"

"County Court Salem June 1682 to Nov. 1685"

Fragment, "Court of Pleas and Sessions 1688–1689"

I. 1692–1709 (General Sessions of the Peace)

II. 1696–1718 (General Sessions of the Peace)

III. 1709–1726 (General Sessions of the Peace)

IV. 1719–1727 (General Sessions of the Peace)

V. 1726–1744 (General Sessions of the Peace)

VI. 1744–1761 (General Sessions of the Peace)

Court Files in boxes, 1636–present, in progress

There is a single copy typescript of seventeenth and eighteenth century court records begun under the auspices of the Works Progress Administration which is available to the researcher in the Clerk's Office.

Essex County Miscellaneous Records:

Essex Deeds, 443 vols. (1671–in progress), VI

Inferior Court of Common Pleas Files, Drawer March–July, 1736

Inferior Court of Common Pleas, 1736–1740

Essex and York, Superior Court of Judicature Minute Book, 1732–1736

Essex Superior Court of Judicature, Minute Book, 1736–1738

Hampshire County. Records of the County Court. Records of the Court of General Sessions of the Peace, Records of the Inferior Court of Common Pleas, Hampshire County Court House, Office of the Clerk of Courts.

I. County Court, 1677–

II. Miscellaneous bundle, General Sessions of the Peace, and Inferior Court of Common Pleas 1726–

III. General Sessions of the Peace and Inferior Court of Common Pleas, 1728–1735

IV. General Sessions of the Peace and Inferior Court of Common Pleas, 1735–1741

V. General Sessions of the Peace and Inferior Court of Common Pleas, 1741–1746

VI. General Sessions of the Peace and Inferior Court of Common Pleas, 1746–1752

Middlesex County. Records of the County Court, Records of the Court of General Sessions of the Peace. Middlesex County Court House. Office of the Clerk of Courts.

Single copy manuscript transcript, "Records of the County of Middlesex, in the Commonwealth of Massachusetts: Transcribed under the Direction of Commisioners of the County of Middlesex, by David Pulsifer MDCCCLI." Volume I, 1649–1663; no volume II, records lost or burned; Volume III, 1671–1680; Volume IV, 1681–1686. V 1689–1699 (original). Changes to Inferior Court of Pleas, p. 155.

General Sessions of the Peace:

I. 1692–1723 (rear of volume contains 1686–1688).

II. 1723–1735

III. 11736–1748

IV. 1748–1761

303 numbered folders variously labeled containing Middlesex Court Files, 1636–ca. 1740.

Plymouth County. Records of the Court of General Sessions of the Peace. Plymouth County Court House. Office of the Clerk of Courts.

I. "Records Sessions of the Peace 1686–1721." Includes some Inferior Court of Common Pleas Records. Records scattered and fragmentary 1713–1721.

II. "Records Sessions of the Peace 1719–1723"

III. "General Sessions of the Peace. Court Records 1723–1730"

IV. "General Sessions of the Peace 1730–1749"

V. "General Sessions of the Peace 1747–1749"

VI. "Records C. Sessions No. 2," 1749–1760

Suffolk County. Records of the County Court, Records of the Inferior Court of Common Pleas. Suffolk County Court House. Superior Court, Office of the Clerk for Civil Business.

Single Copy "Photostatic Copy of Records of County Court, Suffolk 1680–1692," 2 vols., pages numbered consecutively throughout.

Inferior Court of Common Pleas: "Common Pleas" 38 vols., 1692–1752. Volume I, 1692–1698 searched, others only spot checked, no returns.

Suffolk County Court Files. Records of the Court of General Sessions Of the Peace. Suffolk County Court House, Supreme Judicial Court. Office of the Clerk.

I. "Records of the Court of General Sessions of the Peace," 1702–1712.

II. Sessions 1712–1719

III. Sessions, 1719–1725

IV. Sessions 1725–1732

V. Sessions 1743/4–1749

VI. Sessions 1749–1754

Bundle of manuscripts, sessions 1738, 1739

"Court Files Suffolk." 1289 numbered volumes plus three. Includes files of various courts of the Colony and Province held in Suffolk County, files of the Superior Court of Judicature, and the Supreme Judicial Court. Name index and subject index used, volumes 97–98 searched entirely.

Superior Court of Judicature, Assize and General Goal Delivery Supreme Judicial Court, County Court House, Suffolk County, Office of the Clerk of the Supreme Judicial Court.

"Superior Court of Judicature," 34 vols., 1693–1780. Volumes I–XVIII, 1693–1751, searched. First volume contains a few folios of courts from 1686.

Contemporary Books, Pamphlets, Sermons.

(Anon.) Amicus Patriae, *An Address to the Inhabitants of the Province of the Massachusetts-Bay in New England; More Especially, to the Inhabitants of Boston: Occasioned by the late Illegal and Unwarrantable Attack Upon their Liberties, and the unhappy Confusion and Disorders consequent thereon. By a lover of his Country.* (Boston, 1747).

(Anon.) Mylo Freeman, *A word in season to all true lovers of their liberty and their country; Both of which are now in the utmost danger of being forever lost.* (Boston, 1748).

(Anon.) *A Little Pretty Pocket-Book, Intended for the Instruction and Amusement of Little Master Tommy, and Pretty Miss Polly. . . .* (Worcester, 1787). Facsimile.

(Anon.) *The Athenian Oracle. . . .* (Boston, 1705). Attributed to Samuel Sewall that this was reprinted in America. (Allen B. Forbes, M.H.S.).

Bernard, Sir John,. *A Present for An Apprentice: or a sure guide to gain both esteem and estate. With rules for his conduct to his Master and in the World.* (Boston, 1747).

Bradford, William. *Bradford's History "Of Plimoth Plantation." From the original manuscript. With a report of the proceeding incident to the return of the manuscript to Massachusetts. Printed under the direction of the secretary of the commonwealth, by order of the General Court.* (Boston, 1900).

Campbell, John. *After Souls by Death are Separated from their Bodies, the come to Judgement Asserted in a Sermon Deliver'd at Worcester, November 24, 1737. Being the Day of the Execution of John Hamilton, alias Hugh Henderson. With his Confession and Dying Warning.* (Boston, 1738).

Care, Henry. *English Liberties, or the Free-born Subject's Inheritance. . . . Compiled first by Henry Care, and contineued [sic] with large Additions, by W.N. of the Middle-Temple, Esq.* (Boston, 1721).

Coleman, Elihu. *A Testimony against that Anti-Christian Practice of Making slaves of Men. Wherein it is shewed to be Contrary to the Dispensation of the Law and Time of the Gospel, and very opposite both to Grace and nature. Printed in the year 1733.* (New Bedford, Mass., 1825).

Colman, Benjamin. *The Merchandise of a people holiness to the Lord. A Sermon, preached in part at the Publick Lecture in Boston, July 1, 1725. In Part at a private meeting for charity to the Poor, March 6 1726. And now published as a thank-offering to God for repeated surprising bounties from London for uses of Piety and Charity.* (Boston, 1736).

Danforth, John. *The Right Christian Temper In Every Condition, Endeavoured (as the Lord Vouchsafed to assist) to be set forth and recommended; And the due debt of a suitable contentment with our outward lot, humbly demanded, on the behalf of the Divine Providence; in a Lecture upon Heb. 13. 5. Be content with such things as you have.* (Boston, 1702).

Danforth, Samuel. *The Cry of Sodom Enquired Into: Upon Occasion of the Arraignment and Condemnation of BENJAMIN GOAD, For his Prodigious Villany, Together with A Solemn Exhortation to Tremble at Gods Judgements, and to Abandon Youthful Lusts.* (Cambridge, 1674).

Hill, John. *The Young Secretary's Guide or, A Speedy Help to Learning.* (Boston, 1750).

Hill, Thomas. *The Young Secretary's Guide: or, A Speedy Help to Learning.* (Boston, 1730).

Hosmer, James Kendall, ed. *Winthrop's Journal "History of New England" 1630–1649.* In James Franklin Jameson, general ed., *Original Narratives of American History,* Series. 2 vols. (New York, 1908).

Mather, Cotton. *A Faithful Monitor. Offering, an abstract of the lawes in the Province of the Massachusetts-Bay, New England, Against those disorders, the suppression whereof is desired and pursued by them that wish well to the worthy designs of reformation. With some directions and encouragements, to dispense due rebukes, & censures unto all censurable actions.* (Boston, 1704).

____. *A family well-ordered. Or an essay to render parents and children happy in one another. . . .* (Boston, 1699).

____. *Family Religion Excited and Assisted. The Second Impression.* (Boston, 1707).

____. *Magnalia Christi Americana: or, the Ecclesiastical History of New-England From its First Planting in the Year 1620, unto the Year of our Lord, 1698. In Seven Books.* (London, MDCCII).

____. *The Negro Christianized. An Essay to Excite and Assist that good work, the Instruction of Negro Servants in Christianity.* (Boston, 1706).

____. *Pillars of Salt. An History of some Criminals executed in this land, for capital crimes. With some of their dying speeches; collected and published, for the Warning of such as live in destructive courses of ungodliness. Whereto is added, for the better improvement of this History, A Brief Discourse about the dreadful Justice of God, in Punishing sin, with sin.* (Boston, 1699).

____. *Rules for the Society of Negroes, 1693.* (New York, 1888).

____. *Some seasonable advice unto the poor; to be annexed unto the kindnesses of God that are dispensed unto them.* (Boston, 1726).

____. *Theopolis Americana. An essay on the golden street of the holy city; publishing a testimony against the corruptions of the market-place. With some good hopes of Better things to be yet seen in the American world. . . .* (Boston, 1710).

____. *Tremenda. The dreadful sound with which the wicked are to be thunderstruck. In a sermon delivered unto a great assembly, in which was present, a miserable African, just going to be executed for a most inhumane and uncommon murder at Boston, May 25th, 1721. To which is added, a conference between a minister and the prisoner, on the day before his execution.* (Boston, 1721).

____. *A Good Master well served. A brief discourse on the necessary properties of a good servant in every-kind of servitude: and of the methods that should be taken by the heads of a family, to obtain such a servant.* (Boston, 1696).

Mather, Increase. *A Sermon (preached at the Lecture in Boston in New-England the 18th of the 1. Moneth 1674. When two men were executed,* who had murthered their master) wherein is shewed that excess in wickedness doth bring untimely death. The second Impression. . . . (Boston, 1685) Printed originally as *The Wicked Man's Portion.* (Boston, 1675).

____. *A Call to the Tempted. A Sermon on the Horrid Crime of Self-Murder, Preached on a Remarkable Occasion by the Memorable Dr. Increase Mather. And now published from his notes. for a charitable stop to suicides.* (Boston, 1723/4).

Moody, Samuel and Moody, Joseph, eds. *A Faithful Narrative of the wicked life and remarkable conversion of Patience Boston alias Samson; who was executed at York, in the County of York, July 24th, 1735. For the murder of Benjamin Trot of Falmouth in Casco Bay, a child of about eight years of age, whom she drowned in a well.* (Boston, 1738).

Rogers, John. *Death the Certain Wages of Sin to the Impenitent: Lite the sure Reward of grace to the Penitent: Together with the only way for Youth to avoid the Former and attain the Latter. Deliver'd in Three Lecture Sermons; occasioned by the Imprisonment, Condemnation and Execution, of a Young Woman, who was Guilty of murdering her Infant begotten in Whoredom. To Which is Added, an Account of her manner of Life and Death. . . .* (Boston, 1701).

Saffin, John. "A Brief and Candid answer to a late Printed Sheet, entitled, the Selling of Joseph. . . ." in Colonial Society of Massachusetts, *Publications* I (Boston, 1895), 103–111.

Sewall, Samuel. "The Selling of Joseph a Memorial," Massachusetts Historical Society, *Proosedings* first series VII, 161–165 (Boston, 1864).

Wadsworth, Benjamin. *An Essay to do Good: By a dissuasive from Tavern Haunting an excessive Drinking. With a lecture Sermon.* (Boston, 1710).

____. *The Well-Ordered Family: or, Relative Duties. Being the substance of several Sermons, about Family Prayer. Duties of Husbands & Wives. Duties of Parents & Children. Duties of Masters & Servants.* (Boston 1712, 1719).

Willard, Samuel. *A Compleat Body of Divinity in Two Hundred and Fifty Expository Lectures on the Assembly's Shorter Catechism Wherein the Doctrines of the Christian Religion are Unfolded. . . .* (Boston, 1726).

Winship, George Parker, ed. *Boston in 1682 and 1699 A Trip to New England by Edward Ward and a Letter from New-England by J.W.* (Providence, 1905).

Young, Alexander. *Chronicles of the First Planters of the Colony Massachusetts Bay, From 1623 to 1636. Now First Collected From*

Original Records and Contemporaneous Manuscripts, and Illustrated with Notes. (Boston, 1846).

Almanacs

Nichol's Reproductions. Massachusetts Almanacs. 8 vols. 1645–1699. A single copy photographic reproduction. Massachusetts Historical Society.

Clough, Samuel. *Clough's Farewell 1708. An Almanac for the Year of our Lord (According to the common account) 1708.* . . . (Boston, 1708).

Whittemore, N. *Whittemore Revived. An Almanack for the Year of our Lord, 1738.* . . . (Boston. 1738).

Tulley, John. *Tulley 1688. An Almanack for the Year of Our Lord MDCLXXXVIII. Being Bissextile or Leap-year, and from the Creation 5637.* (Boston, 1688).

Newspapers and Magazines

The Boston Evening-Post, 1735–1750.

The Boston Gazette, 1719–1741. Became *The Boston Gazette, or New England Weekly Journal,* 1741. Became *The Boston Gazette, or, Weekly Journal,* 1741–1750.

The Boston News-Letter, 1704–1727. Became *The Weekly News-Letter,* 1727–1750.

The Boston Weekly Post-Boy, 1734–1750. Became *The Boston Post-Boy,* 1750.

The New-England Courant, 1721–1727.

The New-England Weekly Journal, 1727–1741. Incorporated with *The Boston Gazette,* 1741.

The [Boston] *Weekly Rehearsal,* 1731–1735.

The American Magazine and Historical Chronicle, 1743–1746.

Town Records

Published Materials

Bates, Samuel, ed. *Records of the Town of Braintree 1640 to 1793.* (Randolph, Mass., 1886).

Etheridge, George, ed. *Copy of the Old Records of the Town of Duxbury, Mass. From 1642 to 1770.* (Plymouth, 1893).

Perley, Sidney, ed. *Boxford Town Records 1685–1706.* (Salem, 1900).

Muddy River and Brookline Record. 1634–1838. By the Inhabitants of Brookline, in Town Meeting. (n.p., 1875).

Publications of the Brookline Historical Publication Society first series, 10 numbers (Brookline, Mass., 1897).

Records of the Town of Plymouth Published by order of the Town, 3 vols. (Plymouth, 1889–1903), 1636–1783.

Record Commissioners of the Town of Boston, *Reports* 39 vols. (Boston, 1881–1909).

Manuscript Materials

Office of the City Clerk, City of Boston:

"Boston Indentures," 6 vols., 1734–1805, Volume I, 1734–1751.

"City of Boston Office of the City Clerk City Hall Inhabitants—1695 List of & Indentures of Apprentices"

Public Welfare Department, City of Boston:

Files of miscellaneous manuscripts pertaining to Public Welfare and Overseers of the Poor, filed by year.

Church Records

Briggs, L. Vernon. *Church and Cemetery Records of Hanover, Mass.,* 2 vols. (Boston, 1895–1904).

Motte, Ellis Loring, Jenks, Henry Fitch, and Homans, John, eds. *The Manifesto Church Records of the Church in Brattle Square Boston with Lists of Communicants, Baptisms,. Marriages, and Funerals 1699–1872.* (Boston, 1902).

Plymouth Church Records 1620–1859, 2 parts, in Colonial Society of Massachusetts, *Publications* XXII–XXIII (Boston, 1921–25).

Records of the First Church at Dorchester 1636–1734. (Boston, 1891).

Sharples, Stephen Paschall, ed. *Records of the Church of Christ at Cambridge in New England 1732–1830. . . .* (Boston, 1906).

Miscellaneous Records

Published Materials

Massachusetts Historical Society, *Collections,* 79 vols. (Boston, 1802–in progress).

Colonial Society of Massachusetts, *Publications,* 35 vols. (Boston, 1895–in progress).

Historical Collections of the Essex Institute, 87 vols. (Salem, 1859–in progress).

New England Historical and Genealogical Register. (Boston, 1847–in progress), I–L.

Winthrop Papers, 5 vols. (Boston, 1929–1947).

Lechford, Thomas. "Notebook Kept By Thomas Lechford, Esq., Lawyer, In Boston, Massachusetts Bay, from June 27, 1638, to July 29, 1641," American Antiquarian Society, *Archaeologia Americana* VII (Cambridge, 1885).

Maine Historical Society, *Collections* second series X (Portland, 1907).

Miller, Perry, and Johnson, Thomas H., eds. *The Puritans.* (New York, 1938).

The Constitution and By-Laws of the Scots' Charitable Society of Boston with a list of members and officers, and many interesting extracts from the original records of the Society. (Cambridge, 1878).

Hull, John, "The Diaries of John Hull, Mint-Master and Treasurer of the Colony of Massachusetts Bay," American Antiquarian Society, *Archaeologia Americana* III (Boston, 1857), 109–265.

Manuscript Materials

Commonwealth of Massachusetts, Office of the Secretary of State:

Felt Collection 242 volumes

Supplementary Collection, volumes 243–327

Essex Institute, Salem:

Buffum Papers

Essex County Court House, Office of the Clerk of Courts:

Public Notary Books of Stephen Sewall and Mitchell Sewall, 2 vols., 1696–1763.

Harvard University, Baker Library:

"A Collection of Papers Relating to the Iron Works at Lynn and more Particularly to the Suit Between Mr. John Gifford The Agent for the Undertakers of the Iron Works and The Inhabitants of the Massachusetts Bay Colony Dated 1650 et. seq." A single copy typescript of these papers is in the Baker Library.

Massachusetts Historical Society:

Account Book of Hugh Hall, 1728–1733

Account Book of Godfrey Malbone and Abraham Redwood, 1733–1735, Wetmore Collection.

Cushing Family papers

Diary of Josiah Cotton, 1726–1756

Diary of Andrew Eliot interleaved with *Nath'l Ames Almanac for 1744.* (Boston, 1744)

Diary of Ebenezer Parkman, 1728–1729, 1738–1739, photostatic copy, original at American Antiquarian Society

Diary Fragment of Ebenezer Pierson, 1732

Ebenezer Parkman singing book (1721)

Miscellaneous Bound Manuscripts, twenty-one volumes, 1628–1908

Robert Treat Paine papers

Joshua Winslow, Copy Book of Letters

Winthrop Papers. There is a single copy typescript of the forthcoming volume six of *Winthrop Papers.*

Old Colony Historical Society, Taunton, Mass.:

"Documents Very Old," 3 vols.

Book of Thomas Clap

Iron Works account books

Plymouth County Court House, Office of the Clerk of Courts:

"Edward Winslow Notary Public. Benjamin Drew 1741–1759"

Suffolk County Court House, Office of the Clerk of the Supreme Judicial Court:

Bundle of Notarial Records

Broadsides

Massachusetts Historical Society. "Broadsides, Ballads &c Printed in Massachusetts 1639–1800," *Collections* LXXV (Boston, 1922).

Winslow, Ola Elizabeth, ed. *American Broadside Verse From Imprints of the 17th & 18th Centuries.* (New Haven, 1930).

Broadside Collection, Boston Public Library

Secondary Works

Books

√ Adams, James Truslow. *The Founding of New England.* (Boston, 1921).

Akagi; Roy Hidemichi. *The Town Proprietors of the New England Colonies: A Study of their Development, Organization, Activities, and Controversies, 1620–1770.* (Philadelphia, 1924).

Andrews, Charles M. *The Colonial Period of American History.* 4 vols. (New Haven, 1934–1938), I.

Baxter, W.T. *The House of Hancock: Business in Boston 1724–1775.* (Cambridge, 1945).

Bishop, J. Leander. *A History of American Manufactures from 1608 to 1860. . . .* 2 vols. (Philadelphia, 1861–1864).

Bridenbaugh, Carl. *Cities in the Wilderness: The First Century of Urban Life in America 1625–1742.* (New York, 1938).

———. *The Colonial Craftsman.* (New York, 1950).

Bolton, Charles Knowles. *Scotch Irish Pioneers in Ulster and America.* (Boston, 1910).

Calhoun, Arthur W. *A Social History of the American Family from Colonial Times to the Present.* 3 vols. (Cleveland, 1917–1919).

Clark, Victor S. *History of Manufactures in the United States.* 2 vols. (New York, 1929).

Cummings, John. *Poor Laws of Massachusetts and New York.* (New York, 1895).

Dorfman, Joseph. *The Economic Mind in American Civilization 1606–1865.* 2 vols. (New York, 1946).

Douglas, Paul H. *American Apprenticeship and Industrial Education,* in Columbia University *Studies* in History, Economics and Public Law, XCV (New York, 1921).

√ Dow, George Francis. *Every Day Life in the Massachusetts Bay Colony.* (Boston, 1935).

Drake, Samuel Adams. *Old Boston Taverns and Tavern Clubs New Illustrated Edition with An Account of "Coles Inn," "The Baker's Arms," and "Golden Ball" by Walter K. Watkins. . . .*(Boston, 1917).

Ford, Henry Jones. *The Scotch-Irish In America.* (Princeton, N.J., 1915).

Forbes, Esther. *Paul Revere & The World He Lived In.* (Boston, 1942).

Franklin, Benjamin. *The Autobiography of Benjamin Franklin & Selections from his Writings.* Henry Steele Commager, ed. (New York, 1944, Modern Library edition).

Franklin, John Hope. *From Slavery to Freedom: A History of American Negroes.* (New York, 1947).

Furniss, Edgar S. *The Position of the Laborer in a System of Nationalism: A Study in the Labor Theories of the Later English Mercantilists.* (Boston, 1920).

Greene, Lorenzo Johnston. *The Negro in Colonial New England, 1620–1776.* (New York, 1942).

Handlin, Oscar. *The Uprooted: The Epic Story of the Great Migration that Made the American People.* (Boston, 1952).

Herskovits, Melville J. *The Myth of the Negro Past.* (New York, 1941).

Hutchinson, Thomas. *The History of the Colony and Province of Massachusetts-Bay Edited from the Author's own copies of volumes I and II and his Manuscript of volume III, with a Memoir and Additional Notes.* Lawrence Shaw Mayo, ed. 3 vols. (Cambridge, 1936).

Jernegan, Marcus Wilson. *Laboring and Dependent Classes in Colonial America 1607–1783. Studies of the Economic, Educational, and Social Significance of Slaves, Servants, Apprentices, and Poor Folk.* (Chicago, 1931).

Johnson, E.A.J. *American Economic Thought in the Seventeenth Century.* (London, 1932).

Kelso, Robert W. *The History of Public Poor Relief in Massachusetts 1620–1920.* (Boston, 1922).

Lauber, Almon Wheeler. *Indian Slavery in Colonial Times within the Present Limits of the United States,* in Columbia University *Studies* in History, Economics and Public Law, LIV, iii (New York, 1913).

McFarland, Raymond. *A History of the New England Fisheries with maps.* (University of Pennsylvania, 1911).

Moore, George H. *Notes on the History of Slavery in Massachusetts.* (New York, 1866).

Morgan, Edmund S. *The Puritan Family: Essays on Religion and Domestic Relations in Seventeenth-Century New England.* (Boston, 1944).

Morris, Richard B. *Government and Labor in Early America.* (New York, 1946).

Morison, Samuel Eliot. *Builders of the Bay Colony.* (Boston, 1930).

——. *The Maritime History of Massachusetts 1783–1860.* (Boston, 1921).

——. *The Puritan Pronaos: Studies in the Intellectual Life of New England in the Seventeenth Century.* (New York, 1936)

Murdock, Kenneth Ballard. *Increase Mather: The Foremost American Puritan.* (Cambridge, 1925).

Nef, John U. *Industry and Government In France and England, 1540–1640,* in *Memoirs* of the American Philosophical Society Held at Philadelphia for Promoting Useful Knowledge, XV (Philadelphia, 1940).

Osgood, Herbert Levi. *The American Colonies in the Seventeenth Century.* 3 vols. (New York, 1904–1907)

Proper Emberson E. *Colonial Immigration Laws,* in Columbia University *Studies* in History, Economics, and Public Law, XIII, #2 (New York, 1900).

Rose-Troup, Frances. *John White, the Patriarch of Dorchester and the Founder of Massachusetts 1575–1648 With an Account of the Early Settlements in Massachusetts 1620–1630.* (New York, 1930).

Savage, James. *A Genealogical Dictionary of the First Settlers of New England, showing Three Generations of those who came before May, 1692 on the Basis of Farmer's Register.* 4 vols. (Boston. 1860–1862).

Seybolt, Robert Francis. *Apprenticeship and Apprenticeship Education in Colonial New-England & New York,* in Teachers College, Columbia University *Contributions to Education* LXXXVI (New York, 1917).

Shipton Clifford K. *Roger Conant A Founder of Massachusetts* (Cambridge, 1945).

——. *Isaiah Thomas: Printer, Patriot and Philanthropist, 1749–1831* (New York, 1948)

Sibley, John Langdon. *Biographical Sketches of Graduates of Harvard University in Cambridge, Massachusetts,* 8 vols., edited by Clifford K. Shipton from volume IV on (Cambridge, 1873–in progress).

Smith, Abbot Emerson. *Colonists in Bondage: White Servitude and Convict Labor in America 1607–1776* (Chapel Hill, 1947).

Smith, Adam. *An Inquiry into the Nature and Causes of The Wealth of Nations,* Edwin Cannan, ed., (New York, 1937, Modern Library Edition).

Thomas, Isaiah. "The History of Printing In America, With a Biography of Printers and An Account of Newspapers," in American Antiquarian Society, *Archoeologica Americana* V, VI (Albany, 1874).

Tryon, Rolla Milton. *Household Manufactures in the United States. 1640–1860. . . .* (Chicago, 1917).

Weeden, William B. *Economic and Social History of New England 1620–1789,* 2 vols. (Bonton, 1890).

Winsor, Justin, ed. *The Memorial History of Boston Including Suffolk County, Massachusetts. 1630–1880,* 4 vols. (Boston, 1880–1881).

Articles

Adams, Charles Francis. "Some Phases of Sexual Morality and Church Discipline in Colonial New England," Massachusetts Historical Society, *Proceedings, 1880–1891* second series VI, 477–516.

Ainsworth, B. Spofford. "Lotteries in American History," American Historical Association, *Annual Report For the Year 1892* (1893), 173–195.

Albertson, Dean. "Puritan Liquor In The Planting of New England," *The New England Quarterly* XXIII (December 1950), 477–490.

Baker, Ray Palmer. "The Poetry of Jacob Bailey, Loyalist," *The New England Quarterly* II (January 1929), 58–92.

Butler, James D. "British Convicts Shipped to American Colonies," *The American Historical Review* II (October 1896), 12–33.

Dickinson, O.M. contribution to "Trivia," *The William and Mary Quarterly* third series IX (January 1952) 85–86.

Dow, George Francis. "Shipping and Trade in Early New England," Massachusetts Historical Society, *Proceedings, 1930–1932* LXIV, 185–201.

√   Felt, Joseph B. "Statistics of Population in Massachusetts," American Statistical Association, *Collections* (1849), I, 158–170.

Greene, Lorenzo Johnston. "The New England Negro in Newspaper Advertisements," *The Journal of Negro History* XXIX (April 1944), 125–147.

Johnson, E.A.J. "Some Evidence of Mercantilism in the Massachusetts-Bay," *The New England Quarterly* I (July 1928), 371–395.

Lancour, A.H. "Passenger Lists of Ships Coming to North America, 1607–1825," New York Public Library, *Bulletin* XLI (1937) 389–398.

Mathews, Albert. "Hired Man and Help," Colonial Society of Massachusetts, *Publications, 1897–1898* V, 225–256.

Moller, Herbert. "Sex Composition and Correlated Culture Patterns of Colonial America," *The William and Mary Quarterly* third series II, (April 1945), 113–153.

Mook, E. Telfer. "Training Day In New England," *The New England Quarterly* XI (December 1938), 675–697.

Morgan, Edmund S. "The Puritans and Sex," *The New England Quarterly* XV (December 1942), 591–607.

Morris, Richard B., and Grossman, Jonathan. "The Regulation of Wages in Early Massachusetts," *The New England Quarterly* XI (December 1938), 470–500.

√ Parkes, Henry Bamford. "Morals and Law Enforcement In Colonial New England," *The New England Quarterly* V (July 1932), 431–452.

Parkes, H.B. "Sexual Morals and the Great Awakening," *The New England Quarterly* III (January 1930), 133–135.

Pearce, Ray Harvery. "The 'Ruines of Mankind'; The Indian and the Puritan Mind," *The Journal of the History of Ideas* XIII (April 1952), 200–217.

Pierre, C.E. "The Work of the Society for the Propagation of the Gospel in Foreign Parts Among the Negroes in the Colonies," *The Journal of Negro History* I (October 1916), 349–360.

Powell, Chilton L. "Marriage in Early New England," *The New England Quarterly* I (July 1928), 323–334.

Risch, Erna. "Joseph Crellius, Immigrant Broker," *The New England Quarterly* XII (June 1939), 241–267.

√ Shipton; Clifford K. "Immigration to New England 1680–1740," *The Journal of Political Economy* XLIV (April 1936), 225–239.

____. "Secondary Education In the Puritan Colonies," *The New England Quarterly* VII (December 1934), 646–661.

Smith, Abbot Emerson. "Indentured Servants: New Light on Some of America's 'First' Families," *The Journal of Economic History* II (May 1942), II 40–53.

____. "The Transportation of Convicts to the American Colonies in the Seventeenth Century," *The American Historical Review* XXXIX (January 1934), 232–249.

Stavisky, Leonard Price. "Negro Craftsmanship in Early America," *The American Historical Review* LIV (January 1949), 315–325.

____. "Origins of Negro Craftsmanship in Early America," *The Journal of Negro History* XXXII (October 1947), 417–429.

Walcott, Robert R. "Husbandry in Colonial New England," *The New England Quarterly* IX (June 1936), 218–252.

Unpublished Secondary Work

Freiberg, Malcolm. "Boston, Sex, and the Great Awakening," a single copy transcript at Brown University Library.

Towner, Lawrence in Towner, "A Good Master Well Served: A Social History of Servitude in Massachusetts, 1620–1750" (Ph.D. diss., Northwestern University, 1954).

Special, and Guides

Evans, Charles. *American Bibliography A Chronological Dictionary of all Books, Pamphlets and Periodical Publications Printed in The United States of America From the Genesis of Printing in 1639 Down to And Including the Year 1820 with Bibliographical and Biographical Notes,* nine volumes (Chicago, 1903–1925), I–II, 1639–1750. In the process of completion by Clifford K. Shipton, American Antiquarian Society. Used both as a guide, and as a source, when titles indicate the nature of the problem dealt with.

Brigham, Clarence S. *History and Bibliography of American Newspapers, 1690–1820,* 2 vols. (Worcester, Mass., 1947).

Edmonds, John H. *The Massachusetts Archives* (Worcester, Mass., 1922).

Flagg, Charles A. *A Guide to Massachusetts Local History* (Salem, 1907).

Wright, Carroll D. *Report on the Custody and Condition of the Public Records of Parishes, Towns, and Counties* (Boston, 1889).

Index